DIALOGUE
and
DRAMA

DIALOGUE
and
DRAMA

Elements of Greek Tragedy in the Fourth Gospel

JO-ANN A. BRANT

HENDRICKSON
PUBLISHERS

Hendrickson Publishers, Inc.
P. O. Box 3473
Peabody, Massachusetts 01961-3473

ISBN 1-56563-907-3

Cover Art: Actors preparing for a performance. Mosaic from The House of the Tragic Poet, Pompeii. Late first-century C.E. Museo Archeologico Nazionale, Naples, Italy. Photo Credit: Scala / Art Resource, N.Y. Used by permission.

Printed in the United States of America

First Printing — September 2004

Library of Congress Cataloging-in-Publication Data

Brant, Jo-Ann A., 1956–
    Dialogue and drama : elements of Greek tragedy in the Fourth Gospel / Jo-Ann A. Brant.—1st ed.
        p. cm.
    Includes bibliographical references and indexes.
    ISBN 1-56563-907-3 (alk. paper)
    1. Bible. N.T. John—Criticism, interpretation, etc. 2. Greek drama (Tragedy)—History and criticism. I. Title.
    BS2615.52.B73 2004
    226.5′066—dc22
                                                2004009547

TABLE OF CONTENTS

ACKNOWLEDGMENTS

There are many people whom I should thank for providing the foundation for this study of the theatricality of the Fourth Gospel. I will name a few of them here. For my introduction to Shakespeare, I thank Miss Erickson, my fourth-grade teacher, who performed the witch scene from *MacBeth* in front of our class and made me hungry to see more. I thank Norma McCleod and my mother, Thelma Brant, who took me to my first play, a dramatization of Dickens's *Great Expectations* at Theatre Calgary. I thank Stephanie Wong, who, at the age of eighteen, spent her first vacation from employment with me, traveling to Strafford, Ontario, where we watched six plays in four days. I thank Anthony Jenkins, my professor of Twentieth Century British and American Drama at the University of Victoria, for teaching me how to read a play and for describing my prose as "dry, flat, and uninviting," provoking me to devote more attention to my writing.

Over the past six years, I have received encouragement from many colleagues to pursue this line of inquiry. Without it I would have prioritized the immediate demands of undergraduate teaching and kept my ideas to myself. Above all I thank the members of the Ancient Fiction and Early Jewish and Christian Fiction Group of the Society of Biblical Literature, especially Ronald Hock, Dennis McDonald, Judith Perkins, and Richard I. Pervo, for providing an appreciative context in which to share my ideas about the Fourth Gospel as they developed. Early in my career, David Jobling provided significant affirmation of my work and advice that kept me on track. Later in the process, Adele Reinhartz made valuable suggestions on how to proceed towards publication.

I have been fortunate to be surrounded by a supportive community, eager to listen to my inchoate ideas and my frustrations. Many individuals deserve acknowledgment. Menno Friesen never failed to ask how my work was progressing and, when asked to be the first reader of the entire manuscript, answered "Yes." He then set aside other tasks to read the document carefully and to ask questions on behalf of various hypothetical readers. My husband, Joe Springer, offered love and patience and also the invaluable service of his professional skills as a research librarian. My son, Jacob, shares my love of film and became a partner in dialogue about cinematography and intertextuality. Jade was my constant companion throughout the composition of the book and learned to refrain from walking on the keyboard or lying on my notes. My father, Glenn Brant, and my mother opened their homes and provided retreats for me to work in solitude at critical points in my work. My good friends, Mavis Fenn and Cecilia Wassen, lent me courage to continue when the possibility of finishing this project seemed remote.

I owe thanks to Goshen College for meaningful employment for the last ten years and a sabbatical in 2000–2001 to concentrate on this work. I wish to express appreciation to the librarians of Goshen College's Good Library and the Associated Mennonite Biblical Seminary for their assistance in providing the books and articles necessary to my labor and for their patience with my habits and demands.

Finally, I thank the editors of Hendrickson Publishers, James D. Ernest, who accepted the manuscript with excitement, and then Dawn C. Harrell, who supervised the final steps of transforming my manuscript into this volume. I will be forever grateful to Robert Maccini, who, in his capacity as copyeditor, spent a great deal of time correcting my errors and pointing out inconsistencies in my references, thereby sparing me from a great deal of embarrassment. In retrospect, I wish that I had included in this volume some of the many thoughts of praise that I had for his work on women as witnesses in the Fourth Gospel.

When I learned who my copyeditor was, I quickly turned to the pages where I wrote about his work. The way that I handle his contributions, as well as those of many other scholars, obscures a debt. My ideas are not my own invention. They are unleashed by the labors of every author who is named in my bibliography and many others who are not. In some cases, their work has become so much a part of who I am that I am unconscious of the role it plays. And so to any reader who recognizes the foundation that another has laid but for which I have failed to give thanks, I ask for indulgence or forgiveness.

Jo-Ann A. Brant

ABBREVIATIONS

General

B.C.E.	before the Common Era
C.E.	Common Era
d.	died
ed(s).	editor(s), edited by
esp.	especially
ibid.	*ibidem,* in the same place
LXX	Septuagint (the Greek Old Testament)
NRSV	New Revised Standard Version
p(p).	page(s)
trans.	translator(s), translated by
vol(s).	volume(s)

Original Works

Hebrew Bible/Old Testament

Gen	Genesis
Exod	Exodus
Lev	Leviticus
Deut	Deuteronomy
Judg	Judges
Ruth	Ruth
2 Kgs	2 Kings
Esth	Esther

Job	Job
Ps	Psalms
Eccl	Ecclesiastes
Isa	Isaiah
Jer	Jeremiah
Ezek	Ezekiel
Zech	Zechariah

New Testament

Matt	Matthew
Mark	Mark
Luke	Luke
John	John
Acts	Acts
1 Cor	1 Corinthians
Eph	Ephesians
Phil	Philippians
1 Tim	1 Timothy
Titus	Titus
Rev	Revelation

Apocrypha and Septuagint

| Jdt | Judith |
| Sir | Sirach/Ecclesiasticus |

Old Testament Pseudepigrapha

2 Bar.	*2 Baruch (Syriac Apocalypse)*
1 En.	*1 Enoch (Ethiopic Apocalypse)*
3 En.	*3 Enoch (Hebrew Apocalypse)*
Jos. Asen.	*Joseph and Aseneth*
Jub.	*Jubilees*
Let. Aris.	*Letter of Aristeas*
T. Ab.	*Testament of Abraham*

Dead Sea Scrolls

| 1QSa | *Rule of the Congregation* (Appendix a to 1QS) |
| 4QMessAp | *Messianic Apocalypse* |

Philo

Posterity   *On the Posterity of Cain*

Josephus

Ant.   *Jewish Antiquities*
J. W.   *Jewish War*

Mishnah, Talmud, Rabbinic Works

b.   Babylonian Talmud
m.   Mishnah tractate
B. Bat.   *Baba Batra*
Eccl. Rab.   *Ecclesiastes Rabbah*
Nid.   *Niddah*
Pesiq. Rab Kah.   *Pesiqta de Rab Kahana*
Sop.   *Soperim*

Apostolic Fathers

1–2 Clem.   *1–2 Clement*

Other Christian Authors

Augustine
   Tract. Ev. Jo.   *Tractates on the Gospel of John*
Eusebius
   Hist. eccl.   *Ecclesiastical History*
Tertullian
   Spect.   *The Shows*

Classical Authors

Achilles Tatius
   Leuc. Clit.   *Leucippe and Clitophon*
Aeschylus
   Ag.   *Agamemnon*
   Prom.   *Prometheus Bound*
Apuleius
   Metam.   *Metamorphoses*
Aristophanes
   Ach.   *Acharnians*
   Vesp.   *Wasps*

Aristotle
    Poet.   *Poetics*
    Rhet.   *Rhetoric*
Athenaeus
    Deipn.   *Deipnosophistae*
Catullus
    Carm.   *Carmina*
Euripides
    Alc.   *Alcestis*
    Andr.   *Andromache*
    Bacch.   *Bacchae*
    Hec.   *Hecuba*
    Hel.   *Helen*
    Herc. fur.   *Heracles*
    Hipp.   *Hippolytus*
    Iph. aul.   *Iphigeneia at Aulis*
    Med.   *Medea*
    Phoen.   *Phoenician Women*
Herodotus
    Hist.   *Histories*
Hesiod
    Theog.   *Theogony*
Homer
    Il.   *Iliad*
    Od.   *Odyssey*
Petronius
    Sat.   *Satyricon*
Plato
    Rep.   *Republic*
Plutarch
    Mulier. virt. *Mulierum virtutes*
    Pomp.   *Pompeius*
Quintilian
    Inst.   *Institutio oratoria*
Sophocles
    Aj.   *Ajax*
    Ant.   *Antigone*
    El.   *Electra*
    Oed. tyr.   *Oedipus Tyrannus*
    Trach.   *Women of Trachis*
Strabo
    Geogr.   *Geographica*

Secondary Literature

AB	Anchor Bible
AJP	*American Journal of Philology*
AThR	*Anglican Theological Review*
BibInt	*Biblical Interpretation*
BIS	Biblical Interpretation Series
BKP	Beiträge zur klassichen Philologie
BSac	*Bibliotheca sacra*
BTB	*Biblical Theology Bulletin*
CBQ	*Catholic Biblical Quarterly*
ConBNT	Coniectanea biblica: New Testament Series
DJG	*Dictionary of Jesus and the Gospels.* Edited by J. B. Green and S. McKnight. Downers Grove, 1992
EvQ	*Evangelical Quarterly*
ExpTim	*Expository Times*
FF	Foundations and Facets
FRLANT	Forschungen zur Religion und Literatur des Alten und Neuen Testaments
HeyJ	*Heythrop Journal*
HTR	*Harvard Theological Review*
HUCA	*Hebrew Union College Annual*
JBL	*Journal of Biblical Literature*
JSNT	*Journal for the Study of the New Testament*
JSNTSup	Journal for the Study of the New Testament: Supplement Series
JTS	*Journal of Theological Studies*
JTSA	*Journal of Theology for Southern Africa*
LCL	Loeb Classical Library
LS	*Louvain Studies*
MnemosyneSup	Mnemosyne, bibliotheca classica batava: Supplementum
Neot	*Neotestamentica*
NovT	*Novum Testamentum*
NovTSup	Novum Testamentum Supplements
NTS	*New Testament Studies*
NTTS	New Testament Tools and Studies
RNT	Regensburger Neues Testament
SBLDS	Society of Biblical Literature Dissertation Series
SBLEJL	Society of Biblical Literature Early Judaism and Its Literature

SBLMS	Society of Biblical Literature Monograph Series
SBLSymS	Society of Biblical Literature Symposium Series
SBT	Studies in Biblical Theology
SNTSMS	Society for New Testament Studies Monograph Series
ST	*Studia Theologica*
SVTQ	*St. Vladimir's Theological Quarterly*
TBT	*The Bible Today*
TLZ	*Theologische Literaturzeitung*
ZNW	*Zeitschrift für die neutestamentliche Wissenschaft und die Kunde der älteren Kirche*

INTRODUCTION

The setting is an American football game; the play can be at any level: high school, college, or National Football League. As the camera follows the ball in a field-goal kick into the end zone, chances are a sign with "John 3:16" printed on it will come into view. I confess that I am more interested in this sign, which I have seen planted in the middle of cornfields and posted on the sides of barns and in residential windows, than in the game. This sign in the end zone, which may have inspired all the other signs that dot my landscape, has a story. During the 1970s, a fan named Rollen Stewart took to wearing a rainbow wig to games in order to get the camera's attention. After the 1980 Super Bowl, Stewart found Jesus, and thereafter he appeared at games with his wig on his head and a "John 3:16" sign in his hands. Thus, John 3:16 became a part of the theater of a modern spectacle. Stewart's mission came to an end in 1992 when, in zealous anticipation of the rapture, he took a chambermaid hostage in a Los Angeles hotel room. Stewart is now serving time in a State of California Department of Corrections facility.[1]

Many fans have since imitated Stewart and sport the sign at games as though it should mean something as clearly as the team colors speak to fan loyalty. While I can match, for example, the blue and gold paint on a spectator's face with the jersey colors of Notre Dame's football team, there is no cue in the immediate context with which to make the association between John 3:16 and the verse in the Fourth Gospel, "For God so loved the world that he gave his only Son, so that everyone who believes in him may not perish but

---

[1] Rollen Stewart's story is recounted in Sam Green's documentary *The Rainbow Man/John 3:16* (1997), which premiered at the Sundance Film Festival. Awards: Grand Prize, USA Film Festival; Best Documentary, NY Underground Film Festival; Best 8 Indie Films of 1998, selected by the *San Francisco Bay Guardian*; Best Documentary, New York Underground Film Fest; Best Documentary, Chicago Underground Film Fest.

may have eternal life." The sign, by its esoteric allusion, proclaims its bearer to be the possessor of privileged knowledge and invites its audience to enter into its initiation by seeking out the meaning of its reference. This homophoric reference, analogous to an acronym the referent of which is recovered only through common knowledge, in its want of information constructs a community and excludes others. As such, the use of John 3:16 on a sign qualifies for sociolinguist M. A. K. Halliday's category of anti-language.[2]

This phenomenon, whereby a verse of the Fourth Gospel becomes an identity marker in a contest between two opposing forces, setting its bearer apart from the other fans, is an extreme example of the use of Scripture evidenced in readings of the gospel that have become popular in the last several decades. The Fourth Gospel has become the gospel of the anti-language that promotes an antisocial community.[3] Richard Rohrbaugh argues that the attraction of Christian fundamentalists or neotraditionalists to the Fourth Gospel is no accident, for, like modern fundamentalists, alienated from the values and directions of their contemporary society, the group that produced the language of the Fourth Gospel constructed their reality in opposition to prevailing perceptions.[4]

The turn toward defining the language of the Fourth Gospel as anti-language is motivated in part by a reaction against the antagonistic language of the Fourth Gospel. The construction of the Jews, Jesus' vilification of them as the devil's spawn, and conditional threats such as "unless you eat the flesh of the Son of Man and drink his blood, you have no life in you" (6:53) violate some modern sensibilities. This reaction calls for theories of composition that allow those who find the language offensive to distance themselves from the readers who might approve of or need such a polemical gospel. Though I stand on the side of those who are disturbed by the language of this gospel, I find it aesthetically appealing. Like physical violence in modern films such as Arthur Penn's 1967 production *Bonnie and Clyde*, its verbal violence is not gratuitous;

---

[2] M. A. K. Halliday, *Language as a Social Semiotic: The Social Interpretation of Language and Meaning* (London: Edward Arnold, 1978), 164–82.

[3] The concept of anti-language was first introduced to Johannine scholarship by Bruce J. Malina in *The Gospel of John in Sociolinguistic Perspective* (ed. Herman C. Waetjen; Berkeley: Center for Hermeneutical Studies in Hellenistic and Modern Culture, 1985). See also Norman R. Peterson, *The Gospel of John and the Sociology of Light: Language and Characterization in the Fourth Gospel* (Valley Forge, Pa.: Trinity, 1993), 5; Bruce J. Malina and Richard L. Rohrbaugh, *Social-Science Commentary on the Gospel of John* (Minneapolis: Fortress, 1998).

[4] Richard L. Rohrbaugh, "The Gospel of John in the Twenty-First Century," in *What Is John? Readers and Readings of the Fourth Gospel* (ed. Fernando Segovia; 2 vols.; SBLSymS 3, 7; Atlanta: Scholars Press, 1996–1998), 2:257–63.

it is logical to the plot in which an individual places himself beyond the borders of accountability to social norms or civic authority. The language seems appropriate to a gospel in which Jesus' death is not simply an accident of the Roman occupation but the result of a conflict in which one participant seeks a glorious death. Rather than looking to doctrinal logic or to a sociological context, I attribute the debates and conflicts of the gospel to its affinities with a genre equally antagonistic: the ancient Greek tragedy. Numerous other features of the so-called Johannine anti-language, including wordplays, ambiguity and misunderstanding, dualism, and irony and its interpersonal dimensions, are equally characteristic of tragic language.[5]

The relationship between the Fourth Gospel and Greek tragedy comprehends more than a similarity in the degree of conflict. Just as Aeschylus developed tragedy by reducing the role of the chorus and giving speech the leading role (Aristotle, *Poet.* 1448a 16), the author of the Fourth Gospel gives the narrator a limited task and allows the characters to lay out the plot through their speech. He finds what Peter Brook calls "a language of actions, a language of sounds—a language of word-as-part-of-movement, of word-as-lie, word-as-parody, or word-as-rubbish, or word-as-contradiction, or word-shock or word-cry."[6] The language of the Fourth Gospel is different not simply in vocabulary and proclamation; it is different in what it does. The language is dramatic because it shows rather than tells. Though the Fourth Gospel is not a play, the reader feels like he or she is present and watching it all happen. Derek Tovey compares the experience of being a silent observer to being like Scrooge in Charles Dickens's *A Christmas Carol.*[7] We are not the readers of the gospel but its audience.

Beginning with its first scene, the Fourth Gospel distinguishes itself from the beginning of the Gospel of Mark by relying upon the speech of characters rather than narration to tell the story. In Mark, the narrator cites Isaiah; in the Fourth Gospel, the character identified as John says, "I am the voice of one crying out in the wilderness, 'Make straight the way of the Lord,' as the prophet Isaiah said" (1:23). In Mark, the narrator describes John's baptizing activity; in the Fourth Gospel, this information is provided indirectly through the Jerusalem delegation's question "Why then are you baptizing if you are neither the Messiah, nor Elijah, nor the prophet?" (1:25). In Mark, the narrator tells the story of the dove and reports the words of the heavenly voice; in the Fourth Gospel, the Baptist provides this report:

---

[5] This list appears in Malina and Rohrbaugh, *Social-Science Commentary,* 6.

[6] Peter Brook, *The Empty Space* (New York: Atheneum, 1968), 49.

[7] Derek Tovey, *Narrative Art and Act in the Fourth Gospel* (JSNTSup 151; Sheffield: Sheffield Academic Press, 1997), 55.

I saw the Spirit descending from heaven like a dove, and it remained on him. I myself did not know him, but the one who sent me to baptize with water said to me, "He on whom you see the Spirit descend and remain is the one who baptizes with the Holy Spirit." And I myself have seen and have testified that this is the Son of God. (1:32–34)

The narrator of the Gospel of Mark describes the appearance of the Baptist and the content of his proclamation; the Johannine narrator's role in this scene is reduced to the identification of speakers, location, and time. Though the gospel writer is not consistent in his limitation of the narrator, he frequently gives over the construction of action, setting, and character to dialogue, as though he were bound by the tight economy of a theatrical production.

Speaking of the Fourth Gospel as drama has become a habit for Johannine scholars. For the most part, the term "drama" is used to refer loosely to a story fraught with tension between characters with a conflict that arises at its beginning and builds to a crisis. As such, history told in a particular way can be as dramatic as *Hamlet* or *Oedipus Tyrannus*. A number of scholars over the past century have used the term more precisely to refer to the gospel's allegiance to the form and conventions of a work written for performance. In 1907, F. R. Montgomery Hitchcock argued that the plot of the gospel fulfilled the conditions of tragedy by being "one protracted sacrifice" culminating in a reversal of fortune with the choice "Not this man, but Barabbas."[8] In 1923, Hans Windisch contributed an article to the discussion, "Der johanneische Erzählungsstil," in which he contrasted the pericope-based narratives of the Synoptic Gospels with the "broadly elaborated, dramatically presented narratives" of the Fourth Gospel and cast large sections of the gospel into the form of a script.[9] Two years later, Robert Strachan published *The Fourth Evangelist: Dramatist or Historian?* in which he used the term "drama" to refer to the dualism of light and darkness, life and death, and belief and unbelief that gives the gospel a unified structure.[10] This was followed by Clayton Bowen's publication

---

[8] F. R. Montgomery Hitchcock, "The Dramatic Development of the Fourth Gospel," *Expositor* 4 (1907): 266–79. Hitchcock included this material in the fifth chapter of his book *A Fresh Study of the Fourth Gospel* (New York: Gorham, 1911), and he revisited his arguments in "Is the Fourth Gospel a Drama?" *Theology* 7 (1923): 307–17.

[9] Hans Windisch, "Der johanneische Erzählungsstil," in *Eucharisterion: Studien zur Religion und Literatur des Alten und Neuen Testaments* (ed. Hans Schmidt; 2 vols. in 1; FRLANT 36; Göttingen: Vandenhoeck & Ruprecht, 1923), 2:174–213. The article appears in English as "John's Narrative Style," in *The Gospel of John as Literature: An Anthology of Twentieth-Century Perspectives* (ed. Mark W. G. Stibbe; trans. David E. Orton; NTTS 17; Leiden: Brill, 1993), 25–64.

[10] Robert H. Strachan, *The Fourth Evangelist: Dramatist or Historian?* (New York: Doran, 1925).

of "The Fourth Gospel as Dramatic Material," in which he outlined the dramatic sequence of the gospel and suggested that it represented a partially worked pageant.[11] For the most part, these early advocates of comparing the gospel to a drama remained content with an exposition on the overall form.[12] In her review of the ideological motives for describing the gospel as a drama, Colleen Conway contends that these early arguments were driven by the desire to preserve the authority of the gospel in the face of the rise of historical criticism.[13] The association of the Fourth Gospel with drama justified treating it as a unified document in order to counter the arguments of historical criticism that challenged its status as the composition of a single author.

In 1948, C. M. Connick published an argument distinguishing himself from his predecessors on two counts.[14] First, he began to attend to dramatic techniques and patterns, although his analysis was introductory and treated the material in generalities. Second, he concluded that the dramatic character of the gospel was a datum that ought to be considered with regard to its historicity and its anti-Jewish character.[15] Two decades later, in 1968, J. Louis Martyn did just that, in his influential *History and Theology of the Fourth Gospel*, by turning observations about the gospel's dramatic form, in particular John 9, into an argument for its composition history. Martyn contended that the gospel was the product of a Christian community that had been forcefully evicted from the synagogue under the power of the Birkat Haminim—the twelfth of the Eighteen Benedictions in the synagogue service—which asked for heretics (*minim*) to be "blotted out of the Book of Life."[16] According to Martyn, the gospel presents the movement away from a Moses/Messiah typology for understanding Jesus to the notion of the Son of Man as a stage in the growth of faith. Martyn subordinated the question of genre to his

---

[11] Clayton R. Bowen, "The Fourth Gospel as Dramatic Material," *JBL* 49 (1930): 292–305. See also Charles B. Hedrick, "Pageantry in the Fourth Gospel," *AThR* 15 (1933): 115–24.

[12] Others have expounded upon the same theme without developing it: James Muilenburg, "Literary Form in the Fourth Gospel, " *JBL* 51 (1932): 40–53; E. Kenneth Lee, "The Drama of the Fourth Gospel," *ExpTim* 65 (1954): 173–76. Neal Flanagan, "The Gospel of John as Drama," *TBT* 19 (1981): 264–70; Edith Lovejoy Pierce, "The Fourth Gospel as Drama," *Religion in Life* 29 (1960): 453–54.

[13] Colleen M. Conway, "The Politics of the Johannine Drama" (paper presented at the annual meeting of the Society of Biblical Literature, Nashville, Tenn., November 2000).

[14] C. M. Connick, "The Dramatic Character of the Fourth Gospel," *JBL* 67 (1948): 159–69.

[15] Ibid., 169.

[16] J. Louis Martyn, *History and Theology of the Fourth Gospel* (rev. ed., Nashville: Abingdon, 1979), 62.

historical questions. Describing the gospel as a drama legitimized discussing the creative manner in which the gospel writer placed the conflicts of his own community into the context of Jesus' life.

Conway and others now challenge the ideological motivation of a hypothesis that justifies the polemic against the Jews and allows the Jews, albeit those of a generation later than Jesus' own, to remain villains.[17] Besides the fact that the status of the Birkat Haminim in the late first century is a matter of debate, the jump from recognizing that the gospel is a dramatization to the thesis that it is a dramatization of another event altogether—the experience of a hypothetical community—is highly speculative.[18] Conway adds one further point to her critique of Martyn and the school of thought that his work has produced. She argues that the production of the gospel is a datum that reflects the transposition of an oral tradition for a wider audience and suggests an outward rather than a sectarian, inward-looking community.[19]

By returning to the discussion of the dramatic form of the gospel, I may not escape Conway's criticism that identification of the gospel with drama is ideologically driven and justifies the anti-Jewish polemic, but my analysis moves in a different direction than that of my predecessors. I am concerned with the literary fabric of the gospel rather than the historical context of its first or an intended audience.[20] My objective is to unmask the skilled artistry of the gospel, designed to produce a compelling rendition of the story of Jesus capable of finding an audience in a world where Homeric epics and

---

[17] See R. Bieringer, D. Pollefeyt, and F. Vandecasteele-Vanneuville, "Introduction: Wrestling with Johannine Anti-Judaism: A Hermeneutical Framework for the Analysis of the Current Debate," in *Anti-Judaism and the Fourth Gospel* (ed. R. Bieringer, D. Pollefeyt, and F. Vandecasteele-Vanneuville; Louisville: Westminster John Knox, 2001), 11–12.

[18] Adele Reinhartz, "The Johannine Community and Its Jewish Neighbors: A Reappraisal," in Segovia, *What Is John?* 2:111–38; Reuven Kimelman, "Birkat Ha-Minim and the Lack of Evidence for an Anti-Christian Jewish Prayer in Late Antiquity," in *Jewish and Christian Self-Definition* (ed. E. P. Sanders; 3 vols.; Philadelphia: Fortress, 1980–1982), 1:226–44, 391–403.

[19] Conway cites Richard Bauckham, "For Whom Were Gospels Written?" in *The Gospels for All Christians: Rethinking the Gospel Audiences* (ed. R. Bauckham; Grand Rapids: Eerdmans, 1998), 9–48.

[20] In doing so, I join company with the following scholars who have focused upon one or another feature of the gospel's relationship with Greek tragedy: William R. Domeris, "The Johannine Drama," *JTSA* 42 (1983): 29–35; Godfrey C. Nicholson, *Death as Departure: The Johannine Descent-Ascent Schema* (SBLDS 63; Atlanta: Scholars Press, 1983); Mark W. G. Stibbe, *John as Storyteller: Narrative Criticism and the Fourth Gospel* (SNTSMS 73; Cambridge: Cambridge University Press, 1992); Tovey, *Narrative Art and Act*.

Greek tragedies were still read. If I am driven by an ideology, it is the conviction that the reduction of the significance of the gospel to creedal statements that can be summed up on a placard violates the text by ripping lines from their context and ignoring the role they serve in that context. The sign with "John 3:16" written on it suggests that its bearer possesses some certain knowledge. The words "God so loved the world that he gave his only Son," spoken in a context where one character struggles to understand how rebirth is possible, suggest a paradox and the ambiguous relationship between death and what appears to be life. When one reads the gospel attentive to its theatrical language, ambiguity and paradox usurp certitude and clarity.

The following reading of the Fourth Gospel in no way softens its polemic or attempts to target a particular historical identity as the object of that polemic. Instead of a social context, I set the gospel within a literary context in which it must compete not simply with alternate religious ideologies but with the magisterial literature that contains them.[21] When questions of history are addressed, the conclusions are largely negative insofar as I can demonstrate that features of the gospel, including the anti-Jewish polemic and the fear of synagogue eviction, can be explained in terms of the demands of the genre to which the gospel frequently conforms.

I take the argument for reliance upon dramatic conventions as far as I can without violating the form in which we now find the gospel. As Mark Stibbe states, "A drama is a story without a storyteller," and the gospel has a storyteller.[22] The presence of a narrator and his provision of information that is often necessary to the coherence to the plot are the significant features of the gospel that render it unlike a play. In treating the gospel as a performance piece, the narrator becomes a member of the dramatis personae, albeit one who takes on and interprets the parts of other characters as if he were the sole reader. While much of the narrator's role pulls the gospel's identity toward the genre of narrative, aspects of that role contribute to the dramatic structure and theatrical qualities of the gospel. It is not my intent in the following discussion that the contributions of the narrator be ignored, as if the gospel in its early form were a play to which a narrator was affixed in some later redaction. Nevertheless, wherever possible, I focus on what the gospel achieves

---

21 *Didascalia apostolorum* contains an argument that tries to dissuade Christians from reading Greek literature by claiming that Scripture is just as good. Basil, *Address to Young Men on How They Might Derive Benefit from Greek Literature* 2, advocates the study of the Greek classics as preparation for the study of Scripture.

22 Stibbe, *John as Storyteller*, 130. This distinction between narrative and drama may hold true in antiquity, but modern playwrights such as Tennessee Williams and Bertolt Brecht introduce the narrator as one of the dramatis personae who appears regularly in modern and postmodern theater.

without the aid of the narrator. By treating the gospel as a play, I intend to demonstrate at the very least that theater criticism can be a significant heuristic devise for the analysis of the gospel. Beyond this, I intend to demonstrate that although the gospel may not have been intended for the stage, much of its form is that of a performance text and that when we attend to this form, the significance of much of the gospel's content that has provoked discussions about the sacraments, soteriology, and ontology becomes instead a matter of tragic mimesis—the poetic representation of action and people.

One of the limitations of previous discussions of the dramatic form of the Fourth Gospel is the tendency of New Testament scholars to work in isolation from scholars of the Greek and Roman classics and without regard for theater and dramatic criticism. Most seem content with a passing knowledge of the Aristotelian theory that a tragedy is a unified action that contains a reversal of fortune for its hero and provides catharsis for its audience. The descriptive science of drama and theater is no longer dominated by Aristotle. Contributions by structuralists and students of theatrical communication provide a body of theatrical and dramatic theory that directs us to many avenues of research and provides language for fruitful analysis. The use of these tools by scholars who study Greek tragedy, theater, and performance serves as a model for their application to the Fourth Gospel. I draw upon the insights of theorists who do not limit themselves to ancient drama, but here I restrict myself to the Greek tragedians for my comparisons, although I will point to analogous features in Shakespeare or modern pieces to help the reader identify what I see.

The technical vocabulary for my discussion is provided for the most part by structuralists such as Keir Elam and Roman Ingarden. The techniques of semiotics allow us to look at language as multidimensional and serving multiple functions. Statements such as "I am the bread of life," long scrutinized for its symbolic importance and the possible relationship to the name of God, now can become the object of analysis as an index, a verbal gesture. The action of pointing to oneself becomes a facet of characterization that supports or provokes the action of the plot. In particular, I rely upon the distinction, drawn by Roman Ingarden and Eli Rozik, between the fictional, theatrical, and performance axes of the text (see fig. 1).[23] Delineation of these three allows us to distinguish the conventions that build tension and provide unity of plot (those that have been the focus of discussions of Johannine

---

[23] Roman Ingarden, "The Functions of Language in the Theater," in *The Literary Work of Art: An Investigation on the Borderlines of Ontology, Logic, and the Theory of Literature* (trans. George G. Grabowicz; Evanston, Ill.: Northwestern University Press, 1973), 377–96; Eli Rozik, "The Functions of Language in the Theatre," *Theatre Research International* 18 (1993): 104–14.

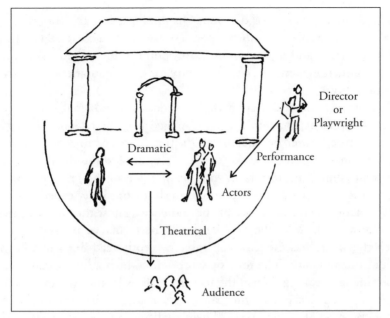

Figure 1: Axes of Text

drama) and those that construct a relationship between the text, the voice of the reader who recites the text, and its audience.

The fictional axis is the relationship between characters in the fictional world of a play. The use of the word "fiction" with reference to the gospel is problematic because many take the action to be the representation of events that actually took place whereas fiction connotes something made up altogether. Although I do not take fiction in this sense, I avoid using the term because of the confusion it might create. I will use the term "dramatic axis" to denote the action that takes place in the represented time and space of the gospel. Attention to this axis is crucial because it demands that one attend to the purpose of utterances within the action. When Jesus states, "You are from your father the devil," not only does he speak to a character; his speech is also an action directed toward another character: he is insulting his conversation partner.

The theatrical axis is the relationship between text and audience—that is, the plane on which the " 'aesthetic' effect on the audience" takes form.[24] An example from the trial scene illustrates the distinction between the first two axes. On the dramatic axis, the effect of enrobing Jesus in purple and crowning him with thorns is to humiliate him and to cause the crowd to see

---

[24] Rozik, "Functions of Language," 105.

him as an object of pity or derision. On the theatrical axis, the effect governed by irony is that the audience sees Jesus' agony as a condition of his exaltation. The robe and the crown of thorns point to his true identity, and the Roman soldiers become the objects of pity for their ignorance or of scorn for their brutality.

The aesthetic effect upon the audience is in no small part a consequence of what happens on the performance axis, the relationship between writer and performer or director and actor. If the performer (our reader) places emphasis upon the word "they"—"*they* dressed him in a purple robe. *They* kept coming up to him, saying, 'Hail, King of the Jews!' and striking him on the face" (19:2–3)—attention can shift from Jesus' experience to the soldier's actions, and the anger of the audience against the victimizer might overshadow anguish for the victimized. The performance axis is the one over which the writer has the least control. An ineptly read line can confuse or mislead the audience. The tone or speed with which a line is delivered can determine its meaning. When the reader vocalizes Pilate's question "What is truth?" he might express either sincere curiosity or extreme cynicism. As George Bernard Shaw observes, "There are fifty ways of saying Yes, and five hundred of saying No, but only one way of writing them down."[25] One means by which the playwright attempts to limit the interpretation of how a performer is to speak or appear is to encode that interpretation on the performance axis of the text. The performance axis is a component of what Ingarden calls the main text; it is not the stage directions but part of the spoken text. In Shakespeare's *The Taming of the Shrew,* when Kate begs her sister to "unknit that threatening unkind brow" (5.2.136), the actress playing Bianca ought not to be wearing a smile. When Jesus says to Mary Magdalene, "Do not hold on to me" (20:17), the reader is directed to imagine a scene in which Mary embraces Jesus.

Aspects of the Synoptic Gospels likewise can be dramatic in this respect. The institution of the Lord's Supper allows the reader to see each action witnessed by the represented gathering of disciples precisely because it is intended to be reenacted; however, moments like that one in the Synoptic Gospels are few, while in the Fourth Gospel they occur in abundance. The Fourth Evangelist's attention to the theatrical and the performance axes, and not simply the dramatic axis (to which most scholars have attended), invites this study.

Chapter 1 begins the unmasking of the gospel's theatricality by examining its dramatic structure. Its prologue and ending function like those in the tragedies by calling an audience into being and taking it into the eternal pres-

---

25 George Bernard Shaw, in the preface to *Mrs. Warren's Profession.*

ent of the represented action and then out again. The epilogue completes the action, calls for applause, and takes the audience out of the present of the action and back into its own world, in which ambiguity and uncertainty are the norms. Within this frame, I expose the similarity of organization, unity, and elements of plots, particularly with reference to their dependence on direct speech, found in the gospel to those found in tragedy. Chapter 2 is devoted to the conventions of drama by which speech constructs the world of the play and its action. Johannine language serves not simply as metaphor or symbol but also as an index pointing to the here and now of the action, the setting in which the action takes place and the world beyond the dramatic space. The long speeches and dialogues of the gospel, like those in Greek tragedy, use antitheses and verbal duels to represent the conflict and to organize the characters' thoughts so that they can be comprehended by an audience and recited by a reader or actor. Chapter 3 examines the techniques by which the gospel writer and the tragedians construct characters with subjective and private consciousness. As in tragedy, the Johannine characters tend to represent themselves through their own speech. Like the tragedians, the gospel writer makes self-identification and discussions of identity central to the action and uses corporate voices to reflect the ambiguity of the dramatic situation. This observation opens up new avenues of inquiry about the characterization of the Jews, the pairing of Simon Peter and the Beloved Disciple, the role of women in the gospel, and the significance of the failure of the gospel writer to give a dramatic role to Satan or demons. In chapter 4, I look at the plot of the gospel and how it draws upon the tropes of "beautiful death" and "marriage to death." By representing Jesus' death as voluntary and glorification rather than victimization or humiliation, the gospel writer creates a commemoration of Jesus' death, a celebration of his death rather than a lamentation.

Tradition and the tendencies of modern scholarship stand in tension with this study of the theatricality of the Fourth Gospel. The *Letter of Aristeas* contains the story of a dream in which Theodectus, a tragic poet, is afflicted with cataracts when he attempts to include a passage from the Bible in a play (*Let. Aris.* 312–321).[26] Theodore of Mopsuestia (d. 428 C.E.) argued for the exclusion of Job from the canon of the Bible because it was an imitation of a

---

[26]Aristeas's letter dates somewhere between the third century B.C.E. and the first century C.E. This attitude toward the theater did not deter at least one Jewish playwright: Ezekiel the Tragedian's *Exagoge*, a dramatization of Exodus, was composed during the same period. Unfortunately, this is our only example of a Hellenistic Jewish play. However, Moses Hadas has demonstrated that the conception of 4 Maccabees is influenced by Greek tragedy in the way it sets a scene and carries action forward through dialogue (*The Third and Fourth Books of the Maccabees* [New York: Harper, 1953], 100–101).

Greek tragedy and therefore a work of fiction.[27] The vehemence with which the early church fathers warn their readers against the evil of attending the theater, the puritanical movement that shut down the theaters of London in the early reign of James I, the pamphlets published within my own Mennonite community equating movies with the world against which Christians ought to set themselves—all these seem to speak against any consideration that the writer of the Fourth Gospel took theatrical pieces as his inspiration for the form of his composition. When the gospel writer begins his work with the words "In the beginning," he not only emulates the opening of Genesis and the canon of the Hebrew Scriptures but also makes a claim to coherence with that tradition.

Proof that the gospel writer made use of the conventions of the Greek tragedies comes in the chapters ahead, but here, before embarking upon this comparison, I must account for how the gospel writer could be well acquainted with these plays and why such imitation would be employed and desired. Dennis MacDonald, in his work on the *Acts of Andrew* and the Gospel of Mark, draws attention to how emulation of the Homeric epics plays a role in the composition of literature in the Greco-Roman era.[28] MacDonald contends that the Gospel of Mark, and Luke's as well, displays direct parallels to passages from Homer. In his analysis he presupposes that the authors of these gospels were trained in mimesis and had before them, either in memory or in physical text, their Homeric models. My argument does not require such direct borrowing from the Greek tragedies, but it does presuppose that the author of the Fourth Gospel may have laid claim to a similar training.

By the first century C.E., most performances in the theater were reduced to spectacle and pantomime. Comedies, including those of Menander, continued to be performed, but the performances of the Greek tragedies as well as the new Roman tragedies of Seneca and Ovid seem to have been limited to readings in private homes.[29] The Greek tragedies had become classics, texts

---

[27] Cited in Moses Hadas, *Hellenistic Culture* (New York: Columbia University Press, 1959), 133–34. Hadas agrees with Theodore's assessment of the influence of tragedy, particularly Aeschylus's *Prometheus*, upon Job but disagrees about its canonical status.

[28] Dennis R. MacDonald, *Christianizing Homer: "The Odyssey," Plato, and "The Acts of Andrew"* (New York: Oxford University Press, 1994); *The Homeric Epics and the Gospel of Mark* (New Haven: Yale University Press, 2000).

[29] There is no record of the performance of the Latin tragedies. Otto Zwierlein, in *Die Rezitationsdramen Senecas* (BKP 20; Meisenheim am Glan: Anton Hain, 1966), presents the argument that Seneca's tragedies were not written with the intention to be performed. This position has prevailed, but it has opponents; see, for example, Dana F. Sutton, *Seneca on the Stage* (MnemosyneSup 96; Leiden: Brill, 1986).

to be copied, emulated, and studied for their rhetorical art. Under the tute-
lage of a teacher of grammar and rhetoric, the Greco-Roman student's sylla-
bus included Homer and the great tragedians Aeschylus, Sophocles, and,
above all, Euripides, as well as the works of Menander, known to us only in
fragments.[30] The goal of this education was not simply erudition; students
prepared to become lawyers, and the study of the classics equipped them with
the rhetorical skills required for forensic oratory.

Much of what we know of Hellenistic education in the Roman Empire
comes to us through the *Institutio oratoria,* the composition of the Spanish-
born Roman teacher of rhetoric Quintilian (35–95 C.E.). Regarding mimesis,
Quintilian writes,

> There can be no doubt that in art no small portion of our task lies in imita-
> tion, since, although invention came first and is all-important, it is expedient
> to imitate whatever has been invented with success. And it is a universal rule
> of life that we should wish to copy what we approve in others. (*Inst.* 10.2.1–2
> [Butler, LCL])

Quintilian goes on to decry blind imitation for its failure in invention and
encourages his student to understand what he imitates and why it is good
(10.2.18). In the imitation of orators and poets, he encouraged the study of
how circumstances and persons were handled, the arrangement of judgments, the manner in which they spoke, procedures, method, the appeal to
emotions, and the manner in which they used applause to serve their case
(10.2.27). The goal was not to commit a speech to memory but, in
Quintilian's words, to reduce "it almost to a state of liquefaction to assist the
process of digestion" so that from this "pulp" something new could be composed (10.1.19). In his long list of appropriate objects for this mimesis, he
holds the poets above the orators (10.1.27), and among the poets, the Attic
dramatics rank alongside Homer. Though he hesitates to judge which tragedian achieved greater perfection of his genre, he recommends Euripides: "But
this much is certain and incontrovertible, that Euripides will be found of far

---

[30] Henri I. Marrou, *A History of Education in Antiquity* (trans. George Lamb;
New York: Sheed & Ward, 1956), 163–64. See Ronald F. Hock, "Homer in Greco-
Roman Education," in *Mimesis and Intertextuality in Antiquity and Christianity* (ed.
Dennis R. MacDonald; Harrisburg, Pa.: Trinity, 2001), 56–77. Hock concludes,
"Homer's role in education was varied, continuous, and profound: names from
Homer were some of the first words students ever learned, lines from Homer were
some of the first sentences they ever read, lengthy passages from Homer were the first
they ever memorized and interpreted, events and themes from Homer were the ones
they often treated in compositional exercises, and lines and metaphors from Homer
were often used to adorn their speeches and to express their self-presentation."

greater service to those who are training themselves for pleading in court" (10.1.67).

What measure of education the writer of the Fourth Gospel attained and how close it came to fulfilling Quintilian's standards are not easily determined. Scholars long ago left behind the conclusions of nineteenth-century form critics that the gospel writers were ignorant and nearly illiterate. The early patristic authors referred to their education in schools of rhetoric and advocated the study of Greek and Roman classics in a "Christian education."[31] Clement of Rome's *First Epistle to the Corinthians* contains a quotation from Sophocles (*1 Clem.* 37:4; quoting *Aj.* 158–161). St. Paul appears to have been able to quote pagan poets such as Menander (1 Cor 15:33) and Epimenides (Titus 1:12), and Luke has him quoting both Epimenides and Aratus (Acts 17:28), although these quotations may reflect familiarity with grammar school primers rather than the original works. The quality of Greek with which the author of the Fourth Gospel expresses himself leads Margaret Davies to claim no more than that he could read.[32] C. K. Barrett credits him with more literary skill:

> In spite of the small vocabulary, the reader never receives the impression of an ill-equipped writer at a loss for the right word; rather that of a teacher who is confident that this message can be summed up in a few fundamental propositions which he has learned to express with studied economy of diction.[33]

Gregory Riley contends that given the fact that the writers of the Gospels could write in Greek, they would have received an education that included memorization and imitation of the Greek heroic literature.[34] Perhaps corroboration that the author of the Fourth Gospel's "studied economy of diction" was gained while studying the Greek tragedies lies in the following demonstration of their similarities.

---

[31] See Clement of Alexandria, "The Witness of Poetry," in *Exhortation to the Greeks* 7; Basil, *Address to Young Men on How They Might Derive Benefit from Greek Literature;* M. L. W. Laistner, in *Christianity and Pagan Culture in the Later Roman Empire* (Ithaca, N.Y.: Cornell University Press, 1951), 49–73, outlines the debate in the first three centuries of the Common Era that led to the standardization of the study of "pagan" authors in the Christian curriculum. Laistner notes that those who argued most vehemently against their study betrayed their own lack of education through their inelegant prose.

[32] Margaret Davies, *Rhetoric and Reference in the Fourth Gospel* (JSNTSup 69; Sheffield, JSOT Press, 1992), 253.

[33] C. K. Barrett, *The Gospel according to St. John* (London: SPCK, 1978), 7.

[34] Gregory J. Riley, *One Jesus, Many Christs: How Jesus Inspired Not One True Christianity but Many: The Truth about Christian Origins* (San Francisco: HarperSanFrancisco, 1997), 69.

The performance of Greek and Roman tragedies in the first century of the Common Era in the form of readings to an audience in a private home provides a model for the publication of the gospel presupposed by this discussion. In *The Gospels for All Christians: Rethinking the Gospel Audiences*, Richard Bauckham and others argue that publication in a written form assumes an audience at a distance and thus a broad audience.[35] Loveday Alexander describes a process by which the "publication" of the small number of copies of the gospel that would have been produced was facilitated. A patron wealthy enough to house a copy in his library would make it available for private study and also provide a "hearth" for its public performance.[36] A public presentation of the gospel through the voice of a reader would then make the use of theatrical conventions expedient. Seneca, in his mimesis of Greek tragedy, remains obedient to the demands of the stage, perhaps without hope of seeing his plays performed. I suggest that the author of the Fourth Gospel liberated himself from such slavish adherence by employing a narrator to help tell the story and so participated in the production of a new genre contemporary with the emerging Hellenistic novel. Nevertheless, he reins in that narrator so that he does not take over the dramatic telling of the story. Just as the medieval church leaders realized that dramatization was necessary in order to make real the stories that provided meanings for the Christian festivals that became the content of faith for European Christians, so the author of the Fourth Gospel recognized the potential power of dramatic literature to make the abstract real, to bring the myth to the present, to allow the audience to envision something other than its own mundane day-to-day reality, and to allow it to see either the absurdity or the sublimity of that reality.

---

[35] See Bauckham, "For Whom Were Gospels Written?" 29–30; Michael B. Thompson, "The Holy Internet: Communication between Churches in the First Christian Generation," in Bauckham, *The Gospels for All Christians*, 69.

[36] Alexander suggests that Theophilus, whom Luke addresses, and the patrons of the Pauline churches fulfilled such a role ("Ancient Book Production and the Circulation of the Gospels," in Bauckham, *The Gospels for All Christians*, 103–4).

CHAPTER 1
Dramatic Structure

Yes, I have tricks in my pocket, I have things up my sleeve;
But I am the opposite of a stage-magician:
He gives you illusion which has the appearance of truth
And I give you truth in the pleasant disguise of illusion.
To begin, I turn back time.

—Tennessee Williams, *The Glass Menagerie*

The Fourth Gospel conforms to many of Aristotle's dictates for the structure of a tragic plot (*Poet.* 1450–1451b). It is complete with a clear beginning, middle, and end, although the gospel may have two of these. The action of the plot has a frame typically labeled with the dramatic terms "prologue" and "epilogue." It is a mimesis of an action that is "heroic and complete and of a certain magnitude" (*Poet.* 1449b). Jesus, the Son of God, asserts his identity, is unjustly rejected and executed, dies a death on behalf of others, and receives restitution in a sequence of events that appears probable or necessary. Though they are episodic, the events of scenes follow in a logical unfolding of the plot, on account of what has preceded, although the awkward sequencing of chapters 5 and 6, the scene with the adulterous woman, and the false ending (20:30) interrupt the plot's progression. Most of my predecessors have concentrated on how the gospel's action occurs in discrete sections that can be broken down into acts and scenes. Finally, much of the action of the gospel is represented through dialogue rather than narration. Although these characteristics are necessary features of the Aristotelian tragic form, they are not unique to tragedy or a play, and their presence in the gospel could be attributed to the conventions of good storytelling if not for the fact that the way that these features are achieved and the purpose they serve render them theatrical as well as suspenseful. The author of the Fourth Gospel plunders a trove of theatrical devices and conventions in order to produce his plot.

Prologue

The formality of the gospel's prologue, the contrast in tone and style with the dialogues and narrative that follow, and the contrast with the beginnings of other gospels led many form critics in the twentieth century to conclude that it was an independent hymn affixed during a stage in the redaction of the gospel's composition.[1] As Charles Giblin notes, the prologue does not contain words of praise or expressions of awe constitutive of a hymn.[2] Most scholars now concede that without the prologue, the gospel's beginning is abrupt; therefore, the prologue is preparatory to what follows. Like the prologue of a Greek tragedy, or any narrative, it prepares the audience to follow its plot. But other functions of this prologue are necessitated by the conditions of performance: they prepare the audience to be an audience. In design and function, the prologue of the Fourth Gospel bears significant resemblance to those of Euripides. The prologue initiates the audience into the privileged realm of knowing that makes irony possible, orients the audience to the broader narrative in which the action is situated and prepares it to enter the action in medias res, and calls the audience into being and gives it a role.

In beginning his plays with a formal prologue, Euripides chooses to restore an archaic convention. Ann Norris Michelini, commenting upon the "artificiality and primitivism" of his prologues, argues that as part of his ironic style Euripides exposes "the mechanisms behind his own magic."[3] By revealing the agency of the gods and the relationship of life and myth, he forces his audience to consider the capacity of words and language to produce contradictions and ambiguity. As Michelini puts it, "Instead of being absorbed into its own world, the Euripidean performance reaches out to the audience, reminding them that the neat elegance of its design was made for

---

[1] Most notably, Rudolf Bultmann (*The Gospel of John* [trans. G. R. Beasley-Murray; Philadelphia: Westminster, 1971], 13–18) considers it a preexisting gnostic hymn devoted to John the Baptist and adapted by the gospel writer. John A. T. Robinson ("The Relation of the Prologue to the Gospel of St. John," in *Twelve More New Testament Studies* [London: SCM, 1984], 65–76) argues that the prologue is a hymn composed by the author after writing the gospel. Raymond Brown (*The Gospel according to John* [2 vols.; AB 29, 29A; Garden City, N.Y.: Doubleday, 1966–1970], 1:21) believes that the prologue was a hymn of the Johannine church later revised and affixed to the gospel.

[2] Charles H. Giblin, "Two Complementary Literary Structures in John 1:1–18," *JBL* 104 (1985): 94.

[3] Ann Norris Michelini, *Euripides and the Tragic Tradition* (Madison: University of Wisconsin Press, 1987), 105.

human minds to inhabit."[4] The revelations of the prologue, what Michelini calls "the pre-conditions for the dramatic action," stand outside the knowledge of the actors or participants in that action.[5] The audience then joins in a sort of collusion with the narrator by sharing privileged knowledge and transcending the finite realm of normal human experience to view what normally cannot be seen: the workings of the cosmic order. The vantage point or "discrepant awareness" between fictional characters and the audience afforded by the prologue allows the audience to enjoy the irony offered by the action of the drama.[6] The design of the Greek theater, in which the audience looked down upon the stage, reinforced this experience of transcendence.[7] From its privileged vantage point, the audience—separated from the participants in the action, who view reality as "a random play of events"—can see the significance of the unfolding action.[8] Provided with information about Jesus' identity (the Word of God incarnate and God's only Son [1:14, 18]) and a summary of the plot (he comes into the world to his own people, who do not accept him [1:10–11]), the audience of the gospel similarly recognizes the implications of actions and the "truth" that lies behind veiled or unwitting assertions. Whatever the provenance of the prologue, without it the audience of the gospel would enter the action without orientation and be left to respond to Jesus' signs and assertions with the same bewilderment shown by characters within the gospel.[9]

Euripidean prologues rarely give away as much of the plot as does that of the Fourth Gospel. In the prologue to *Hecuba*, the ghost of Polydorus, son of Priam and Hecuba, appears and recounts the sacrifice of his sister Polyxena and his own murder at the hands of Polymestor, into whose care he had been entrusted. In the action that follows, Polyxena's sacrifice takes place. Such prologues not only set the stage but also prepare the audience to feel the pathos of the unsuccessful arguments that follow. Just as we know that Hecuba's attempts to persuade Odysseus to spare her daughter in the first half of the play will fail, we know that Jesus will not persuade the crowd of his identity.

---

4 Ibid., 106–7.

5 Ibid., 105.

6 Manfred Pfister, *The Theory and Analysis of Drama* (trans. J. Halliday; Cambridge: Cambridge University Press, 1988), 50. Cf. Paul D. Duke, *Irony in the Fourth Gospel* (Atlanta: John Knox, 1985), 24.

7 David Wiles, *Tragedy in Athens: Performance Space and Theatrical Meaning* (Cambridge: Cambridge University Press, 1997), 177.

8 Michelini, *Euripides and the Tragic Tradition*, 124–26.

9 Morna Hooker ("John's Prologue and the Messianic Secret," *NTS* 21 [1974]: 42–43) compares the function of Mark 1:1–13 to that of John 1:1–18 to make this point.

Given that Greek plays deal with traditional material from the Homeric epics and Greek mythologies, the Euripidean prologue need not summarize the story as much as situate the plot in the appropriate narrative and then provide important cues to the audience to help prepare for any departures or contradictions. The prologue of Euripides' *Helen*, delivered by Helen, begins by providing a summary of her birth narrative and the events that lead to the war with Troy, and then introduces a startling revelation: the Helen who was taken by Paris to Troy is a double, "an airy delusion," conjured up by Hera in a complicated plot of revenge against Aphrodite, her rival for the title of the most beautiful. Similarly, in Euripides' *Iphigenia among the Taurians*, the audience meets the daughter of Agamemnon living years after her apparent death as a sacrificial victim to the Trojan War. In the prologue, Iphigenia explains how Artemis replaced her with a deer and stole her away to the land of the Taurians (24–31). The first line of John's prologue, "In the beginning was the Word" (1:1), grounds the historic present in Hebraic myth; the historical Jesus is linked to the mythic origins of creation. With its echoes of the wisdom tradition, the prologue may assist the audience in recognizing the continuity between the incarnation and orthodox tradition. As Wayne Meeks notes, the line "He was in the world, and the world came into being through him; yet the world did not know him" (1:10) contains the central theme of the Jewish wisdom myth; but Meeks also points out that in most Jewish versions of the myth, wisdom finds acceptance by Israel in the Sinai covenant.[10] Nothing in Jewish tradition prepares the audience for the idea that God would send his preexistent Son to restore humanity to the status of children of God. The prologue therefore marks a significant departure from the myth and alone prepares the audience to follow the rationale of Jesus' words and deeds in the gospel.[11] The Fourth Gospel's departures from the chronology and events of the Synoptic version of Jesus' life, together with the differences in the content of Jesus' preaching, typically are treated as data pointing to the development of a Johannine community in isolation from the communities of the Synoptic tradition.[12] The miracle at the wedding at Cana is the inaugural event of Jesus' public ministry. The cleansing of the temple occurs

---

[10] Wayne Meeks, "The Man from Heaven in Johannine Sectarianism," *JBL* 91 (1972): 61.

[11] Elizabeth Harris (*Prologue and Gospel: The Theology of the Fourth Gospel* [JSNTSup 107; Sheffield: Sheffield Academic Press, 1994], 45) makes the same argument.

[12] See D. Moody Smith, *John among the Gospels: The Relationship in Twentieth-Century Research* (Minneapolis: Fortress, 1992), for an account of the development of this consensus.

at the beginning of the story and does not precipitate Jesus' death sentence. Lazarus, the principal of a parable in Luke, and his resurrection take on the role of catalyst for the arrest. Jesus' speeches defend his claim to divine status rather than describe the nature of the kingdom of heaven. If the first audience was familiar with the Synoptic tradition, the prologue may have served to prepare it, as it does contemporary readers, for such departures by providing significant clues about what to expect: certainly not a peripatetic preaching career interrupted and terminated by a conflict based upon the sanctity of the temple.

As in the prologue to Euripides' *Bacchae,* in which Dionysus gives an account of how he came to be in Thebes, the gospel's prologue explains how the divine came to be striding about Judea and the Galilee. This explanation then provides the conditions for the antagonism that greets Jesus. The bold claims of Jesus to possess an authority that goes beyond that of a prophet and an ancestry that is other than human will clash with what is known of Jesus' parentage and birthplace by those who inhabit the story. In *Bacchae,* Dionysus lays out the tension of claims about his status more baldly. He begins by proclaiming his divinity: "I am the son of Zeus, Dionysus. Semele, the daughter of Cadmus, bore me once in a birth precipitated by the lightening flame" (1–2 [Morwood]). His incarnation is necessitated by the refusal of some to believe, among them his mother's sisters, who deny that he is the son of Zeus and accuse Semele of using Zeus to hide her seduction by a mortal (27–29). Similarly, Amphitryon explains the tensions of divine parentage in the prologue to *Heracles.* In order to dwell within the homeland of his mortal father, Heracles must perform labors, the last of which is to descend to Hades, where he is when the play begins and from which he will return in the course of the action with the once-dead Theseus. Early in the play, Heracles' antagonist, who seeks to kill his family, voices the obvious challenge of one who does not possess the knowledge shared by Amphitryon in his prologue. Lycus asks, "Do you believe that the father of these children, who lies dead in Hades, will return?" (145–146 [Kovacs, LCL]), and he accuses Amphitryon of seeking glory by boasting that Zeus shared his wife and fathered his son (148–149). These plays, like the gospel, begin by bringing sharply into focus the ambiguity of the hero's situation in a world of blind violence. Heracles himself becomes subject to this confusion of truth and appearance when Hera sends madness to seize him, and he slays his children and wife, thinking that they belong to Eurystheus, his taskmaster. In *Bacchae,* Agave, in a similar fit of madness, participates in the dismembering of her own son Pentheus, whom she has taken for the animal prey of a frenzied hunt. In the gospel, the metaphorically blind leaders, thinking that he is a man subject to the finality of death, crucify the Son of God.

Mark Stibbe, in *John as Storyteller*, provides a detailed comparison of the similarities of content between the prologues of the gospel and *Bacchae*. Both describe the incarnation of a divine being who chooses to reveal himself to people who fail to recognize him and refuse to worship him. In both prologues, one person—Cadmus in *Bacchae* and John the Baptist in the gospel—is identified as an exception.[13] Both of these characters then assume important roles in the initial action prior to the entrance of their deities. Neither Stibbe nor I suggest that the gospel writer had a particular prologue, let alone that of *Bacchae,* before him. Stibbe argues that the similarities reflect the mythos of tragedy, a form embedded in the cultures of both Euripides and the evangelist.[14] The introduction of the plot line in which a deity who has become incarnate will be rejected prepares the audience for the tragic consequences of the failure of recognition.

A prologue, formally separate from the action and a seemingly contrived beginning, facilitates the drama by taking the audience a certain distance into the action. A play, unlike a biography, for example, begins in medias res, and so the audience must be prepared to step into its flow. The prologue therefore introduces the first characters to appear and sets the mood of the first scene. When Polydorus closes his prologue with the line "But now I shall get out of the path of aged Hecuba, for she is coming out from the tent of Agamemnon, frightened at the sight of me in her dream" (*Hecuba* 52–54 [Kovacs, LCL]), the audience knows who enters and the reason for her disposition. The gospel's prologue twice introduces John (1:6–8, 15) and the role he will play in the plot.[15] Johannine scholars continue to question the integrity of the prologue and ask whether these verses served as the original introduction to which the poem later was appended or whether they are the later insertions. The first hypothesis seems untenable. Alone, these verses establish John's role in relation to Jesus, but they do not prepare for the pathos of the gospel. The verses may be a later insertion, but they are a necessary

---

[13] Mark W. G. Stibbe, *John as Storyteller: Narrative Criticism and the Fourth Gospel* (SNTSMS 73; Cambridge: Cambridge University Press, 1992), 136–37. Although the gospel identifies the Baptist only as John, I will use the longer title to prevent confusion with John the supposed author, even though I refrain from referring to the author by any given name.

[14] Ibid., 137.

[15] Harris (*Prologue and Gospel,* 38) notes that vv. 6–8 function like the *parodos* of a Greek tragedy, the song accompanying the entrance of the chorus, and that Sophocles similarly interrupts his informal prologue to *Electra* with the *parodos*. Harris does not press the point beyond suggesting that the gospel writer may be following a convention. The comparison to a *parodos* may be unnecessary, given the tendency of Euripidean prologues to include the introduction of characters.

one. When the action of the gospel begins, the narrator provides information about who speaks, but the prologue has provided the crucial information about the Baptist's role as a witness rather than a forerunner.

Historical critics make much of the supposed rivalry between the disciples of Jesus and those of the Baptist by contrasting John's denial with Jesus' confession, but if we focus upon the actual plot of the gospel, the prologue allows the story to begin with a short scene that prepares for Jesus' entrance. In contrast to the Gospel of Mark, the narrative of which also begins with the Baptist by marking the continuity between the call to repentance—the substance of John and Jesus' ministry—and expectations, the prologue anticipates and describes tension. Those whom God has sent are not, and do not do, what people expect. Moreover, the struggle is between the individual, John, who testifies to the light, and the group, the world, who thinks it knows the truth but actually knows the darkness. Jesus can step into this duel about dualism without narration providing context or background. The stage is set for conflict, not a preaching ministry in Galilee.

Although the Fourth Gospel's prologue bears little direct resemblance to the form of those of Euripides, characterized by prosaic rather than poetic structure, one organizational principle renders their forms comparable. Through counterpoint, the prologues of both the tragedies and the gospel strike the chords of tension with which the action begins. In the gospel, the language of light versus darkness and reception versus rejection sounds the opposing themes that will dominate the action.[16] Although the tragedies do not begin with comparably elaborate chiastic and parallel stanzas, similar sets of polar opposites appear. Poseidon, in *The Trojan Women,* juxtaposes his divine construction of Troy with its destruction by Hera and Athena. The reported images of temples running with blood and Priam's dead body at the base of the altar (βάθροις) of Zeus, Protector of the House (15–17), grotesquely portray the tension between the city's glory, with its honor to the gods, and the defeat of its men, with the ensuing impiety to the gods in the treatment of its women. The prologue ends with words that link destruction with the loss of piety: "So, towers of dressed stone, city once prosperous, farewell! If Zeus' daughter Pallas had not destroyed you, you would still be standing firm on your foundations [βάθροις]" (45–47 [Kovacs, LCL]). The word βάθροις is used earlier to refer to the city's altars. In *Iphigenia among the Taurians,* Iphigenia contrasts her former status as a sacrifice to Artemis by the

---

[16] Herman Ridderbos ("The Structure and Scope of the Prologue of the Gospel of John," *NovT* 8 [1966]: 191) anticipates J. Louis Martyn by arguing that this conflict of opposing forces is not "pious meditation" or "theological speculation" but a reflection of the struggle in which the *evangelist* stands.

Greeks with her present role as the priestess of Artemis who sacrifices Greeks (1–41). Iolaus, in *Children of Heracles,* begins with the contrast of the man who is just to his neighbors with one who is good only to himself. He then begins a speech, describing his and the children's predicament, that moves through a chiastic ordering of the following topics: the honor of his former share in Heracles' labors, Heracles' dwelling in heaven, his own exile, and his current state of weakness and shame (1–54). The language of dualism in all of these prologues is a semantic feature of their plots. In *Children of Heracles,* the plot begins where the prologue leaves off, with the abuse of Iolaus, who, in the course of the play, along with the Athenians, responds with an act of bravery that restores his honor. The play ends with the ignoble death of his adversary, thereby bringing the opposing themes of the prologue full circle. Similarly, in the gospel, the dualism of light versus darkness and acceptance versus ignorance provides structure to the plot. Those who fail to recognize Jesus stand in darkness and act upon their ignorance, but instead of Jesus' light being overcome, death becomes the occasion for his glory to be made visible.

The functions of a prologue identified above serve the needs of a narrative as well as that of a performance piece. In the context of a performance, the prologue takes on a number of additional roles unique to the theatrical axis. The first of these is to signal its beginning. The act of reading is initiated with a clearly intentional act; one picks up the text and reads. The act of listening requires an interruption; the audience must be quieted and its attention turned to the action on stage.[17] In a Greek theater, where no lights could be dimmed or curtain drawn, the prologue was designed to do this and therefore had to be strong or energetic. Moreover, its design had to move in repetitive or circular patterns so that an inattentive listener would not miss something crucial. In *The Frogs,* Aristophanes dramatizes Euripides' rationale for the prologue by having Euripides complain about Aeschylus's habit of "raving haphazardly, and rushing into the thick of things."[18] In *Bacchae,* Euripides attends to the needs of members of his audience who may have missed Dionysus's first lines, which tell that he has assumed the form of a man and has come to Thebes (1–4), by having the deity repeat the important information in lines 23 and 53–54. In the context of ancient worship or a gathering of Christians, a reading of the gospel would require some sort of similar interruption. "In the beginning," then, serves as a double entendre: it refers both to time (the beginning of the story) and to itself (the beginning of the

---

[17] Peter D. Arnott, *Public and Performance in the Greek Theatre* (London: Routledge, 1989), 6–7.
[18] Cited ibid., 7

gospel). Key concepts, the coidentity of the Word and God (1:1, 18) and the role of the Word in creation (1:3, 10), are repeated later in the prologue, in part, through the facilitation of its chiastic structure.[19]

Perhaps the most significant task of the dramatic prologue is to bridge the distance of time and place between the action of the play and the situation of the audience. The prologue invites the audience into the eternal present of the stage. Thorton Wilder describes this phenomenon:

> On stage it is always now; the personages are standing on that razor edge, between the past and the future, which is the essential character of conscious being; the words are rising to their lips in immediate spontaneity. . . . The theater is supremely fitted to say: "Behold! These things are."[20]

By addressing the audience, the Euripidean prologue invites it to treat the events on stage as though they were unfolding before its eyes. The tragedies were not written as though a fourth wall were erected and the audience were not present. The character that delivers the prologue reaches out to the audience and establishes a relationship with it, and in this way extends a hand that invites the audience into the drama's time and place. The character that gives the prologue enters into collusion with the audience by revealing himself or herself to the audience and assigning it a role. In *Alcestis*, Apollo begins,

> House of Admetus? In you I brought myself to taste the bread of menial servitude, god though I am. Zeus was the cause: he killed my son Asclepius, striking him in the chest with the lightning-bolt, and in anger at this I slew the Cyclopes who forged Zeus's fire. (1–6 [Kovacs, LCL])

As easily as the actor becomes Apollo by alluding to his myth and perhaps by carrying a bow, the symbol by which the god was identified, the audience becomes the House of Admetus. In Aeschylus's *Eumenides*, the audience is identified with visitors to the shrine. The Pythia begins with a prayer in honor of the gods (1–30) and then turns to the audience and addresses it: "Where are the Greeks among you? Draw your lots and enter" (31 [Fagles]). Given that the first audience of the play was Greek, the line cleverly invites the viewers to identify with the role they are given.

The sudden use of the first-person plural pronoun in the gospel's prologue functions in a similar way. When the audience hears, "The Word be-

---

[19] Charles H. Talbert ("Artistry and Theology: An Analysis of the Architecture of Jn 1,19–5,47," *CBQ* 32 [1970]: 365) argues that the chiastic structure serves this need of the audience as well as assisting the memory of the author or reader.

[20] Quoted in Malcolm Cowley, ed., *Writers at Work: The Paris Review Interviews* (New York: Viking, 1958), 58.

came flesh and lived among us, and we have seen his glory" (1:14), it is prepared to become a witness to the events and to Jesus' divine majesty. Readers of the Fourth Gospel have tended to conflate the identity of the prologue's assigned narrator with its author and have attributed the use of the first-person plural pronoun in the prologue to the authorial voice. But a line at the end of the gospel, "This is the disciple who is testifying to these things and has written them, and we know that his testimony is true" (21:24), suggests that the author of the gospel and the narrator have two different identities. Scholars have resorted to theories that attribute this split to stages of composition in which early drafts of the gospel were supplemented by the contributions of an editorial committee. The existence of an editorial committee then explains use of the first-person plural pronoun in one verse of the prologue: "And the Word became flesh and lived among us, and we have seen his glory, the glory as of a father's only son, full of grace and truth" (1:14). The identification of the narrator's voice with the author reflects the habit of reading the gospel as though it were written for solitary consumption rather than public performance. In a public reading, the prologue would be read by an identifiable person who continues in the role of narrator, and the use of the first-person plural pronoun recognizes that the reader stands before an audience, in contrast to the disembodied narrator of the gospels of Matthew and Mark. The "us" and "we" denote the shared status of narrator and audience as denizens of the world into which the Word came. The use of the first person in the prologue then functions in much the same way as the statements of self-identification in tragic prologues, except that the identity of the narrator belongs to whoever reads the text, and thus remains unassigned until a recital. This puzzling use of the first-person plural at the beginning and end of the gospel is thereby solved if one pictures the publication of the gospel as a recitation by a reader to an audience. Treating the text as a performance text requires that we distinguish between the author and the narrator, that we conflate the identities of the narrator and the reader (the reader takes on the person of the narrator through the locution of the text), and that we make a distinction between reader and audience.

The movement of the prologue in the Fourth Gospel is toward the audience, toward the visible, toward incarnation, down a vertical axis from heaven to earth and along a horizontal axis from past to present.[21] The abstract language, with its obscured signification, resonates with the opacity of

---

[21] Ed L. Miller ("The Logic of the Logos Hymn: A New View," *NTS* 29 [1983]: 552–56) describes four strophes "suitable for antiphonal recitation" that progress on the temporal axis from the Logos in a preexistent state, at creation, in the incarnation, and then in the present.

our vision of the divine and the primordial order. As the language gains lucidity, its focus becomes the seen and the known, the world. It connects the experience of the audience with the mythic order by means of the lines "And the Word became flesh and lived among us, and we have seen his glory, the glory as of a father's only son, full of grace and truth," and "From his fullness we have all received, grace upon grace." The prologue ends with the assertion "No one has ever seen God." What follows in the gospel, as in Peter Brook's "holy theatre," is an art that offers the conditions whereby the invisible, Jesus' divine glory, is made visible to an audience.[22]

The Organization of Plot

The prologue takes the audience into the perpetual present of the action. The action itself is structured along a second temporal principle, that of sequence.[23] The playwright must tell the story in such a way as to reduce or manipulate it into a set of actions that can be dramatized as a succession of dialogues between central figures. Moreover, the time in which key events unfold and the time in which the dramatized action takes place must appear to be the same. Greek tragedies, plays in general, and the Fourth Gospel tend to do this by limiting the number of episodes and having each follow logically from the action that precedes it. On stage, the story must unfold sequentially in particular locations populated by identifiable characters. In the Synoptic Gospels, precisely when or where something happens or who says something does not necessarily affect the coherence of the narrative. For example, in Luke, Jesus' saying about the narrow door is introduced by these two verses: "Jesus went through one town and village after another, teaching as he made his way to Jerusalem. Someone asked him, 'Lord, will only a few be saved?'" (Luke 13:22–23). Sometime, somewhere, for some unstated reason, someone speaks. The Fourth Evangelist, in contrast, is as attentive as a dramatist to where and when something happens and to who speaks. This formal similarity is generated by a number of constitutive characteristics of drama: the relationship between episodes and the movement of characters within the dramatic space, transitions designed to measure the tension or

---

22 Peter Brook, *The Empty Space* (New York: Atheneum, 1968), 56.

23 Keir Elam (*The Semiotics of Theatre and Drama* [London: Routledge, 1980], 117–18) identifies four temporal levels: present, sequence, chronological time (the amount of time that has passed), and historical time (a definite time transformed into now).

mood of the dramatic action, strategic ordering of information to build suspense, and unity of time and place.

The Episodic Structure

In part, the episodic nature of the tragedies and the gospel is the result of the movement of characters on and off stage. In Greek tragedy, the episodic structure is necessitated by the fact that there are as many as three actors or as few as one to play all the principal parts. Peter Arnott counts twenty-three parts in Aristophanes' *Birds,* divided between three actors.[24] The chorus in *Oedipus Tyrannus* interrupts a heated exchange between Oedipus and Creon with the words "Cease, my lords! In timely fashion I see Iocaste here coming from the house" (631–633 [Lloyd-Jones, LCL]). Sophocles maintains a brief exchange between all three actors long enough for Iocaste to be apprised of the nature of the conflict. The actor playing Creon then exits, and when he appears again, he has assumed the part of the messenger. The chorus, as well as the actors, changes rolls and can function as a group of citizens, attendants, or suppliants. The gospel writer also seems to limit himself to two or three principals and then a crowd or the disciples as a group. Dialogues are then the encounters between Jesus and one other individual or a crowd.

Entrances and exits are constitutive of drama.[25] The arrival of a person to a setting begins a dialogue. A third party entering can end a conversation, for the dialogues are seldom exchanges between more than two characters, and when all principal actors exit, the actions comes to an end. While the evangelist uses the narrator to stitch dialogues together and is not always careful about how scenes end, he is attentive to the movement of people in and out of scenes, and that movement carries the action forward. When Nicodemus arrives, the dialogue begins. The Samaritan woman does not approach until the disciples have left to find food, and the disciples do not engage in dialogue until the woman departs. By recording what they do not say, the narrator underscores the fact that the disciples do not interact with the woman: "They were astonished that he was speaking with a woman, but no one said, 'What do you want?' or, 'Why are you speaking with her?'" (John 4:27). The dialogue with the disciples over the bread-of-life discourse begins only when the crowd is gone, for the disciples are seldom around when Jesus is interacting with others.

---

24 Peter Arnott, *An Introduction to Greek Theatre* (New York: St. Martin's, 1967), 27.

25 See Oliver Taplin, *Greek Tragedy in Action* (Berkeley: University of California Press, 1978), 31.

The clearest example of the gospel's adherence to this stage convention occurs in John 9, which contains seven distinct scenes demarcated by the change in personae:

Scene 1: Jesus speaks with the disciples and to the blind man. (9:1–7)

Scene 2: The man, now sighted, reports his healing to his neighbors. (9:8–12)

Scene 3: The man speaks with the Pharisees. (9:13–17)

Scene 4: The Pharisees speak with the man's parents. (9:18–23)

Scene 5: The Pharisees speak with the man. (9:24–34)

Scene 6: Jesus speaks with the man. (9:35–38)

Scene 7: The Pharisees speak with Jesus. (9:39–41)

J. Louis Martyn treats the chapter as the dramatic expansion of the healing story in vv. 1–7.[26] A similar pattern of change of characters gives shape to the structure of the healing of the lame man, the resurrection of Lazarus, and Jesus' trial. In John 11, Jesus speaks with Martha, Martha exits to call Mary, with whom she speaks privately, and Mary exits to find Jesus. The narrator underscores that the logic of this movement is carried by the dialogue when he tells us that the Jews misinterpret Mary's intent and think that she is going to the tomb, so they follow her (11:31b). After speaking with Mary, Jesus exits to the tomb, where he speaks with Martha. The action is more cinematic than in a classical tragedy in that the character exiting one scene enters the next scene in a new setting. In a Greek tragedy, Jesus would exit the first scene to allow Mary to enter and speak on stage with her sister. Nevertheless, the gospel writer clearly is following a theatrical convention as a way of handling the centrality of dialogue to the action of the gospel.

If we look at the Synoptic Gospels, we find a sharply contrasting picture of how characters enter and exit scenes. In Matt 8, for example, Jesus heals a leper in one setting and a centurion's servant in another; spends time in Peter's mother-in-law's house, where he heals her; moves to an undisclosed setting where a scribe approaches and prompts the "foxes have holes" saying; gets into a boat and stills a storm; and then encounters the Gadarene demoniacs. None of these episodes are carried by the dialogue. They tend to end in pronouncements that do not call for a continuation of the action, and the next brief encounter is not prompted by its predecessor. Later in the gospel, Jesus is talking to the disciples and violating the Sabbath when some Pharisees pop up in a grain field to confront him (Matt 12:1). These chance en-

---

[26]J. Louis Martyn, *History and Theology in the Fourth Gospel* (rev. ed.; Nashville: Abingdon, 1979), 26–27.

counters render the Synoptic Gospels more like the romance novels than a Greek tragedy.[27] Contingency plays a less significant role in the Fourth Gospel. As in drama, each character has a motive or a purpose for being present, and each is strategically positioned in anticipation of the conclusion of the story. Perhaps this concession to logic requires the Fourth Evangelist to take Jesus to Jerusalem three times rather than allowing the citizens of Jerusalem to habituate Galilee.

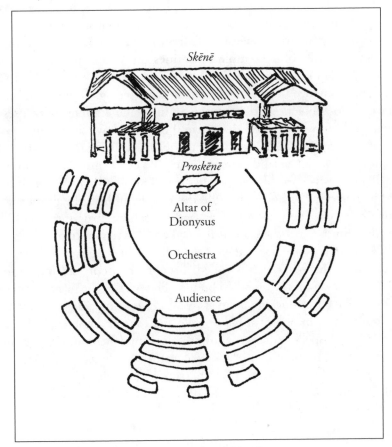

Figure 2: The Greek Theater

Exits and entrances do not simply demarcate scenes and acts, nor are they simply necessitated by the limited numbers of actors; they give shape

---

[27] Mikhail Bakhtin, "Forms of Time and of the Chronotope in the Novel," in *The Dialogic Imagination: Four Essays* (ed. Michael Holquist; trans. Caryl Emerson and Michael Holquist; Austin: University of Texas Press, 1981), 94.

to what one sees. Exits and entrances serve to isolate Jesus as well as other characters upon the stage and thereby make visible the conflict or intimacy between characters. Nicodemus's entrance dramatizes the alienation that he experiences from his voluntary association and prepares the audience for the way that he separates himself from the group later in the gospel. The movement of Pilate from inside the praetorium, where he speaks with Jesus, to outside, where he speaks with the Jews, dramatizes his attempt to control the action. While appearing to speak as Jesus' advocate, he actually is orchestrating the Jews' affirmation of the authority that he represents. Jesus' isolation during the trial scene accentuates the conflict between the uncompromising attitudes of the temple authorities and Jerusalem crowd, those of Jesus, and Pilate's own political machinations and motives. If this scene were to be dramatized upon the Athenian stage (see fig. 2), it would bear resemblance to the action in *Agamemnon* in which Clytemnestra uses her powers of manipulation and deceptive speech to draw characters into the interior of her palace. The exterior is the realm of dialogue where first Agamemnon and then Cassandra are persuaded to enter into the interior space that Clytemnestra controls and where she will murder them. Agamemnon is lured by flattery; Cassandra, by a desire to have fulfilled the prophecy that no one believes. The interior action and Cassandra's true intent is hidden from the chorus until the door is opened and Clytemnestra emerges upon the *ekkyklēma* (ἐκκύκλημα), a device that allows the audience to see interior space. When the *ekkyklēma* is rolled through the door and out onto the *proskēnē* (προσκηνή), the bloodied bodies of her victims lie in a tableau upon it. Pilate, like Clytemnestra, controls what the Jews outside see by bringing Jesus out first as an object of his ridicule and then as an object of his judgment.[28] The gospel's audience, allowed to see into the interior space of the praetorium, witnesses Pilate's lack of control over Jesus. The conflict between truth and politics is made clear. Truth is found only in the private encounter with Jesus, and the manipulation and appeasement of the desire of the crowd are found in public.[29]

Transitions

The way that the author of the Fourth Gospel handles transitions between episodes, by employing the narrator to provide a short bridge that

---

[28] For a detailed examination of how the direct speech in this scene controls the action, see chapter 2, pp. 86–87.

[29] For more discussion of the significance of public and private space, see chapter 3.

moves Jesus from one setting to the next, bears no resemblance to the transitions between major scenes in the tragedies. The way that he ends some episodes, however, seems to be guided by a tragic convention. In Greek tragedy, episodes are divided by a *stasimon* (στάσιμον), a choral ode in which the chorus comments upon or reacts to the preceding episode. The gospel writer frequently provides comments that function in a manner similar to that of the *stasimon* by measuring the mood of the action.[30] Sometimes they are provided by the narrator, and sometimes by a collective voice.

The *stasima* in Sophocles' *Ajax* illustrate how the temper of the chorus measures the development of mood in the play. The play begins with Ajax bent upon self-destruction, and so the chorus, comprised of his sailors, comments in the first *stasimon*, "I am greatly anxious and am fearful, like the troubled glance of the winged dove" (139–140 [Lloyd-Jones, LCL]). After Ajax appears to have relinquished his suicidal mania, the chorus expresses its exuberance:

> I thrill with longing, and leap up in my delight! Hail, hail, Pan, Pan! Pan, Pan, wandering over the sea, appear from the snow-beaten rocky ridge of Cyllene, lord who directs the dances of the gods, so that you can be with me and tread the Mysian and Cnosian measures that you have taught yourself! No, it is my wish to dance! And may Apollo, lord of Delos, come over the Icarian sea and be with me, forever kindly! (693–705)

When Menelaus and Teucer exit the scene in which Ajax's death is discovered, the joy of the chorus gives way to anguish:

> What will be the final number of the wandering years? When will their count end, the years that bring for me the ceaseless torment of the sufferings of battle, in the wide land of Troy, a mournful reproach for the Greeks? . . . And before my shield against nocturnal fear and arrows was mighty Ajax. But now he is made over to a hateful god. What joy, what joy yet remains for me? I wish I were where the wooded cape, beaten by the surf, projects over the sea, beneath the high plateau of Sunium, so that I could salute sacred Athens! (1185–1222)

Although the audience follows the plot knowing all along that Ajax intends to kill himself, the action moves through moods of apprehension, joy, and then grief.

---

[30] Neal Flanagan ("The Gospel of John as Drama," *TBT* 19 [1981]: 267) suggests, "The narrator functions like a Greek chorus to move action along and to comment on its significance." Paul Duke (*Irony in the Fourth Gospel*, 140–41) concedes that these reflections are in the style of those offered by the tragic chorus and that the gospel writer was acquainted with the Greek tragedies, but he insists, "It would be ridiculous, of course, to suppose the author intended to write anything like a play."

When Johannine scholars examine the comments of the narrator and the collective characters following an episode in the gospel, attention tends to focus upon whether they mark acceptance or rejection of Jesus, while the effect upon the tone of the action is ignored. The first scenes of the gospel pass swiftly through a demonstration of Jesus' power with no open conflict, and the words of the Samaritans at the end of the episode with the woman at the well give voice to the mood of the action: "It is no longer because of what you said that we believe, for we have heard for ourselves, and we know that this is truly the Savior of the world" (4:42). Exuberance gives way to ambivalence by the end of the Festival of Booths as disciples desert Jesus and as family members and authorities oppose him. The concluding comments of the crowd in Jerusalem express this turn toward uncertainty:

> Is not this the man whom they are trying to kill? And here he is, speaking openly, but they say nothing to him! Can it be that the authorities really know that this is the Messiah? Yet we know where this man is from; but when the Messiah comes, no one will know where he is from. (7:25–27)

By the end of Jesus' public discourses, the shift in mood that makes his execution possible is marked by a comment of the narrator: "Although he had performed so many signs in their presence, they did not believe in him" (12:37). He calls this disbelief a fulfillment of Isa 53:1 and 6:10 and then concludes,

> Isaiah said this because he saw his glory and spoke about him. Nevertheless many, even of the authorities, believed in him. But because of the Pharisees they did not confess it, for fear that they would be put out of the synagogue; for they loved human glory more than the glory that comes from God. (12:41–43)

Though we cannot ignore that these closing comments are an indictment against the Pharisees, we should observe that they also serve to end the dialogue with a sense of bitter resignation. The comments at the end of episodes, like the *stasima* of a tragedy, register the shifts in emotions as the action progresses.

The Unity of Plot

The ostensible lack of unity in the composition of the Fourth Gospel has been the occasion for theories of displacement, various sources, and multiple editions. Those who argue that the gospel is the composition of one individual must contend with differences in style, inconsistencies in sequence, and unevenness in the finish of scenes.[31] Nevertheless, these problems do not obscure the unity that drives the gospel's plot. The gospel's sequence of episodes unmistakably moves toward a climax. Although Aristotle would not have commended it for its elegance, he would have spared it his worst criticism, reserved for the episodic plot in which one episode does not necessarily follow from another (*Poet.* 1451b 34–35). The Gospel of Matthew, in which miracle follows miracle without any apparent organizing principles, would earn Aristotle's censure. In the Fourth Gospel, signs of Jesus' power prompt dialogues in which Jesus repeatedly attests to his own authority with increasing insistence and clarity, and as a result, his dramatic audience becomes more hostile. Though the evangelist may have rushed his composition, his gospel may have suffered some mishap leading to disarrangement, and editors may have laid their hands to it, the impulse toward unity is evident especially when the devices that unite its parts are examined in the light of the glorious achievement of unity in the Greek tragedies.

This unity of action in the tightly managed economy of a play is achieved through attention to a strategic ordering of information. Keir Elam borrows the Russian formalists' differentiation between *fabula* (story) and *sjuzet* (plot) to explain how the represented actions and events—the plot—with their heterogeneity (some enacted and others reported), discontinuity (shifts in scenes from one setting to another), and incompleteness (gaps in the action) must be coherent enough for the spectator to follow the logic of the action. What is more, this same spectator must be able to abstract what Elam calls a "paraphrase of a pseudo-narrative" in order to recount a story.[32] In order to condense action and events essential to the maintenance of their story and the unity of the plot, the Synoptic authors avail themselves of summaries.[33] Paragraphs such as the following occur frequently in Matthew:

> Jesus went throughout Galilee, teaching in their synagogues and proclaiming the good news of the kingdom and curing every disease and every sickness among the people. So his fame spread throughout all Syria, and they brought to him all the sick, those who were afflicted with various diseases and pains, demoniacs, epileptics, and paralytics, and he cured them. And great crowds followed him from Galilee, the Decapolis, Jerusalem, Judea, and from beyond the Jordan. (Matt 4:23–25)

---

[31] For a more detailed examination, see Brown, *The Gospel according to John,* 1:xxiv–xxxiv.

[32] Elam, *Semiotics of Theatre and Drama,* 119–20.

[33] Matt 4:23–25; 9:35–36; 15:29–31; 19:1–2; Mark 1:45; 6:53–56; Luke 2:52; 4:14–15; 5:15–16; 8:1–3.

The author of the Fourth Gospel eschews such iterative and repetitive summaries. As with a play that builds a story for its protagonist without narration through the comments of characters, the audience learns from the comments of characters about Jesus' background (1:46; 6:42; 7:41), that he had a preaching ministry that involved baptism (4:1), that he maintained a number of friendships (11:3, 11), and that he performed many other healing miracles (3:2; 7:3). The audience then contextualizes into this story the plot in which Jesus comes into conflict with "the Jews" and Jerusalem authorities.

Another dramatic device that provides unity is the suspense by which the tone of action that occurs toward the end of a piece is brought forward into earlier action of a different temper. Susanne Langer provides a cogent account of this constitutive element of drama:

> Before a play has progressed many lines, one is aware not only of vague conditions of life in general, but of a special situation. Like the distribution of figures on a chessboard, the combination of characters makes a strategic pattern. In actual life we usually recognize a distinct situation only when it is reached, or nearly reached, a crisis; but in the theater we see the whole setup of human relationships and conflicting interests long before any abnormal event has occurred that would, in actual life, have brought it into focus. Where in the real world we would witness some extraordinary act and gradually understand the circumstances that lie behind it, in the theater we perceive an ominous situation and see that some far-reaching action must grow out of it. This creates the peculiar tension between the given present and its yet unrealized consequent, "form in suspense," the essential dramatic illusion.[34]

Frequently, when Johannine scholars speak of the drama of the gospel, they refer to its suspense—that is, the way that the beginning and subsequent episodes anticipate its conclusion. While the action in the first four chapters of the Fourth Gospel is without conflict, the ominous direction it will take is foreshadowed by Jesus' allusions to his own death (1:51; 2:4, 19; 3:14). Explicit references to time, such as in Jesus' remark at the wedding in Cana "My hour has not yet come" (2:4), mark its progression toward a *telos* not immediately apparent in the action. As Jesus increasingly antagonizes his dialogue partners, his imminent death is constantly brought into view through his allusions to it (3:14; 5:25; 6:39, 51, 70; 7:7, 19, 33–34; 8:14, 21, 28; 10:17; 12:32). Oedipus, in *Oedipus Tyrannus*, also alludes to the coming hour of his fate, albeit unaware of what that hour will actually bring:

> Already, when I compute the passage of the days, I am troubled, wondering how he fares; for he has been away longer than is natural, beyond the proper

---

[34] Susanne K. Langer, *Feeling and Form: A Theory of Art Developed from Philosophy in a New Key* (New York: Scribner, 1953), 311.

time. But when he comes, then I shall be a wretch if I fail to take any action that the god may indicate. (73–77 [Lloyd-Jones, LCL])

Oedipus's dialogues mark his progressive understanding of who he is and what his fate will be. In both gospel and play, one senses that the movement of time is unambiguously a movement toward the final crisis of the story.

In order to generate this dramatic tension in a way perceptible to the spectator, a play is written backwards. As in theatrical fencing where parries precede thrusts, we find that word of the impending conflict and doom precedes the act itself. Prophetic words and ironic statements that are truer than their speaker knows are germane to the tragedies. This is nowhere clearer than in *Oedipus Tyrannus* when Oedipus proclaims, "It will not be on behalf of a distant friend, but for my own sake, that I shall drive away this pollution; whoever killed him [Laius] may well wish to turn the same violence against me" (137–140), and does not know that he is the one who has killed Laius and will go into exile after blinding himself. At the level of story, the prophecies that Oedipus will kill his father and bed his mother precede the acts that precipitate the current crises. Paradoxically, this arrangement of word before deed generates suspense while ensuring that the audience's expectations of a logical plot are met. In the gospel, characters repeatedly prognosticate about the future: "Where does this man intend to go that we will not find him? Does he intend to go to the Dispersion among the Greeks and teach the Greeks?" (7:35); "If we let him go on like this, everyone will believe in him, and the Romans will come and destroy both our holy place and our nation" (11:48); "it is better for you to have one man die for the people than to have the whole nation destroyed" (11:50). Moreover, the hostility toward Jesus is anticipated by his own defensive reaction to his interlocutors. Jesus announces the crowd's intention to kill him before they are shown to have formed the intent (7:19–20). On the theatrical axis, the audience's enjoyment of irony is coupled with the disturbing anticipation of the fulfillment of these words.

Another aspect of this backward construction is the direction of causation between deed and word. The signs seem to lead to the discourses, but in actual fact the discourses have caused the signs. The discourses are the true action of the gospel, just as dialogue is the action of a drama. The Fourth Evangelist presents a limited number of the many signs to which Nicodemus refers and with which the royal official seems familiar, selected to anticipate the thematic focus of the discourses. The explicit designation of some actions as *sēmeia* (σημεῖα) and repetition render this pattern in the gospel obvious. Its use in the tragedies is subtler. Perhaps the clearest example is the role that the crimson tapestry plays in *Agamemnon*. When Agamemnon arrives at the palace, Clytemnestra has her women spread out a red tapestry on which he is to walk. The carpet is irrelevant to the plot because Agamemnon will enter the palace whether he walks on it or not.[35] Rather than causing Agamemnon's death, the placement of red cloth serves as an omen of it and allows Clytemnestra to speak her mind about the pursuit of justice while Agamemnon and the chorus think that she refers to the carpet and the palace before them (900–976). Like the signs of the Fourth Gospel, the tapestry becomes the occasion for dialogue and an index of events to come.

The demands that a dramatic performance places upon the spectator to follow the action leads Aristotle to insist that the dramatist adhere to two principles: the unity of time and the unity of place. A dogmatic reading of Aristotle gives rise to the misconceptions that unity of time means that the action happens in one day and unity of place means that it happens in one locale. By these standards, the gospel writer violates the principles of unity and would seem to deviate from the genre of the tragic play. But closer examination of the way that the tragedians adhere to these two principles makes possible a comparison to the gospel.

Unity of time does not mean that the action happens in the course of one day, although Aristotle's favorite play, *Oedipus Tyrannus,* and many of the Greek dramas appear to take place between one sunrise and sunset. Unity of time is a linear sequence of the events of a single plot line that moves through a continuous present to a climax and closure. Contemporaneous action is not dramatized but reported so as not to interrupt the linear flow. True unity of time, in which the plot time seems to be identical to the performance time, is rarely attempted in drama. This feat may have been accomplished for the first time in film with Stanley Kramer's 1952 production *High Noon,* in which the 105 minutes of story time, marked by frequent shots of a clock, is captured in 85 minutes of reel time. In Aeschylus's *Prometheus Bound,* the protagonist remains on stage throughout the entire performance without any apparent ellipses of time or jump in action, but references to time made by characters suggest a discrepancy between the passage of time on stage and the length of time that the audience has been watching. Time is accelerated for Prometheus. For example, when Oceanus arrives, about three hundred verses into the play, he begins, "Here at last! Prometheus, I have come a long way to visit you" (284–285 [Vellacott]). Given that the play begins with Prometheus's arrival at the rock upon which he is pinned, more time has passed than what could be measured by a clock.

---

[35] Lutz Käppel, *Die Konstruktion der Handlung der Orestie des Aischylos: Die Makrostruktur des "Plot" als Sinnträger in der Darstellung des Geschlechterfluchs* (Zetemata 99; Munich: Beck, 1998), n.p.; cited in a review of Käppel by Mischa Meier, *Bryn Mawr Classical Review,* September 5, 1999.

Since the passage of stage time does not correspond to real time, references to time keep the audience abreast with the action. Anne Ubersfeld calls these "informing micro-sequences, which signal the progress of the action, the march of time, the succession of events."[36] In film, the passage of time can be marked with glimpses of clocks, especially when the plot involves the suspense of a deadline or the anticipation of news, or with a succession of shots of a particular setting showing the progression of seasons. For example, in the 1999 film *Notting Hill*, directed by Roger Michell, a full year passes in one scene in which the male lead walks down Portobello Road. Through clever editing, the scene appears to have been taken in one camera shot in which summer turns to fall and then winter and then spring. A pregnant woman appears early in the scene and reappears at its end with the baby in her arms.

In Greek tragedy, the passage may be signaled with references to time or its lapse made by characters in the dialogue. For example, in *Iphigenia among the Taurians*, the heroine marks the passing of a night between one exit and her next entrance by referring to a dream that she saw "in the night whose darkness has just departed" (150–151 [Kovacs, LCL]). When Euripides needs to make a leap in the time, he often employs a messenger who recounts what has passed between episodes. At the end of one episode, Iphigenia exits with her brother Orestes and his friend Pylades after explaining her intent to sacrifice them at the seaside. When the next episode begins, a messenger recounts how the trio has fled to the country and embarked on a Greek ship (1289–1292). Sometimes this unity comes at a price. In *Agamemnon*, the continuous action that begins with the watchman spotting the last in a series of beacons that run from Troy, set to bring immediate news of the defeat of the Trojans to Argos, moves without temporal ellipsis to the arrival of a herald who has traveled from the battlefield. His description of his journey home reveals the inconsistency between the lapse in stage or plot time (minutes) and that of story time (days, if not weeks, of travel).

Rather than using the words of a character to mark the passage of time, the Fourth Evangelist uses the narrator's preoccupation with a clock or a calendar to maintain a sense of its flow by measuring or marking any lapses. Thomas Brodie remarks, "The text moves, imperceptibly almost, from a flow of days to a flow of feasts to a flow of years."[37] The narrator first notes the passage of several days by beginning new scenes with the phrase "the next

[36] Anne Ubersfeld, *Reading Theatre* (trans. Frank Collins; Toronto: University of Toronto Press, 1999), 136.

[37] Thomas Brodie, *The Gospel according to John: A Literary and Theological Commentary* (New York: Oxford University Press, 1993), 21.

day" (1:29, 35, 43), and then a leap of three days by beginning the narration of the wedding at Cana with "on the third day" (2:1). He marks greater lapses of time by referring to annual Jewish festivals, and the audience counts the passage of three years by the passing and arrival of three Passovers.[38]

Although the gospel's author avails himself of temporal ellipses and narrative insertions, in long sections of the text plot time runs uninterrupted. The action at the Festival of Booths spans three chapters (7:10–10:21). The farewell supper invites comparison to Louis Malle's 1981 film *My Dinner with Andre* insofar as the lapse of time in both supper scenes allows for the consumption of an actual meal. Within these long scenes the evangelist generates a sense of continuous flow, despite his own narrative interruptions and ellipses, through his distinctive use of the particle οὖν. Οὖν occurs 195 times in the Fourth Gospel, only 8 of which appear in direct discourse.[39] Martha Reimer reviews observations by numerous grammarians and draws the conclusion that the evangelist uses οὖν to mark "continuation or consequence, either temporal or logical, between the elements that οὖν relates."[40] Reimer observes that the use of οὖν not only signals continuity but also "monitors the tension" as the oppositions within the plot structure develop. The οὖν appears at points of temporal or local setting (4:46; 12:1; 20:19), when new participants are introduced (3:25; 13:4–6), and before a leading question, statement, or action (4:9; 4:47–49; 6:5; 6:66–68; 7:3–6; 21:5, 15). It also marks a positive or a negative reaction to Jesus' words or actions (4:28, 40, 45; 5:8–10; 6:14, 60; 7:43; 11:45–53). Reimer finds the greatest concentration of οὖν in John 18–19, where "almost every piece of distinctive information that moves both the plot and the theme toward the culmination of the climax is marked with an οὖν."[41]

The effect of the presence of οὖν cannot easily be captured in English translation. In John 11:1–44, where the use of οὖν is dense, the NRSV translators use "so" to express causation (11:3, 36, 41) or "after," "then," or "when" to express temporal relations (11:6, 14, 17, 20, 32, 33, 38), or ignore it in translation (11:12, 16, 21, 31). The temporal choices lend the narration a backward-looking tone, as though this is a series of events that happened in

---

[38] 2:13, Passover; 5:1, a festival of the Jews; 6:4, Passover; 7:2, Booths; 10:22, Dedication; 12:1, six days before Passover.

[39] Edwin A. Abbott (*Johannine Grammar* [London: Black, 1906], 479) observes that in the LXX of Genesis through Chronicles, the use of οὖν in narrative is almost nonexistent.

[40] Martha Reimer, "The Functions of οὖν in the Gospel of John," *START* 13 (1985): 29.

[41] Ibid., 35.

the past. The following translation of a passage from the episode reveals a mechanic that pulls the audience forward into the action:

> So straightway [ὡς οὖν; ὡς denotes a quick succession of events], having heard that Lazarus was ill, then [τότε μὲν] he stayed two days longer in the place where he was. Thereupon he says [ἔπειτα μετὰ τοῦτο λέγει; ἔπειτα marks sequence] to his disciples, "Let us go to Judea again." The disciples say [λέγουσιν] to him, "Rabbi, the Jews were just now trying to stone you, and you are going there again?" Jesus answered, "Are there not twelve hours of daylight? Those who walk during the day do not stumble because they see the light of this world. But those who walk at night stumble because the light is not in them." And with this he says to them [ταῦτα εἶπεν, καὶ μετὰ τοῦτο λέγει αὐτοῖς], "Our friend Lazarus has fallen asleep, but I am going there to awaken him." Then [οὖν] the disciples said to him, "Lord, if he has fallen asleep, he will be all right." [Here the narrator interrupts.] Jesus, however, had been speaking about his death, but they thought that he was referring to sleep. [The dialogue resumes.] Then [τότε οὖν] Jesus told them plainly, "Lazarus is dead." (11:6–14)

Derek Tovey perceives that in the Greek text, οὖν gives the narrator's speech "the almost breathless energy of a first-hand or anecdotal report," as though the narrator were an eyewitness.[42] If we consider the effect upon the audience, we see that the narrator moves each line into the position of immediacy: each οὖν draws the reader into the next moment as if traveling through the event with the narrator.

Where the use of οὖν is not prevalent, the use of the historic present is.[43] Mark also frequently uses the historic present, coupling it with καί with monotonous results, whereas the Fourth Evangelist gives vigor to the narrative through the use of asyndeton (the absence of subordinating conjunctions between clauses).[44] In narrating the wedding at Cana, the call of the disciples, the conversations with the Samaritan woman, Martha, and Mary Magdalene, and the conversations with Peter at the footwashing and the resurrection, the narrator slips in and out of the present and the aorist tenses. If the narrator interjects background material into this flow of action, he often signals the interruption with a δέ and slips into the imperfect tense.[45] When he returns to the dialogue and the passage of events, he resumes the use of the historic present or aorist tense.[46]

---

[42] Derek Tovey, *Narrative Art and Act in the Fourth Gospel* (JSNTSup 151; Sheffield: Sheffield Academic Press, 1997), 180.

[43] See J. J. O'Rourke, "The Historic Present in the Gospel of John," *JBL* 93 (1974): 585–89.

[44] See Abbott, *Johannine Grammar*, 70.

[45] For example, 18:15a: Ἠκολούθει δὲ τῷ Ἰησοῦ Σίμων Πέτρος. . . .

[46] Reimer, "Functions of οὖν," 30.

The NRSV translators tend to use the past tense when presented with the historic present. By rendering the footwashing scene with the tenses that appear in the Greek text, we can see how the narrator originally strove for a movement through a present or a series of presents:

> He gets up [ἐγείρεται] from the table, he takes [τίθησιν] off his outer robe, having tied [λαβὼν] a towel around himself. Then he pours [βάλλει] water into a basin and began [ἤρξατο] to wash [νίπτειν] the disciples' feet and to wipe [ἐκμάσσειν] them with the towel that was tied [διεζωμένος] around him. He comes [ἔρχεται] to Simon Peter, who says [λέγει] to him, "Lord, are you going to wash my feet?" Jesus answered [ἀπεκρίθη] and he said [εἶπεν] to him, "You do not know now what I am doing, but later you will understand." Peter says [λέγει] to him, "You will never wash my feet." Jesus answered [ἀπεκρίθη] him, "Unless I wash you, you have no share with me." Simon Peter says [λέγει] to him, "Lord, not my feet only but also my hands and my head." Jesus says [λέγει] to him, " One who has bathed does not need to wash except for the feet, but is entirely clean. And you are clean, though not all of you." (13:4–10)[47]

R. Alan Culpepper, citing Boris Uspensky's analogy, likens the effect to a slide show that places readers within scenes.[48] Derek Tovey observes that this has "the effect either of transporting the reader into the past, or bringing the past alive in the reader's present," the purpose of which is "to create 'a sense of eyewitness authority.'"[49] Tovey looks to Chariton's first-century C.E. Greek romance *Chaereas and Callirhoe* for instances where a narrator shifts from a past tense to the use of the present for reported speech, and argues that the Fourth Gospel's technique represents a refinement of what he calls a "figural narrative situation."[50]

Tovey overlooks another and earlier precedent for this weaving of tenses within ancient storytelling: the messenger speeches of the tragedies. In the speech that reports how the Corinthian princess has been poisoned by Medea's gifts of a robe and a crown, the messenger turns to the historic present to make his hearer into what Irene de Jong calls a "pseudo-eyewitness":[51]

> Taking the gorgeous robe, she dressed herself in it,
> Putting a golden crown round her curly locks,
> She arranges the set of the hair in a shining mirror,

---

[47] Adapted from the NRSV translation.

[48] R. Alan Culpepper, *Anatomy of the Fourth Gospel: A Study in Literary Design* (FF; Philadelphia: Fortress, 1983), 30.

[49] Tovey, *Narrative Art and Act*, 177.

[50] Ibid., 183–85.

[51] Irene J. F. de Jong, *Narrative in Drama: The Art of the Euripidean Messenger-Speech* (MnemosyneSup 116; Leiden: Brill, 1991), 39, 42.

Smiling at the lifeless image of her body;
Then rising from her chair, she walks about the room
With her gleaming feet stepping most soft and delicate.
(*Medea* 1159–1165)[52]

The messenger's language reenacts the princess's actions before the mirror. By encouraging the imaginative act of reconstructing the action in the mind's eye, this language enacts as it reports.

The Fourth Evangelist is not consistent in his use of either the historic present or the particle οὖν, but there is sufficient frequency to make the effect clear. Like a Euripidean messenger speech, the narrator's reportage is designed to continually draw the audience back into the present and forward flow of events.

Unity of place is not simply that everything happens in one location but that the movement in space is made logical by what is said. H. D. F. Kitto attributes the unity of space in which all action occurs in one setting to convenience rather than necessity.[53] *Iphigenia among the Taurians*, for example, happens exclusively in front of the temple of Artemis. The *skēnē* represents the temple; *eisodos* (εἴσοδος) A leads to the seashore, and *eisodos* B leads to the palace of Theos. In contrast, Aeschylus's *Eumenides* begins in Delphi, and the action moves to Athens, where it takes place in various locales, including the Acropolis, the Areopagos, and the Panathenaia.[54]

Action in the Fourth Gospel is not confined to one place. The narrator provides the setting for each scene, and as a consequence, problems with continuity arise. In John 5, Jesus is in Jerusalem at the Sheep Gate, from where he goes to the other side of Galilee for John 6. The fact that the narrator does not tell how Jesus came to be in Galilee to go to its other side leads some scholars, such as Rudolf Bultmann, and some less eager to rearrange, including Rudolf Schnackenburg and Alfred Wikenhauser, to argue that the order of John 5 and 6 ought to be reversed.[55] In John 6, the Jews turn from following Jesus to rejecting his ideas while, in John 5, they seem more antagonistic when they persecute him for violating the Sabbath; thus, the reversal of these two chapters would serve an argument about the logical development of a unified plot. But

---

[52] Most translators turn the participles, all of which are aorist active, and the present tense into the aorist tense. Here I have adapted Rex Warner's translation.

[53] H. D. F. Kitto, *Greek Tragedy: A Literary Study* (2d ed.; New York: Doubleday, 1950), 177.

[54] Arnott (*Public and Performance*, 137) uses statements made by characters to identify these locations.

[55] Bultmann, *The Gospel of John*, 10–11, 209–10; Rudolf Schnackenburg, *The Gospel according to St. John* (trans. Kevin Smyth; New York: Herder & Herder, 1968), 53–58; Alfred Wikenhauser, *Das Evangelium nach Johannes* (3d ed.; RNT 4; Regensburg: Pustet, 1961), 118–21.

this rearrangement is not necessary, nor is it my point. Were it not for the fact that the gospel writer so assiduously follows the demand for unity of space by charting Jesus' movement, the order of the chapters would not be a problem. In contrast, the Gospel of Matthew sets scenes in grainfields, synagogues, houses, or mountains without identifying where they are located. Given that Matthew provides no point of departure, it seems reasonable that Jesus sends his disciples on their mission without a prescribed itinerary. Having no map at all, the reader of Matthew does not feel disoriented and does not wonder how Jesus or his opponents come to be where they are. The Fourth Gospel, on the other hand, provides an itinerary. Its references to locations are like those scenes in old movies in which a map is projected onto the screen and a line is drawn signifying that the characters have traveled from one locale to another. Consequently, when roads on the map do not line up, the audience is left not knowing how characters get from one point to the next.

The Johannine attempt at unity of space and time produces the sort of structure that invites critics to presuppose that the passage of time or the movement through the landscape is the defining organizational principle of the gospel. For example, Fernando Segovia picks up Wayne Meeks's description of the "man from heaven" and then compares the gospel to ancient biographies. Jesus, the Word of God, travels into the world to launch his polemic against it and to introduce God's will into the hostile environs.[56] In contrast, Thomas Brodie focuses upon time as the primary element, with space and geography performing a complementary function.[57] The three years of the gospel form a typology of human experience, the journey of a human through three stages of life. The first Passover signifies the positive and easy belief of youth; the second, the cognizance of sin and ambivalence of middle age; and the third, old age, when death, with its threat to life and belief, approaches.[58] In the light of the tragedies, these patterns of space and time may appear not to be the intentional design of the gospel so much as a consequence of the goal of unity.

Plot Elements

When Aristotle asks what sort of action is appropriate to drama, he identifies three means of moving the soul to pity and fear (the emotions that drama ought to arouse): reversal *(peripeteia)*, recognition *(anagnōrisis)*, and

---

[56] Fernando F. Segovia, "The Journey(s) of the Word of God: A Reading of the Plot of the Fourth Gospel," *Semeia* 53 (1991): 47.

[57] Brodie, *The Gospel according to John*, 26–27.

[58] Ibid., 33.

suffering *(pathos)* (*Poet.* 1450a 34–35; 1452b 8). Most undergraduates are taught the following oversimplified version of his discussion of the elements of plot. The tragedy is the story of a heroic protagonist with some fatal flaw whose fortune is reversed, and at the moment of self-recognition, he or she suffers. The audience entertained by the arousal of fear and pity ought to experience a catharsis, a purging of these emotions, by the end of the play. Neither the plots that Aristotle studied nor Aristotle's own analysis is so simple, nor should Aristotle's prescriptions be seen as definitive of tragedy. Yet Aristotle's delineation of plot elements has become so entrenched in the Western psyche that it is difficult to avoid recognizing them in our literature. I am no literary theorist, and thus I succumb to the lure of Aristotle's siren by examining the representation of *peripeteia, anagnōrisis,* and *pathos* in the Fourth Gospel. My objective is not to demonstrate that the gospel follows the dictates of a tragic plot but rather to show how the evangelist uses the craft of the Greek tragedians to represent these plot elements when they occur.

Peripeteia

The idea of *peripeteia* as a single event or a simple reversal of fortune belies the complexity of how reversals are handled in the Greek tragedies. In some plays, the reversals are subtle and may be in relationships as frequently as in fortune. For example, in Sophocles' *Philoctetes*, the dramatic reversal of status for the protagonist occurs in the story that precedes the action. Philoctetes, heir to Heracles' bow, en route to the battle of Troy is bitten on the foot by a serpent, and when his wound festers, his constant complaining causes his comrades to leave him on the deserted island of Lemnos. As the play begins, these same comrades, compelled by the words of a seer that only Heracles' bow can defeat Troy, have returned to Lemnos to steal that weapon from Philoctetes. Several reversals happen in the course of the action. First, Neoptolemus is persuaded to pretend to befriend the castaway in order to gain access to the bow, but then, with the bow in hand, he is moved to compassion by Philoctetes' suffering and exchanges the guise of friendship for true friendship. Odysseus then thwarts this reversal by stealing the bow. In the final turn of events, Heracles appears as a *deus ex machina* in a vision and commands Philoctetes to return to Troy, and thus he restores Philoctetes' status as a hero; but in the action of the play, this reversal is decidedly anticlimactic.

In the plot of the Fourth Gospel, reversals abound. Jesus, Son of God, is abused and murdered and then restored through resurrection.[59] Characters

---

[59] Culpepper (*Anatomy of the Fourth Gospel,* 88) identifies Jesus' death as the gospel's *peripeteia,* "the falsification of expectations."

with whom he interacts have changes of heart: strangers become followers, and followers become strangers; and at least one of these, Simon Peter, is restored to friendship. The question at hand, however, is not whether reversals occur but how they occur or what is akin to the tragedies in the representation of their occurrence. These reversals are achieved, in no small part, through dramatic devices comparable to a pair, identified by Jean-Pierre Vernant, at work in *Oedipus Tyrannus*.[60] First, in the course of the action, terms used for the hero are inverted. Oedipus, who describes himself at the onset as "on the track" (220), "flushing out" the "wild beast at large in the mountains," is in the end represented as an animal when he howls like a wild beast and flees to the wilds of Cithaeron.[61] The one who solves the riddle of the Sphinx about the stages of life becomes its incarnation, at once brother to his own children and husband to his own mother.[62] Oedipus the savior becomes the pollution that he has sworn to drive from the city. Second, characters redirect to the honor of the gods terms they once used to glorify Oedipus.[63] In line 14, the priest applies the title κρατύνων to Oedipus, and the chorus restores it to Zeus in line 903. The chorus heralds Oedipus as its σωτήρ in line 48, but the priest appeals to Apollo as σωτήρ in line 150. Eventually, the title of πατήρ, the power of dominion, and the capacity to help are transferred from Oedipus to one or another of the gods.[64]

The principal reversal of the Fourth Gospel, which runs both parallel to that of *Oedipus Tyrannus,* insofar as one proclaimed king is ostracized, and counter to the tragedy, insofar as his humiliation is his glorification, is supported by the use of both devices identified by Vernant. In the first half of the gospel, language and actions associated with a savior or royal figure dominate as Jesus proclaims himself to be a life-bringing agent—"I am the bread of life" (6:35), "I am the light of the world"(8:12), "I am the resurrection and the life" (11:25)—and performs acts that bring wine, bread, and healing; but by the end of the gospel, Jesus becomes the affliction whose death brings security. Affirmations of Jesus' role as king tend to come after his healing miracles. The narrator says that after the miraculous provision of bread, the crowd intends to seize Jesus and make him king (6:15). When Jesus enters Jerusalem, on account of the resurrection of Lazarus, as the narrator later confirms (12:18), the crowd greets him shouting, "Hosanna! Blessed is the

---

[60] Jean-Pierre Vernant, "Ambiguity and Reversal: On the Enigmatic Structure of Oedipus Rex," in *Myth and Tragedy in Ancient Greece* (ed. Jean-Pierre Vernant and Pierre Vidal-Naquet; trans. P. du Bois; New York: Zone Books, 1988), 113–39.
[61] Ibid., 122.
[62] Ibid., 138.
[63] Ibid., 123.
[64] Ibid., 123.

one who comes in the name of the Lord—the King of Israel!" (12:13). In the Synoptic tradition, Jesus provokes this greeting by assuming the identity of the royal figure of Zech 9:9, who rides into Jerusalem on a donkey. In the Fourth Gospel, Jesus mounts the donkey in response to this greeting as though claiming the title. The narrator sets the reversal in the plot line as early as John 5 when he explains, "the Jews were seeking all the more to kill him, because he was not only breaking the sabbath, but was also calling God his own Father, thereby making himself equal to God" (5:18). In the direct discourse, the reversal is more gradual and begins with the questions "Is not this Jesus, the son of Joseph, whose father and mother we know? How can he now say, 'I have come down from heaven'?" (6:42). The questions are followed by the identification of Jesus as someone suffering from suicidal demon possession and therefore as someone unclean (7:20). The gospel brings the two roles of savior and intolerable pollution into juxtaposition when Jesus says, "I have shown you many good works from the Father. For which of these are you going to stone me?" (10:32), and the Jews argue, "It is not for a good work that we are going to stone you, but for blasphemy, because you, though only a human being, are making yourself God" (10:33). The tension between king and pollution is resolved when Jesus is designated as the scapegoat, the individual whose expulsion saves the community. The chief priests and Pharisees identify the king as one who brings destruction rather than salvation: "What are we to do? This man is performing many signs. If we let him go on like this, everyone will believe in him, and the Romans will come and destroy both our holy place and our nation" (11:47–48). The fact that Jesus' signs point toward his status as monarch becomes the cause of his execution when Caiaphas ordains, "it is better for you to have one man die for the people than to have the whole nation destroyed" (11:50). Vernant stresses that whether divine king or scapegoat, Oedipus "is responsible for the collective salvation of the group . . . the *pharmakos* [scapegoat] is . . . the king's double."[65] In the gospel, this coidentification of Jesus as king and scapegoat is made complete by the crowning of Jesus as a fool's king.[66]

The gospel adds a twist to this ironic reversal. By expelling Oedipus as the *pharmakos*, the city rids itself of the pollution caused by the murder of its

---

65 Ibid., 132.

66 P. Wendland ("Jesus als Saturnalien-könig," *Hermes* 33 [1898]: 175–79) argues that the soldiers reenact the crowning of the false king of the Saturnalia. David Rensberger (*Johannine Faith and Liberating Community* [Philadelphia: Westminster, 1988], 94) observes that Pilate "uses Jesus to make a ridiculous example of Jewish Nationalism."

king. Jesus' death as the *pharmakos* is the murder of the king and his exaltation.[67] Jesus must become the *pharmakos* in order to fulfill his role as divine king. Oedipus's wound, obtained when his father has his ankles pierced with a lead spike, is a symbol of his status as *pharmakos*. The sight of Jesus' wounds elicits from Thomas the supreme confession of the gospel: "My Lord and my God" (20:28).[68]

In the gospel, the transfer of titles follows two trajectories. Jesus boldly and rapidly adopts divine prerogatives. After his first Sabbath violation, he claims that "the Son gives life to whomever he wishes (5:21), "the Father judges no one but has given all judgment to the Son" (5:22), and "all may honor the Son just as they honor the Father" (5:23). The attribution of authority to Jesus by others follows a different course. At the onset of the action, several titles are granted to Jesus: Andrew calls him "Messiah" (1:41); Nathanael, "Son of God," "King of Israel" (1:49); the Samaritans, "Savior of the world" (4:42); and the crowd at Tiberias, "the prophet who is to come into the world" (6:14). These acclamations are followed by a dramatic shift in which his identity comes into question. The Jews ask, "Is not this Jesus, the son of Joseph, whose father and mother we know?" (6:42), and, "How can this man give us his flesh to eat?" (6:52). The crowd cannot decide whether he is a good man or he is deceiving them (7:12), whether he is the prophet or the Messiah, or if it is possible that the Messiah could come from Galilee (7:40–41). The title "rabbi" disappears from use, and Jesus is subjected to insults: "you are a Samaritan and have a demon" (8:48). The Pharisees call for the reversal: "Give glory to God! We know that this man is a sinner" (9:24). Lazarus's resurrection prompts a brief return to the language of adoration when Martha professes, "Yes, Lord, I believe that you are the Messiah, the Son of God, the one coming into the world" (11:27); but the crowd that is eager to call Jesus "king" after the resurrection of Lazarus (12:13) quickly strips Jesus of honorific titles when he talks about being "lifted up from the earth" (12:32). By referring to the Messiah and the Son of Man in the third person—"We have heard from the law that the Messiah remains forever. How can you say that the Son of Man must be lifted up? Who is this Son of Man?" (12:34)—they deny Jesus the status of Messiah and do not treat "Son of Man" as an honorific title. This trajectory ends when the chief priests grant the title of king to another: "We have no king but the emperor" (19:15). The reversal that happens abruptly in the Synoptic tradition

---

[67] See Duke, *Irony in the Fourth Gospel*, 113.

[68] For further discussion of Jesus as *pharmakos*, see René Girard, *Things Hidden since the Foundation of the World* (trans. Stephen Bann and Michael Meteer; Stanford, Calif.: Stanford University Press, 1987), 167–70.

after the temple incident spans the entire course of the Fourth Gospel and is encoded in the language used by characters to describe the significance of Jesus' actions and his status.

Johannine scholars frequently attend to who speaks and the significance of particular titles in order to deposit characters into the categories of true or quasi-believers and sinners.[69] Insofar as it is clear that the affirmations of Jesus come from followers who presumably remain loyal to him and the denunciations come from those who reject him, these attributions are logical. The evangelist has placed the words on the lips of those motivated to speak as they do. Someone must necessarily utter the speeches that constitute the reversal that gives structure to the gospel, but by trying to line the utterances up with categories of faith in some hypothetical community, we ignore the relationship of language to dramatic structure.

Vernant argues that reversal is the "keystone of the dramatic structure," "the matrix of its dramatic construction and language"; therefore, tragedy unites and opposes irreconcilable terms.[70] Examining *Oedipus Tyrannus*, we see how reversal of status from king to exile is also achieved through the complicated use of binary language regarding sight and blindness. According to Claude Calame, the reversals in the play turn upon two sources of knowledge: one dependent on "the voice of a god" possessed by Tiresias the blind prophet, and one dependent upon the "vision of a man," in this case Oedipus.[71] At the beginning of the play, knowledge is based on words: Oedipus brings salvation by solving the riddle of the Sphinx. Faced with the new threat that besets the city, Oedipus turns to the authority of knowledge gained by human vision, claiming, "Well, I shall begin again and light up the obscurity [ἐγὼ φανῶ]" (132 [Lloyd-Jones, LCL]). Given that ἐγὼ φανῶ can mean both "It is I who will bring the criminal to light" and "I shall discover myself to be the criminal," Oedipus does not know where the truth in his own words lies.[72] When Tiresias reveals that Oedipus is the one guilty of killing Cadmus, Oedipus enters into a debate with those who have previously been his compatriots over the power of sight and the truth of words, in which he now puts no stock. Oedipus says to Tiresias, "Tell me as much as you

---

69 For example, Rensberger (*Johannine Faith and Liberating Community*, 70) concludes that John the Baptist and Nicodemus symbolize two groups that claim some knowledge of Jesus but whose knowledge is inadequate by the standards of the evangelist. Nicodemus symbolizes "secret Christians."

70 Vernant, "Ambiguity and Reversal," 120–21.

71 Claude Calame, "Vision, Blindness, and Mask: The Radicalization of the Emotions in Sophocles," in *Tragedy and the Tragic: Greek Theatre and Beyond* (ed. M. S. Silk; Oxford: Clarendon, 1996), 21.

72 Vernant, "Ambiguity and Reversal," 118.

please, since your words will be wasted" (365), and he accuses Tiresias of being without truth: "You are without it, since you are blind in your ears, in your mind, and in your eyes" (370–371). Tiresias provides a parallel response: "You have sight, but cannot see" (413). Incapable of recognizing the truth of Tiresias's speech, Oedipus complains, "How riddling and obscure in excess are all your words!" (439). The next reversal occurs when Oedipus, acknowledging the truth of Tiresias's words, pleads, "All is now clear! O light, may I now look on you for the last time" (1182–1183). The chorus ends its own lament with a play on two oppositions, of sight versus blindness and life versus death:

> Ah, son of Laius, would that I had never set eyes on you! For I grievously lament, pouring from my lips a dirge. To tell the truth, you restored me to life and you lulled my eyes in death. (1214–1222)

Now in possession of the sight that words can bring, Oedipus finds the light of divine knowledge too bright to bear and blinds himself in order to enter into a solitary darkness.

The reversals in the Fourth Gospel also are achieved through a complex of dualistic language, and the dramatic debates with the authorities also work their way around the ambiguous language of sight and blindness and around poles of knowledge based upon one's vision and knowledge based upon the divine word. The plot turns from the reception of Jesus as a wonder-worker, whose signs they see and commend, to his rejection as a blasphemer, whose words they hear and condemn.

At the beginning of the gospel, sight is associated with knowledge. Jesus says to Nathanael, "Do you believe because I told you that I saw you under the fig tree? You will see greater things than these. . . . Very truly, I tell you, you will see heaven opened and the angels of God ascending and descending upon the Son of Man" (1:50–51). And he tells Nicodemus, "we speak of what we know and testify to what we have seen" (3:11). Once Jesus begins to perform the signs that point to his identity, the word supplants sight in the epistemology of belief. In the dialogue with the Samaritan woman, Jesus' words produce belief (4:42), and when the royal official begs Jesus to perform his role as wonder-worker, Jesus seems to lament: "Unless you see signs and wonders you will not believe" (4:48). In the next episode, Jesus makes explicit the priority of voice over sight when he states, "anyone who hears my word and believes him who sent me has eternal life" (5:24). Jesus accuses his interlocutors of being willing to rejoice in John the Baptist's shining light but, by failing to believe him, of not hearing God's voice or seeing his form or having his word abide in them (5:35–38). The shift to knowledge gained through words heralds the turn in the gospel toward conflict. In the first real debate of the gospel—the dialogue with the crowd that gathers after the feeding of the five thousand—Jesus declares, "you have seen me and yet do not believe" (6:36). The problem for the Jews is precisely the fact that they have seen him in his capacity as the son of Joseph. The knowledge gained through human vision contradicts the knowledge that Jesus' words seek to impart.

In the long episode at the Festival of Booths in John 8–10, sight is once more equated with knowledge, at which point debate escalates into hostility. In these dialogues the ambiguity of the language of sight is exploited. Jesus proclaims himself to be the "light of the world." and the Pharisees question the validity of his testimony—that is, his words (8:12–13). When he restores the vision of the blind man, he proclaims, "I came into this world for judgment so that those who do not see may see, and those who do see may become blind" (9:39). The Pharisees retort, "Surely we are not blind, are we?" (9:40). Jesus counters, "If you were blind, you would not have sin. But now that you say, 'We see,' your sin remains" (9:41). Speech comes to denote blindness. In the end, Jesus' opponents attribute his words to madness and demonic possession, but those who remain uncertain note the tension between what a demon does (tells lies) and what Jesus has done (open the eyes of the blind).

In the final reversal, in which mourning turns to joy, we find a continuation of the play on knowledge based on sight versus knowledge based on divine voice. Mary is incapable of recognizing Jesus until she hears him call her by name. In the next scene, in contrast, Jesus says to a group of disciples, "Peace be with you," but according to the narrator, it takes a show of Jesus' wounded hands and side before they seem to recognize him (20:20–21). In the scene with Thomas, the doubting disciple predicates knowledge upon sight and touch by saying, "Unless I see the mark of the nails in his hands, and put my finger in the mark of the nails and my hand in his side, I will not believe" (20:25). Jesus counters with an epistemology based on revelation—that is, words: "Have you believed because you have seen me? Blessed are those who have not seen and yet have come to believe" (20:29). This apparent inconstancy of epistemology may reflect the paradox underscored in the language of the prologue. The Word becomes incarnate, the object of sense perception, in order that we may see his glory. While belief based upon reception of the word is affirmed, that word—the content of the gospel—is based upon the eyewitness account of the Beloved Disciple. In the arch of the gospel's plot, one grand reversal occurs. Seen through the blind vision of human eyes, it appears to be the story of the fall of a man from acclaim to humiliation. Viewed from the perspective provided by the witness of the Beloved Disciple, the reversal is from the ambiguity that is inherent in the human predicament to illumination.

Christian readers have habitually treated the dualism of the gospel as soteriology, concluding that those who believe Jesus, including perhaps the readers, are saved while those who reject him, who include most of the characters in the story, are damned. It seems possible to me that we have mistaken the dualism of the gospel for a message rather than recognizing the role it plays as ambiguous language in the dramatic construction of reversals. The victims of the ambiguity are those who place Jesus upon the cross. Just as Oedipus kills his father and sleeps with his mother without knowing that he has committed parricide and incest, the Jewish and Roman authorities do not know that they commit deicide. The Jewish authorities, from the human point of view, condemn a human being for impious speech. The gospel, composed of words, asserts itself to be the repository of truth. Paradoxically, by presenting us with accounts of the resurrection appearances and appealing to the eyewitness authority of the Beloved Disciple, the gospel seems to concede to the fact that human beings, in the end, depend upon vision for their knowledge.

Anagnōrisis

R. Alan Culpepper describes the story of the Fourth Gospel as "a death struggle over the recognition of Jesus as the revealer."[73] In his book *The Gospel and Letters of John,* he argues that recognition is used throughout the gospel as a recurring scene, "not merely as the climactic scene."[74] Andrew Lincoln criticizes Culpepper's use of the term *anagnōrisis* for its lack of resemblance to Aristotle's category because the gospel does not entail a major event that brings new information to light, changing the situation of the protagonist.[75] Insofar as the gospel's recognition scenes bear no resemblance to the *anagnōrisis* of *Oedipus Tyrannus,* he is correct. Aristotle extols this particular play for having the recognition occur at the same time as the *peripeteia,* but he does not limit his delineation of recognition to one type, nor does he suggest that a play have only one recognition scene. I agree with Culpepper that "*anagnōrisis* permeates the plot."[76] In *The Gospel and Letters of John,* he examines whether identity is disclosed or discovered and shows how failed or partial *anagnōrisis* mobilizes the opposition against Jesus and drives the plot.[77]

---

73 Culpepper, *Anatomy of the Fourth Gospel,* 84.
74 R. Alan Culpepper, *The Gospel and Letters of John* (Nashville: Abingdon, 1998), 71.
75 Andrew T. Lincoln, *Truth on Trial: The Lawsuit Motif in the Fourth Gospel* (Peabody, Mass.: Hendrickson, 2000), 162.
76 Culpepper, *Anatomy of the Fourth Gospel,* 84.
77 Culpepper, *Gospel and Letters of John,* 77–86.

My own interest lies not simply in the presence and purpose of *anagnōrisis* but in its management, especially on the theatrical axis of the text.

Recognition is a cognitive act and therefore something private. In a narrative, an omniscient narrator can reveal what occurs in a character's head. In a performance piece, recognition must be played out on the dramatic and theatrical axes so that the audience can see or hear the event happen. Two of the principal means of making it visible are the action that follows and the way that characters speak when the moment of recognition occurs.

When recognition occurs in Greek tragedy, the audience frequently witnesses changes in the relationship between characters because the new understanding either resolves or generates conflicts or does both. Iocaste acts out her recognition of the irreconcilable fact that her husband is her son by killing herself, thereby resolving the tension by ceasing to be either mother or wife. When Iphigenia recognizes her brother in *Iphigenia among the Taurians*, antagonism between the siblings ends, but Iphigenia then must align herself with her brother against the Taurians. When Electra recognizes her brother Orestes, she ceases to be the victim of her mother's plotting and plots the victimization of her mother. The change in relationship, then, effects the course of the plot.

As Culpepper notes, recognition in the Fourth Gospel signifies the moment when Jesus' identity becomes clear to another person.[78] As in the tragedies, more often than not, it alienates rather than unites people. For example, in the Fourth Gospel, the focus upon Jesus' person rather than his message necessitates distance between John the Baptist and Jesus. In the Synoptic Gospels, Jesus stands in continuity with John the Baptist, who brings a ministry of baptism and repentance. That repentance—the recognition of one's sinfulness and need for moral reorientation—then becomes the focus of Jesus' preaching. In the Fourth Gospel, in order to recognize who Jesus is, characters and audience must mark the discontinuity rather than continuity with the Baptist. John's first lines therefore distance him from Jesus by denying roles that could be attributed to Jesus: he is not the Messiah, not Elijah, not the prophet (1:20–21). Again the sharp division between the world that rejects Jesus and the individual who accepts him can be seen as a function of the relationship of *anagnōrisis* to plot. When characters recognize Jesus, they must realign their relationships with others. John the Baptist must decrease, Nicodemus must be from Galilee, and the blind man is driven out from the company of the Jews. The private cognitive act is made visible in social conflict.

Within the scene in a tragedy in which recognition takes place, the change from one cognitive state to another is often visible or audible in the representation of emotions. Cedric Whitman puts it well: "Characters who

---

[78] Culpepper, *Anatomy of the Fourth Gospel,* 88–89.

are strangers in mourning" become "characters who share an intimacy lifted into rapture by the restoration of the dead."[79] With their faces masked, the Athenian actors could not have employed the "method" of Konstantin Stanislavski or Lee Strasburg, in which the actor presents the appropriate emotions by drawing upon his or her own emotional memory; they relied upon the words supplied by the playwright.[80]

If we compare two lengthy recognition scenes, Electra's recognition of Orestes in both Euripides' and Sophocles' versions of *Electra,* to the short scene in the garden where Mary recognizes Jesus, we find many of the same techniques of language used to express and control the emotional *peripeteiai* that signify *anagnōrisis.* The techniques do not come into play in the same order in either tragedy or in the gospel, so I will disassemble Sophocles' and Euripides' works and follow the arrangement provided by the gospel writer. The narrator provides description of the emotions and action that parallels the information provided on the performance and theatrical axes, but we will disregard it.

Commentators have tended to be puzzled by Mary's failure to recognize Jesus and her mistaking him for the gardener. Bartholomew the Apostle (fifth–seventh century) gives the gardener a name, Philogenes, and a history: his son was healed by Jesus.[81] Tertullian describes the report that Jesus' body was stolen by a gardener who was disgruntled because visitors to the tomb were trampling his cabbage.[82] Is this an elaborate literary allusion to ancient royal and messianic themes, as Nicolas Wyatt contends?[83] Does this signify that Jesus' body has been transformed in appearance, as Raymond Brown suggests?[84] Hans von Campenhausen, citing S. Kraus, argues that John 20:15 is dependent upon a Jewish legend that a gardener by the name of Judah removed the body. Mary's mistake, then, is an apologetic counter to the legend.[85] This line of inquiry attends more closely to the narrator's comment than the construction of the dialogue and relies upon material external to the text. The logic of her failure may reside within the action of recognition itself.

The dialogue begins with a series of questions put to Mary by the angels and Jesus. Both the angels and Jesus ask, "Woman, why are you weep-

[79] Cedric H. Whitman, *Euripides and the Full Circle of Myth* (Cambridge: Harvard University Press, 1974), 13.

[80] Ibid., 13.

[81] *The Book of the Resurrection of Christ by Bartholomew the Apostle* 1.6–7.

[82] Tertullian, *Spect.* 30.

[83] Nicolas Wyatt, "Supposing Him to Be the Gardener (John 20,25): A Study of the Paradise Motif in John," *ZNW* 81 (90): 21–38.

[84] Brown, *The Gospel according to John,* 2:1009.

[85] Hans von Campenhausen, "The Events of Easter and the Empty Tomb," in *Tradition and Life in the Church* (trans. A. V. Littledale; Philadelphia: Fortress, 1968), 66–67.

ing?" (20:13, 15a), and Jesus adds, "Whom are you looking for?" (20:15b). The repetition of the questions is important on the dramatic axis because it provides Jesus with a disguise. Euripides uses a similar technique in the recognition scenes in *Electra*. Orestes begins the scene knowing his sister but is a stranger to her, someone whom she suspects means her harm. By referring to himself in the third person, Orestes delays the possibility that she recognize him.

> I have come with word of your brother. . . .
> He goes about in misery, with no single city as his home. . . .
> Are you alive? he asks. And if living, what are your fortunes? (228–238
>   [Kovacs, LCL])

The delay provided by the language allows Orestes to exact the information that he needs about his sister's predicament before her joy can obscure her anguish. By echoing the words of the angels, "Woman, why are you weeping?" Jesus aligns himself with those who have no prior relationship with Mary. He presents himself as someone whom she ought not recognize.[86] Moreover, his added question, "Whom are you looking for?" distinguishes him from the object of her weeping.

The purpose of this disguise is not merely dramatic; it is theatrical in that it gives Mary time to express her grief in dialogue. Just as characters in tragedies describe each other's and their own emotions, first the angels and then Jesus tell the audience that Mary is weeping. Given that the characters and the audience know the answer to the questions, the purpose of the inquiries is not to solicit information upon which Jesus or the angels will act or to inform the audience but to lay out the emotion upon which the action of recognition will turn. The questions of the dialogue also serve a function on the performance axis. Speaking while crying is a difficult task, so rather than having characters cry, the dramaturge makes them speak about crying. Sophocles' Orestes describes his own speechlessness: "Ah, ah, what can I say? Where can I go, since words fail me? I can no longer control my tongue!" (*El.* 1174–1175 [Lloyd-Jones, LCL]). One method of producing speech out of emotion is to use questions. The one who asks the questions then expresses sympathy and the one questioned is forced to speak through the emotion. Sophocles' Electra asks Orestes questions and makes assertions to which he responds with short expressions of his extreme agitation.

---

[86] Alison Jasper ("Interpretative Approaches to John 20:1–18: Mary at the Tomb of Jesus," *ST* 47 [1993]: 111) suggests that his questions are a gardener's questions and thus are "a piece with the disguise."

ELECTRA: What is your trouble? Why do you say that?

ORESTES: Is it the illustrious person of Electra that is here?

ELECTRA: This it is, and in a sorry state.

ORESTES: Alas, then, for this miserable disaster!

ELECTRA: Surely it is not over me that you are lamenting, stranger!

ORESTES: O body dishonored and godlessly ruined! (1176–1181)

The pattern in the gospel is much less apparent insofar as it is restricted to the repetition of the question "Why are you weeping?" by the angels and Jesus and Jesus' additional question, "Whom are you looking for?" but the effect is evident. The language of other characters solicits speech while representing her tears so that Mary can speak in spite of her grief.

The expression of grief in a theatrical piece requires careful attention to the demands of the performance axis lest the emotion obscure what the actor is saying. The content of the speech must carry or complement the emotion. Two aspects of Mary's speech serve this purpose. A person is seldom articulate when in a state of distress; nevertheless, Mary's speech follows an antithetical pattern so that the thoughts are organized. When she utters a petition, her anguish is articulated in the form of speech-act suited to the emotion:

They have taken away my Lord,	[A] Ἦραν τὸν κύριόν μου,
and I do not know where they have laid him.	[B] καὶ οὐκ οἶδα ποῦ ἔθηκαν αὐτόν.
Sir [Lord], if you have carried him away,	[A] Κύριε, εἰ σὺ ἐβάστασας αὐτόν,
tell me where you have laid him,	[B] εἰπέ μοι ποῦ ἔθηκας αὐτόν,
and I will take him away.	[A] κἀγὼ αὐτὸν ἀρῶ.
(20:13, 15)	

In Electra's long lament prior to Sophocles' recognition scene, when she thinks that she holds in her hands a vessel containing Orestes' ashes, emotion is sustained through a careful balancing of words and antitheses. Though this is a far more eloquent and far longer speech than that of Mary, the reliance upon antithesis and the move to petition serve the same function here as in the Fourth Gospel:

O remaining memorial of the life of the dearest of men to me,
Orestes, how far from the hopes
With which *I sent you off* [A] do *I receive you back* [A].
Now you are nothing [B], and *I hold you in my hands* [C];
But *you were glorious, brother, when I sent you from the house* [D].

How I wish that I had departed from life
Before *I stole you with these hands* [C],
Saving you from murder and sent you to a *foreign land* [E],
So that you should have died and lain here on that day,
Getting a share in your father's tomb [F]!
But now you have died miserably, far from home,
An exile in another land, without your sister [E].
And *I,* unhappy one, *did not wash you with loving hands* [C]
Or take up the sad burden, as is proper, from the blazing fire.
But you were given burial . . . *by foreign hands* [E/C],
And come as a little substance in a little urn [D].

. . . .

Therefore do you receive me into this mansion of yours,
Receive *me who am nothing into nothingness* [B],
So that in future *I may live* [G] with *you below* [H].
Yes, for *when you were above* [H], I shared your fate,
And *now I desire to die* [G] and *not to be excluded from your tomb* [F];
For I see that the dead suffer no pain. (1126–1143, 1165–1170 [Lloyd-
    Jones, LCL]; italics added)

The emotions of grief and despair set the stage for the dramatic turn to joy
that makes the recognition recognizable to the audience.

Sophocles manages the turn from lament by the diminution of lines to
mere phrases to express joy:

ELECTRA: [I]t is the body of Orestes that I hold here. . . .

ORESTES: Look at this seal that was my father's and learn whether I speak the
    truth!

ELECTRA: O dearest light!

ORESTES: Dearest, I too can witness!

ELECTRA: Voice, have you come?

ORESTES: Ask it of no other.

ELECTRA: Do I hold you in my arms? (1216, 1223–1226)

The stichomythia of the Fourth Gospel achieves its emotional turn with even
more punctuated joy:

JESUS: Mary!

MARY: Rabbouni! (20:16)

With dramatic economy and without the interjections of an omniscient narrator, the gospel represents the private experience of recognition through public displays of emotion.

The act of recognition in the gospel ends, as do many such scenes, with an embrace. In classical tragedy, the embrace makes visible on the theatrical axis the fact that the character who has come to a new understanding feels great joy and affection for the one whom he or she now holds. In order to achieve this goal, the tragedian encodes directions to the actors on the performance axis of the text to make clear who initiates the embrace and to ensure that the embrace takes place. In *Electra*, Sophocles picks up the language of the sister's lament when she thinks that she is holding Orestes' ashes, which the audience ought to view with irony, and turns the act of holding into an expression of joy:

ELECTRA: Do I hold you in my arms?

ORESTES: So may you always hold me! (1226 [Lloyd-Jones, LCL])

The Fourth Gospel's recognition scene ends in a similar embrace that, as necessary in classical drama, is not narrated but is an action encoded in Jesus' speech: "Do not hold on to me, because I have not yet ascended to the Father" (20:17). Mary's act of holding Jesus fulfills her intent to "take him" in a way that she has not intended but that the audience has anticipated. Jesus' words baffle exegetes. Many take them as a command not to touch him and speculate about the ontology implied by the words. Is Jesus demanding more respect for his glorified body, as Chrysostom contends and Ceslas Spicq affirms?[87] Is H. Kraft correct in assuming that Jesus is concerned that she avoid ritual impurity?[88] If this is the case, then Mary Rose D'Angelo must be correct in concluding that his body must undergo some changes by the time he encounters Thomas, whom he invites to have physical contact.[89] When this text is viewed as dramaturgy, the ontological questions vanish, and the line signifies what action takes place on the performance axis.[90] Jesus' command

---

[87] D. C. Fowler, "The Meaning of 'Touch Me Not' in John 20:17," *EvQ* 47 (1975): 17.

[88] H. Kraft, "John 20:17," *TLZ* 76 (1951): 570.

[89] Mary Rose D'Angelo, "A Critical Note: John 20:17 and Apocalypse of Moses 31," *JTS* 41 (1990): 481–503.

[90] In *Iphigenia among the Taurians* (769–711), when Orestes tries to embrace his sister, he is reproved for defiling a priestess. In Euripides' *Ion,* Ion spurns Xuthus's embrace with the line "Stop! If you touch the god's fillets, you may break them with your hand!" (523 [Kovacs, LCL]). In Euripides' *Bacchae,* Cadmus asks Agave, "Why do you fling your arms round me, my wretched child, as a young swan shelters the old one, hoary and helpless?" (1364–1366 [Morwood]).

"Do not hold on to me" is not a prohibition against embracing but forms an antithetical parallelism with the command "Go to my brothers and say to them, 'I am ascending to my Father and your Father, to my God and your God'" (20:17).

Diana Culbertson observes that the Greek tragedies "betray an imperative to bring the self into correspondence with the universe or reality that the self was to mirror." Thus, "recognition was a function of plot." Only later was it "perceived as an aspect of character."[91] Modern readers have a tendency to treat recognition in the Fourth Gospel as a function of character rather than plot. Nicodemus's failure to recognize Jesus is treated as a failure of character. If we situate the patterns of recognition found in the Fourth Gospel within the context of the tragic tradition, this failure becomes a plot element. The logic of which characters are chosen to overcome this ambiguity (e.g., the Samaritan woman) and which characters remain mired in it (e.g., the Jewish authorities) may also prove to be a function of plot. The characters who recognize Jesus have no power to prevent the plot from unfolding as it must.

The Necessity of *Pathos*

In Aristotle's theory of tragedy, *pathos* is not simply suffering but rather actions by which suffering is wrought. Just as *anagnōrisis* and *peripeteia* are not discrete plot elements, *pathos* winds its way through, and is constitutive of, the twists and turns of a plot. The reversals that follow recognition provoke *pathos*—that is, the actions that lead to destruction or distress—and this in turn arouses fear or pity in the audience.[92] For example, in Sophocles' *Electra*, one form of agony is replaced with another: Electra the victim becomes Electra the avenger. Sophocles provides the audience access to Electra's thoughts about this transformation by having her pray:

> Lord Apollo, hear them [Oresetes and Pylades] favorably, and hear me also, who have often stood before you in supplication, making an offering from what I had. But now, Lycian Apollo, with the things I have, I ask, I fall before you, I implore, be an active helper in this play and show mortals with what wages the gods reward impiety. (1376–1383 [Lloyd-Jones, LCL])

For Electra, her release from lament for her brother and the misery of her life necessitate Clytemnestra's pathetic end. In the Greek tragedies, *pathos* is born

---

91 Diana Culbertson, *The Poetics of Revelation: Recognition and the Narrative Tradition* (Macon, Ga.: Mercer University Press, 1989), 2.

92 Aristotle, *Poet.* 1452b 13–14.

of necessity. W. H. Auden draws the following distinction between Greek and Christian tragedy:

> Greek tragedy is the tragedy of necessity; i.e., the feeling aroused in the spectators is "What a pity it had to be this way": Christian tragedy is the tragedy of possibility, "What a pity it was this way when it might have been otherwise."[93]

Auden's dichotomy perhaps holds true for the Synoptic Gospels, but an examination of the language of the Fourth Gospel shows that the possibility of the outcome being otherwise is contradicted at every turn. The language of necessity found on the lips of characters, especially those of Jesus, leads the characters to enact suffering without recourse to other possibilities.

The study of the techniques whereby *pathos* is dramatized is, then, the study of the language of necessity. In his analysis of tragic language in both Greek and Shakespearean plays, M. S. Silk identifies three aspects of this language, "compulsion, excess and identity," which he argues are "irreducible determinants" that propel tragic action forward through the plot.[94] These same determinants can be isolated within the complex of Johannine speech that drives the plot of the gospel toward the destruction of its protagonist. In the following analysis, I will pursue the first two aspects identified by Silk and leave the language of identity for the discussion of Jesus' characterization.

In the dialogue between Antigone and Polynices in *Oedipus at Colonus,* Antigone tries to persuade her elder brother to turn back from a fatal confrontation with their brother Eteocles. Antigone speaks the language of volition and possibility; Polynices speaks of compulsion:

> ANTIGONE: Polynices, I beg you to let me persuade you in a certain matter!
> . . . Turn back your army at once to Argos, and do not destroy yourself and the city!
>
> POLYNICES: Why, that cannot be! For how could I bring back the army again, when I had once shown cowardice?
>
> ANTIGONE: Why must you be angry once more, brother? What profit do you gain by the ruin of your country?
>
> POLYNICES: To run away is shameful, and it is shameful for me, the senior, to be mocked like this by my brother!

---

93 W. H. Auden, "The Christian Hero," in *Tragedy: Vision and Form* (ed. Robert W. Corrigan; San Francisco: Chandler, 1965), 143.

94 M. S. Silk, "Tragic Language: The Greek Tragedians and Shakespeare," in Silk, *Tragedy and the Tragic,* 465.

ANTIGONE: Then do you see how you are fulfilling the prophecies of this man [Oedipus], who declared that you should die at one another's hands?

POLYNICES: Yes, that is his wish; and must we not comply? (1414–1426 [Lloyd-Jones, LCL])

Polynices reduces decision to fate: "These things depend on fate, to go one way or another" (1443). His compulsion is the need to protect his own honor. In this play, Antigone argues the part of free will, but in Sophocles' play named for her, she will appeal to the necessity of piety when she risks her life to bury this same brother. The two ways of thinking about the future, as the product of either choice or compulsion, frequently become the topic of debate in Greek tragedy and serve in part to shine a light upon the fact that necessity is the force that wins out.[95] Although the compulsion to which characters appeal varies from play to play, the demands of justice, divine will, revenge, self-preservation, and victory, along with honor and piety, appear with great frequency.

We find a comparable use of the topic of necessity and choice in the discussions of the Fourth Gospel. When John the Baptist's disciples point out that his following is deserting him for Jesus, John responds as though their comment is intended to urge him to take action against this trend. He defends his lack of action with an appeal to necessity: "He must increase, but I must decrease" (3:30). In a brief dialogue with himself as an imaginary conversation partner—itself a theatrical device—that has been compared to the Synoptic account of the agony in Gethsemane, Jesus denies the possibility of deliberating about his course of action: "Now my soul is troubled. And what should I say—'Father, save me from this hour'? No, it is for this reason that I have come to this hour" (12:27).[96] He acknowledges no choice; he is compelled by a sense of divine mission. In contrast, the Jesus of Matthew's Gethsemane petitions God, "My Father, if it is possible, let this cup pass from me," and he indicates that in following God's will, he relinquishes his own (Matt 26:39). In the dialogues leading to the decision to have Jesus executed,

---

[95] Other examples of this topic of debate include Euripides, *Med.* 148–266; *Hec.* 251–331; and Sophocles, *El.* 1482–1507. In Aeschylus's *Eumenides*, the Furies argue for the necessity of revenge and justice, while Apollo argues for free will. Athena provides the compromise upon which Athenian democracy is based: judgment at the end of a trial. In Euripides' *Hecuba*, the heroine laments both that she is luckless and that mortals do not learn thoroughly the art of persuasive speaking (812–819). I will return to the topic of free will versus necessity at the end of chapter 3 and the discussion of characterization.

[96] Sophocles employs this device of a character putting questions to himself when Ajax reviews his options and concludes that he has none (*Aj.* 457–480).

necessity is treated as a compelling argument. The Pharisees' question "What are we to do?" (John 11:47) presupposes that what they decide can affect the course of the future.[97] Caiaphas responds with an argument for expedient necessity: "You know nothing at all! You do not understand that it is better for you to have one man die for the people than to have the whole nation destroyed" (11:49–50). A few verses later, the Pharisees echo Caiaphas's conclusion: "You see, you can do nothing. Look, the world has gone after him!" (12:19). Necessity precludes choice. In the trial, the Jews couch this compulsion in language of legal necessity: "We have a law, and according to that law he ought to die because he has claimed to be the Son of God" (19:7). Since Pilate is under no compulsion to follow this statute, they find another compelling reason—his loyalty to Caesar—and argue, "If you release this man, you are no friend of the emperor. Everyone who claims to be a king sets himself against the emperor" (19:12). By first stating that he finds no case against Jesus and offering to release either "the King of the Jews" or Barabbas (18:38–40), Pilate speaks as though he is guided by his free will rather than external compulsion. Given that Barabbas is an enemy of the Roman state, the option of freeing him signifies Pilate's freedom from the bounds of civil law. Pilate makes his belief in his freedom to exercise choice explicit by saying to Jesus, "Do you not know that I have power to release you, and power to crucify you" (19:10). Jesus, in turn, denies Pilate's free will by denying him responsibility, in this case, for his own action: "You would have no power over me unless it had been given you from above; therefore the one who handed me over to you is guilty of a greater sin" (19:11). These dialogues underscore the unrelenting movement of the plot toward destruction.

Closely linked with the language of necessity is the language of excess—that is, language that lacks moderation and oversteps the bounds of human reason. The Samaritan woman claims, "He told me everything I have ever done" (4:39). The Pharisees claim that if Jesus is not stopped, "everyone will believe in him" (11:48), and they call the crowd in Jerusalem that heralds Jesus as the king of Israel the "world" (12:19). The alternatives that Caiaphas presents to the council are the death of one man and the destruction of the entire nation (11:48–51). In the Greek tragedies, characters who are about to enact *pathos* speak with comparable flourishes. In *Hecuba*, before the wife of Priam exacts vengeance for her son's murder, she states that no woman has suffered such misfortune "unless you named Lady Misfortune herself" (785 [Kovacs, LCL]). She proclaims, "No mortal is free!" (865), and pointing to the tent containing female captives, she makes the exaggerated claim that it "conceals a throng of Trojan women" (880) who will aid her in her plot.

---

[97] In *Antigone*, Creon asks a version of the same question: τί δῆτα χρὴ δρᾶν; (1099).

The tragic hero excludes a middle ground in his or her speech. Jesus tends to render conditions absolute: "For this I was born, and for this I came into the world, to testify to the truth. Everyone who belongs to the truth listens to my voice" (18:37).[98] His speech is peppered with the words "everyone" or "no one" and "never," "always," or "forever." Sophocles colors Antigone's and Oedipus's perceptions of life by having them speak in similar terms. *Antigone* begins with a dialogue between Oedipus's two daughters in which Antigone paints events with absolutes: "No, there is nothing painful or laden with destruction or shameful or dishonoring among your sorrows and mine that I have not witnessed" (4–6 [Lloyd-Jones, LCL]). When she reveals to her sister that Creon has prohibited the burial of Polynices, she claims that Ismene's response to this ordinance will show whether her "nature is noble" or she is "the cowardly descendant of valiant ancestors" (37–38). For Oedipus, either Tiresias is blind or he himself is wrong; the middle is excluded. This speech of excess is a condition of *pathos*, for the characters who cast conditions and alternatives in such absolute terms are driven to act in a dangerous and reckless manner.

Silk points to how the language of "too late" expresses resignation to necessity.[99] In *Agamemnon*, the chorus seeks to determine if a crime has been committed, and Clytemnestra responds,

> [Y]ou try me like some desperate woman. My heart is steel, well you know. Praise me, blame me as you choose. It's all one. Here is Agamemnon, my husband made a corpse by this right hand—a masterpiece of Justice. Done is done. (1425–1430 [Fagles])

Pilate's words "What I have written I have written" (19:22) attest to the same concept, that there is no going back; he has no regret by which he would be motivated to alter the trajectory of the action. The realized eschatology of the gospel found on the lips of Jesus is a facet of his insistence upon the necessary consequence of a given action:

> Those who believe in him are not condemned; but those who do not believe are condemned already, because they have not believed in the name of the only Son of God. (3:18)

> Very truly, I tell you, anyone who hears my word and believes him who sent me has eternal life, and does not come under judgment, but has passed from death to life. Very truly, I tell you, the hour is coming, and is

---

[98] See also John 3:3, 13–15, 18; 4:13, 48; 5:19, 24, 29, 37–38; 6:35, 51, 53; 8:12, 24, 47, 52; 11:25.

[99] Silk, "Tragic Language," 468.

now here, when the dead will hear the voice of the Son of God, and those who hear will live. (5:24–25)

When conditions are absolute and a character acts by necessity, the conclusion seems predetermined and thus to be a fact before it has happened.

Dramatic speech often oversteps the limits of ordinary language by accomplishing the deed in speech before act. Jesus, yet alive, speaks as if beyond the grave. Such prochronistic or proleptic speech is endemic to tragic characters bent upon dying.[100] In her examination of dramatic death speeches, Fiona MacIntosh finds that characters begin to die in speech earlier than they do in body:

> The process of a character's death begins early in the tragedies—indeed, it could be maintained that the cost of tragic status is exclusion from the full process of living. . . . During the course of the big speech [a character's last words], it becomes clear that the dying characters have only the most tenuous of links with their immediate surroundings: it is as if they already occupied the liminal world beyond the world of the living.[101]

The following speech by Heracles illustrates how a dying character uses the present tense rather than the future: "Ah, ah, misery, I am done for! I am dead, I am dead, there is no longer light for me! Ah me, I know now in what a calamity I stand! Go, my son—your father is no more" (Sophocles, *Trach.* 1143–1146 [Lloyd-Jones, LCL]). Characters who refer to themselves as dead frequently mask the anachronism of their speech by referring to themselves in the third person.[102] When Jesus refers to himself as if already dead or resurrected, "Now the Son of Man has been glorified, and God has been glorified in him," he uses the third person, and then he restores the first person to return to the present time of the action: "Little children, I am with you only a little longer" (13:31–33). At other points, the distinction between future and present collapses altogether:

> The hour is coming, indeed it has come, when you will be scattered, each one to his home, and you will leave me alone. Yet I am not alone because the

---

[100] Gérard Genette (*Narrative Discourse: An Essay in Method* [trans. Jane E. Lewin; Ithaca, N.Y.: Cornell University Press, 1980], 40) defines prolepsis as "a narrative manoeuvre that consists of narrating or evoking in advance an event that will take place later." Adele Reinhartz ("Jesus as Prophet: Predictive Prolepses in the Fourth Gospel," *JSNT* 36 [1989]: 3–16) identifies prolepsis as idiosyncratic to Jesus' speech and argues that Jesus' ability to proclaim the future points to his unique identity as the Son of God.

[101] Fiona MacIntosh, "Tragic Last Words: The Big Speech and Lament in Ancient Greek and Modern Irish Tragic Drama," in Silk, *Tragedy and the Tragic*, 415.

[102] Ibid., 419.

Father is with me. I have said this to you, so that in me you may have peace. In the world you face persecution. But take courage; I have conquered the world! (16:32–33)

When the future becomes the present, the possibility of either chance or making another decision and thereby turning the course of events seems to disappear.

Placed in the context of the dramatic conventions that represent *pathos*, the doctrinal import of Jesus' pronouncements loses some of its clarity. Of course, some distinction must be made between Antigone's accusation of cowardice against Ismene and Jesus' accusation that those who do not believe in him are dead. Antigone has no resurrection to vindicate her exclusion of a middle course. Philip Vellacott observes, "The more elated, the more poetically expressed, the hero's confidence becomes, the more poignant is the audience's awareness that this hope is groundless and his reason blind."[103] The prologue and the narrator, as well as a possible conviction that Jesus has risen, inoculate the audience against this sort of pity. Nevertheless, Jesus' language produces a sense of inevitability about his death. Given that he is uncompromising, he forces his dialogue partners to act in an equally uncompromising manner. The language is designed to drive the plot and is not necessarily based upon a sectarian ideology or intended to be encapsulated in a creedal statement by which the world is divided into the categories of innocent and condemned.

In a play such as *Oedipus Tyrannus,* in which characters act to evade the fulfillment of oracles and by doing so set into motion the events that will lead to the prediction coming true, Auden's description of tragic necessity seems reasonable. Nevertheless, it is inadequate. By resisting the oracle, Laius and Iocaste set into place the conditions by which their son will fail to recognize his relationship to them and as a result can kill the one and marry the other without knowing that he violates his duty as a son. The parents did not have to abandon their son, and oracles are notoriously misleading. Although Jesus speaks as if remorse or future conversion is not possible, his actions toward Simon Peter at the end of the gospel suggest that people change. The language of necessity in both tragic literature and the gospel is a feature of the plot, and as such, it ought not be used as sole evidence for the representation of a deterministic universe. I will return to the discussion of free will and necessity at the end of chapter 3, on characterization, in which other dramatic and theatrical features of the gospel invite more nuances in the representation of the world offered by the gospel.

---

[103] Philip Vellacott, *Ironic Drama: A Study of Euripides' Method and Meaning* (Cambridge: Cambridge University Press, 1975), 3.

Epilogues and Endings

The double ending of the Fourth Gospel is yet another compositional puzzle for Johannine scholars, yet another datum for redaction theories. Although I have found no precedence for two epilogues in the tragedies, I find it striking how the two sets of closing lines taken together with John 21 fulfill the functions of a theatrical epilogue and contain elements by which the audience is invited to express approval of the performance just witnessed and is returned to its own time and place.

A quick glance at Euripides' prologues and epilogues reveals a consistent pattern in which the dramatist makes direct references to the literary and selective nature of the composition. Perhaps Euripides strove to make the artifice of his work unmistakable by using the same epilogue or *exodos* (ἔξοδος)—the song with which the chorus makes its final exit—in five plays:

> There are many shapes of divinity, and many things the gods accomplish against our expectation. What men look for is not brought to pass, but a god finds a way to achieve the unexpected. Such was the outcome of this story.[104]

Both of the gospel's epilogues end with a similar concession that the evangelist's work is a literary composition based upon selection:

> Now Jesus did many other signs in the presence of his disciples, which are not written in this book. But *these are written* so that you may come to believe [πιστεύσητε or πιστεύητε] that Jesus is the Messiah, the Son of God, and that through believing you may have life in his name. (20:30–31; italics added)

> This is the disciple who is testifying to these things and *has written them,* and we know that his testimony is true. But there are also many other things that Jesus did; if every one of them were written down, I suppose that the world itself could not contain the books that would be written. (21:24–25; italics added) [105]

---

[104] Euripides, *Alc.* 1159–1163 [Kovacs, LCL]; *Bacch.* 1387–1394; *Med.* 1415–1419; *Hel.* 1689–1690; *Andr.* 1284–1288.

[105] The last epilogue of the Fourth Gospel has some parallels in Hebraic literature (Eccl 12:9–12). For example, Rabbi Johanan ben Zakkai says, "If all the heavens were sheets of paper, and all the trees were pens for writing, and all the seas were ink, that would not suffice to write down the wisdom I have received from my teachers; and yet I have taken no more from the wisdom of the sages than a fly does when it dips into the sea and bears away a tiny drop" (*Sop.* 16:8), and Philo comments, "Were he to choose to display his riches, even the entire earth, with the sea turned into dry land, would not contain them" (*Posterity* 144).

The repeated mention of the act of writing (which I have emphasized in the quotations) and the existence of a text distance the voice of the narrator from the content of his utterances. Moreover, when the gospel becomes an object to be considered rather than a script to be read, the recital clearly is over.

In the setting of Greek theater, this self-conscious ending serves a very practical purpose: it calls for applause by announcing that the play is over and pointing out what the playwright and actors have accomplished. Two of Euripides' plays end with direct appeals for the favor of the judges. At the end of *Iphigenia among the Taurians,* the chorus leader appeals to Athena, "O most august lady Victory, may you have my life in your charge and never cease garlanding my head!" (1497–1498 [Kovacs, LCL]). The appeal for the prize at the end of the *Phoenician Women* is even more blatant: "Victory, may you have my life in your charge and never cease garlanding my head!" (1765 [Kovacs, LCL]). Sophocles issues more subtle invitations by ending with calls to rally round some moral vision and selecting language that cues the audience. For example, Orestes' final words to Aegisthus in *Electra* invite the agreement of the audience's assenting applause: "This punishment should come at once to all who would act outside the laws—death. Then crime would not abound" (1505–1507 [Lloyd-Jones, LCL]). The chorus then rounds off the play with a double entendre that refers to both the story's and the performance's end: "Seed of Atreus, after many sufferings you have at last emerged in freedom, made complete by this day's enterprise" (1508–1510). The Greek text ends with the word *teleōthen,* which, like the announcement "The End" in amateur theatrics, serves as a verbal bow and makes clear that the play is over and the time for the audience's applause has begun.

The two epilogues of the gospel also invite the audience to judge the composition worthy of praise and marshal opinion in favor of its claims. The first epilogue draws attention to the rationale or virtue of the gospel's construction by stating that Jesus did many things but the gospel lifts out those things that bring "life in his name." Scholars tend to treat the clause ἵνα πιστεύ[σ]ητε ὅτι Ἰησοῦς ἐστιν ὁ χριστός (20:31) as a statement of the purpose of the gospel and conclude that the gospel was written to bring its readers to faith, but the Greek text presents difficulties and subtleties that permit an interpretation that is coherent with the form of the entire gospel. We are faced with two textual witnesses: one provides the present subjunctive πιστεύητε, "may continue to believe," and the other provides the aorist subjective πιστεύσητε, "may come to believe."[106] Evidence for the former is more

---

[106] Brown (*The Gospel according to John,* 2:1056) provides the following lists of textual witnesses and critical editions. Present subjunctive: Vaticanus, Sinaiticus*, 𝔓66 (probably), Westcott, Bover, Nestle, Merk, Tasker NEB, Aland Synopsis. Aorist

compelling, and its use follows logically from ἵνα. The focus is not on what will happen for the audience but what it has just experienced: the exaltation of Jesus' name through the dramatization of his death and resurrection. While the gospel affirms that belief in Jesus brings eternal life, it also provides an experience of Jesus that validates this belief. These things are written in such a way that for a time one lives in the presence of Jesus and witnesses the glory of his actions and affirms that his name ought to abide as the object of praise on the lips of the audience.

In the second epilogue, the narrator marshals the opinion of the audience by articulating it: "we know his testimony is true." As Craig Koester suggests, although members of the community of the gospel (what I call the audience, a looser sociopolitical identity) shared a common Christian faith, their various backgrounds (Jewish, Samaritan, and Greek) entailed various outlooks, and so the pronouns "you" in 20:31 and "we" in 21:24 are exercises in communication "intended to shape the stance of its readers."[107] The narrator then offers his own opinion: "I suppose [οἶμαι] that the world itself could not contain the books that would be written" (21:25). The word οἶμαι invites the audience into the mind of the narrator and casts the assertion into a form of assessment. By implication, the evangelist's task of sorting through the material and weighing it would have been a Herculean labor deserving of applause.

Besides encouraging the audience to affirm that what it has just witnessed has merit, the final words of the tragedy end the eternal present action of the plot by sending the characters on stage off to a life in the mythic or historic past and by returning the audience to its own present. Francis M. Dunn notes how Euripides changes the meter from iambic to anapestic, a marching rhythm, when he moves from dialogue to epilogue, thereby giving "a self-contained metrical shape to the gesture of emptying the stage."[108] Although the gospel writer employs no such change in rhythm, he does use techniques similar to those of Euripides. He does not place the final words on the lips of a principal character. In the final lines of Euripides' plays that do not include the epilogue that we noted earlier, a god often appears as a *deus ex machina* to deliver prophetic speeches that cross the bounds of human knowing and provide a retrospective view of the hero's life if it has not come to an end on

---

subjunctive: Bezae, Alexandrinus, Byzantine tradition, Von Soden, Vogels, American Bible Society Greek NT.

[107] Craig Koester, "Spectrum of Johannine Readers," in *What Is John? Readers and Readings of the Fourth Gospel* (ed. Fernando Segovia; 2 vols.; SBLSymS 3, 7; Atlanta: Scholars Press, 1996–1998), 1:10.

[108] Francis M. Dunn, *Tragedy's End: Closure and Innovation in Euripidean Drama* (Oxford: Oxford University Press, 1996), 15–16.

stage, making clear that the action of the tragedy is complete. The chorus then sings a brief *exodos,* such as "Farewell! The mortal man who can fare well and suffers no misfortune is indeed blessed" (*El.* 1357–1359 [Kovacs, LCL]) or "We go now with pity and in tears: we have lost our greatest friend" (*Herc. fur.* 1427–1428 [Kovacs, LCL]), rendering the departure of the principal characters final and affirming that the action is over. The Johannine narrator's concluding words consign the characters of the gospel to the past and do not point to a continuation of the action. When the Gospel of Matthew, in contrast, ends with Jesus' words "And remember, I am with you always, to the end of the age" (Matt 28:20), the action of the gospel continues into a yet-to-be-narrated future. The gospels of Mark and Luke end in medias res with a summary narration of the ongoing story. Some ancient manuscripts of the Gospel of Mark end with the young man directing the women to tell the disciples that they will meet Jesus in Galilee and then the women leaving in fear and silence (Mark 16:7–8). Two later manuscript traditions end with descriptions of an evangelical mission (Mark 16:9, 19–20), and Luke moves the disciples' activity to Jerusalem and the temple, where the action of Acts will begin (Luke 24:52–53). The lack of openness to ongoing action at the conclusion of the Fourth Gospel contributes to the thesis that a Johannine community has closed itself off from a mission to the world.[109] Such a conclusion, however, ignores the gospel's adherence to the conventions of storytelling that call for an ending that is complete and does not encourage the audience to wonder what happens next.

As the Fourth Gospel moves toward its conclusion, words addressed to characters within the action form a continuum between the dramatic axis and the theatrical axis. For example, the audience can claim the blessing that Jesus describes for Thomas: "Blessed are those who have not seen and yet have come to believe" (20:29). The belief of the audience not only is commensurate with that of the witnesses within the story but also is in some way happier or more fortuitous. Dunn points to a similar passage in Euripides' *The Suppliant Women.*[110] The chorus leader invites the chorus to make its final exit and go perform a task in honor of Athens and its mythic founder, Theseus, a character in the play, for having restored common law to Hellas, a role that the Athens of Euripides proudly claimed for itself. The dramatic locution directs its praise to the Athens of the past; the theatrical locution praises the Athens of the present. In the gospel, on the dramatic axis, Jesus' locution refers to some unnamed recipients of the report of his resurrection. On the theatrical axis, the locution refers to those believers sitting in the audience.

---

[109] See Rensberger, *Johannine Faith and Liberating Community,* 28.
[110] Dunn, *Tragedy's End,* 76.

Set in the context of the dramatic frame of the gospel, the closing action also bridges the time of the play with the present in a manner similar to the aition found in Euripidean endings. In his analysis of Euripidean closing aetiologies, Dunn notes that these tragic endings spell "out the connection between past and present by showing that events of the play survive in some specific way into the present world of the audience."[111] For example, in Medea's final speech in the play bearing her name, she announces, "I shall enjoin on this land of Sisyphus a solemn festival and holy rites for all time to come in payment for this unholy murder" (1381–1383 [Kovacs, LCL]). At the end of *Iphigenia among the Taurians*, Athena directs King Thoas to build a temple when he arrives in Athens and set up the statue of Artemis and a cult to the goddess with a prescribed ritual in which the neck of a man would be grazed to draw blood (1453–1457). The cult of Artemis Tauropolos in the Attic deme of Hala, with its mock sacrifice, would have been part of the religious observances of Euripides' audience.[112] In the gospel, the belief that the resurrection appearances engender in their witnesses is sustained in the belief of the gospel's audience. The witness of the Beloved Disciple stands at the end of the gospel like a monument proving that the action of the gospel is connected to the experience of the audience.

The aition is more than a Kipling *Just So Story* about how the leopard got its spots, in that it serves the theatrical purpose of leading the audience out of the mythic or historical world of the drama.[113] Though the authority of an institution, such as the Areopagus, may be affirmed by Aeschylus's *Eumenides*, that affirmation is not the purpose of the play. Recent scholars of the tragedies have revised the theory of the Cambridge school of thought that argued that tragedies were rituals that enacted their own legendary origins.[114] The Athenian adage "Nothing to do with Dionysus" calls for another explanation of the relationship between the tragedies and ritual. Dunn describes the revival of an anthropological approach that emphasizes the homology between ritual and tragedy as social and civic structures that define one's place in the social order.[115] The performance of the gospel bridges the distance between the audience and the gospel story. The "then" of the story becomes the "now" of the audience in much the same way as the performance of the Eucharist collapses the span of time that divides contemporary worship from

---

[111] Ibid., 46.

[112] Ibid., 48.

[113] Ibid., 58.

[114] For example, Gilbert Murray, *Euripides and His Age* (Home University Library of Modern Knowledge 73; New York: Holt, 1913), 41.

[115] Dunn, *Tragedy's End*, 61.

the Last Supper. The aition serves as a threshold that, once crossed, returns the audience to its own time.

If the gospel does rely upon the conventions of tragic endings, the seemingly awkward jump from Jesus' predictions to the narrator's reflections may be more the result of clumsy mimesis than inelegant editing. As we noted earlier, the *deus ex machina* frequently connects the mythical plot of the play to the world of the audience though a prophecy addressed to a character. At the end of *Orestes*, Apollo tells Orestes that he will not be forgotten and that the name Oresteion will be given to the town in which he will dwell. In *Hecuba*, Polymestor recounts the prophecy of Dionysus that Hecuba "will become a dog with fiery eyes." When Hecuba asks, "Shall I fulfill the prophecy by dying here or living?" Polymestor answers, "By dying, and your grave will receive the name . . . 'Hound's Grave,' a mark for sailors to steer by" (1265–1273 [Kovacs, LCL]). Strabo substantiates the fact that the audience could connect this aition with its own experience when he refers to Cynossema, a geographical landmark with which the Athenians were familiar, as Hecuba's tomb.[116] The audience that knows of the existence of Oresteion and Cynossema then acknowledges the fulfillment of the prophecy, and the future of the story is connected to the present of the audience through its memory. In the final chapter of the gospel, the prophecy regarding Peter's old age and the ambiguous remark about the fate of the unnamed disciple also serve to connect the past to the present. Peter can only guess at what Jesus' poetic words about his own future mean, and he can have no idea about what the future holds for the unnamed disciple, but the first audience of the gospel surely knew. The two asides on the part of the narrator (21:19, 23), which most critics assume to be later additions intended to clear up any uncertainty about these references, make this discrepant awareness explicit. For the audience, these privileged glimpses into the future connect the action of the gospel, removed by some six or seven decades, to its own experience and memory.

This discussion of the gospel's endings has implications for the tenableness of J. Louis Martyn's strategy of reading the story of Jesus as the story of the Johannine community, a community recently expelled from the synagogue. The endings call the audience to assent to the truth of what they have witnessed, that is, the truth of the story of Jesus. Adele Reinhartz points to a number of texts, including 20:31–32, that confirm that this is the true story of the sojourn of the Son of God in the world and not the story of the community. The editorial statement that the witness to the emission of water and blood from Jesus' wound "knows that he tells the truth" (19:34–35) and the

---

[116] Strabo, *Geog.* 7.55; 13.28.

pattern of prophecy and fulfillment that impute historicity to the events—both point to the narrative strategy of treating the story as "true." She also takes note of the way that the narrator bridges the gap between the time of Jesus and the gospel's audience by using the second-person plural. She suggests that the audience as a community may claim that the Paraclete, anticipated in 14:26, 15:26, and 16:7–11, resides with them and that Jesus' prayer for divine protection in 17:1–25 and his blessing in 20:29 apply to them.[117] These strategies have purpose if the Gospel is intended to help the audience see how the story of Jesus connects to them. They would be redundant if the story were a mirror of the community's own experience.

Thomas Brodie compares the effect of the final epilogue to the "technique of a movie camera which, at the end, withdraws and allows the viewer to see a much larger scene." The gospel writer "now provides a view of how the Gospel originated, how it was received, and how it was recorded."[118] Euripides' generic moral ending calls for reflection and an end to the action. The gnomic quality of the gospel's final assertion, "we know that [the disciple's] testimony is true," with its platitudinous flourish, "if every one of [the things that Jesus did] were written down, I suppose that the world itself could not contain the books that would be written," signals that the action is complete and that the time has come for the audience to reflect upon the meaning of the story.[119] If the prologue takes the audience into the perpetual present of the discourse time of the play, the epilogue takes it out again.

Conclusion

Our modern experience of the theater, particularly the cinematic theater, might leave us with the impression that a theatrical performance has more to do with entertainment than with religious faith. Aristotle tells us that tragedy has its origin in the cult of Dionysus, but the Athenian proverb "Nothing to do with Dionysus" and the absence of evidence to corroborate Aristotle's claim suggest that the connection of their content to the worship of Dionysus was unclear when the tragedies were first performed. Recently the relationship between theater and ritual worship has been revived in the fields of theater criticism and ritual studies in an examination of their affec-

---

[117] Adele Reinhartz, *Befriending the Beloved Disciple: A Jewish Reading of the Gospel of John* (New York: Continuum, 2001), 48–51.

[118] Brodie, *The Gospel according to John*, 595.

[119] Dunn, *Tragedy's End*, 17–18.

tive rather than genetic relationship.[120] The Greek tragedies, performed within Dionysus's temple precincts during a seven-day festival, were framed by ritual. The theater was transformed into a sacred place when the corpse of a sacrificed pig was carried around the performance space. Even without these trappings of religiosity, the audience participated in the performance in a manner more analogous to religious worship than the voyeuristic experience of watching a play after the curtain representing a fourth wall is raised.

Richard Schechner, drawing upon the work of Victor Turner, describes the structure of dramatic performance as that of a ritual, beginning with gathering and ending with dispersal, between which a social drama is performed. Turner identifies four actions within rituals that enact social dramas: breach, crisis, redressive action, and reintegration. A breach is a situation that disrupts social unity; the crisis is an event that requires that this breach not be overlooked; some redressive action must be taken so that schismatic elements are reintegrated into the social unit or a new social unit is established.[121] A typical modern Western wedding follows this pattern. Those dearly beloved to the families of the bride and groom gather. The bride enters on her father's arm, and he gives her away, enacting both the breach of the family unit caused by her relationship to the groom and the crisis, her lack of connection to a patriarchal structure; a performative utterance must follow to integrate her into a new social unit. Once husband and wife leave the church, the gathering disperses.

The tragedies and the gospel, as a performance piece rather than a collection of confessional statements, like rituals, generate an audience, a sense of communal unity, and then draw the audience across a liminal zone from its time and space to another and then back out again to its own time. The audience becomes a witness of what it otherwise cannot see or, in some cases, cannot normally bear to look at. The theater is an inversion of reality. What one sees—the diversity and conflict that are characteristic of the world out of which the audience comes—is enacted in the theatrical space, and the audience comes together and for a time becomes a united witness to an event sharing one perspective of the unfolding action. The conventions by which that action and its time and place are constructed do not create the illusion that what the audience sees is really what is happening. The action of theater may represent very real experiences of life and death, but what people do

---

[120] See Michael Hinden, "Drama and Ritual Once Again: Notes toward a Revival of Tragic Theory," *Comparative Drama* 29 (1995): 184.

[121] Richard Schechner, *Performance Theory* (London: Routledge, 1988), 168–69, 187.

or say on the stage is highly stylized and formal. A film such as Steven Spielberg's *Schindler's List* (1994) frames the suffering of the *Shoah* within an aesthetically pleasurable experience not to make the *Shoah* a thing of beauty—even though the film itself may be just that—but to make the suffering accessible by giving the viewers distance so that they can bear to watch it and thereby come to some understanding of it. Spielberg's use of black and white and the intrusion of color that highlighted the story of one little girl in the scene in which the members of the Warsaw ghetto are rounded up for deportation are instrumental to this end.[122] The audience sees the past come alive again with tragic awareness bought by irony, and it witnesses either what is to come to pass or a vision of powers at work not normally seen, or both. Shakespeare's *Othello* brings to light the workings of jealousy and revenge. *Oedipus Tyrannus* depicts the tragic outcome of confusion about one's true identity. The Fourth Gospel reveals the tentative nature of understanding in the world—the contingency of knowledge upon what is to come rather than what has happened in the past or what seems to be the case in the present. The gospel makes visible the confusion generated by the presence of the divine in this world and by the world's resistance to the paradox or challenge to human institutions that God might bring. The audience sees the world out of which it has come and into which it will return.

Tragedies, by their conventions, call attention to themselves by employing irony so that the audience's relation to the action is different from that of the characters represented in the *orchēstra* or on the *skēnē*. The management of voices—formal prologue and epilogue, reported action, dialogue as contest, the corporate chorus, and so on—brings into being the appearance of action unfolding before the eyes of the audience but at the same time reminds the audience that its experience is contrived. Similarly, the gospel constitutes its audience by its prologue and then presents the unfolding action of Jesus' conflict with the Jews and the *pathos* that results from that conflict. The audience enjoys the mutual experience of irony, knowing what the characters in the action cannot know, recognizing levels of meaning that characters do not intend, and understanding the implication of words and actions before events unfold. In the performance time of the gospel, the disunity of

---

[122] *Schindler's List* has been the subject of much negative criticism for its maudlin treatment of the Holocaust, but its viewing remains for many North Americans their only contact with the suffering of the Jews during World War II. In my opinion, the French film *Train de vie* (1999), directed by Radu Mihaileanu, in which a Jewish village evades deportation by buying its own train and making a journey by rail to Palestine, traveling through Germany and across the front lines of the German and Soviet armies, achieves that end more effectively by using humor and an improbable plot.

an audience is dispelled and the conflicts that characterize its experience unfold upon the stage.[123] By facilitating a liminal experience, the gospel alienates its audience from the world, even if for a short time. Those who have viewed the Fourth Gospel as the manifesto of a sectarian community have treated this capacity of the gospel to alienate its reader as instrumental in providing members of the community with an identity. In an examination of irony and sectarianism, Trond Skard Dokka, however, suggests that "the linguistic fluctuations of this gospel—from mother tongue to metaphor to mother tongue and so on endlessly—would have tended to subvert all linguistically fixed marks of identity, for the group as for individuals. . . . If a community ever lived this, it probably did not survive very long." If such a community did exist, it left no trace in the historical record of the early church.[124] Like the community of the theater, that of the gospel disperses once the reading is over. Beyond the experience of the text, it does not possess ironic knowledge but returns to the ambiguity and conflict of the world.

---

[123] See Oddone Longo, "The Theater of Polis," in *Nothing to Do with Dionysos? Athenian Drama in Its Social Context* (ed. John J. Winkler and Froma I. Zeitlin; Princeton, N.J.: Princeton University Press, 1990), 19.

[124] Trond Skard Dokka, "Irony and Sectarianism in the Gospel of John," in *New Readings in John: Literary and Theological Perspectives* (ed. Johannes Nissen and Sigfred Pedersen; JSNTSup 182; Sheffield: Sheffield Academic Press, 1999), 106–7.

CHAPTER 2
Speech as Action

MR. SMITH: There, it's nine o'clock. We've drunk the soup, and eaten the fish and chips, and the English salad. The children have drunk English water. We've eaten well this evening. That's because we live in the suburbs of London and because our name is Smith.

—Eugène Ionesco, *The Bald Soprano*

In the final act of Shakespeare's *Macbeth*, Macduff's line "I have no words, my voice is in my sword" (5.7.8) risks exposing the mechanics of theatrical action. While denying the power of language, Macduff and the playwright who gives him his voice achieve a great deal with words. Shakespeare's text places a sword in Macduff's hand but draws the audience's attention away from that sword to the voice that Macduff claims he does not have, and with these words Macduff threatens Macbeth and provokes a duel.[1] In both Shakespearean and ancient Greek drama, working without stage directions and with minimal scenery, the word is the predominant device by which the dramaturge represents another time and place and by which actions are accomplished.[2] Worlds and events exist within words. One of the most important questions that the reader of classical tragedy should ask is, "What is brought before our eyes by characters' speech?" Through their speech, the

---

[1] This line was drawn to my attention by Dana Chetrinescu, "The Other's Evil: Warfare and Propaganda in Shakespeare's Plays," University of Helsinki, Faculty of Arts, http://www.eng.helsinki.fi/doe/ESSE5–2000/dana.chetrinescu.htm (accessed August 25, 2000).

[2] See Jindrich Honzl, "The Hierarchy of Dramatic Devices," in *The Semiotics of Art: Prague School Contributions* (ed. Ladislav Matejka and Irwin Titunik; Cambridge: MIT Press, 1976), 125.

actors orient the audience to the stage space and to the world supposed to exist beyond its architecture. In speech, objects appear and gestures are anticipated, and the tension and the conflict of the drama unfold through speech-acts.

In the analysis of performance pieces, the Prague school of semiotics distinguishes between the role of two different receptors: the stage artists, who must turn the words into a performance, and the audience, whose role is to watch and make sense of the language and its relationship to what is seen and heard within performance time. When the object of study becomes the performance text, these two roles are fused together. Shakespearean scholar Harry Berger Jr. distinguishes the experience of "the Slit-eyed Analyst" who reads Shakespeare from that of the "Wide-eyed Playgoer" who sees a performance.[3] The latter, short on time and patience, cannot be expected to sift through the surplus of words and unpack the layers of meaning. This observation gives rise to a debate in Shakespearean scholarship over whether the text or the performance is the appropriate object of study. The simple distinction between reader and playgoer cannot be rendered absolute. Some readers possess the powers of what Harry Berger calls "imaginary audition" and can conjure a performance in their mind's eye, while some playgoers possess the quickness of mind or the habits of an oral culture that make sense of subtle patterns in speech.[4] Nevertheless, this distinction between the habits of the reader to find meaning in language and to search for the author's intent and the audience's experience of the play as a spectacle has bearing upon the analysis of the text of a play. One ought to distinguish between word as referent and word as spectacle. In examining the details and the nuances of words to determine what they mean, one also ought to ask what they do. How do the words on the page orient a reader to the conditions of performance, and how do the words uttered by the performer orient an audience to the realities and action within the space and time represented on stage?

The prominent role that dialogue and direct speech play in the Fourth Gospel calls for attention to the capacity of language to perform multiple functions in one literary context; therefore, I am attentive to the imperatives identified by Berger. From a pragmatic perspective, the analytical tools provided by those who study dramatic language provide heuristic devices for differentiating and identifying the various services rendered by Johannine

---

[3] Harry Berger Jr., *Imaginary Audition: Shakespeare on Stage and Page* (Berkeley: University of California Press, 1989), 9–44.

[4] Ibid., 38–39, 45–46. On the "problem" of retaining and retrieving knowledge in a primary oral culture, see Walter J. Ong, *Orality and Literacy: The Technologizing of the Word* (London: Routledge, 1982), 34.

dialogue in the construction of its dramatic world and action. From a hermeneutical perspective, these tools may fit passages with readings that make good sense of what is happening in them.

The following analysis of the various activities of the word takes two approaches to language: the first examines speech as gesture, and the second examines speech as act.[5] In the context of theater, gestures are linguistic devices that communicate to the performer and audience the information needed to identify the context in which the action takes place. They connect the action on stage to the world of the play. For example, when the actor playing the part of Cassandra in *Agamemnon* directs the chorus, "No, no, look there!" (1115), the actor ought to point toward the *skēnē*, the chorus knows to turn toward it, and the audience recognizes that the "there" to which she gestures is not the *skēnē* of the theater but the house of Agamemnon, because the play's characters have consistently referred to the space as such. In narrative, the represented world of the story is described by external commentary; in drama, it is revealed in the words of the individuals who reside within it.[6] The analysis of speech as act examines how dialogues or monologues enact the conflict or suffering of the drama and influence the direction or shape the form that future action takes. For example, Cassandra's visions of the violence within the house to which she points are not simply a report of the murder of Agamemnon; her prophetic vision is her suffering. At the beginning of the dialogue, the chorus is under the influence of Apollo's curse—he has given Cassandra the gift of prophecy with the condition that no one will believe her—and unable to make sense of her words, the chorus believes her to be mad. Cassandra's violent language hits the chorus like a slap in the face that brings it to its senses. In the end, she utters a prophecy that the chorus believes, and she is thereby empowered and ceases to be the victim of the god or the Trojan War.

The treatment of speech as action is indebted to John Austin's theory of speech-acts, in which he distinguishes between descriptive utterances that report some state of affairs and performative utterances that do things such as bless or curse, praise or criticize.[7] In the act of saying something, utterances or locutions can be invested with an illocutionary force designed to have an effect upon the person or persons to whom the utterance is directed or to ef-

---

[5] The difference between speech as gesture and speech as act is more a matter of degree and function than kind. Gestures tend to be the small acts that interpret the world rather than change it.

[6] See Keir Elam, *The Semiotics of Theatre and Drama* (London: Routledge, 1980), 103–12.

[7] J. L. Austin, *How to Do Things with Words* (New York: Oxford University Press, 1962), 4–7.

fect a change of some sort.[8] In the Fourth Gospel, for example, the words of the resurrected Jesus to the disciples "Receive the Holy Spirit. If you forgive the sins of any, they are forgiven them; if you retain the sins of any, they are retained" (20:22–23) do not describe the power that the disciples have; rather, they are words of initiation whereby the power to forgive is granted them. Austin's theory delineates the conditions that render a speech-act effective or felicitous.[9] A speech-act works because of social conventions. For example, first, the individual must have the power or authority to execute the act, and the act must be executed properly or completely. Second, he or she must be sincere. A promise is not a promise if one does not intend to fulfill it. An illocutionary act can bring about a perlocutionary effect.[10] For example, when the chief priests demand that Pilate write, "This man said, 'I am King of the Jews'" (19:21), they expect him to do so. Pilate's failure to comply points to the infelicity of the command insofar as the priests have no authority over Pilate. If they did have authority, their illocution would be felicitous, and Pilate's refusal would be an act of disobedience. Austin recognizes that his dichotomy is provisional because a descriptive utterance can be performative in some contexts.[11] Thus, when Jesus states, "I am the bread of life" (6:35), he not only describes his identity but also asserts it. The following discussion, accordingly, is concerned not with dividing up utterances in the Fourth Gospel into categories but with exploring the way that language works in a manner comparable to theatrical discourse.

Speech as Gesture

When Clement of Alexandria described the intent of the author of the Fourth Gospel to compose a "spiritual gospel" to complement those setting forth the "outward facts," he seems to have presupposed a distinction, not unlike that found in semiotic analysis, between artificial and natural language.[12] Discussion of the "spiritual" nature of Johannine language has been one of the keystones in accounting for the differences between the Fourth

---

[8] Austin (ibid., 99) uses the term "illocutionary act" to signify the "performance of an act *in* saying something as opposed to performance of an act *of* saying something."

[9] Ibid., 14–15. Austin calls "the doctrine of the *things that can be and go wrong* on the occasion of such utterance, the doctrine of the *Infelicities.*"

[10] Ibid., 101–6.

[11] Ibid., 132–46.

[12] Clement cited in Eusebius, *Hist. eccl.* 6.14.

Gospel and the Synoptic tradition. Charles Sanders Peirce provides a tripartite typology of artificial language—icon, index, and symbol—the first and third of which tend to receive a great deal of attention from Johannine scholars. [13] The category of icon, which includes metaphor, consists of signs that bear resemblance to that which they signify, whereas a symbol denotes through the association of ideas that may be arbitrary or conventional and may require some sort of interpreter in order for the connection to be made. For example, the story of Jesus' crucifixion explains how the cross can be a symbol of salvation rather than an instrument of execution. The Fourth Evangelist often exploits both the metaphoric and the symbolic potential of his language: bread is a metaphor for Jesus' ability to bring life, but it is also symbolic of his authority insofar as it can be associated with the manna from the exodus tradition or the eschatological banquet of intertestamental literature. The symbols of the Fourth Gospel frequently rely upon the conventions of the Judaic tradition to make sense.

It is the oft neglected second category of Peirce's typology that concerns us here.[14] Peirce defines the index as "a sign that refers to the object it denotes by virtue of being really affected by the object."[15] Smoke is usually an index of fire, a cough may be an index of a cold, and weeping can be an index of powerful emotion. The index is not limited to signs that are parts of larger events. Like a finger pointing beyond itself, the index may be a response to some environmental cause. For example, an umbrella may signify that it is raining, or a lamp may indicate that it is night.

Performance texts rely heavily upon signs that are indices in order to represent a world upon a stage or a screen. Cartoons tend to use fixed conventions, such as a rooster crowing as an index of daybreak and a rural setting. In film, the musical score has become a conventional means of indicating mood. Some of these have become so familiar to us that they are part of our everyday language. A small child will cry, "Ta-da!" when rendering a hidden object visible, and an adolescent will sing the musical motif from *The Twilight Zone*, although he or she may have never seen the program, to signify that something strange is going on. Indices may be intrinsic

---

[13] Charles Sanders Peirce, *Elements of Logic* (vol. 2 of *The Collected Papers of Charles Sanders Peirce;* ed. Charles Hartshorne and Paul Weiss; Bristol: Thoemmes, 1997), §247.

[14] There have been a few exceptions. Gary A. Phillips addresses the use of index in " 'This Is a Hard Saying. Who Can Be Listener to It?' Creating a Reader in John 6," *Semeia* 26 (1983): 30–37; and more recently, Derek Tovey, *Narrative Art and Act in the Fourth Gospel* (JSNTSup 151; Sheffield: Sheffield Academic Press, 1997), 178–81.

[15] Peirce, *Elements of Logic*, §248.

to the action of a drama and therefore subtle; for example, a knock at the door points to the presence of someone outside it.[16] In classical drama, which employs no stage directions, the indices are embedded in speech. Romeo's line "But, soft! what light through yonder window breaks?" (*Romeo and Juliet* 2.2.2) points to a window, which may or may not be represented in the set, and to the darkness in which the scene takes place. In the open-air, daylight productions of the Elizabethan and Greek theater, such spatial and temporal indices are crucial for the audience.

The Fourth Gospel makes more use of this sort of language than do the Synoptic Gospels even though the presence of a narrator renders the use of indices in direct speech unnecessary in many cases. In the following analysis, three aspects of the use of indices will be examined: deictic language, language that signifies a movement, and language that points to properties and geography of dramatic space.

Deixis

Within the category of index lies a group of words that linguists place in the subgroup of deixis. The principal role of these words is to point to subjectivity (who is speaking and to whom), temporality (past, present, and future with the dramatic present as the point of reference), spatiality (the presence of the speaker and the orientation of space and referents to him or her), and modality (things such as attitude or ambiance). Personal and demonstrative pronouns such as "I," "you," "this," and "that" and adverbs such as "here" and "now" serve to attract the audience's attention and to identify the contextual elements of speaker, addressee, time, and location (see fig. 3).[17] Keir Elam maintains that "the drama consists first and foremost precisely in this, an *I* addressing a *you here* and *now*," and assigns these little words the status of "most significant linguistic feature—both statistically and functionally—in the drama."[18] A line from *Oedipus Tyrannus* illustrates how these words serve as verbal markers of place and individuals. Iocaste and the messenger are on stage when Oedipus enters and says, "My dearest wife, Iocaste, why have *you* summoned *me here* from the house?" (950–951 [Lloyd-Jones, LCL]; italics added). The line serves a double duty: it initiates the dialogue, and it also orients the audience to the action. In narrative, the narrator can provide the information that identifies the time and place of the

---

16 This example comes from Elam, *Semiotics of Theatre and Drama*, 22.

17 Ibid., 22–27.

18 Ibid., 139–40, 27. Elam cites Alessandro Serpieri, who counts five thousand deictic words in the twenty-nine thousand words that constitute Shakespeare's *Hamlet*.

action, and who is speaking and the manner in which he or she speaks, but in a classical performance piece, direct speech must supply these contextual elements. Moreover, the repetition of deictic terms continually draws the audience's attention to the here and now of the stage world. In the course of performance, the here and now keeps changing as the present becomes the past and the future becomes the present, and the deictic language continuously reasserts the eternal present of the stage.[19] As we will see in the following discussion, the Fourth Gospel uses deictic and language gestures in speeches in ways peculiar to drama when narration does or could provide the same information.

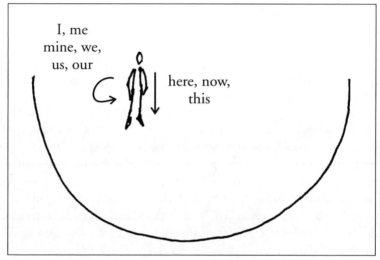

Figure 3: Deixis Materializing the Dramatic Subject
in an Actual Body, Place, and Time

Some aspects of the Johannine narrator's speech make sense only if decoded on the performance axis, and some represent the space that the narrator occupies as if it were the dramatic space of the characters he describes. When the narrator sets up the context for the dialogue with the Samaritan woman, he explains, "Jacob's well was there, and Jesus, tired out by his journey, was sitting by the well [ὁ οὖν Ἰησοῦς κεκοπιακὼς ἐκ τῆς ὁδοιπορίας ἐκαθέζετο οὕτως ἐπὶ τῇ πηγῇ]. It was about noon" (4:6). The NRSV translation omits the word οὕτως because it is awkward to translate and makes no sense in a silent, private reading. The Greek text reads literally, "Jesus . . . sat

---

[19] Jiří Veltrusky, "Basic Features of Dramatic Dialogue," in Matejka and Titunik, *The Semiotics of Art,* 128.

thus." The οὕτως makes good sense only if it is accompanied by a gesture performed by the reader indicating what "thus" signifies.[20] A second instance occurs in the description of the position of the Beloved Disciple during the final supper: ἀναπεσὼν οὖν ἐκεῖνος οὕτως ἐπὶ τὸ στῆθος τοῦ Ἰησοῦ (13:25). Again the translators of the NRSV ignore the word οὕτως and provide this rendering: "So while reclining next to Jesus . . ." If we attend to the presence of οὕτως, a more literal translation would begin, "Leaning in this way . . . ," again calling for some sort of gesture to make sense of the language. Although the use of οὕτως on these occasions is by no means unequivocal in its purpose, these two cases arouse suspicion that any reading of the gospel ought to be attentive to other possible uses of language as gesture.

The Fourth Evangelist's penchant for using the demonstrative pronouns ἐκεῖνος and οὗτος as personal pronouns sets him apart from the authors of the Synoptic Gospels.[21] In reported speech, these demonstrative pronouns function deictically by inviting the hearer to trace a path from the verbal gesture to the thing indicated.[22] For example, when John the Baptist spots Jesus, he points to him with these words: οὗτός ἐστιν ὑπὲρ οὗ ἐγὼ εἶπον ("This is he of whom I said"; 1:30); and after he narrates his vision of the descent of the Spirit, he gestures toward him again: οὗτός ἐστιν ὁ υἱὸς τοῦ θεοῦ ("this is the Son of God"; 1:34). If the chief priests had their way and the inscription on the cross were to read, ἐκεῖνος εἶπεν· Βασιλεύς εἰμι τῶν Ἰουδαίων ("This man said, I am King of the Jews"; 19:21), the ἐκεῖνος would function as an arrow pointing toward Jesus as the speaker. The narrator makes similar use of these demonstrative pronouns as if he is able to point to the thing or person to which he refers. The first occurrences are in the prologue, in which οὗτος refers to "the Word" and ἐκεῖνος to John: "In the beginning was the Word. . . . This [Word] was in the beginning [οὗτος ἦν ἐν ἀρχῇ] with God" (1:1–2), and "That [man] was not the light [οὐκ ἦν ἐκεῖνος τὸ φῶς]" (1:8) (author's translations). Throughout the narrative sections, demonstrative pronouns are used periodically in lieu of personal pronouns to identify characters.[23] In the denial scene, the narrator refers to Peter twice as ἐκεῖνος (18:17, 25), as if to differentiate him from the other disciple, who was known to the high priest, by their proximity to himself. In the final

---

[20] Edwin Abbott (*Johannine Grammar* [London: Black, 1906], 26) suggests that the meaning is, "he sat down just as he was," as "he sat thus" is unintelligible.

[21] The exceptions are Luke 18:14 and Mark 16:10.

[22] See Charles J. Fillmore, "Towards a Descriptive Framework for Spatial Deixis," in *Speech, Place, and Action: Studies in Deixis and Related Topics* (ed. Robert J. Jarvella and Wolfgang Klein; Chichester, N.Y.: Wiley, 1982), 46.

[23] For the use of οὗτος as a personal pronoun, see also 1:7, 41; 3:2; 6:71; for ἐκεῖνος, 2:21; 9:9, 11, 25, 36; 11:13, 29, 49; 13:25, 27; 19:15; 20:13, 15, 16.

epilogue, the narrator provides a bridge between the dramatic space and time and the location of his narration by pointing to the Beloved Disciple: "This [οὗτος] is the disciple who is testifying to these things" (21:24). The use of this deictic language does not necessitate that the object to which it points be present. It is anaphoric; it refers back to things just treated in the discourse or ahead to things immediately to be treated and points to things found not in the space of perception but in the discourse, but it gains its emphatic power by its representational power.[24]

Within the speech of characters, deictic language is used with striking force (see fig. 4). Although the personal inflection of Greek verbs makes the use of personal pronouns unnecessary, the author of the Fourth Gospel frequently includes them in sentence constructions. Ὑμεῖς ("you" plural) appears in John as often as in all three Synoptic Gospels put together, σύ ("you" singular) more frequently, and ἐγώ ("I") twice as often.[25] The increased occurrence of ἐγώ is not solely the result of Jesus' tendency to talk about himself; John the Baptist, the man at the pool, the man born blind, Martha, and Pilate all add ἐγώ to their statements.[26] The effect of the pronoun use is lost in English translation; in order to capture it, emphasis must be put on the pronouns, as if the speaker were either touching his or her breast when using the first-person pronoun or pointing to the person or group being addressed when using the second- or third-person pronouns. The first dialogue establishes the pattern when the Jerusalem delegation asks John, "Who are you?" (σὺ τίς εἶ; 1:19), and he replies, "I am not the Messiah" (ἐγὼ οὐκ εἰμὶ ὁ χριστός; 1:20), "I am the voice" (ἐγὼ φωνὴ; 1:23), "I baptize with water" (ἐγὼ βαπτίζω ἐν ὕδατι; 1:26). When Jesus first speaks to Peter, his use of first-person pronouns renders his statements "You [σύ] are Simon son of John" and "You [σύ] are to be called Cephas" (1:42) as identifications rather than descriptions. In exchanges such as the dialogue following the feeding of the five thousand, the use of pronouns functions like a spotlight upon characters, singling them out. When the crowd asks, "What sign are you going to give?" (τί οὖν ποιεῖς σὺ σημεῖον; 6:30), it points to the distinction between Moses' and Jesus' identities.

We find a comparable use of personal pronouns in tragic dialogue, particularly when an exchange begins to get heated. For example, in Sophocles'

---

24 See Karl Bühler, "The Deictic Field of Language and Deictic Words," in Jarvella and Klein, *Speech, Place, and Action*, 20–30. Bühler calls anaphoric deixis "deixis at phantasma."

25 Bruce J. Malina and Richard L. Rohrbaugh (*Social-Science Commentary on the Gospel of John* [Minneapolis: Fortress, 1998], 12) identify this as a characteristic of the anti-language of the gospel.

26 In chapter 3 I will address Jesus' habit of talking about himself.

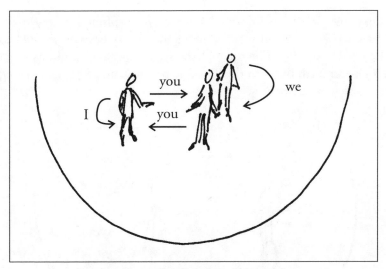

Figure 4: Deixis Signifying Interpersonal Action

Antigone, as Antigone and Ismene square off and take opposing positions regarding Polynice's burial, ἐγώ and σύ sharpen the tips of their sentences as they score verbal repartees. Falling back on her status as a woman and claiming that she has no choice but to consent to Creon's prohibition against the burial, Ismene states, "I shall beg [ἐγὼ μὲν οὖν αἰτοῦσα] those beneath the earth to be understanding" (65 [Lloyd-Jones, LCL]), to which Antigone retorts, "But I shall bury him [κεῖνον δ' ἐγὼ θάψω]. It is honourable for me to do this and die" (71–72), and counters, "As for you, if it is your pleasure [σὺ δ' εἰ δοκεῖ], dishonour what the gods honour" (76–77). Ismene protests, "I [ἐγὼ μὲν] am not dishonouring them" (78), and Antigone rebuts, "You [σὺ μὲν] may offer that excuse, but I shall go [ἐγὼ δὲ] to heap up a tomb for my dearest brother!" (80–81). Each sentence, with its pronounced use of the first and the second person, keeps the focus upon the back-and-forth action of the exchange. The presence of ἐγώ, ἡμεῖς, σύ, and ὑμεῖς plays a comparable role in the gospel's trial scene. The following texts are characteristic of the entire dialogue:

PILATE: Are you [Σὺ] the King of the Jews?

JESUS: Do you [σὺ] ask this on your own, or did others tell you about me?

PILATE: I [ἐγὼ] am not a Jew, am I? (18:33–35)

PILATE: You [ὑμεῖς] take him and crucify him; I [ἐγὼ] find no case against him.

THE JEWS: We ['Ημεῖς] have a law. (19:6–7; author's translation)

A comparable density of first- and second-person pronouns appears in the dialogues between the Jewish authorities and the man born blind and his parents (9:19–21, 24–34). The force of the second-person pronouns hurls the lines back and forth between the dialogue partners, and the first-person pronouns are defensive gestures.

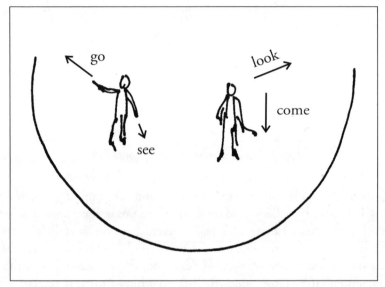

Figure 5: Deixis Signifying Movement

Deictic language provides an ordering schema that generates the reality on stage. When the words of the text are spoken, they are lifted out of a past time and another place to the here and now. Characters in the Fourth Gospel consistently point to the present time and to the space they occupy. Not only is the contrast between the use of νῦν ("now") and ἄρτι ("presently") in the Fourth Gospel and the Synoptic Gospels numerically significant; the manner in which these words are employed differs.[27] In the Gospel of Matthew, the word νῦν appears only four times: once in a poetic way of saying "never" (24:21), once by Caiaphas to mark the witness of Jesus' blasphemy (26:65), and twice in taunts to Jesus on the cross (27:42, 43). In Luke, νῦν appears in prayers or beatitudes or marks a contrast rather than the temporal location

---

[27] Νῦν occurs four times in Matthew, three times in Mark, twelve times in Luke, and twenty-eight times in John. Ἄρτι appears in Matthew seven times, three of which are in narrative, and in John twelve times, all of which are in direct speech.

of action.[28] In the Fourth Gospel, Martha, like other characters, uses deictic language to emphasize the location and moment in which she speaks: "Lord, if you had been here [ὧδε], my brother would not have died. But even now [καὶ νῦν] I know that God will give you whatever you ask of him" (11:21–22).[29] Besides deictic adverbs such as ὧδε, characters ground the action in their own time and place with deictic motion verbs such as "look," "come," and "go" (see fig. 5). For example, when Jesus tells the Samaritan woman, "Go, call your husband, and come back" (4:16), both commands situate the action with reference to where Jesus stands.[30] This sort of deictic language is part of natural speech, but its concentration in dramatic dialogue, particularly at the beginning of scenes, is crucial to the establishment of a dramatic context. *Oedipus Tyrannus*, a play without a prologue, opens with a speech by Oedipus that points to his position as the center of the action:

> Children, latest to be reared from the stock of Cadmus, why do you sit like this before me, with boughs of supplication wreathed with chaplets? . . . Thinking it wrong to hear this from the report of others, my children, I have come myself, I who am called Oedipus, renowned to all. (1–8 [Lloyd-Jones, LCL])

When characters call attention to their own presence, the dramatic context enters the primary world in which action is in progress.[31]

Indices of Movement

Working without stage directions, the classical playwright maintains some control over the performance axis as well as the interpretation of actions by the audience on the theatrical axis by including references to movements in dialogue while they are being carried out. Even in modern screenplays, characters continue to talk about what they are doing in unnatural ways so that the audience understands what is happening. In the television program *Law and Order*, for example, when the detectives examine the murder victim, they explain their actions with lines such as "I'll look in his wallet to see if he has any I.D." In classical drama, such a line also tells the

---

[28] For νῦν in contrasts such as "then and now" and "from now on," see Luke 5:10; 11:39; 12:52; 16:25; 19:42; 22:18, 36, 69.

[29] See also John 14:29–30; 17:4–5. Luke uses the word ὧδε far more than any other gospel writer, but the Fourth Gospel also uses ἐντεῦθεν, ἐνάδε and ἰδέ to point to location.

[30] See also John 1:39, 46; 7:3; 9:7; 11:34; 21:3.

[31] See Elam, *Semiotics of Theatre and Drama*, 140.

actor what to do. For example, when Ion makes his appearance in Euripides' *Ion*, he sings to himself:

> Come, O broom fresh-grown,
> servant made of lovely laurel,
> sweeper of Phoebus' altar . . .
> with you I sweep the god's temple floor (112–114, 121 [Kovacs, LCL])

The cessation of this sweeping action and the initiation of the act of cleansing the floor are marked by a turn in his song:

> But I shall cease my labor of sweeping
> with these laurel branches,
> and from a vessel of gold I shall cast
> the water the earth produces, (145–147)

Such vivid and expressive lines signify a development in dramatic writing from a declamatory style in which the actor merely recited the lines to one that called for gesture.[32] Aristotle complained that actors, thinking the words insufficient to convey meaning to the audience, struck the pose or performed the actions for which the words called.[33] Aristotle preferred declamation of the epics to performances of the tragedies and grumbled that actors, by paying attention to how they expressed words, were winning more praise than the poets who wrote them.[34]

We have already examined how the action of embrace is an index of emotion in recognition scenes and how the words of a character indicate the gesture. Jesus' line "Do not hold on to me" (John 20:17) can be taken as an index of an action rather than as a line fraught with profound theological or ontological implications. Encouragement to place this line on a performance axis can be found by examining other pieces of Johannine dialogue that clearly contain gestures. By comparing the way that direct speech is handled at the end of the trial in the Gospel of Matthew to its treatment in the Fourth Gospel, we can see how the words of the Johannine characters stand for actions. In Matthew, Pilate and the crowd engage in a dialogue in which questions are answered with suggestions:

PILATE: Then what should I do with Jesus who is called the Messiah?

CROWD: Let him be crucified!

---

[32] See Peter Arnott, *Public and Performance in the Greek Theatre* (London: Routledge, 1989), 48.
[33] Aristotle, *Poet.* 1461b–1462a.
[34] Aristotle, *Rhet.* 3.1403b.

PILATE: Why, what evil has he done?

CROWD: Let him be crucified! (Matt 27:22–23)

In the Fourth Gospel, the deictic language is pronounced, and words accompany implicit gestures and movement. As Pilate approaches the Jewish authorities, he describes what he is doing: "Look, I am bringing him out to you to let you know that I find no case against him" (19:4). With the line "Behold the man!" (19:5b), Pilate points to Jesus as standing next to him or nearby.[35] The chief priests and police follow with a chanted imperative, "Crucify him! Crucify him!" (19:6b), that signifies movement in the opposite direction of Pilate's gesture. In the modern political theater of protest, the words call for fists thrust forward into the air. Pilate responds by using deictic language that shifts the attention back to the Jews and then again to himself, thereby setting himself in opposition to them: "Take him yourselves [λάβετε αὐτὸν ὑμεῖς] and crucify him; I [ἐγὼ γὰρ] find no case against him" (19:6c). When Pilate approaches the Jews for the last time, he once more points to Jesus: "Here is your King!"(19:14), and accents the relationship between those whom he addresses and Jesus as well as Jesus' presence. The crowd responds with a gesture directed at Pilate that pushes Jesus off the stage: "Away with him! Away with him! Crucify him!" (19:15). Not only do the characters describe what they are doing; their words also tell other characters what to do.

Other examples of direct speech that requires movement or gesture occur throughout the gospel. John the Baptist points to Jesus and directs the attention of the Jerusalem delegation and then of his disciples to Jesus with the words "Look, the Lamb of God" (ἴδε ὁ ἀμνὸς τοῦ θεοῦ; 1:29, 36). The NRSV translation obscures the subjective and spatial qualities of the deictic language by rendering 1:29 "Here is the Lamb of God." Jesus' and Philip's invitations "Come and see" (1:39, 46) are gestures that beckon. Jesus' directions to the servants at the wedding in Cana indicate their actions, some of which, but not all, the narrator reiterates:

Direct Speech	Narrative
JESUS: Fill the jars with water.	And they filled them up to the brim.
JESUS: Take it to the chief steward.	So they took it. (2:7–8)

Jesus' words on the cross "Woman, behold your son" (γύναι, ἴδε ὁ υἱός σου; 19:26) and "Behold your mother" (ἴδε ἡ μήτηρ σου; 19:27) require that

---

35 This the RSV translation; the NRSV translates ἰδοὺ ὁ ἄνθρωπος "Here is the man!"

Jesus' head turn from one character to the other.[36] When Jesus directs Thomas, "Put your finger here and see my hands" (20:27), Jesus ought to hold out first one hand with its wound for Thomas to touch and then both hands for him to see.

We find many of the same forms of indices in a dialogue in *Alcestis* in which Heracles persuades Admetus to take the resurrected and veiled Alcestis into his home. After Heracles repeatedly insists that Admetus "take this woman," Admetus commands his servants, "Take her in, since I must receive her into my house." An exchange then begins about whose and which hand will take her:

> HERACLES: I will not release the woman into the hands of servants.
>
> ADMETUS: Take her into the house yourself, if you like.
>
> HERACLES: No, I shall put her into your hands.
>
> ADMETUS: I will not touch her. She may go into the house.
>
> HERACLES: I trust only your right hand.
>
> ADMETUS: My Lord, you compel me to do this against my will.
>
> HERACLES: Have the courage to stretch out your hands and touch the stranger.
>
> ADMETUS: There, I stretch it out, as if I were cutting off a Gorgon's head.
>
> HERACLES: Do you have her?
>
> ADEMTUS: Yes, I have her. (1110–1119 [Kovacs, LCL])

The invitation to receive the woman is met with Admetus's statements that send her away. The sense of the repeated references to hands is completed by the action of reaching out and grabbing hold of Alcestis. With the words "Look at her! See whether she bears any resemblance to your wife" (1121), Heracles makes clear that he has lifted her veil, and he directs Admetus' eyes. The line serves as an index of the position of Admetus's face and makes sense only if Admetus is directing his gaze away from her. The presence of so much deictic language in this play and in the Fourth Gospel turns dialogue into a series of actions between characters rather than an exchange of ideas.

---

[36] Once again the NRSV obscures the deictic qualities of the language by translating ἴδε, "here is."

As in Greek tragedy, the Johannine propensity to let characters' speech represent the world behind the text can be meteoric in speed and effect. At the wedding in Cana, the action of running out of wine is brought to the reader's attention by words from Jesus' mother: "They have no wine" (2:3b). These simple words accomplish much more than gesture to what is happening at the moment; they replace the annunciation narratives of Matthew and Luke. Jesus' mother's speech is an index of her precognition of Jesus' status. What she believes he is capable of accomplishing is unclear, but her words to Jesus and to the servants anticipate something extraordinary. Jesus' last utterance before his death, "It is finished" (19:30a), announces the action of dying and indicates his control over his own death. The line of narrative that follows, "Then he bowed his head and gave up his spirit" (19:30b), echoes what has already been represented in direct speech.

In the Greek tragedies, characters typically die off stage, but Euripides offers a number of exceptions, most notably the death of Alcestis, in which speech serves as an index of expiration. Alcestis does not give up the ghost as quickly as does Jesus; her words signify a more gradual process and point to the presence of death and the identity of her addressee:

> Someone is taking, is taking me (don't you see him?) away to the court of the dead. It is winged Hades, glowering from beneath his dark brows. [To death:] What do you want? Let me go! Ah, what a journey it is that I, unhappiest of women, am making! . . . [To her servants:] Let me go, let me go now! Lay me back. I have no strength in my legs! Hades is near and night creeps darkly over my eyes. [To her children:] Children, children, your mother is no more, no more! Farewell, my children, joy be yours as you look on the light of the sun! (*Alcestis* 259–271 [Kovacs, LCL])

Alcestis has more to say. For readers versed in Shakespearean drama, she brings to mind Desdemona, as she has the ability to speak seemingly from the other side of death. When she finally expires, her lines become as terse as those of Jesus:

ALCESTIS: I am gone.

ADMETUS: What are you doing? Are you leaving me?

ALCESTIS: Farewell.

ADMETUS: I am utterly undone.

CHORUS LEADER: She is gone. Admetus' wife is no more. (391–393)

Although her words are more descriptive of the experience of death than those of Jesus, they serve the same purpose on the theatrical axis: they inform the audience that death has come. The chorus's confirmation of that death is comparable to the Johannine narrator's descriptive echo of Jesus' words.

The incongruity between Jesus' verbal gesture in "Rise, let us be on our way" at the end of John 14 and the continuation of the farewell speech for another three chapters calls for some explanation. Raymond Brown favors the idea that these words signal the conclusion of an early version of the discourse to which a later editor added what follows.[37] C. H. Dodd argues that Jesus is speaking of "a movement of the spirit, and interior act of will" to meet his assailant, the archon of this world, rather than a physical movement.[38] Don Carson perpetuates the tendencies of earlier commentaries by suggesting that the discourse continues as they walk to the garden, and the various references to viticulture are indices of the vineyards and activities that they see as they walk.[39] Brown criticizes such efforts as "a romantic approach . . . dependent on unrecorded stage directions."[40] Given the absence of any overt references to their surroundings in John 15–17, Brown probably is correct on this last point, but the treatment of 14:31 as an index pointing to the conclusion of the speech may miss the effect of the failed gesture. At the end of Samuel Beckett's *Waiting for Godot*, Vladimir asks, "Well? Shall we go?" and Estragon answers, "Yes, let's go," but neither moves. Their immobility at the end of the play represents the ineffectuality of intent in an absurd world. Jesus' immobility, despite his stated intention to leave, may be an indication of his disinclination to stop talking. He later verbalizes this sentiment by saying, "I still have many things to say to you, but you cannot bear them now" (16:12). The line, then, serves as an index of modality rather than signifying a physical movement inconsistent with the ongoing action.

Indices of Setting

The last category of this analysis of language as gesture includes speech that points to objects, temporal setting, and the features and geography of physical setting. In classical drama, characters speak about the objects in their

---

[37] Raymond E. Brown, *The Gospel according to John* (2 vols.; AB 29, 29A; Garden City, N.Y.: Doubleday, 1966–1970), 2:656.

[38] C. H. Dodd, *The Interpretation of the Fourth Gospel* (Cambridge: Cambridge University Press, 1953), 407–9.

[39] D. A. Carson, *The Gospel according to John* (Grand Rapids: Eerdmans, 1991), 479.

[40] Brown, *The Gospel according to John*, 2:583.

hands and what they see around themselves. They also describe the nature of the place they inhabit and the character of the space that lies beyond the sphere of their activity. This sort of speech is a form of code by which performers orient themselves on stage and audiences translate what they hear and see on stage into a world of its own.

In classical drama, the speech of the characters generates the meta-discourse from which the stage manager constructs a set with properties. References to objects become important indices of how a set should look or what properties should be upon it. Shakespeare provides a comic picture of this aspect of stagecraft in the scene in *A Midsummer Night's Dream* in which Bottom and his band of amateur thespians rehearse the play *Pyramus and Thisbe*. The play calls for a wall, so Snout the joiner takes the part, and in the performance Pyramus speaks to the wall as if it were a character by making requests of it and giving it thanks. Classical Greek drama, on the whole, requires very few properties, but performances could include animals and chariots when references by characters call for them. For the most part, the Johannine narrator supplies the description of details with which a reader constructs a mental picture of the setting of action. In the temple scene, the narrator provides the cattle, sheep, doves, and coins, and Jesus merely points to them with his words: "Take these things out of here!" (2:13–16). In the scene in which Mary washes Jesus' feet, the narrator relates that Mary has a pound of costly nard and that she anoints Jesus' feet and wipes them with her hair. If we were to rely solely upon what the characters provide, we would see only the expensive perfume. This is not the case in the scene in which Jesus predicts his betrayal. The bread, the act of dipping, and the dish are all brought before the eye by the words of Jesus: "It is the one to whom I give this piece of bread when I have dipped it in the dish" (13:26a). At first glance, the comparable scene in the Gospel of Matthew contains the same objects, but upon closer scrutiny, we see that the management of action is very different. Matthew narrates, "When it was evening, he took his place with the twelve; and while they were eating, he said, 'Truly I tell you, one of you will betray me. . . . The one who has dipped his hand into the bowl with me will betray me'" (26:20–23). At some moment in the time narrated, the action has already taken place. In the Fourth Gospel, the action happens after Jesus speaks: "So when he had dipped the piece of bread, he gave it to Judas son of Simon Iscariot" (13:26b). In Matthew, the bowl need not be in view when Jesus speaks, but in the Fourth Gospel, the bowl and the bread must be in view.

Details such as the description of the pool with five porticoes at Beth-zatha (5:2) or the snapshot of Jesus walking in the portico of Solomon in the temple (10:23) suggest to some that the gospel is an eyewitness account or even historically accurate.[41] To others, the gospel's play between Judea and Galilee/Samaria suggests a theological or ideological use of topography rather than historical concern.[42] No one disputes the gospel writer's interest in location, but here the focus is upon how the characters talk about the space that they inhabit and how space is constructed by their speech. If we approach the text with the analytical tools of scholars who study theatrical space, it becomes evident that the author of the gospel manages scenographic detail with some finesse. Michael Issacharoff distinguishes between mimetic space, "that which is made visible to an audience and represented on stage," and diegetic space, that which "is described, that is, referred to by the characters" (see fig. 6).[43] Issacharoff qualifies this dichotomy by noting that when "discourse is focused on the mimetic space, it acquires an indexical function."[44] The mimetic space itself is created by the diegetic power of the set design and properties in consort with the language of the drama. The direct speech and the narrator of the Fourth Gospel seem to construct both these types of space. We have already noted that in the episodic structure of the gospel, scenes are set in particular locations and Jesus' travels are not part of the narrative. The scenographic details seem to function to suggest setting or mimetic space, while references to broader geographic territory or to cities situate the mimetic space within the context of diegetic space in a manner characteristic to stage space and not necessary to narrative.

If we compare the handling of the cleansing of the temple in Matthew and in the Fourth Gospel, we find that the language that generates the mimetic space and the relationship of that space to the action are very different. Besides the fact that there is more activity in the Fourth Gospel, the relationship of action, dialogue, and space is much more tightly crafted.[45] In Matthew, the action precedes the representation of place:

---

41 Martin Hengel (*The Johannine Question* [Philadelphia: Trinity, 1989], 110) contends that the Gospel of John was written by a Judean eyewitness; C. H. Dodd (*Historical Tradition in the Fourth Gospel* [Cambridge: Cambridge University Press, 1963], 233–47) believes that these details may reflect authentic memories.

42 See Wayne A. Meeks, "Galilee and Judea in the Fourth Gospel," *JBL* 85 (1966): 159–69; Robert T. Fortna, "Theological Use of Locale in the Fourth Gospel," *AThR* 3 (1974): 58–95.

43 Michael Issacharoff, "Space and Reference in Drama," *Poetics Today* 23 (1981): 215.

44 Ibid., 216.

45 Jeffrey L. Staley (*The Print's First Kiss: A Rhetorical Investigation of the Implied Reader in the Fourth Gospel* [SBLDS 82; Atlanta: Scholars Press, 1988], 90) draws attention to the use of near alliterations in John 2:14–16 (e.g., καὶ εὗρεν ἐν τῷ ἱερῷ τοὺς πωλοῦντας βόας καὶ πρόβατα καὶ περιστερὰς καὶ τοὺς κερματιστὰς καθημένους, καὶ . . . κολλυβιστῶν ἐξέχεεν τὸ κέρμα . . . τοῖς τὰς περιστερὰς

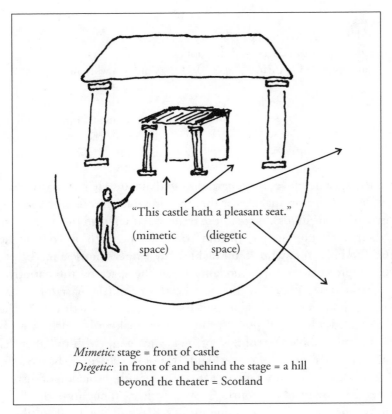

Fig. 6: Theatrical Space

Action	Space
Then Jesus entered	the temple
and drove all who were selling and buying	in the temple,
and he overturned	the tables of the money changers and the seats of those who sold doves. (21:12)[46]

The Johannine narrator brings the mimetic space into view before action takes place in it:

πωλοῦσιν εἶπεν) and the use of sounds made "by forcing air out of the lungs" that complements Jesus' action.

[46] The same order is found in the Greek text.

Space	*Action*
In the temple he found people selling cattle, sheep, and doves, and the money changers seated at their tables.	
	Making a whip of cords, he drove all of them
out of the temple, both the sheep and the cattle.	
	He also poured out the coins of the money changers and overturned their tables. (2:14–15)

When the episode moves from narration to dialogue, characters, by pointing to it with their words, make clear that they inhabit this mimetic space. Jesus uses spatial deixis in his charge to the dealers that refers to the mimetic space and their economic activity within it: "Take these things out of here!" (2:16a), and his command "Stop making my Father's house a marketplace!" (2:16b) represents the same modality given the space by the narrative description in verses 14–15. In the Matthean version, the narrator leaves the identity of Jesus' audience vague, and Jesus' speech "It is written, 'My house shall be called a house of prayer'; but you are making it a den of robbers" (21:13) contains only the contrast of "my" and "you," with no other deictic terms. His words "house of prayer" and "den of thieves" describe what he encounters in terms that do not correlate directly with the action of disrupting commercial activity. In the Fourth Gospel, both the thoughts of the disciples, "Zeal for your house will consume me" (2:17), and the words of the Jews, "What sign can you show us for doing this?" (2:18), refer to Jesus, what he has done, and the location in which he is doing it. In the Gospel of Matthew, the narrative turns to activities that are not specific to the temple: "The blind and the lame came to him in the temple, and he cured them" (21:14); and the chief priests respond to the words of the children, "Hosanna to the Son of David," which, though spoken in the temple, make no reference to it or to Jesus' actions. The remaining dialogue in Matthew contains no language that orients the audience to the action's physical setting, and when Jesus exits, the narrator describes him leaving "them" and the city (21:17). In contrast, the last two lines of the Johannine dialogue keep the physical space intact and in view by repeated reference to the temple: "Jesus answered them, 'Destroy this temple, and in three days I will raise it up.' The Jews then said, 'This temple has been under construction for forty-six years, and will you raise it up in three days?'" (2:19–20). Within Johannine dialogues, characters often refer to aspects of the mimetic space in a similar manner, although seldom as vividly as they do in the temple scene. In the dialogue with the Samaritan woman, the setting at the well is kept in view by references to drawing water from it (4: 7, 11, 15). When the disciples return, Jesus directs their attention to the fields surrounding the well (4:35). The mimetic space in the Fourth Gospel is more complete and intrinsic to the action than that of a Synoptic Gospel.

Mark A. Matson suggests that the temple continues to be the "conceptual backdrop" for the discourses set in Jerusalem until Jesus' farewell address. Once Jesus has established himself as the replacement for the temple in 2:19, he begins to use imagery that refers to the eschatological temple: "Let anyone who is thirsty come to me. . . . 'Out of the believer's heart shall flow rivers of living water'" (7:37–38); "I am the light of the world" (8:12).[47] These statements, then, implicitly point to Jesus' physical surroundings as though Jesus were saying, "I, not this temple, am the light of the world."

The way that the Johannine author chooses to represent mimetic space is comparable to that demanded by the classical stage. For example, in Euripides' *Ion*, the stage space mimetically represents the temple of Apollo and is signified in speech, with the placement of an altar and perhaps with the presence of a statue of the god. When Ion enters for the first time, he marks the spot by noting that the "smoke of dry incense rises up to Phoebus' rafters" (90–91 [Kovacs, LCL]), and then he occupies the mimetic space by describing in great detail his activity of purifying the entrance, cleaning the floor, and shooing birds away as he performs each task (100–183). Each line connects his action with its mimetic space. When the chorus enters, it describes in detail all that it sees: a frieze of Heracles cutting off the Hydra's head, Bellerophon riding upon Pegasus, and other scenes of mythic violence. References to the chorus's own eyes and the action of looking aid in the production of mimetic space: "My eyes dart in all directions. Look at the rout of the Giants carved on the stonework!" (205–207). These graphic references to a real place are designed not to make the story appear true—the temple at Delphi was not decorated with these scenes—but to render the mimetic space and to connect it to the themes of violence and being earthborn that belong to the diegetic space.[48] As in the Johannine temple scene, the continuous references to the temple and the orientation of actions and characters in its space point over and over again to the here and now of the unfolding action.

---

[47] Mark A. Matson, "The Temple Incident: An Integral Element in the Fourth Gospel's Narrative," in *Jesus in Johannine Tradition* (ed. Robert T. Fortna and Tom Thatcher; Louisville: Westminster John Knox, 2001), 150–51. Matson argues that the distinctive features of the Fourth Evangelist's account of the temple incident, especially the use of Ps 69 and Zech 14, signify that it is based on an interpretation of a Jesus tradition independent from that in Mark. These differences may be the result of the way that he uses space rather than sources from which he draws.

[48] See Cedric H. Whitman, *Euripides and the Full Circle of Myth* (Cambridge: Harvard University Press, 1974), 76–77.

In American television, the conventions for establishing diegetic space are easy to spot. The opening credits of programs that are set in New York City, such as *Law and Order*, feature the skyline of the city and landmarks, such as the New York Supreme Court, which are indices of the relationship of the show's mimetic space (a crime scene or a courtroom) to its diegetic space (New York City). In order to maintain the realism of this diegetic space, dialogue frequently is set on busy streets of New York City. When the mountains that surround Canmore, Alberta, near Banff National Park and Calgary, where I grew up, appeared in the film *Mystery Alaska,* I became conscious that the mimetic space of the film (a town set in the mountains) could no longer sustain the illusion of the diegetic space (Alaska) to which the characters continually refer.[49] In stage plays, only the language of the actors establishes and maintains diegetic space. Duncan's line "This castle hath a pleasant seat" (*Macbeth* 1.6.1) points to the mimetic space of the stage, which his speech represents as the front of a castle, and to the diegetic world beyond the stage or theater, now a promontory upon which the castle sits (see fig. 6). The watchman's opening speech in Agamemnon begins by establishing the mimetic space, "the roofs of Atreus," and then conjures up a diegetic world complete with stars in the night and a line of torches that race from distant Troy to Argos. Nothing in the speech of other characters or the action on stage challenges the location of the mimetic space in a larger dramatic reality.

In the Fourth Gospel, Galilee, Judea, and heaven are represented as diegetic space. Jesus does not wander through the landscape as he does in the Synoptic Gospels, and incidents do not happen as he walks along the road. In the Fourth Gospel, either the action takes place in specific locales within the Judean or Galilean landscape identified by the narrator, sometimes after the fact (see 1:28) but usually before the dialogue begins, or characters ground with deictic language the action in the spot where they stand and refer to a world out there. For example, in Jesus' brief interaction with his brothers, the brothers' line "Leave here and go to Judea" (7:3) sets up a dichotomy between the space in which the action takes place and the space beyond. Jesus and the disciples speak in a comparable way when he discusses his intention to go to Judea:

---

[49] The more "realistic" modern film conventions become, the more potential for disruption of the relationship of mimetic and diegetic space and the experience of the audience. My husband's enjoyment of Ron Howard's *A Beautiful Mind* (2001) was tarnished when he spotted in the film, in a kitchen set in the 1950s, a Tupperware container of the same design and color as one in our kitchen cupboard and made in the 1980s.

JESUS: Let us go to Judea again.

DISCIPLES: Rabbi, the Jews were just now trying to stone you, and are you going there again?

JESUS: Our friend Lazarus has fallen asleep, but I am going there to awaken him.

DISCIPLES: Lord, if he has fallen asleep, he will be all right.

JESUS: Lazarus is dead. For your sake I am glad I was not there, so that you may believe. But let us go to him.

THOMAS: Let us also go, that we may die with him. (11:7–16; abbreviated)

The dichotomous references to space in this exchange become more pronounced when contrasted with how the Gospel of Matthew handles location in the passage in which Jesus announces his intention to go to Jerusalem:

While Jesus was going up to Jerusalem, he took the twelve disciples aside by themselves, and said to them on the way, "See, we are going up to Jerusalem, and the Son of Man will be handed over to the chief priests and scribes, and they will condemn him to death; then they will hand him over to the Gentiles to be mocked and flogged and crucified; and on the third day he will be raised. (20:17–19)

Matthew's action happens while moving through space rather then setting up a contrast between here and there. Moreover, the references to death are pure prophecy whereas in the Fourth Gospel the predictions from Thomas's lips generate dramatic irony and the tension between here and there becomes part of the suspense of the action.

Comparable dialogues in the tragedies, in which one character discusses plans to go to another location or remain in the present one and another character tries to influence the first character one way or the other, are too expansive to reproduce here. In *Oedipus at Colonus*, Sophocles writes one dialogue after another centered upon the desire for, or resistance to, a character moving from his or her present location to another one. Oedipus begins by refusing to leave a sacred grove or his seat upon a rock. When Creon cannot move him, the dialogue turns to Creon's intent to take Antigone and Ismene away. The action ends with a dialogue between Polynices and Antigone in which the brother declares his intent to leave Athens and to return to Thebes, where he will either die or expel Creon and Eteocles. In the concluding dialogues, Oedipus determines to return to Thebes, a place to which he refers as his tomb and Hades, and after his death, his daughters persuade

Theseus to allow them to return home to their father's tomb. The contrast between the safety of the mimetic space and the dangers of the diegetic space is a motif that repeats itself in many of the tragedies and is present in the Fourth Gospel.

As Adele Reinhartz has illustrated, the Fourth Gospel comprises more than one metanarrative.[50] In the historical narrative, Jesus is born in Nazareth to Joseph and his mother, who appears in the action, and is charged with blasphemy in Judea and crucified as an insurrectionist against Rome. In the cosmological narrative, Jesus is the Word of God from heaven, incarnate in flesh, whose death is his glorification in heaven. The language that characters use to identify the diegetic space in which the action takes place facilitates the production of these narratives. Jesus refers to the space of the cosmological narrative (heaven), while other characters refer to the space of the historical narrative (Judea and Galilee). The sharp contrast that characters make between mimetic and diegetic space and the contrast between the modality attributed by Jesus to space and that attributed by others are integral to the conflicts of the gospel.

The difference between Jesus' use of diegetic language and that of other characters is already pronounced in Jesus' first brief dialogues, which occur when he calls the disciples. Beginning in 1:43, the narrator refers to Jesus' intention to go to Galilee and then makes that space more substantial by identifying Bethsaida as the hometown of Philip, Andrew, and Peter. The dialogue then fills in more details in this rough map of Galilee when Philip tells Nathanael about "Jesus son of Joseph from Nazareth." Nathanael's response, "Can anything good come out of Nazareth?" (1:46), adds modality to the map: Nazareth is a backwater place. When Jesus announces the arrival of Nathanael, he identifies him as a citizen of the diegetic space, "Here is truly an Israelite in whom there is no deceit!" (1:47), a denizen of the physical world, "I saw you under the fig tree" (1:48), but he abruptly expands this diegetic space to include the cosmic order when he predicts, "you will see heaven opened and the angels of God ascending and descending upon the Son of Man" (1:51). After this, Jesus continues to speak of diegetic space that spans the heavens, while other characters tend to refer to their regional settings. The Samaritan woman asks, "How is it that you, a Jew, ask a drink of me, a woman of Samaria?" (4:9), and she sets the well in its historical context in the Jacob tradition (4:12) and on Mount Gerizim and marks the distance from Jerusalem in language that emphasizes the difference between Jesus' national identity and her own: "Our ancestors worshiped in this mountain, but

---

50 Adele Reinhartz, *The Word in the World: The Cosmological Tale in the Fourth Gospel* (SBLMS 45; Atlanta: Scholars Press, 1992).

you [Jews] say that the place where people must worship is in Jerusalem" (4:20). Jesus, in contrast, speaks of worship "in spirit and truth" (4:23–24). In general, when characters other than Jesus refer to the diegetic space, the horizon broadens to include Judea, Samaria, or Galilee. The Pharisees and Caiaphas speak of the greater political reality of Rome and its threat to their temple and nation (11:48). When Jesus speaks, the diegetic space expands beyond the confines of the Roman provinces; the heavens and the whole world lie beyond his stage.

Jesus also has a habit of taking an aspect of the mimetic space and turning it into a referent for his cosmological narrative. He takes something concrete from the location of the action and moves it into the abstract realm from which he comes, or he takes something located temporally in the present of the action and moves it into eternal time. The dialogue with the Samaritan woman provides an example of the latter when Jesus contrasts the water in the well with his water: "The water that I will give will become in them a spring of water gushing up to eternal life" (4:14). Later in the dialogue, Jesus provides an example of the former when he moves from references to worship on "this mountain" to worship "in spirit and truth" (4:21–24). Several tragic characters share a similar habit of speech where they see beyond the action that takes place in the mimetic space to a broader physical or temporal context.[51] The chorus in *Prometheus Bound* extends the agony that Prometheus experiences, pinned upon his rock, to the entire world:

> Now every country cries aloud in grief:
> The peoples of Europe mourn
> For you and the Titan race,
> Your glorious, ancient rule and honour;
> And all the settled tribes
> That grace the fields of holy Asia
> Weep loudly for you and share your suffering. (406–412 [Vellacott])

In *Agamemnon*, Cassandra looks with her words at the mimetic space representing the palace and sees a curse from its past at work in the dramatic present: "See, my witnesses—I trust to them, to the babies wailing, skewered on the sword, their flesh charred, the father gorging on their parts" (1094–1096 [Fagles]). These are the children of Thyestes, Agamemnon's uncle, who were murdered by Agamemnon's father and fed surreptitiously to his brother and whom she now sees sitting dead on the steps holding out pieces of their own flesh, which their father takes and eats (1223–1229). She sees the

---

[51] See Arnott, *Public and Performance,* 153–55.

supernatural world rather than the physical world in which the palace sits: "See, Apollo himself, his fiery hands—I feel him again, he's stripping off my robes, the Seer's robes!" (1285–1286). When she looks at the door of the palace and speaks, "I address you as the Gates of Death" (1314), the diegetic space is not its interior but Hades. Peter Arnott calls Cassandra, as well as Prometheus and his chorus, "a nodal figure" that draws together past, present, and future, and he compares her to a shaman who channels all time into the present moment through ritual.[52] This collapse of time and space is so obvious in Jesus' speech that in some cases he seems to have ceased to be located in the mimetic space or represented time of the action. After his last comment explicitly directed to Nicodemus (3:12), Jesus seems to speak into space and as though the time of the action is past. The movement to retrospective references to the time of the dramatic action, coupled with Jesus' use of the third person, has led many scholars to conclude that the voice of Jesus has been replaced with that of the narrator or evangelist.[53] Placed in the context of dramatic conventions, Jesus' language marks him as a "nodal figure" who resides both in the mimetic and diegetic spaces represented by other characters' speech and in another world represented by his own speech.

When, from time to time, characters refer to the world as the broader context for the action, their speech often is ironic. When Jesus' brothers goad him, "show yourself to the world" (7:4), the world to which they refer is not a global geophysical reality but one to be understood in opposition to the private realm. They mean, "Go public." But in Jesus' speech, "The world cannot hate you, but it hates me because I testify against it that its works are evil" (7:7), it stands in opposition to the heavenly realm. When the Pharisees comment on the size of the crowd that greets Jesus' when he arrives in Jerusalem for the last time, they say, "The world has gone after him" (12:19). For the Pharisees, the world is the Passover pilgrimage, but by speaking hyperbolically, their language points to Jesus' hyperreality.

In Euripides' *Ion,* the use of diegetic space, with its oracles and divine intrusions, supports its own "cosmological tale" about Ion and Athens' imperial and autochthonic identity. The story of that identity is told in a dialogue

---

[52] Ibid., 155–57. Arnott includes other examples: Cassandra, Tiresias in *Oedipus Tyrannus,* and the chorus in *Bacchae.*

[53] Raymond Brown (*The Gospel according to John,* 1:149) lists Tillmann, Belser, Schnackenburg, Wescott, Lagrange, Bernard, Van den Bussche, Braun, and Lightfoot. See also John Painter, *The Quest for the Messiah: The History, Literature, and Theology of the Johannine Community* (Nashville: Abingdon, 1993), 198. Thomas Brodie (*The Gospel according to John: A Literary and Theological Commentary* [New York: Oxford University Press, 1993], 195) describes this as a "distancing phenomenon."

between Ion and Creusa in which both are ignorant of their relationship. Creusa, Ion's mother, is the daughter of Erechtheus, whose forebear "sprang from the earth" (267 [Kovacs, LCL]), and Ion is the product of a secret liaison with Apollo, who raped Creusa, a fact that she managed to conceal from her father by exposing the child at birth. Ion is therefore both of divine descent and earthborn. Creusa accompanies her husband, Xuthus, who has come to ask the oracle at Delphi whether they are to remain childless, and meets Ion, who has been raised as a servant of Apollo in the temple. Ion then tells her his own story, and its similarity to her own prompts Creusa to tell the tale of her son's conception, but she disguises the fact that she speaks about herself, and Ion has no reason to suspect that he is the child in the story. Both Ion and Creusa continue to believe that Ion is the product of some other unknown woman who has been wronged. The truth of Ion's identity, then, belongs to the diegetic space of the tale and must be mediated to the plot of the mimetic space, where confusion reigns, by divine agents.

When the truth is received in the mimetic space, characters tend to misinterpret it. The oracle provides Xuthus with a slightly misleading prediction that the one who will meet him when he leaves the temple is his son, or so Xuthus reports (535–537). When Xuthus comes from the oracle, who resides in the diegetic space, onto the stage, he greets Ion, "My son, I wish you joy!" (517). Ion is irritated and threatened by Xuthus's overtures of affection until Xuthus explains what the oracle has told him. Eventually he is persuaded to join a celebration of his birth, where Creusa unsuccessfully tries to poison him because she believes that he is the son of some slave woman with whom Xuthus lay and therefore not worthy to rule over the Athenians.

In both *Ion* and the Fourth Gospel, crossing the boundary between the mimetic and diegetic spaces signifies death for those who are ignorant and true life for those in the know. In *Ion*, the *skēnē*, representing Apollo's temple, and *eisodos* B, which leads to other altars and the place where Ion's birthday is celebrated, introduces the diegetic space of the plot. *Eisodos* A leads to the home where Xuthus and Creusa are staying, beyond that to the cave of Trophonius, and eventually to Athens, the diegetic space of the story world. Ion's initial joy at learning that he is Xuthus's son gives way to apprehension when he realizes that his supposed father intends to take him across the threshold of his home through *eisodos* A to a foreign space. Ion begins his argument for why he should not leave the temple by observing, "Things do not look the same close up as from a distance" (585). He continues to point to the virtues of the mimetic space over the diegetic: "Hear, father, what good things I have enjoyed here. . . . As I consider these things, I think it is better here than in Athens, father. Let me live here" (633–646). The chorus reacts with suspicion to an oracle that would make possible such border crossing:

"Strange is the word of the god and strange the things it reports to me. There is some clever trickery in this boy raised here and begotten elsewhere. Who would deny it?" (690–694). It is hostile to the plan: "Never may the boy come to my city; ere then may he leave his young life behind. The city would have good reason to keep off an incursion of strangers. Enough have been admitted by our old ruler, King Erechtheus" (721–724). The boundary ought not be crossed, and one who attempts to do so ought to die. Confused about Ion's true identity, the chorus calls for his death lest he presume to claim citizenship in the diegetic realm. Creusa, who misinterprets the oracle to signify that she will not be the mother of the child and is goaded into attempting to murder Ion with the Gorgon's poisonous venom, punctuates her plot with the line "If it passes down his throat, he will never come to glorious Athens but will die and remain here" (1037–1038).

The reversal of the action happens when the prophetess carries his cradle and its contents, signs that point to Ion's true identity and right to claim Athens as his home, from the diegetic space onto the stage. The most important of these signs is a wreath from Athena's sacred olive tree on the Acropolis; the vitality of this wreath authenticates that it comes from the diegetic space of the tale of divine origin. Creusa's ignorance is dispelled when Apollo's priestess brings the wicker cradle that is a token of Ion's true birthright; but Ion, still under the spell of his circumstances, sees her rush to embrace him as a sign of madness brought on by her contact with some god. When Creusa persuades him that he is indeed her son, he doubts that he is Apollo's son, and wonders if her tale is self-serving until Athena, a *deus ex machina*, appears as Apollo's messenger to confirm that Ion will rightfully rule her land. Xuthus is allowed to continue under the delusion that Ion is his own offspring. The final lines of dialogue emphasize that Ion's movement from the mimetic space to the diegetic space is ascension:

CREUSA: My son, let us go home.

ATHENA: Go, both of you, and I shall follow.

ION: Yes, a fit guardian of our way.

CREUSA: And one who loves the city.

ATHENA: Mount the ancient throne.

ION: It is right for me to possess it. (1616–1619)

In order to become who he truly is, Ion must leave the illusion of the mimetic space and return to the truth of the diegetic space, Athens.

In the Johannine corollary to this use of space, Jesus, his signs, John the Baptist, and the divine voice (12:28) are witnesses sent from the diegetic space of the cosmological tale to substantiate Jesus' claim to divine parentage. Similarly, the residents of the mimetic space find it difficult to understand these communications or to accept their truth, and they attribute them to madness or blasphemy. Again, I am not suggesting that the author of the gospel had *Ion* or any particular tragedy in front of him but rather that he exploits the same dichotomy between mimetic and diegetic space in his composition. The hero's claim to belong to another, more exalted realm when he appears to belong to the mundane one makes him subject to death. When Jesus makes claims to his right to his throne, he uses deictic language that emphasizes the distinction between the space that he occupies dramatically and the space to which he refers:

> My kingdom is not from *this world*. If my kingdom were from *this world,* my followers would be fighting to keep me from being handed over to the Jews. But as it is, my kingdom is not from *here.* (18:36; italics added)

The implications of this formal similarity between a Greek tragedy and the Fourth Gospel for current Johannine studies may be significant. The scholarly consensus tends toward the hypothesis that the language of the gospel—this world, with its ignorance, lies, death, and sin, is set in strong opposition to the heavenly realm of knowledge, truth, life, and freedom—reflects a dualism that characterized the sectarian beliefs of a Johannine community. However, if the gospel writer was following the conventions of a drama, the genre itself promotes language that divides earthly from heavenly realities. Because a play presupposes the spatial medium of a theater, the characters mark the distinction between the space of the stage and the reality beyond by pointing to the latter with binary terms. Some terms are value neutral, such as "here" versus "there," but others, such as "above" and "below," reflect cultural values that give a preference to one over the other. Given the design of Greek theaters, language of "below" refers to the stage space, while "above" points to the roof of the *skēnē*, upon which the gods appear. The audience also sits above the stage and looks down on the action from on high, and it shares, by implication of the language and the ironic elements of the drama, the positive pole of the vertical axis.[54] David Wiles argues that Greek tragedies seek to reconcile this dualistic vision of space in the design of the theater and the dramas through the presence of a focal point

---

[54] David Wiles, *Tragedy in Athens: Performance Space and Theatrical Meaning* (Cambridge: Cambridge University Press, 1997), 176.

in the orchestra, either an altar or a tomb.[55] The opposition between the immortal and mortal realms is breeched through a centripetal space. Though it is impossible to draw a direct line between the Greek stage and the Johannine dualism, it is clear that the Fourth Gospel is drawn upon this same vertical axis with a focal point, Jesus, where binary opposites, divine and human, mortal and immortal, collide and converge.

Ambiguous Indices and Conflict

In the context of drama, the ambiguous nature of language, with its capacity to mislead and bewitch as well as to clarify and describe, is exploited to generate conflict. The duplicity between the audience and a character is achieved when one character constructs a world using the referents that other characters use to refer to a different reality, and the audience recognizes both meanings. As Froma Zeitlin puts it,

> Tragedy is the art form, above all, that makes the most of what is called discrepant awareness—what one character knows and the other doesn't or what none of the characters know but that the audience does. Several levels of meaning operate at the same time. Characters speak without knowing what they say, and misreading is the typical and predictable response to the various cues that others give.[56]

When the antagonists believe that they are talking about the same reality as the protagonist when they actually are not, in the terminology of speech-act theory, the fit of word to world is infelicitous and they appear foolish. When the protagonist uses deceptive or ambiguous language that can fit both the world of the antagonists and the world of the speaker, the antagonist is again the victim. In *Ajax*, Sophocles exploits the ambiguity of referents to allow his protagonist to fulfill his own desires while appearing to obey the will of others. Ajax, in a fit of madness, mistakes a flock of sheep for his enemy and slaughters it; and when he becomes cognizant of what he has done, he is overwhelmed by shame and a desire to kill himself. In order to leave the hut in which his friends have imprisoned him to protect him from himself, Ajax tells them that he has been persuaded not to leave his wife a widow and his son an orphan. He announces his intention:

---

[55] Ibid., 66–72.

[56] Froma I. Zeitlin, "Playing the Other: Theater, Theatricality, and the Feminine in Greek Drama," in *Nothing to Do with Dionysos? Athenian Drama in its Social Context* (ed. John J. Winkler and Froma I. Zeitlin; Princeton, N.J.: Princeton University Press, 1990), 74.

I shall go to the meadows by the shore where I can wash myself, so that I can clean off the dirt upon me and escape the grievous anger of the goddess. I shall come to where I can find untrodden ground and conceal this sword of mine, most hated of all weapons, digging a hole in the ground where none can see it, but let the darkness of Hades guard it down below [ἀλλ᾽ αὐτὸ νὺξ Ἅιδης τε σῳζόντων κάτω]. (654–660 [Lloyd-Jones, LCL])

His friends take his words as a sign that he no longer harbors suicidal intent, but there is more than one way that Ajax can cleanse himself and that a sword can dig a hole leading to Hades. Once Ajax is free of his friends, he makes his intent more explicit. He plants the sword in the ground with the sharpened blade pointing up, and then he buries the blade in his own side, proclaiming, "This is the last word Ajax speaks to you; the rest I shall utter in Hades to those below [τὰ δ᾽ ἄλλ᾽ ἐν Ἅιδου τοῖς κάτω μυθήσομαι]" (864–865). The chorus is left to berate itself for being deaf to the meaning of Ajax's earlier words (911).

The author of the Fourth Gospel exploits the ambiguity of reference to an almost comic end. The failure of Jesus' dialogue partners to understand the referents of his language when he alludes to his departure makes them appear foolish. They try to fit Jesus' word to their world. Jesus announces his intent to leave for the realm of his own diegetic speech: "I will be with you a little while longer, and then I am going to him who sent me. You will search for me, but you will not find me; and where I am, you cannot come" (7:33–34). The crowd assumes that he refers to their own world:

Where does this man intend to go that we will not find him? Does he intend to go to the Dispersion among the Greeks and teach the Greeks? What does he mean by saying, "You will search for me and you will not find me" and "Where I am, you cannot come"? (7:35–36)

A similar pair of statement and response marked by ambiguity about referents occurs in the dialogue preceding the healing of the man born blind. Jesus states, "I am going away, and you will search for me, but you will die in your sin. Where I am going, you cannot come" (8:21). The listeners are baffled: "Is he going to kill himself? Is that what he means by saying, 'Where I am going you cannot come'?" (8:22). Jesus' continued use of ambiguous language, "You are from below, I am from above; you are of this world, I am not of this world. I told you that you would die in your sins, for you will die in your sins unless you believe that I am he," prompts the obvious question "Who are you?" (8:23–25). Thomas underscores the discrepancy between his understanding and Jesus' references after Jesus asserts, "You know the way to the place where I am going," when he objects, "Lord, we do not know where you are going. How can we know the way?" (14:4–5). When Jesus remarks,

"A little while, and you will no longer see me, and again a little while, and you will see me," the disciples concede, "What does he mean . . . ? We do not know what he is talking about" (16:16–18). After Jesus puts it another way, the disciples claim that they have finally figured it out: "Yes, now you are speaking plainly, not in any figure of speech! Now we know that you know all things, and do not need to have anyone question you; by this we believe that you came from God" (16:29–30). Jesus finds their confidence dubious and predicts their reaction to the arrest and crucifixion, which makes clear the continued inadequacy of their understanding:

> Do you now believe? The hour is coming, indeed it has come, when you will be scattered, each one to his home, and you will leave me alone. Yet I am not alone because the Father is with me. I have said this to you, so that in me you may have peace. In the world you face persecution. But take courage; I have conquered the world! (16:31–33)

The world to which Jesus refers is not the world to which his antagonists, including his own disciples, refer.

Another form of conflict generated by the ambiguity of reference comes in statements and questions that challenge the fit of Jesus' language to the world of his dialogue partners:

> JEWS: Is not this Jesus, the son of Joseph, whose father and mother we know? How can he now say, "I have come down from heaven"? (6:42)

> DISCIPLES: This teaching is difficult; who can accept it? (6:60)

> PHARISEES: You are testifying on your own behalf; your testimony is not valid. (8:13)

> PHARISEES: Where is your Father? (8:19)

> JEWS: Are we not right in saying that you are a Samaritan and have a demon? (8:48)

> JEWS: Now we know that you have a demon. Abraham died, and so did the prophets; yet you say, "Whoever keeps my word will never taste death." (8:52)

> MANY: He has a demon and is out of his mind. Why listen to him? (10:20)

> OTHERS: These are not the words of one who has a demon. Can a demon open the eyes of the blind? (10:21)

JEWS: It is not for a good work that we are going to stone you, but for blasphemy, because you, though only a human being, are making yourself God. (10:33)

CROWD: We have heard from the law that the Messiah remains forever. How can you say that the Son of Man must be lifted up? Who is this Son of Man? (12:34)

POLICE OFFICER: Is that how you answer the high priest? (18:22)

PILATE: What is truth? (18:38)

In part, the ambiguity of Jesus' speech helps generate the illusion that his world of discourse is the divine realm. If language is the means by which we understand reality and if the divine reality is incomprehensible to mortals, then Jesus' incomprehensible speech is divine. The conflict between the speakable and the unspeakable confirms the existence of two worlds, for what is unspeakable in the world of one discourse is speakable in the world of the other.

The irony of the tragedies is dependent upon this sort of ambivalent signification, and those characters who fail to recognize the multivalent potential of language or attempt to limit the meaning of language in order to control events accuse each other of speaking the unspeakable. Given that the action of a drama is speech, it is not surprising that characters speak about their speaking and about the conflict that speaking produces. As Vimala Herman notes, "The evaluation of each other's utterances becomes the drama."[57] The Synoptic Gospels' habit of letting Jesus speak without interruption or giving him the last word without recording how his audience reacts is perhaps the principal factor that renders their writings less dramatic than the Fourth Gospel. Euripides' *Alcestis* provides a typical exchange in which characters struggle to find a common ground for their language. Heracles returns from Hades with Admetus's wife, Alcestis. Alcestis is veiled, but the audience knows who she is while Admetus does not. When Heracles says, "I wish I had the power to convey your wife to the light from the halls below and could do you this service" (1072–1074 [Kovacs, LCL]), the audience knows that Heracles' wish is infelicitous because the deed has been done. Admetus, in contrast, believes that the wish is infelicitous because it asks for the impossible: "I know that you would wish to. But what is the good of such a wish? It is not possible for the dead to come back to the light"

---

[57] Vimala Herman, *Dramatic Discourse: Dialogue as Interaction in Plays* (London: Routledge, 1995), 132.

(1075–1076). Heracles offers the veiled woman to Admetus as a bride, with words of consolation, "A woman and a new union will put an end to your longing," to which Admetus responds, "Hush! What a shocking thing you have said! I should never have thought it of you" (1087–1088). The truth of Heracles' words, apparent to the audience, are an offense to Admetus, who must believe that this is another woman, given his lack of belief in resurrection. When Jesus announces, "Now is the judgment of this world; now the ruler of this world will be driven out. And I, when I am lifted up from the earth, will draw all people to myself" (12:31–32), the crowd rejects Jesus' words with the same logic: "We have heard from the law that the Messiah remains forever. How can you say that the Son of Man must be lifted up? Who is this Son of Man?" (12:34). Jesus, like Heracles, seems to speak in violation of convention.

In *Oedipus Tyrannus*, Tiresias can speak of Oedipus's identity as the son of Iocasta, but Oedipus cannot conceive of the truth of Tiresias's words because he has the facts wrong. Because Oedipus takes Corinth for his home, rather than Thebes, and takes Polybus to be his father, rather than Laius, he cannot make sense of Tiresias's suggestion that his relationship with Iocaste is shameful:

> OEDIPUS: Is it bearable that I should hear these words from this man? . . . I did not know that your words would be foolish; else I would hardly have summoned you to my house.
>
> TIRESIAS: That is what I am; foolish, as you think, but the parents who gave you birth found me wise.
>
> OEDIPUS: What parents? Wait! Who among mortals gave me birth?
>
> TIRESIAS: This day shall be your parent and your destroyer.
>
> OEDIPUS: How riddling and obscure in excess are all your words! (429–439 [Lloyd-Jones, LCL])

As Oedipus is soliciting the information that will correct his understanding of the facts and render Tiresias's words meaningful, other characters try to silence speech. When Iocaste realizes that the story that the messenger tells makes her the mother of Oedipus, she pleads, "Why ask of whom he spoke? Take no thought of it! Let these words go for nothing and not be remembered!" (1056–1057). To prevent Oedipus from connecting the story line of Iocaste's exposed child with his own, the shepherd tries to stop the messenger: "A plague on you! Will you not be silent?" (1146). The similar disjunction between Jesus' words and the known facts regarding Jesus' parentage causes other characters to question the appropriateness of his speech. When Jesus says, "I am the bread that came down from heaven," the Jews respond, "Is not this Jesus, the son of Joseph, whose father and mother we know? How can he now say, 'I have come down from heaven'?" (6:41–42). They too try to silence him, but instead of using words, they use deadly force.

The Fourth Gospel adds a complicating factor that distinguishes its action from that of *Oedipus Tyrannus* and also the gospels of Matthew and Luke. The Jews do not have their facts wrong. The statement that Jesus is the son of Joseph rests upon the brute fact that he was born to the wife of Joseph. Jesus appeals to a different kind of fact, the kind that depends upon human institutions.[58] His acts require divine power; therefore he is the agent of a divine power. Power is passed down in hierarchical religious and political institutions from father to son; therefore Jesus is the Son of God. As John Searle observes, for institutional facts to be taken as true, they must exist at some level on top of some brute physical facts.[59] In *Oedipus Tyrannus*, the institutional fact of Oedipus and Iocaste's impurity is based upon the brute fact that Iocaste is Oedipus's mother. In the Fourth Gospel, the institutional fact of Jesus' status as a divine agent does not rest upon the story of a birth, as it does in Matthew and Luke, but upon the resurrection.

Redundant Narration

The fact that the narrator provides most of the references to objects, time, and place in the Fourth Gospel places it in the genre of narrative rather than play, but a significant amount of the information given by the narrator is redundant because characters provide what is needed. The characters frequently speak as though they were in a play. The Samaritan woman reports that she and Jesus are at Jacob's well (4:12). The narrator explains that the Samaritans believe because of Jesus' words, and then the Samaritans themselves state the same thing (4:41–42). Back-to-back lines of narrative and Jesus' direct speech report that the disciples were afraid when they saw Jesus walking on the water (6:19–20). Immediately after the narrator relates, "As he walked along, he saw a man blind from birth," the disciples bring the blind man into view with the question "Rabbi, who sinned, this man or his parents, that he was born blind?" (9:1–2). The narrator states that some in the Festival of Booths crowd wanted to arrest him but did not do so (7:44). In the dialogue that follows, when the chief priests and Pharisees ask, "Why did you not

---

[58] For the distinction between brute and institutional facts, see John R. Searle, *The Construction of Social Reality* (New York: Free Press, 1995), 27.
[59] Ibid., 35.

arrest him?" we learn from them that the temple police had failed in their duty. The police then provide a motive for their reported failure: "Never has anyone spoken like this!" (7:46). This dialogue allows the audience to supply the same metanarrative as that provided by the narrator.

At points, the repetition of information in narrative and direct speech seems clumsy or even comic. In both Sabbath healings, the narrator and the characters provide the temporal context. In the first instance, no sooner has the narrator said, "Now that day was a sabbath," than the Jews say to the once lame man, "It is the sabbath; it is not lawful for you to carry your mat" (John 5:9b–10). In the account of the healing of the man born blind, the revelation of the temporal context is delayed in direct speech, but the narrator spoils the dramatic effect by blurting out, "Now it was a sabbath day when Jesus made the mud and opened his eyes" (9:14). Otherwise, the audience would grasp the significance of why the blind man is asked to repeat the description of his healing, "The man called Jesus made mud, spread it on my eyes, and said to me, 'Go to Siloam and wash'" (9:11), only after he gives it again for a third time (9:15), when the Pharisees say, "This man is not from God, for he does not observe the sabbath" (9:16). When the narrator sets the scene for the raising of Lazarus, he provides a temporal frame of reference: "When Jesus arrived, he found that Lazarus had already been in the tomb four days" (11:17). Fortunately, this communication is separated by sufficient action so as not to undermine the humor of Martha's words of warning to Jesus, "Lord, already there is a stench because he has been dead four days" (11:39). Again, an omniscient and intrusive narrator can easily subvert the dramatic or comic effect of the timing of the information supplied by characters to the audience. In some cases, the author of the gospel could have spared himself the problem of a narrator who knows more than he should and tells more than is necessary. When Jesus states that his opponents are seeking opportunities to kill him (7:19), he reveals his omniscience, and his words seem prophetic. When the narrator reports that "the Jews were seeking all the more to kill him" (5:18), the information precedes both the motivation and the action and is untimely.

Reported Action

In Greek tragedy, events such as death or battle often are reported rather than staged. To some extent, this is a matter of economy, given the limits of time and the physical constraints of the stage. Synchronous action is handled by having one character tell what he or she is seeing or has seen. For example, in *Iphigenia at Aulis*, Clytemnestra tries to persuade Agamemnon not to sacrifice Iphigenia while Achilles goes to stop the soldiers. When

Achilles returns, he enters the tent, describing what happens outside it, and then recounts how the soldiers received his attempt to intercede (1345–1358). The action of major battle scenes is not suited to the stage, and so characters narrate their passage after the fact. The limits of the stage, however, are not the principal reason most events are reported rather than enacted; the perspectives of characters who report the action and the debate that ensues replace events with dialogue.

The distinct difference between the attention given to events and that given to dialogue in the Fourth Gospel gives rise to hypotheses about the sources upon which the gospel writer based his document. With the exception of the Passion Narrative, the events have been attributed to a signs (*semeia*) source, and the dialogues to something known as the *Offenbarungsreden,* or revelatory discourse source. One of the most persistent advocates of the signs source is Robert Fortna, who describes the narrated deeds and speeches as "very nearly contradictory modes of Jesus' activity." The deeds, which he describes as "vivid, brief and earthy," he ascribes to an early stratum of the Jesus tradition that he calls the "Signs Gospel," and he contends that the discourses, containing the "portrait of the Jesus of universal Christianity," are a major amplification of a second source.[60] Tom Felton and Tom Thatcher have subjected the material that Fortna assigns to the "Signs Gospel" to statistical analysis and have detected significant differences in style from the remaining material in the Fourth Gospel.[61] Though it may be true that the gospel writer drew from different sources, the differences in style and content may also reflect the relationship between the events and the dialogues they prompt. The events, which may reflect the passage of several hours, reported in brief narratives whereas, in the dialogues, the action unfolds at a leisurely pace of the conversation.

Most of the events of the Fourth Gospel are narrated, but many are brought to the audience's eyes by characters' speech. John the Baptist reports the descent of the Spirit upon Jesus (1:32). The slaves report the healing of the royal official's son (4:52). The Jews report that the temple has been under construction for forty-six years (2:20). The lame man describes what happens when he tries to get into the pool (5:7). The boy who has five barley loaves and two fish appears only in Andrew's speech (6:9). Although Jesus

---

[60] Robert T. Fortna, *The Fourth Gospel and Its Predecessors: From Narrative Source to Present Gospel* (Philadelphia: Fortress, 1988), 1–7. For a more recent affirmation of his belief in the signs source, see Fortna's "Jesus Tradition in the Signs Gospel," in Fortna and Thatcher, *Jesus in Johannine Tradition,* 199–208.

[61] Tom Felton and Tom Thatcher, "Stylometry and the Signs Gospel," in Fortna and Thatcher, *Jesus in Johannine Tradition,* 209–18.

performs a limited number of miracles, both Nicodemus and Jesus' brothers make the audience aware of other signs or works (3:2; 7:3).

The logic behind the presentation of the descent of the Spirit in a report rather than narration may lie in the observation made by Jindrich Honzl that a dramatist can attempt to control the number of meanings that an audience might give to an action or deed by having a character describe the action, thereby giving it his or her interpretation.[62] Placed on the lips of John the Baptist, the interpretation of Jesus' experience takes precedence over the event itself. The action is the Baptist's witness. Three features of this report—the inclusion of direct speech, the distinction between the focalization of the event when it happened and its focalization as narrated, and the subjectivity in which the factual report is framed—are devices employed within the messenger speeches in tragedies.

In the context of messenger speeches, the use of direct speech makes the description of an event more vivid and produces an eyewitness effect although the messenger is not an objective witness but a subjective participant in the event.[63] The messenger in *Andromache* begins his account of the death of Neoptolemus with references to his own experience of the events as a member of Neoptolemus's retinue. He then quotes Orestes' words that had aroused hostility against Neoptolemus as if merely reporting what he heard as the events unfolded. The messenger goes on to report the suspicion and hostility of the men of Delphi, his failure to perceive it, and how he later came to learn of it (1088–1099).[64] He has inserted Orestes' speech into the order of events not as he witnessed them but as he later understands them. By indicating how he understood the event then and how he sees it now, the messenger underscores his subjectivity.[65] We find a similar retrospective quality in John the Baptist's account of the descent of the Spirit. The Baptist reports his own speech, "This is he of whom I said, 'After me comes a man who ranks ahead of me because he was before me'" (1:30), but if he is referring to what he said the previous day, "the one who is coming after me; I am not worth to untie the thong of his sandal" (1:27), he either reports speech that the gospel's audience has not heard or inaccurately represents his own speech insofar as he is qualifying his words. The latter seems plausible because in the remainder of

---

62 Honzl, "The Hierarchy of Dramatic Devices," 125.

63 Irene J. F. de Jong, *Narrative in Drama: The Art of the Euripidean Messenger-Speech* (MnemosyneSup 116; Leiden: Brill, 1991), 131.

64 This pattern of retrospective awareness is evident in a number of messenger speeches, including that of Talybius in *Hecuba* (517–520) and the account of Orestes' murder of Aegisthus in Euripides' *Electra* (777–780).

65 Jong, *Narrative in Drama*, 29.

the speech John acknowledges that his understanding of what he has witnessed is shaped by a revelation. He explains that he has seen the Spirit descend as a dove from heaven and remain on Jesus, but by his own admission, this vision does not provide sufficient information with which to positively identify Jesus. He states, "I myself did not know him, but the one who sent me to baptize with water said to me, 'He on whom you see the Spirit descend and remain is the one who baptizes with the Holy Spirit'" (1:33). Based on this reported speech, John the Baptist then testifies that Jesus is the Son of God. In the reporting of the events, he imposes his later cognition upon the meaning of his earlier statements.

The Baptist's repeated insistence upon the subjectivity of the focalization is pronounced: "I saw the Spirit . . . the one who sent me . . . said to me . . . I myself have seen and have testified that this is the Son of God" (1:32–34). When the messenger in *The Suppliant Women* describes the victory of the Athenians over the Theban army, he also reminds his audience continually that the event is focalized through his own experience. He begins, "I stationed myself to watch at the Electan gate on a tower commanding a good view. I saw the three divisions of the army. The hoplites extended themselves upwards to a hill (Ismenus' Hill, I have heard it called)" (651–655 [Kovacs, LCL]). Later in the report he reminds his audience that his words are based upon his authority as an eyewitness: "Since I stood at the spot where both chariots and cavalry were fighting, I saw first-hand the many travails that took place there. I do not know what I should mention first" (684–687). He tells of his own reaction to the victory: "I raised a shout of joy, leapt into the air, and clapped my hands" (719–720), and he ends with his own evaluation of Theseus's performance as the army's general (726–730). The subjectivity of the messenger's description of Theseus's gallantry becomes a foil for questions from Adrastus, the king of Argos, about the more gruesome aspects of the carnage and the shamefulness inherent in Theseus's task of having to carry the corpses that he has fought to recover. Throughout the play, Euripides continues to juxtapose the themes of heroism and the tragedy of life. Similarly, the subjectivity of the Baptist's witness sets the stage for more questions about the validity of subjective witness.

If we accept the Baptist's witness on par with that of the omniscient narrator in the Synoptic version of Jesus' baptism, then the Holy Spirit did descend upon Jesus and did pronounce him to be the Son of God. If we treat this as drama, however, John's witness becomes more problematic and consequently a plot element. His witness is something that characters can accept or reject. If his partners in conversation remain the Pharisees (the text is not explicit), then the credibility of the witness is seriously diminished by the way it is subjectively represented. There can be no corroboration. If he addresses his own disciples, then his identification of Jesus is fraught with sufficient ambiguity to render their later apparent lack of understanding logical.

We find a second example later in the gospel that also illustrates how the evangelist uses reported speech to serve dramatic action. When the man who was lame repeats Jesus' words, he accurately reports that Jesus said, "Take up your mat and walk" (5:8, 11). He neglects to report Jesus' first words, "Stand up," the command by which the healing is performed and the compliance with which is not a Sabbath violation. On the lips of the healed man, Jesus' command no longer refers to the consequences of the healing—the man is now able to leave the pool—but instead becomes an admonition to violate the Sabbath by carrying his bed.

Speech as Deed

When the verbal gestures of the protagonist that interpret reality collide with those of other characters, conflict develops, and speech becomes the principal action of the drama. The action of the plot of the Fourth Gospel, like the action of classical tragedy, ought not be confused with the action of its story. Jesus' miracle at Cana, the three healings, the feeding of the five thousand, and the resurrection of Lazarus are analogous to the murders and battles of the tragedies. The dialogues refer deictically to these events, but they themselves constitute the dramatic action.[66] Consequently, the task of an audience listening to a dialogue or a monologue in a play is different from the task of an audience listening to a lecture. The questions that an auditor of a play must answer involve not only what language means but also what language does. What has happened in the course of the speech? Christian exegetical tradition has set as its primary task the extraction of doctrine from the stream of utterances through which the action of the Fourth Gospel progresses. The mechanics or poetics of the construction of its speeches and dialogues, until recently, have not been of primary interest unless their patterns could provide the key to unlock meaning.[67] In the following analysis of speech as act, I will demonstrate that Johannine dialogues follow a number of conventions found in Greek tragic dialogue, including the use of antitheses, flyting contests, and formal debates. These patterns, as in Greek drama, are not necessarily the purveyors of meaning but of plot. Jesus, as the protago-

---

[66] See Elam, *Semiotics of Theatre and Drama*, 157.
[67] Studies done in the rhetoric of honor and shame (e.g., Jerome Neyrey) and oral traditions (e.g., that on riddle by Tom Thatcher) mark new directions.

nist, uses words to achieve his ends by provoking responses and challenging characters to take action, thereby moving the plot along.

Patterns and conventions in dramatic speech serve multiple functions on the various axes of the text. On the dramatic axis, the conflict develops gradually. On the performance axis, the lines are more easily committed to memory, and the emotions of the conflict do not overwhelm the speech. On the theatrical axis, when ideas are reiterated and movement is thematic, the audience is given enough leisure to make sense of the tension and reactions.

Much of the material from the Fourth Gospel scrutinized in the following discussion has been used as evidence in the ongoing development of J. Louis Martyn's hypothesis that the polemic of the gospel addresses the situation of the Johannine community. Compared with the Matthean Jesus, for example, the Johannine Jesus makes very few substantive arguments. He does not question the adequacy of the Jewish leaders' methods of applying the rules of vows, tithes, or Sabbath observance, and he does not accuse them of hypocrisy for fulfilling some laws and violating other principles. Instead, Jesus takes his opponents' concerns about Sabbath violation and rules of witness and makes the conflict personal by accusing them of rejecting him and by rejecting them in turn. This polarization of identity supports the hypothesis that the conflict is between Christians who accept Jesus and Jews who reject Christians after some definitive split in the communities, such as the issuance of the Birkat Haminim. Moreover, the seemingly advanced Christology of the gospel suggests to those who support the hypothesis a lengthy period of development for the gospel's language. Rodney Whitacre observes that the ideas are not necessarily advanced but, rather, "the way they are so tightly interwoven" suggests a period of reflection.[68] The following comparison of Jesus' speech with the action of the tragedies presents an alternative and literary account of the polemic. If the gospel writer is employing the conventions of tragic dialogue, those conventions push both the polemic in the direction of interpersonal conflict and Jesus' statements about his own identity toward more outrageous or offensive limits, and the mimesis of those conventions produces the tight weave of the polemic.

Antithesis

One of the most prevalent patterns upon which the tragedians organize speech is antithesis. A strong rhetorical rhythm rather than an exchange of ideas provides organization to a speech or the illusion of a natural movement

---

[68] Rodney A. Whitacre, *Johannine Polemic: The Role of Tradition and Theology* (SBLDS 67; Chico, Calif.: Scholars Press, 1982), 9.

of thought. For example, when characters correct themselves by negating what they have just said, their speech takes on a natural quality, as though they were thinking on their feet. [69] Jesus does this a number of times. After stating, "Everyone who has heard and learned from the Father comes to me," he snatches his words back by qualifying them with "Not that anyone has seen the Father except the one who is from God" (6:45–46). In an argument with the Pharisees, Jesus states, "You judge by human standards; I judge no one. Yet even if I do judge, my judgment is valid" (8:15–16). [70] If Jesus' speech is scrutinized for consistency of thought, such repairs require an accounting in logic. For example, Thomas Brodie suggests that the first pair of assertions refers to Jesus' immediate purpose and the second to the eventual consequence of his presence. [71] If his speeches are considered as movements in dramatic discourse, they are simply the artifice of living speech. In contrast to their role in poetry, where they create logical or conceptual balance, speeches that follow an antithetical pattern enact the conflict that constitutes the drama and arouse strong opposing reactions from those with whom the speaker interacts. [72] Antitheses allow characters to lay out the conflicting propositions or commitments that give rise to their plight or provoke antagonism. In *Prometheus Bound*, Aeschylus constructs Prometheus's first monologue using this strategy: [73]

> *Thesis: To speak* of this is painful for me;
>
> *Antithesis: to keep silence* is no less pain.
> On every side is suffering.
> When first among the immortal gods anger broke out
> Dividing them into two factions,
>
> *Thesis:* of which *one resolved to unseat* the power of Chronos,
> and make Zeus absolute king—mark that!—
>
> *Antithesis:* While *the opposing side resolved no less*
> that Zeus should never rule the gods—

---

69 See Keir Elam, *Shakespeare's Universe of Discourse: Language Games in the Comedies* (Cambridge: Cambridge University Press, 1984), 316.

70 See also John the Baptist's self-correction in John 3:32–33.

71 Brodie, *The Gospel according to John*, 324.

72 See Elam, *Semiotics of Theatre and Drama*, 177.

73 I have altered the line breaks found in *Prometheus Bound*, translated by Philip Vellacott in *Aeschylus: Prometheus Bound, The Suppliants, Seven against Thebes, and The Persians* (Harmondsworth: Penguin, 1961), 26–27, in order to make the antithetical pattern clearer.

Thesis: At that time *I,* offering the best of all advice,
      Tried to convince the Titan sons of Heaven and Earth,

Antithesis: And failed.

. . . .

Antithesis: That was the help that I gave the king of the gods;

Thesis: and *this is my reward—*

Antithesis: this is his black ingratitude.

. . . .

Antithesis: Of wretched humans *he* took no account,
      Resolved to annihilate them and create another race.
      This purpose there was no one to oppose

Thesis: But I: *I dared.*
      I s*aved the human race* from being ground to dust,
      from total death. (197–208, 223–224, 233–237 [Vellacott]; italics added)

A comparable pattern runs through the end of Jesus' dialogue with Nicodemus:

Antithesis: Indeed, God did *not* send the Son into the world
      to condemn the world,

Thesis: but in order that *the world might be saved* through him.

Thesis: Those who believe in him are not condemned;

Antithesis: but *those who do not believe are condemned* already,
      because they have not believed in the name of the only
      Son of God.
      And this is the judgment,

Antithesis: that the light has come into the world,
      and people loved darkness rather than light because
      their deeds were evil.
      For all who do evil hate the light
      and *do not come to the light,*
      so that *their deeds may not be exposed.*

Thesis: But those who do what is true come to the light,
      so that it *may be clearly seen* that *their deeds*
      have been done in God. (3:17–21; italics added)

In both speeches, the antithetical construction sets the deeds or position of one agent in diametric opposition with that of another, thereby establishing the grounds for conflict.

The technique of moving the speech along through thesis and antithesis often is combined with repetition and chiasmus. The following speech from *Antigone* uses antithesis and chiasmus to turn an inquiry into her transgression into a claim of innocence and a charge against the gods:

> What justice of the gods have I transgressed?
> Why must I still look to the gods, unhappy one?
> Whom can I call on to protect me?
> *For by acting piously,*
> *I have been convicted of impiety.*
> Well, if this is approved among the gods,
> I should forgive them for what I have suffered, [A]
> since I have done wrong; [B]
> but if they are the wrongdoers, [B]
> may they suffer worse evils [A]
> than those they are unjustly inflicting upon me! (922–928
>   [Lloyd-Jones, LCL]; italics added)

Antigone's speech is part of a longer dialogue in which she maintains her opposition to Creon and asserts her vision of justice against his. Her speeches are not designed to persuade Creon of her innocence but rather to move her closer to her death by sharpening their conflict.

Jesus' speech in John 6:44–58 provides a comparable example of a speech that uses the rhythms of antithesis and repetition not to advance an argument but to intensify a conflict:

> No one can come to me unless drawn by the Father who sent me;
> and I will raise that person up on the last day. . . .
> Everyone who has heard and learned from the Father comes to me. . . .
> whoever believes has eternal life.
> I am the bread of life.
> *Your ancestors ate the manna in the wilderness, and they died.*
> This is the bread that comes down from heaven, so that one may eat of it
> and not die.
> I am the living bread that came down from heaven.
> *Whoever eats of this bread will live forever;*
> and the bread that I will give for the life of the world is my flesh. . . .
> unless you eat the flesh of the Son of Man and drink his blood,

you have no life in you.
Those who eat my flesh and drink my blood have eternal life,
and I will raise them up on the last day;
for my flesh is true food and my blood is true drink.
Those who eat my flesh and drink my blood abide in me,
and I in them.
Just as the living Father sent me,
and I live because of the Father,
so whoever eats me will live because of me.
This is the bread that came down from heaven,
not like that which your ancestors ate, and they died.
But the one who eats this bread will live forever. (6:44–58; italics added)

Repetition and the use of negative and positive terms create a pattern in which Jesus continually affirms that he is the source of eternal life and he will raise up those who come to him. The movement or development of the speech, however, is not toward an invitation but toward exclusion of his dramatic audience from the life Jesus offers.

The repetition and development in John 6:44–58 have been treated by various historical critics as evidence for stages in its composition history. Raymond Brown divides the bread-of-life discourse between vv. 50 and 51 on the grounds that vv. 44–50 pick up and repeat the terms of vv. 35–40 and because he sees duplication of vv. 44–50 in vv. 51–59, where eating is equated with believing, as editorial activity.[74] Brown works on the presupposition that if "repetition is not pedagogic," it would appear "to be the result of two different traditions of the same words."[75] He attributes vv. 51–58 to a final redactor who created a second, sacramental bread-of-life discourse to supplement the first, sapiential discourse.[76] The treatment of repetition by historical critics may attend too closely to what the words mean and fail to recognize what the act of repeating oneself does or signifies. In drama, repetition, either in a dialogue between two speakers or in a set speech, points to stasis or even the death of language.[77] Repetition of an idea using the same language does not signify an openness to the development of thought, for, by turning talk back on itself, the character speaks as though the dialogue is going nowhere. In both Antigone's and Jesus' speeches, rather than explicating their meaning, repetition cuts off the possibility of dialogue. Antigone's

---

74 Brown, *The Gospel according to John,* 1:268, 281.
75 Ibid., 1:xxv.
76 Ibid., 1:287.
77 Herman, *Dramatic Discourse,* 157.

speech begins with questions about what she has done wrong, but when in the second assertion she matches the charge against her with a countercharge of wrongdoing by the gods, she stands in competition rather than cooperation with them.[78] When Jesus moves from the invitation to believe to an invitation to eat, he ends the speech with a proposition to which his dialogue partners cannot assent. On the dramatic axis, he kills the conversation.

The repetition and antithetical patterns of these and other tragic speeches also serve a practical purpose on the performance axis. In order to retain and retrieve the lines of carefully constructed speech, the actor relies upon the rhythmic and balanced patterns of repetition and antithesis.[79] Oral traditions use the same principles in order to render thoughts memorable. It is plausible that the antithetical construction of Jesus' sayings in the Synoptic tradition reflects a period of oral transmission. In the case of the Fourth Gospel, the same techniques seem to render longer speeches either memorable or suited for recital, or both.[80]

Nicholas Hytner, director of many Shakespearean productions, identifies the balancing of opposites as one of Shakespeare's favorite techniques for making language during performance comprehensible.[81] In speeches where the dramatic context calls for powerful emotions, the actors control grief or rage with the organization of thought. The language, then, expresses the emotions rather than allowing the emotions to obscure the language. In *Antigone,* when Creon asks if she has transgressed his command, Antigone delivers the defiant "yes" for which the plot calls, in a speech that ends with these balanced lines:

> I knew that I would die, of course I knew, even if you had made no proclamation.
> But if I die before my time, I account that gain.
> For does not whoever lives among many troubles, and I do, gain by death?
> So it is in no way painful for me to meet with this death; if I had endured that the son of my own mother should die and remain unburied, that would have given me pain, but this gives me none.
> And if you think my actions foolish, that amounts to a charge of folly by a fool! (460–470 [Lloyd-Jones, LCL])

---

[78] Ibid., 155.

[79] See Ong, *Orality and Literacy,* 34.

[80] Source critics of the Fourth Gospel do not describe a discourse rather than a sayings source. Raymond Brown (*The Gospel according to John,* 1:xxxiv–xxxv) rejects the source theory and posits a process whereby sayings and stories about Jesus were molded into Johannine patterns to meet the needs of preaching or incipient liturgy.

[81] Hytner made these comments during an interview following the PBS telecast of his production of *Twelfth Night* at Lincoln Center on August 30, 1998.

The author of the Fourth Gospel uses the same device of balancing lines in the dialogue with the disciples following the bread-of-life discourse. Jesus meets the disciples' question "This teaching is difficult; who can accept it?" with lines that match their disdain with his own:

> Does this offend you? Then what if you were to see the Son of Man ascending to where he was before?
> It is the spirit that gives life; the flesh is useless.
> The words that I have spoken to you are spirit and life. But among you there are some who do not believe. . . .
> For this reason I have told you that no one can come to me unless it is granted by the Father. . . .
> Did I not choose you, the twelve? Yet one of you is a devil. (6:61–70)

The content of his speech points to the tension between Jesus and his followers, but the antithetical structure of these lines, with their positive assertions, signifies maintenance of Jesus' self-control. In the prayer with which he ends his farewell speech, Jesus delivers a long series of carefully balanced lines that, from the beginning, "glorify your Son so that the Son may glorify you" (17:1), to the end, "the world does not know you, but I know you" (17:25), match the themes of glory and unity with his measured and majestic delivery.[82] These are lines to be recited rather than words on a page to be scrutinized.[83]

In longer dialogues the Greek tragedians often set the chiastic and antithetical movement of the language within a broader structure of paired speech-acts in order to control the development of the conflict so that it does not escalate into a shouting match or come to a conclusion too precipitously. In Oedipus's dialogue with Tiresias, the action moves from Oedipus's request for

---

[82] John 17 has been compared to other biblical prayers that come at the end of farewell addresses (Gen 49; Deut 32–33; see also *Jub.* 22:7–23), but the sentence structure of none of these bears the same distinct antithetical pattern produced by repetition and clauses. The repetition in the lines of Deut 32–33 and *Jub.* 22:7–23 takes the form of step parallelism, typical of Hebrew poetry, in which a statement is repeated with different words. For example, "May my teaching drop like the rain, my speech condense like the dew; like gentle rain on grass, like showers on new growth" (Deut 32:2). Bultmann's comparisons of John 17 to Manichaean hymns is based on the vocabulary and themes rather than the poetic syntax; see Bultmann, *The Gospel of John* (trans. G. R. Beasley-Murray; Philadelphia: Westminster, 1971), 489 n. 8.

[83] Fiona Macintosh ("Tragic Last Words: The Big Speech and Lament in Ancient Greek and Modern Irish Tragic Drama," in *Tragedy and the Tragic: Greek Theatre and Beyond* [ed. M. S. Silk; Oxford: Clarendon, 1996], 423) describes "the repetition, recall and recognition" of the speeches "intrinsically pleasurable activities . . . for both participant and spectator."

information and Tiresias's refusal to Tiresias's request to be dismissed and Oedipus's refusal, and from Oedipus's accusation that Tiresias participated in the planning of Laius's murder to Tiresias's counteraccusation that Oedipus is the culprit (Sophocles, *Oed. tyr.* 300–462). True to the irony of the play, the counteraccusation provides the answer to Oedipus's request and leads to the granting of Tiresias's own request. The course of two of the longer uninterrupted dialogues in the Fourth Gospel can be charted on this grid of paired speech-acts. The dialogue with the Samaritan woman begins with Jesus' supplication "Give me a drink" (4:7), followed by a dialogue that questions the propriety of a Jew making a request of a Samaritan woman. The conversation turns on the inversion of the supplication: the woman then asks Jesus for the drink (4:15); and in the dialogue that follows, the conditions that make her request felicitous are revealed: the coming of the Messiah renders the worship practices that divide Jews and Samaritans obsolete. In the bread-of-life discourse, Jesus offers the bread of life (6:32), the crowd makes supplication to Jesus (6:34), Jesus denies them the bread of life (6:36), and the crowd rejects Jesus (6:66).

We habitually treat the dualism of the gospel doctrinally and divide its terminology between those who have sight, understand, come to the light, and have life and those who are blind, misunderstand, dwell in darkness, and are condemned to death. Greek tragedy's dualist language or binary terminology serves a dramatic function by providing antithetical structure to conflict. In *Oedipus Tyrannus,* Sophocles plays with both the opposition of sight versus blindness and truth versus falsehood in a manner comparable to that of the gospel:

> OEDIPUS: Have you so shamelessly started up this story? How do you think you will escape its consequences?

> TIRESIAS: I have escaped; the truth I nurture has strength. . . .

> OEDIPUS: Do you believe that you will continue to repeat such things and go scot-free?

> TIRESIAS: Yes, if the truth has any strength.

> OEDIPUS: It has, except for you; you are without it, since *you are blind* in your ears, in your mind, and in your eyes. . . .

> You are *sustained by darkness* only, so that you could never harm me or *any other man that sees the light.* . . .

> this wizard hatcher of plots, this crafty Beggar, who has *sight only when it comes to profit,* but *in his art is blind!* . . .

TIRESIAS: And I say, since you have reproached me with my blindness, that *you have sight*, but *cannot see* what trouble you are in. (354–413 [Lloyd-Jones, LCL]; italics added).

Oedipus provokes Tiresias into revealing that Oedipus is the king's murderer by questioning his love of the truth and then responds to the revelation with a death threat. He equates the falsehood of the prophecy with Tiresias's blindness, to which Tiresias responds that Oedipus has eyes but is blind. This insult secures for Tiresias his desired release, for Oedipus can fight Tiresias's prophecy only with a curse and expulsion from the city. Jesus' dialogue with the Pharisees in John 9 provides a parallel use of themes of blindness:

JESUS: I came into this world for judgment so that those who do not see may see, and those who see may become blind.

PHARISEES: Surely we are not blind, are we?

JESUS: If you were blind, you would not have sin. But now that you say, "We see," your sin remains. (9:39–41)

Again, the lines are carefully balanced in order to express the tensions between the two parties. An earlier dialogue between the Jews and Jesus that plays with the pairs God versus Satan, truth versus falsehood, and freedom versus bondage also provides a parallel to Oedipus and Tiresias's dialogue. Jesus' claim that "the truth will make you free" (8:32) is met with the protest that as descendents of Abraham, the Jews have never been slaves. When the Jews claim that they are God's children, Jesus counters, "You are from your father the devil" (8:44), in order to pit the lies of the devil against the truth he tells. The logic of the antithetical claims is not found in history—that the Jews once were slaves in Egypt is central to their faith—but in the dramatic construction.[84] The logic of the accusation that they are from the devil ought to be placed in the same context.

Flyting

The exchanges of insults that occur in the Fourth Gospel may not simply be pieces of reciprocal verbal abuse. Such interactions in Greek tragedy belong to a literary type of scene and category of dramatic dialogue known as "flyting," after the Scottish tradition of demonstrating linguistic

---

[84] Whitacre (*Johannine Polemic*, 69) probably is correct in concluding that the Jews do not mean political freedom but the freedom from idolatry, and thus sin, granted through the covenant with Abraham.

prowess through the exchange of curses and insults. The purpose of the volley of insults is not the vilification of any one character but a show of wits and provocation; but unlike a debate over a principle, idea, or point of law, flyting is "verbal contesting with an *ad hominem* orientation."[85] In literary flyting, found from the Homeric epics through Beowulf to Shakespeare, the contest contains insults, boasts, riddles, and miniature stories, and the merit of a verbal charge is measured by whether it remains within the limits of the facts.[86] A key component of literary flyting is irony, for it is the reader or audience who determines whether a point has been scored. In the Homeric epics, combatants pump themselves up with self-presentational flyting before battles; in the tragedies, the flyting replaces the battles, and the physical violence is its aftermath and often occurs offstage. [87] Bruce Malina and Richard Rohrbaugh suggest that the "challenge and riposte" of the gospel is based upon "the never-ending game of challenge-response that characterized nearly all social interaction" of ancient village life.[88] In Greek drama the tragedians and comedians transcribed these challenge games into the action of their plays. Malina and Rohrbaugh categorize the puns and riddles of the gospel's verbal melees as examples of the "antilanguage" of the Johannine "antisociety."[89] Given the organization of these exchanges and their centrality in the action of the gospel, a literary influence is not simply another possible source for this language but seems the probable source.

In a major study of verbal duels in Homeric and Anglo-Saxon narrative poetry, Ward Parks explains how flyting fits into a narrative in which combat is central. Though my focus in the following section is upon flyting, I will summarize Ward's delineation of the broader literary framework in which flyting is placed, because a number of its elements will factor into my analysis of characterization (chapter 3) and Jesus' death (chapter 4). Flyting is a preparatory act that follows the engagement of two heroes in adversarial roles and precedes physical combat. While flyting, the heroes contend for honor and glory in an eristic display and determine the terms of physical engagement. Because flyting is a contest for honor, in the Homeric epics participation is restricted to men. Parks identifies five types of movement within the flyting:

---

[85] Ward Parks, *Verbal Dueling in Heroic Narrative: The Homeric and Old English Traditions* (Princeton, N.J.: Princeton University Press, 1990), 6. See also Elam, *Shakespeare's Universe of Discourse*, 9.

[86] See Carol J. Clover, "The Germanic Context of the Unferth Episode," *Speculum* 55 (1980): 459.

[87] Claude Calame, *Poétique des mythes dans la Grèce antique* (Hachette Université: Langues et civilisations anciennes; Paris: Hachette, 2000), 288.

[88] Malina and Rohrbaugh, *Social-Science Commentary*, 147–48.

[89] Ibid., 7–14, 81, 158.

Identification: The heroes identify each other as opponents.

Retrojection: The hero boasts about past accomplishments and genealogy and casts aspersions upon those of his opponent.

Projection: The hero boasts about what he will do and predicts failure for his opponent.

Attribution-Evaluation: The hero marshals the narrative evidence from the previous two categories and brings it to bear on his state of honor, usually in the form of self-praise, and that of his opponent, usually in the form of abuse.

Comparison: The hero attempts to prove that he has more courage or ability than his opponent.[90]

On occasion, one hero will contract to resign from the contest and will perform an act of appeasement, such as clasping his opponent's knees, which redefines the relationship as one of master and servant rather than matched adversaries.[91] In some cases, a hero will offer a conditional contract that takes on eristic overtones and perpetuates the flyting.[92] In other cases, the flyting produces a contract in which the means—a trial by arms or some other display of potency—for establishing the claim to superior prowess or status are fixed. After the physical conflict, the eristic element of the flyting can be picked up once more in the ritual resolution of the contest, in which the hero's victory is declared through vaunting (boasts over the fallen enemy and praise of the hero's superiority) and symbolic actions that usually show disrespect to the body of the enemy.[93] In the following discussion of the verbal contests of the Fourth Gospel, I will draw from Parks's work and will use Homeric parallels as well as some from the Greek tragedies. In some cases, the Homeric parallels are clearer and may reflect the possibility that both tragedies and the gospel are dependent upon the Homeric paradigm. When the flyting is integrated into the tragedies and the gospel, it becomes less formal and appears to be part of the give-and-take of heated discussion rather than a necessary prelude to battle.

.   Because of the power of words to generate worlds and possibilities, flyting in drama often exploits the different meanings of words so that insults

---

[90] Parks, *Verbal Dueling in Heroic Narrative*, 105–14.

[91] Ibid., 101–2. For example, Lykaon takes Achilles by the knees and pleads for his life (Homer, *Il.* 21.71).

[92] Ibid., 103.

[93] Ibid., 56. The plot of a number of Greek tragedies, including *Antigone* and *The Suppliant Women,* follows the consequence of these symbolic acts.

can be subtle or clever. For example, in an argument between Tiresias and Creon in Sophocles' *Antigone*, the word "profit," which can refer to either salvation or material advantage, takes center stage:

TIRESIAS: I am well disposed to you, and my advice is good; and it is a pleasure to learn from a good adviser, if his advice brings profit [κέρδος].

CREON: Aged man, all of you shoot at me like archers aiming at a target, and I am not unscathed by your prophetic arts; long since I have been sold and exported by your tribe! Make your profits [κερδαίνετ'], import electrum from Sardis if you wish, and gold from India! . . . And even men who are clever at many things fall shamefully, aged Tiresias, when they skillfully speak shameful words in the pursuit of gain [λέγωσι τοῦ κέρδους χάριν]! . . .

CREON: I do not wish to reply rudely to the prophet.

TIRESIAS: Yet you speak rudely, saying that my prophecies are false.

CREON: Yes, all you prophets are an avaricious race.

TIRESIAS: Rulers, also, are prone to be corrupt.

CREON: Do you know that those whom you rebuke have power?

TIRESIAS: Yes, for it is through me that you saved this city.

CREON: You are a skillful prophet, but given to dishonesty.

TIRESIAS: You will provoke me into telling you things that should not be dug up!

CREON: Do so, only do not speak for the sake of profit [μὴ 'πὶ κέρδεσιν λέγων]!

TIRESIAS: That is what you already think I do.

CREON: Know that you will never be able to trade on my judgment!
(1030–1063 [Lloyd-Jones, LCL])[94]

In this exchange Creon takes the upper hand, although by the end of the play he concedes that Tiresias is wiser. In tragic flyting, both opponents tend to be

---

[94] See Karl Reinhardt, "Illusion and Truth in Oedipus Tyrannus," in *Modern Critical Interpretations: Sophocles' Oedipus Rex* (ed. Harold Bloom; New York: Chelsea House, 1988), 76.

equally clever with words, and the factor that determines whom the audience judges to be superior is how closely the words match the true state of affairs.

The exploitation of divergent meanings of a single word or the discordant meaning of homonyms or phonetically similar words is a device that in broad comedy produces laughter.[95] Ernst Cassirer calls this sort of linguistic bandying "pure self-activity of the word."[96] The pattern in which one person makes a direct statement and the other takes the unintended meaning of the statement and renders it absurd or confusing is a stock trick in comedy. One of the best-known examples of this occurs in *Cyclops*, Euripides' only extant satyr play, in an expansion of the "no man" speech from Homer's *Odyssey*, in which Euripides plays upon the capacity of a word to serve as a proper name as well as to mean something. Odysseus calls himself Noman; therefore, when the Cyclops tries to explain what has happened and refers to Odysseus by name, the chorus takes him to mean that no man has caused him harm:

CHORUS: Why do you shout so, Cyclops?

CYCLOPS: I am ruined!

CHORUS LEADER: You *do* look ugly.

CYCLOPS: And miserable as well!

CHORUS LEADER: Did you fall in a drunken stupor into the coals?

CYCLOPS: Noman [Οὖτίς] destroyed me,

CHORUS LEADER: No one [Οὖτίς], then, has done you wrong.

CYCLOPS: Noman [Οὖτίς] has blinded my eye.

CHORUS LEADER: So you are *not* blind.

CYCLOPS: ow sharp the pain!

CHORUS LEADER: And how could no one make you blind?

CYCLOPS: You mock me. But this Noman [Οὖτίς], where is he?

CHORUS LEADER: Nowhere, Cyclops. (668–676 [Kovacs, LCL])

---

95 Elam, *Shakespeare's Universe of Discourse*, 174.
96 Cited ibid., 9.

The scene continues its comedic thrust by having the chorus use deictic language dependent upon sight to give directions, such as "over there," to which the blinded Cyclops responds by bumping into walls.[97]

In the Fourth Gospel, Jesus makes extensive use of word plays and riddles in a contest in which his opponents frequently are unwitting participants and he emerges the winner. Tom Thatcher identifies an abundance of statements by Jesus designed to set others on the wrong course, often with humorous results.[98] For example, when the disciples return to the Samaritan well with food and urge Jesus, "Rabbi, eat something," Jesus refuses, saying, "I have food to eat that you do not know about," to which the disciples respond, "Surely no one has brought him something to eat?" (4:31–33). When Jesus asks Philip, "Where are we to buy bread for these people to eat?" (6:5), his question is rhetorical, but Philip takes it literally: "Six months' wages would not buy enough bread for each of them to get a little" (6:7). When Jesus tells the disciples, "Our friend Lazarus has fallen asleep, but I am going there to awaken him" (11:11), the disciples, comically, take him at his word and reply, "Lord, if he has fallen asleep, he will be all right" (11:12). These exchanges with the disciples are brief, and they do not develop into contests because the disciples seem to concede to Jesus' preeminence. In the exchanges with "the Jews" and their representatives, however, participants in the dialogues square off and ad hominem attacks fly until they become grounds for physical action.

The first hint of flyting occurs in Jesus' exchange with Nicodemus. Although it does not escalate into a full-fledged verbal combat—only Jesus moves to ad hominem remarks—or a contract for physical engagement, it establishes Jesus' supremacy as the master of such contests before the stakes become high. Nicodemus begins with an identification—"Rabbi, we know that you are a teacher who has come from God; for no one can do these signs that you do apart from the presence of God" (3:2)—that seems like a contractual statement establishing grounds for agreement rather than a basis for antagonistic engagement. There is no general consensus about whether the character of Nicodemus's opening is sincere or insincere, and his purpose in approaching Jesus is unclear. The setting of the dialogue at night suggests to many that although Nicodemus's praise may be sincere, he gives it privately.

---

97 The comedy team Abbott and Costello provide an extended example of this pattern in their "Who's on first?" routine—banter based upon the capacity of the word "who" to serve as a proper name as well as a pronoun.

98 Tom Thatcher (*The Riddles of Jesus in John: A Study in Tradition and Folklore* [SBLMS 53; Atlanta: Scholars Press, 2000], 213–29) places John 6:5 and 11:11 in the category of "dramatic riddles."

In the cultural setting of the Homeric epics, Greek tragedy, or the Gospels, in order for excellence or honor to be established, it must be publicly recognized.[99] Many flyting contests begin with an address filled with praise for the opponent that turns out to be a form of self-aggrandizement for the one who gives it. When Asteropaios answers Achilles' question "Who are you?" by greeting him with "High-hearted son of Peleus" (Homer, *Il.* 21.153 [Lattimore]), he is not being deferential but rather seeks to establish that Achilles' status is honorable before introducing himself as the grandson of the rivers of Axios. The two men are therefore worthy and formidable opponents. If we set Nicodemus within the context of what we know of Pharisaic dialogue, in which arguing different positions regarding a point of law was common fare, his opening might serve as an invitation to debate.

Jesus responds to Nicodemus's greeting with a subtle boast containing a potential insult as well as a potential trap in the form of a word play: "no one can see the kingdom of God without being born from above [ἄνωθεν]" (3:3). Nicodemus picks up the second, unintended meaning of ἄνωθεν, "again," and asks, "How can anyone be born after having grown old? Can one enter a second time into the mother's womb and be born?" (3:4). It is impossible to tell whether Nicodemus is insensible to Jesus' intended meaning or whether he is actually engaging in the flyting and trying to foul Jesus by accusing him of crossing the bounds of truth and thereby violating the rules of play. Jesus' ensuing statement "Do not be astonished. . . . The wind blows where it chooses, and you hear the sound of it, but you do not know where it comes from or where it goes. So it is with everyone who is born of the Spirit" (3:7–8) seems like a contract for disengagement on the basis of agreement, but Nicodemus rejects the terms by asking, "How can these things be?" (3:9). Jesus comes back with an attributive-evaluative move, "Are you a teacher of Israel, and yet you do not understand these things?" (3:10), leaving Nicodemus silent while Jesus continues with a series of moves. He draws a comparison in which he praises himself: "we speak of what we know and testify to what we have seen; yet you do not receive our testimony" (3:11). He follows with a retrospective observation that serves as an attribute and evaluation of Nicodemus's present status: "If I have told you about earthly things and you do not believe, how can you believe if I tell you about heavenly things?" (3:12). The claims that "no one has ascended into heaven except . . . the Son of Man" and "just as Moses lifted up the serpent in the wilderness, so must the Son of Man be lifted up" (3:13–14) are boasts. The first is a retrospective claim to a past accomplishment, and the second is a comparison based upon retrospective praise of a past hero and projective self-praise of Jesus, both of

---

[99] Parks, *Verbal Dueling in Heroic Narrative*, 29.

which end with a contract: whoever concedes to this praise of Jesus will have eternal life (3:15). The final statements of Jesus' speech continue to articulate this contract and to speak of the consequences of rejecting the contract as if the final trial were over: "Those who believe in him are not condemned; but those who do not believe are condemned already, because they have not be-lieved in the name of the only Son of God" (3:18). The speech resembles the vaunting at the end of a battle, in which the result of the armed combat is treated as a reflection of the merits of the flyting—that is, the one whose claim to honor is strongest will necessarily defeat the opponent.[100] Achilles boasts over the dying Asteropaios that his genealogical advantage has deter-mined their fight's outcome:

> Lie so: it is hard even for those sprung of a river
> to fight against the children of Kronos, whose strength is almighty.
> You said you were of the generation of the wide-running river,
> but I claim that I am the generation of Zeus.
> The man is my father who is lord over many Myrmidons,
> Peleus, Aiakos' son, but Zeus was the father of Aiakos.
> And as Zeus is stronger than rivers that run to the sea, so
> the generation of Zeus is made stronger than that of a river.
> For here is a great river beside you, if he were able
> to help; but it is not possible to fight Zeus, son of Kronos. (Homer, *Il.* 21.184–193 [Lattimore])

As an act of poetic justice, Achilles consigns Asteropaios's body to a watery grave. Although Jesus' claims are not a prelude to mortal combat, the stakes he puts forth are life and death, and like a combatant, he offers his opponent life in exchange for acknowledgment. Failure to acknowledge him is a sign of the ignorance and inferiority of his opponent. The question of whether Nicodemus concedes to Jesus' claims or whether he persists in failing to substantiate his praise of Jesus by never openly proclaiming it is a matter of debate.

In the light-of-the-world discourse, both sides engage in all-out flyting that ends with a gesture on the part of the Jews that defines the terms of the physical conflict. Jesus begins with the offer of a contract that would establish peace by requiring his opponents to honor him, in return for which he will grant them a gift: "If you continue in my word, you are truly my disciples; and you will know the truth, and the truth will make you free" (8:31–32). In heroic contests in which opposing communities are engaged in what Parks calls "guest-host bonding," the conflict often ends with the giving of gifts, al-

---

[100] Ibid., 60.

though gifts normally are offered to the victor.[101] Here the offer is an induce-
ment for the opponent to resign, but the Jews reject his offer and commence
the flyting. The repetition by others of Jesus' assertion in the form of a question, "What do you mean by saying, 'You will be made free'?" (8:33b), is a
method of trying to humiliate an opponent by challenging the truth of what
he has said.[102] Their appeal to their pedigree is a retrospective boast: "We are
descendants of Abraham and have never been slaves to anyone" (8:33a). Lineage is perhaps the most frequent content of retrospective boasts in Homeric
verse. In an exchange between Glaukos and Diomedes in which Diomedes
states that he will fight with him only if he is human, Glaukos boasts of his
line by claiming that plenty of men know it and then gives a long genealogy
filled with praise of his ancestors (Homer, *Il.* 6.144–231). He begins with a
piece of folk wisdom: "The wind scatters the leaves on the ground, but the
live timber burgeons with leaves again in the season of spring returning. So
one generation of men will grow while another dies" (Homer, *Il.* 6.143–149
[Lattimore]). By virtue of the virility and heroism of past generations,
Glaukos finds no reason to doubt that he will prevail in a conflict with
Diomedes. Similarly, by virtue of their past, the Jews see no need of the gift of
freedom in the present.

The dialogue then moves into a series of rhetorical arguments made by
Jesus in which he denies their claim to Abrahamic descent, toward the end of
which he delivers an insult regarding their genealogy: "You are from your
father the devil. . . . He was a murderer from the beginning. . . . he is a liar
and the father of lies" (8:44). At this point, the flyting has crossed the bounds
of the paradigm and slipped into what Parks and others call "dozens" or
"sounding"—a game not bound by truth in which the sole aim is creativity
and the subject of the insults often is the opponent's mother.[103] One of the
conventions of sounding is that opponents know that the insults are untrue.
If we recognize this contest paradigm as a dimension of the gospel's literary
structure, then the contention that "the Jews" are the devil's spawn may also
belong in the same category as the line about Jesus being a Samaritan. In
sounding, addressees defeat the insult by surpassing it. The Jews counter with
an insult of the same sort, put in the form of a question that presupposes an
affirmative answer: "Are we not right in saying that you are a Samaritan and

---

[101] See Homer, *Od.* 8.208–211.

[102] Herman, *Dramatic Discourse,* 154. Children often engage in this form of
flyting by repeating every word that the dialogue partner speaks.

[103] Parks, *Verbal Dueling in Heroic Narrative,* 111–12, 114. One of the liveliest
and most extended examples of sounding occurs in a scene in Steven Spielberg's
Hook (1991) in which Peter Pan must reestablish his role as leader of the lost boys by
vanquishing their new leader, Rufio, in a sounding contest.

have a demon?" (8:48). In light of their earlier statement regarding Jesus' parentage (6:42), the first part of this insult is not grounded in truth, and Jesus ignores the accusation that he is a Samaritan. In flyting, because the insult is intended to be truth, the address must offer a self-defense.[104] By denying that he has a demon and taking the insult as a challenge to his honor, Jesus reengages the norms of flyting.

Jesus begins to lay down the terms of a contract in which his opponents would resign when he says, "I do not seek my own glory; there is one who seeks it and he is the judge. Very truly, I tell you, whoever keeps my word will never see death" (8:50–51). The first part is a common boast in which the hero contends that he brings honor to a higher principle, his god or his country. In a flyting match with Aineias, Achilles begins by accusing him of seeking his own aggrandizement, and Aineias belittles Achilles' words as insults designed to frighten a baby and then defends himself by describing the honor of his family, the source of which he imputes to Zeus: "Zeus builds up and Zeus diminishes the strength of men, the way he pleases, since his power is beyond all others" (Homer, *Il.* 20.243 [Lattimore]). In both Jesus' and Aineias's arguments, the fact that this higher power is the judge of the contest is an implicit assertion that his opponent cannot win. Jesus then lays down the conditions by which his opponents can be spared. His opponents reject the offer by reiterating the slur that he has a demon, this time in the form of a statement, and then they attempt to mock Jesus' statement that those who keep his word "will never see death" by changing the words to "will never taste death." Jesus then mounts a volley of boasts and insults that provoke a physical response. He contends that God glorifies him, and he contrasts his opponents' lack of knowledge of God with his own knowledge. He then uses a retrospective claim to honor by saying, "Your ancestor Abraham rejoiced that he would see my day; he saw it and was glad" (8:56). The Jews contest the validity of his boast, "You are not yet fifty years old, and have you seen Abraham?" (8:57), and Jesus defends his seemingly outrageous claim, "Very truly, I tell you, before Abraham was, I am" (8:58), thereby provoking anger that overwhelms the Jews' ability to continue in the flyting.[105] They then establish the terms of the physical conflict by picking up stones to throw at him.

If we examine the use of flyting in Euripides' *Bacchae*, we find a similar use of insults and boasts designed to provoke conflict rather than to win a de-

---

104 Ibid., 114.

105 Thatcher (*Riddles of Jesus in John*, 219–29) places these statements in the category of "mission riddles," but given that they are designed to win the contest, I place them in his category "neck riddles."

bate. In Pentheus's first exchange with Dionysus, Pentheus first tries to ridicule Dionysus, who is disguised as a bacchant dressed in a fawnskin with a fennel-wand, by first insulting his appearance. He then interrogates Dionysus with a series of question designed to make him seem foolish, but like the Johannine Jews, he fails, first because he is ignorant of Dionysus's real identity and second because Dionysus's earnest, albeit ambiguous, replies are insulting and point to Pentheus's inability to fluster him. His strategies for winning are not unlike those of Jesus. The exchange begins with Pentheus's earnest inquiries about the bacchanalia:

> PENTHEUS: What benefit do the rituals bring to the sacrificers?

> DIONYSUS: It is not right for you to hear, but it is worth knowing.

> PENTHEUS: You faked that answer skillfully to make me want to hear.

> DIONYSUS: The rituals of the god hate a man who practices impiety.

> PENTHEUS: The god, just what was he like? Tell me, for you saw him clearly.

> DIONYSUS: He appeared in the form he chose. I did not arrange this.

> PENTHEUS: Here again you have sidetracked me with fine but empty words.

> DIONYSUS: An ignorant man will think another's wise words folly. (474–480
> [Morwood])

When Pentheus risks being humiliated by Dionysus's evasive answers and insults, he engages in flyting by returning volleys:

> PENTHEUS: Do you perform your sacred rituals at night or by day?

> DIONYSUS: Mainly by night. The night has solemnity.

> PENTHEUS: This is your insidious method of corrupting women.

> DIONYSUS: You can find immorality by daylight too. (485–488)

Once Pentheus loses this exchange, he spells out the terms of the impending conflict, "You must pay the penalty for your wicked sophistries," and Dionysus offers symmetrical terms: "And you must pay for your ignorance and your impiety towards the god." Dionysus resumes the flyting by challenging Pentheus to offer another boast: "Tell me what I must suffer. What fearful thing will you do to me?" Pentheus makes a series of projective claims, each of which is challenged by Dionysus:

PENTHEUS: First I shall cut off your love-locks.

DIONYSUS: My hair is sacred. I grow it for the god.

PENTHEUS: Now give me this thyrsus from your hands.

DIONYSUS: Take it from me yourself. I carry it for Dionysus.

PENTHEUS: We shall guard your body inside in prison.

DIONYSUS: The god will free me whenever I wish. (493–498)

They then flip roles, and Pentheus challenges Dionysus's claims to the god's protection:

PENTHEUS: When you stand among the bacchae and call him.

DIONYSUS: He is here close by even now and sees what I suffer.

PENTHEUS: And where is he? He is not manifest to my eyes.

DIONYSUS: He is where I am. In your impiety you cannot see him.
   (499–502)

When Pentheus once more asserts the grounds for action and his power to defeat Dionysus by commanding his men, "Lay hold on him. He is showing contempt for me and for Thebes," Dionysus challenges the basis for his claim to power: "You do not know what your life is, or what you are doing, or who you are." Pentheus returns with a boast based on genealogy, "I am Pentheus, the son of Agave and of my father, Echion," and Dionysus rejects it with a veiled projective claim to victory: "You have a name fit to sorrow for" (503–508). In the immediate context, Pentheus appears to prevail because he succeeds in arresting his opponent, but in the broader context of the play, Dionysus has baited Pentheus into performing the act of injury for which Dionysus can seek revenge.

Jesus participates in a similar sort of baiting designed to goad the Jews into requesting the act, crucifixion, by which Jesus can demonstrate his glory and for which Jesus can seek remediation, resurrection. He lures them into dialogues designed to confuse and to insult. The illustration, or *paroimia* (παροιμία; John 10:6), of the good shepherd, the telling and interpretation of which serve to silence Jesus' dialogue partners, can be set in the context of this flyting contest. Like parables of the Synoptic tradition, it is a story within a story, but unlike the parables, with perhaps the exception of the parable of the Wicked Tenants (Mark 12:1–12; Matt 21:33–46; Luke 20:9–19), John 10:1–18 is a *mise en abyme*. In a manner analogous to the performance of "The

Murder of Gonzago," the play within a play in *Hamlet* about regicide and infidelity, Jesus tells a story similar to the story in which he appears that serves various purposes on the different axis during a reading of the gospel. On the theatrical axis, the *paroimia* and its interpretation produce both suspense, by deferring the reaction of the Pharisees to the charge of blindness, and dramatic irony, by alluding to Jesus' imminent death. On the dramatic axis, the story and its interpretation function like a trap. Jesus has no argument with which to justify his allegations against the Pharisees, but their reaction to the semantic indeterminacy of the *paroimia* corroborates Jesus' accusation and indicts them by aligning them with the malevolent figures in the story.

Many scholars have offered allegorical interpretations of this text, relating its various parts to individuals and institutions or political events during Jesus' career, to the experience of the Johannine community, or to a combination of these. Other readers ignore the historical context as well as the narrative context, focusing upon either an abstracted Johannine theology or a reconstructed nascent Gnosticism.[106] Adele Reinhartz points out that all "share the methodological assumption that the elements of the *paroimia*, and the interrelationships among them, correspond to some structure outside the *paroimia* itself, either within the historical tale of the gospel, or outside it, in the political or theological background of first-century Judaism and Christianity."[107] Rudolf Bultmann, Barnabas Lindars, C. K. Barrett, and C. H. Dodd conclude that the confusing references within the *paroimia* are the result of excessive editorial work in which the evangelist has reworked as many as four different parables.[108] Adolph Jülicher, whose work set the guidelines for most current analysis of parables, rejects such assessment on the basis of the "unnatural conditions" described in the *paroimia*. Johannes Quasten accuses Jülicher of not having sufficient understanding of Palestinian customs, but as Reinhartz points out, Quasten can find evidence of these customs only in the *paroimia*.[109] In contrast, Robert Kysar adopts a literary approach and argues that the variations in the pattern of negative and positive images are designed to keep the reader "off guard and surprised" and the rapid transitions of images are a challenge to the reader.[110]

---

106 Adele Reinhartz (*The Word in the World*, 51–56) provides a survey of the scholarly debate.

107 Ibid., 56.

108 For a summary of their conclusions, see Robert Kysar, "Johannine Metaphor—Meaning and Function: A Literary Study of John 10:1–18," *Semeia* 53 (1991): 81–111.

109 Johannes Quasten, "The Parable of the Good Shepherd: Jn. 10:1–21," *CBQ* 10 (1948): 6; Reinhartz, *The Word in the World*, 57.

110 Kysar, "Johannine Metaphor," 88.

The problem with most of these readings is that they treat the audience of the *paroimia* as the reader of the text. Kysar's observations about the challenge of the *paroimia* ought to be directed to Jesus' narrative audience. As Reinhartz demonstrates, the riddle of the *paroimia* can be solved only when set within the context of the cosmological narrative, to which only the narrator and the audience of the gospel are privy. Tom Thatcher places the *paroimia* into the category of "catch riddle," which trips up its narrative audience by failing to provide it with the key to its solution and depends upon "overlapping performance contexts" to qualify as a legitimate riddle—that is, one with a solution. The task of solving the riddle falls to what Thatcher calls "the real world audience."[111] The *paroimia* is a true riddle on the theatrical axis, but on the dramatic axis it plays a different role. When one tells riddles without solutions, one does not intend the riddle to be solved but to give offense.[112] In Judg 14:14, Samson uses an unsolvable riddle to demonstrate his prowess or superiority over those to whom he addresses his puzzle. In *Oedipus Tyrannus*, Tiresias does not wish to be the one to make plain to the king that he has killed his father and wed his mother, but he does intend to intensify Oedipus's anger and be dismissed. Consequently, he speaks in language that Oedipus describes as "riddling and obscure in excess" (439 [Lloyd-Jones, LCL]). Jesus' choice of language similarly ignores his antagonists' demand to speak plainly (10:24), and the *telos* of the *paroimia* is to insult.

Although we have no example of a *paroimia* in the tragedies comparable in content or form to the story that Jesus tells, the plays provide many examples of references to short *paroimiai* by which characters obscure the meaning or intent of their speech to demonstrate or to gain power.[113] In Sophocles' *Ajax*, Ajax fills a speech, by which he persuades his captors to release him, with illustrations of conventional wisdom that seem to speak to his coming to his senses:

> No, the saying [παροιμία] of mortals is true, that the gifts of enemies are no gifts and bring no profit. Therefore for the future we shall learn to yield to the gods, and we shall learn to reverence the sons of Atreus. They are commanders, so that we must bow to them, how else? Why, the most formidable and the

---

111 Thatcher, *Riddles of Jesus in John*, 190.

112 See Tom Thatcher, "The Riddles of Jesus in the Johannine Dialogues," in *Jesus in Johannine Tradition* (ed. Robert T. Fortna and Tom Thatcher; Louisville: Westminster John Knox, 2001), 266–67.

113 See Homer, *Il.* 9.189 for an example of *mise en abyme* in the Greek epic tradition. Achilles sings of the deeds of heroes. Aristophanes makes frequent use of the device of a play within a play (e.g., *Ach.* 440–445).

most powerful of things bow to office; winter's snowy storms make way before summer with its fruits, and night's dread circle moves aside for day drawn by white horses to make her lights blaze; and the blast of fearful winds lulls to rest the groaning sea, and all powerful Sleep releases those whom he has bound, nor does he hold his prisoners forever. (664–676 [Lloyd-Jones, LCL])

These pieces of folk wisdom, like Jesus' illustration of the sheepfold, represent their speaker as the bearer of common sense. The Johannine narrator describes the lack of reaction to the illustrations as a failure to understand what Jesus is saying to them (10:6). They are baffled or nonplused by Jesus' obliqueness, for these statements seem to have nothing to do with what they have been talking about. The various pieces of 10:1–5 can be taken as pieces of conventional wisdom related to tending sheep and need not be taken as allusions to Jesus. The *paroimia* has become a trap: Jesus uses their lack of understanding, a sign of weakness, as an opening to present them with confusing and opposing interpretations in which he employs the terms of the *paroimia*. By making his audience strain to understand first a puzzle that they cannot solve and then solutions that are equally puzzling, he confirms his accusation that the Pharisees are blind.

The effect of the explication of the *paroimia* may not be limited to insulting their intelligence. Its terms may also be understood as insults directed against their persons, but the abundance of scholarly interpretations warns against ascribing any certainty to any account of their referents. The *paroimia* presents a space, the sheepfold, normally associated with safety, and a space beyond a gate where hungry wolves prowl, an area normally associated with danger. In the Synoptic parables of the lost sheep, the shepherd seeks to return the sheep to the fold. In the Johannine story, the action inverts the values of the space when thieves and robbers enter the fold and the sheep are killed and destroyed, and the shepherd leads the sheep out to safety and to life. Jesus first identifies himself with the boundary between the two spaces: the gate. As Ruth Padel points out in her discussion of theatrical space, a "door is a pragmatically universal image of ambiguous temptation, uncertain invitation, and hesitation."[114] In Jean-Paul Sartre's *No Exit*, the characters cannot bring themselves to open and walk through the door to their prison,

---

[114] Ruth Padel ("Making Space Speak," in *Nothing to Do with Dionysos? Athenian Drama in Its Social Context* [ed. John J. Winkler and Froma Zeitlin; Princeton, N.J.: Princeton University Press, 1990], 358) observes, "The half opened tragic door crystallizes the ambiguities that 'door' in itself evokes, at least in Western tradition." She cites Gaston Bachelard (*The Poetics of Space* [trans. M. Jolas; Boston: Beacon, 1969], 222–24), who argues that the door offers "images of hesitation, temptation, desire."

so they cling to the certainties of their hell rather than the ambiguity of what lies beyond. Jesus seems to be challenging his narrative audience to think of the known as the dangerous and ambiguous, and the unknown as the realm of certitude. When he aligns himself with the good shepherd, for whom the realm beyond the fold becomes a place of danger and death, he makes explicit once more his attitude toward his opponents. The insult embedded in the *paroimia* is a comparison: if Jesus is like a good shepherd, they are like hired hands who are irresponsible and endanger the lives of their charges, or like thieves whose claim to authority is illegitimate.[115] If they treat Jesus' words as an allusion to Isa 56:5–12, as John A. T. Robinson suggests, they could associate the terms of the first explanation with Isaiah's description of God's life-giving temple, and the terms of the second explanation with Isaiah's accusation that Israel's rulers are corrupt and without understanding.[116] If this is the case, Jesus' *paroimia* is a subtle reiteration of his accusation in 9:39–41 that they are blind sinners. However they might understand Jesus' terms, the effect of his words is measured by their response, in which many of them insist that he has a demon (10:19–21). They discount his words in order to protect their own integrity, for one cannot be insulted by the words of a madman.

The flyting contest continues in John 10:22–39, when Jesus reintroduces the terms of the *paroimia* in answer to the demand "If you are the Messiah, tell us plainly" (10:24) by saying, "I have told you, and you do not believe . . . because you do not belong to my sheep" (10:25–26). He ends by making the claim "The Father and I are one" (10:30). The conflict then escalates, and his opponents replace words with stones, but Jesus sustains the verbal engagement by demanding an account of its contractual terms: "I have shown you many good works from the Father. For which of these are you going to stone me?" (10:32). This question is designed not to disarm the Jews but to delay them.[117] When the Jews answer in sincerity that it is not for a good work but for the blasphemy of making himself a god that they seek to stone him, Jesus appeals to Ps 82:6: "Is it not written in your law, 'I said, you are gods'? If those to whom the word of God came were called 'gods'—and the scripture cannot be annulled—can you say that the one whom the Father has sanctified and sent into the world is blaspheming because I said, 'I am God's Son'?" (10:34–36). He then reiterates his claim that he and the Father are coterminous (10:38), and the Jews attempt to arrest him.

---

[115] See Quasten, "Parable of the Good Shepherd," 153.

[116] John A. T. Robinson, "The Parable of John 10:1–5," *ZNW* 46 (1955): 233–38.

[117] Thatcher (*Riddles of Jesus in John,* 219–29) categorizes this as a "neck riddle" in that it "saves Jesus' neck" by deflecting his opponents.

In the 1960s scholars looked at how, in the Jewish exegetical tradition, the term "gods" in Ps 82 was understood to refer to angels, Melchizedek, judges, or Israel at Sinai and argued that Jesus meant that if Scripture could call a person "god," he did not speak inappropriately when he claimed, "The Father and I are one" (10:30).[118] The context in the gospel speaks against this explanation. It seems unlikely that at this point Jesus would argue that he is not making an unusual claim for himself. Jerome Neyrey argues that John 10:34–36 anticipates Jewish midrash by understanding Ps 82 to mean that Israel could be called "god" because, when they received the Torah at Sinai, they became holy and sinless and thus deathless, but they subsequently sinned and died as a result.[119] By citing Ps 82, Jesus equates himself with Israel at Sinai and thereby denies that he has sinned. If this is the case, Jesus is saying something like, "Those who are holy are called gods, and I am holy; therefore I can be called a god." Neyrey treats the citation as an apologetic within the forensic dynamics of John 10 but limits its purpose to confounding his accusers and not substantiating his claims in 10:28–30.[120]

I suspect that the interpretation of Ps 82 supported by Neyrey may have been current at the time of Jesus' ministry or the writing of the gospel, but what is compelling about his account is the fact that it makes the reaction that follows logical. Jesus has not provided the Jews with an argument against their charges; he has provided yet another claim about his status as God's agent with which they can take issue. He invites them to arrest him. In the game of wits, he shows that he is not concerned about how they take his words or what they do in response. Moreover, if Jesus intends to invoke all of Ps 82, in which God speaks critically of human judges who have "neither knowledge nor understanding" but "walk around in darkness" (Ps 82:5), he may be ridiculing their judgment. Given that Jesus has argued earlier, "whoever keeps my word will never taste death" (John 8:51), and has accused the Pharisees of being blind (9:41), his opponents ought to realize now that he is denying their capacity to judge him and reminding them of their own immortality.

The judge of theatrical flyting contests is, ultimately, the audience. As the benefactors of the irony that runs through much of the flyting, any audience of the gospel ought to concede that Jesus scores the most points, if not all of them. But more often than not, the winner of the flyting contest is the loser of the dramatic struggle. In *Romeo and Juliet*, Mercurio bests Tybalt with his words but loses his life. When words begin to win the day, those who face defeat must resort to violence to silence their opponent.

---

[118] Summarized by Jerome Neyrey, " 'I Said: You Are Gods': Psalm 82:6 and John 10," *JBL* 108 (1989): 647–49.

[119] Ibid., 656.

[120] Ibid., 661.

The Agōn

The conflicts of the Fourth Gospel, with their accusations of legal infractions, testimonies, scrutiny of witnesses, and rendering of judgment, contain forensic language apropos of a trial.[121] Andrew Lincoln suggests, "This metaphor of a lawsuit on a cosmic scale is the most distinctive characteristic holding many of the elements of its plot and discourse together."[122] Lincoln ties the "I am" sayings that appear throughout the gospel to the covenantal lawsuit of Isa 44:6–8, in which Israel puts God on trial and God testifies on his own behalf.[123] In Isaiah, the purpose of the lawsuit is to demonstrate that although God's sovereignty has been called into question by the Babylonian conquest, God is really in control. In the Fourth Gospel, the crucifixion and death of Jesus put this sovereignty once more into question and require that God's agent, Jesus, take the stand.[124] I find no reason to argue with Lincoln's conclusions until he comes to the question of genre. Following Richard Burridge, Lincoln describes the gospel as an ancient biography, a life of Jesus, for which the motif of the trial provides emplotment.[125] Biographies tend to cover a life from birth to death and contain episodes formative of a person's character and career as well as events leading to major accomplishments or crises. Having drawn this conclusion, he makes an interesting remark about the frame of the gospel:

> The frame helps the reader to enter into and to exit from the narrative world. In the Fourth Gospel, crossing the threshold into the world of the lawsuit and moving from an external to an internal perspective are aided by the narrator's use of the first-person plural in the prologue (1:14, 16). Readers are in this way included as among those who have true insight into the main character in the trial. The transition back into the world of the reader is achieved in a similar fashion . . . 21:24.[126]

---

[121] Jerome Neyrey ("The Trials [Forensic] and Tribulations [Honor Challenges] of Jesus: John 7 in Social-Science Perspective," *BTB* 26 [1996]: 107–24) finds patterns of forensic proceedings in John 5:17–45; 7–8; 9; 10:22–35; 11:45–53; and in the trial before Pilate.

[122] Andrew T. Lincoln, *Truth on Trial: The Lawsuit Motif in the Fourth Gospel* (Peabody, Mass.: Hendrickson, 2000), 13.

[123] Ibid., 43–44.

[124] Ibid., 49–50.

[125] Ibid., 170–71. Lincoln cites Richard A. Burridge, *What Are the Gospels? A Comparison with Graeco-Roman Biography* (SNTSMS 70; Cambridge: Cambridge University Press, 1992), 41–42.

[126] Ibid., 172.

These two functions for the trial structure—organization of both the plot of the gospel and the experience of the reader—resemble the use of the trial motif within the Greek tragedies. Moreover, the form and content of the evangelist's and the tragedians' debates are comparable.

Peter Arnott observes that the sustained contention and exchanges of abuse in both Greek tragedy and comedy sometimes "embarrass" Western directors whereas "for the average Greek and Roman they were part of the normal cut and thrust of conversation."[127] Political life in Athens centered upon public debate. Even dramatic performances were a contest in which merits were judged and winners and losers pronounced. The agonistic discourse within Greek society also leaves its mark upon the plots of those Greek plays that contain a formal or informal trial, in which a plaintiff brings a case, the defendant responds, and a judgment is rendered, and those that express conflict as formal debate.[128] The formal debate, or agōn (ἀγών), containing two balanced arguments, seems to have been a favored formal convention of Greek theater. Arnott argues that the dramatist found in the debates of the Athenian law court an "informing image" that allowed the plot to unfold in an argument, such as a court case does, to which the audience would be responsive.[129] Moreover, in plays such as *Hecuba*, the dispassionate form of the debate becomes a context for passionate language, whereby in her anguish Hecuba can be reasonable and eloquent.[130]

The formal agōn of the tragedies, particularly those of Euripides, who uses this convention more than do Sophocles and Aeschylus, typically begins with a provocative act or proposal to which a plaintiff responds in a long speech that moves through a series of legal, logical, or moral arguments. The plaintiff tends to round off the speech with an appeal to the character of the judge or a condemnation of the character of the defendant. The opponent or defendant to whom this charge is made then responds with an equally long speech in which he or she typically defends his or her character and provides counterarguments and countercharges. When the agōn occurs in the context of a formal or informal trial, the judge makes a shorter speech rendering a verdict against the defendant or against the plaintiff. In some plays, the reply to the first speech is reduced to a few lines or takes the form of a refusal to speak.[131] Although Jesus dominates the discourse, and his plaintiffs or the defendants

---

[127] Arnott, *Public and Performance,* 105.

[128] Formal trials occur in Euripides' *Hecuba, Trojan Women,* and *Hippolytus,* and in Aeschylus's *Eumenides.*

[129] Arnott, *Public and Performance,* 112–13.

[130] Ibid., 109–10.

[131] See, for example, Euripides, *Med.* 1323–1360. See Michael Lloyd, *The Agon in Euripides* (Oxford: Clarendon, 1992), 10.

against his charges have little opportunity for rebuttal, many aspects of this tragic convention seem to govern the form and content of Jesus' arguments.

The most pronounced evidence of the possible influence of the convention of the *agōn* upon the composition of the gospel occurs in John 8:12–59. Given that I have already argued that 8:12–59 follows the conventions of a flyting contest, I may appear to be contradicting myself, and my reader could justifiably demand to know whether it is a flyting contest or an *agōn*. In the tragedies, flyting and *agōn* are not genres but patterns that fit into or weave into each other to form the conflict. In *Alcestis,* Euripides sets up a confrontation between Admetus and his father, Pheres, by having Admetus initiate an *agōn* that devolves into a flyting contest. The *agōn* consists of two balanced arguments. In the first, Admetus accuses his father of failing in his duty by refusing to take his son's place in death, and in the second, Pheres defends himself. Legal and moral arguments then give way to vitriolic insults:

PHERES: We must live with a single life, not with two.

ADMETUS: And may yours be longer than Zeus's!

PHERES: Do you curse your father, though he has done you no wrong?

ADMETUS: Yes, for I see you lusting for length of days.

PHERES: But is it not you who are burying this corpse in your stead.

ADMETUS: Yes, the sign of your cravenness, you coward.

PHERES: She did not die at my hands. You cannot say that.

ADMETUS: Oh! If only you might come to need my help some day!

PHERES: Woo many wives so that more may die! (712–719 [Kovacs, LCL])

The flyting ends with a symbolic death when Admetus renounces his relationship with Pheres. In the tragedies, the *agōn* and the flyting move the plot toward the same end: the death of one of the adversaries. The dialogue in John 8:12–59 does not follow the formal demands of an *agōn*, but Jesus' longer speeches resemble its sustained arguments. Within the logic of the argumentation about who is a credible witness are patterns similar to those along which the legal and moral points of the *agōn* are laid. The gospel writer seems to have borrowed from the contents of the *agōn* without making use of its entire form and blended it into the design of a larger contest. In the following discussion, I will use the word *agōn* to describe Jesus' speeches, but I acknowledge that the word is more descriptive of the action than definitive of the literary form.

Both Neyrey and Lincoln examine the forensic language in John 8:12–59 in detail. Neyrey sets it into the context of the second of two strata of the gospel's forensic material. In the earlier of the two, Jesus is formally charged with violating the Sabbath (5:16), and he defends himself (5:30–47). In the second stratum, which Neyrey ascribes to a period of high Christology, Jesus is charged with blasphemy, and he defends himself by arguing that by virtue of his powers of creation and judgment, he is equal to God (5:19–29).[132] Neyrey breaks the discourse into three units based upon Jesus' role. In the first, 8:12–20, Jesus appears as plaintiff; in the second, 8:21–30, he assumes the role of eschatological judge, a role that he continues to fulfill in the third part, 8:31–59. Lincoln takes note of changes in the narrative audience of the arguments. In 8:12–20, Jesus addresses the Pharisees; in 8:21–30, comments are directed to the Jews; in 8:31–47, the audience contains Jews who once believed in Jesus; and in 8:48–59, he once again addresses the Jews.[133] In a comparison with the *agōn*, both these criteria for dividing the discourse become valid. The text of 8:12–59 seems to contain two discrete debates that contribute to the extended conflict governing the entire plot. In the first *agōn* (8:12–30), the Pharisees appear as plaintiff, and Jesus takes the role of defendant by responding to them (8:12–20) and then presents a countercomplaint against the Jews, the larger party whose interests the Pharisees represent (8:21–30). In the second *agōn* (8:31–59), Jesus is the plaintiff and directs his charges to the Jews who had believed in him (8:31–47), the defendant's speech is reduced to a countercharge (8:48), and Jesus then defends his position as plaintiff against the Jews (8:49–59).

The first *agōn* (8:12–30) begins with a provocative proposal in which Jesus claims, "I am the light of the world. Whoever follows me will never walk in darkness but will have the light of life" (8:12). In response, the Pharisees charge that by testifying on his own behalf, his testimony is invalid (8:13), and Jesus begins his defense. He cannot refute the fact that he is testifying on his own behalf; therefore he argues that his testimony is valid because he knows the facts of the case (8:14). Unlike his opponents, he does not have to determine whether a witness is true or false: "You judge by human standards; I judge no one" (8:15). He backtracks from this point by arguing that as God's agent, he is an authoritative judge (8:16). He then appeals to law and argues that he has two witnesses: himself and God (8:17–18). When

---

[132] Jerome Neyrey, *An Ideology of Revolt: John's Christology in Social-Science Perspective* (Philadelphia: Fortress, 1988), 9–36.

[133] Lincoln, *Truth on Trial*, 82.

the Pharisees interject the question "Where is your Father?" Jesus ends his argument with a condemnation of his opponents for their failure to know both him and his Father (8:19).

In the *agōn* in *Alcestis*, Pheres' response to Admetus's accusation that he has failed his duty as a father by refusing to die in Admetus's stead follows a pattern similar to the last half of Jesus' argument. Once again the act is not disputed—Pheres did refuse to die—what is at issue is the validity of the act. Like Jesus, his identity is part of his defense. Pheres begins with a statement that counters Admetus's argument that he has not behaved like a father: "Son, whom do you imagine you are berating with insults, some Lydian or Phrygian slave of yours, bought with money? Do you not know that I am a freeborn Thessalian, legitimately begotten of a Thessalian father?" Like Jesus, he argues that no law has been violated; there is no Greek custom that obliges him to die for his son. He asserts that he has fulfilled his duty by doing what his own father had done (Jesus also asserts that he acts in accord with his Father) and denies that any injustice has been done; he has robbed Admetus of nothing. Like Jesus, he ends with a condemnation of his accuser by arguing that Admetus is the coward for persuading his wife to die in his place (675–705 [Kovacs, LCL]).

Neyrey notes that the themes and arguments of 8:21–30 stand in discontinuity with 8:12–20 in significant ways and therefore ought to be treated as a separate unit. With its focus upon Jesus' departure and the Jews' sin, this debate seems to cast Jesus in the role of judge.[134] If this were a formal trial, Jesus' speech could be construed as a judge's verdict, but Jesus renounces the role of judge in 8:15–16. In an *agōn* that provides structure to a more personal conflict, the defendant often speaks as though he or she were the plaintiff's judge. If we set this *agōn* into the frame of the trial that Lincoln describes, Jesus' argument in 8:21–30, with its proleptic references to the crucifixion and resurrection, serves as part of his defense by exonerating him and convicting the Jews. Jesus begins with a reference to his exaltation, "I am going away, and you will search for me," then pronounces the verdict and sentence, "you will die in your sin" (8:21), and goes on to state the basis for this sentence: "You are from below, I am from above; you are of this world, I am not of this world" (8:23). The next statement repeats the judgment in two forms. The first casts it into the past tense, "I told you that you would die in your sins," and seems to justify the judgment by arguing that "the Jews" were warned. He then expresses the judgment in a conditional form, "for you will die in your sins unless you believe that I am he" (8:24), making the punishment a logical consequence of the offense. He also amplifies the

---

134 Neyrey, *An Ideology of Revolt*, 40.

gravity of the offense by charging that he has much to condemn (8:26), implying that their offense exceeds the count specified. He ends by referring to his crucifixion, which will serve as confirmation of their sin and of his authority and duty to act as the Father has instructed him (8:28–29).

If we line up Jesus' speech against the judgment that Agamemnon renders at the end of the *agōn* in which Polymestor accuses Hecuba of treacherously murdering his sons (Euripides, *Hec.* 1240–1251), we find that elements of Agamemnon's speech are comparable to those of Jesus. Agamemnon's addressee is also the plaintiff because the plaintiff, not the defendant, is found guilty. He begins by commenting upon his duty to judge: "Though the troubles of other men are burdensome for me to judge, yet I must do it" ([Kovacs, LCL]). Agamemnon gives his verdict, that Polymestor has killed his guest, and provides the basis for his judgment, that Polymestor is motivated by gold and lies to suit his case. He then marks the enormity of the crime of killing a guest, "Perhaps in your country it is a small thing to kill guests, but to us Greeks this is an abominable deed," and characterizes Polymestor's suffering as the logical consequence of his own guilt. But this sort of condemnation of a plaintiff is also found in a defendant's speech. In Euripides' *Andromache*, Hermione begins by condemning Andromache to death for usurping her place with her husband, Neoptolemus, when he takes her as his prize after the Trojans' defeat and the death of Hector, Andromache's husband. Andromache replies not by pleading for her life or professing her innocence, but by giving an account of why Neoptolemus rejects his wife, and she ends with a warning to Hermione to avoid the path of her mother, Helen, who committed a moral sin for love of a mortal man (147–273).

The way that Jesus speaks as eschatological judge rather than as a character caught in the temporal order of the plot line makes his arguments difficult to follow. This correspondence between the nature of his judgment and his characterization as eschatological judge remains true to the purpose of the dramatic convention of the *agōn*. Where judgments are rendered, they often say more about the character of the judge than the guilt or innocence of the accused. When Menelaus pronounces his verdict of guilty against Helen in Euripides' *Trojan Women*, he argues that Helen's punishment is designed to show that Menelaus is a man. By being stoned, Helen is to learn not to besmirch his honor (1036–1041). In painting such a self-serving picture of justice, Euripides seems to be inviting the audience to question the integrity of Menelaus's judgment. When the play ends with hints of the couple's future reconciliation, the necessity of violence for the reestablishment of honor continues to be in question. Jesus' argument that his crucifixion and its negative consequences will confirm his integrity as eschatological judge finds corroboration in the unfolding of the plot.

In the second *agōn* (8: 31–59), Jesus contests the Jews' claim to the status of being free as descendants of Abraham. Neyrey once more assigns him the role of judge, but I am inclined to see this as a response, rather than a judgment, that seeks to discredit the Jews' claim to be free and thus their status as witnesses. In the context of the immediate *agōn*, Jesus is the plaintiff, but in the context of the larger contest, Jesus is discrediting the testimony of his opponents and supporting his own testimony. The critical issue remains that of who is capable of giving valid and true testimony. In discrediting their claim that Abraham is their father, Jesus uses hypothetical syllogism—a form of rhetoric typical of legal arguments in both the tragedies and Greco-Roman jurisprudence. This is a form of argument in which the speaker puts forth the conditions that would substantiate an adversary's position and then disproves that position by demonstrating that the conditions are not fulfilled. Jesus argues that if the Jews were Abraham's children, they would do what Abraham did. By trying to kill an honest man—something Abraham did not do—they prove that someone else is their father. Then, by putting forward another hypothetical syllogism, he counters their claim that they are not illegitimate children but that God is their father. First, he establishes the condition: if they were God's children, they would love him (8:42). Then he inserts a counterclaim: they do their father's desire, and their father is the devil, who is a murderer and a liar (8:44). Then he reverts to his syllogistic argument, arguing that if they were children of God, they would believe the truth but they do not hear God's word because they are not from God (8:45–47).

Though the arguments in the tragedies are seldom so blatantly tautological, they tend to share formal similarities. In the following comparison, I return to *Alcestis* and the first speech of the *agōn* between Admetus and his father. Admetus's accusations are similar in form and content to those of Jesus. Just as Jesus argues that the Jews do not fulfill the conditions of true children, Admetus argues that Pheres does not fulfill the conditions of true fatherhood. He argues that if Pheres were his true father, he would have died for him, and he charges him with being a coward for clinging to the short period of life left to him rather than dying for his own son. He argues that Pheres has already received his due in life, including respect from his son, and has failed to show repayment. He affirms that he is not Pheres' son by stating that he will not bury him, that he is the child of his savior. He ends with the observation that old men are insincere in praying for death because they cling to life (629–672). Admetus's argument is not fraught with explicit hypothetical syllogisms; instead, it is one implicit syllogism: "If you were a true father, you would do what your child asks; you did not do what I asked; therefore, you are not a true father." Here, as in many of Euripides' debates, the tragedian obscures the formal rhetoric of the argument by rendering it a natural self-expression of a character's situation in the drama.[135]

The defense of the Jews is limited to the countercharge that Jesus is a Samaritan and has a demon—that is, Jesus is not a reliable or valid witness. As we noted earlier, the allegation that Jesus is a Samaritan is spurious and requires no response. Jesus does respond to the implicit allegation that he is not a valid witness by providing arguments to prove his credibility that follow lines of defense typical of the tragedies (8:49–58). He begins by testifying to the quality of his own character: "I do not have a demon; but I honor my Father, and you dishonor me." He argues that he does not seek his own glory but that of God. He ends this part of his speech with the statement that whoever keeps his word will never see death—that is, whoever agrees with him exercises good judgment by believing in him. In the tragic *agōn*, the playwright often facilitates the transition to a new argument by having the speaker answer an imaginary objection.[136] The gospel writer allows Jesus' speech to be interrupted by having the Pharisees raise the objection that Jesus is making himself greater than Abraham and the prophets. Jesus responds by providing the flip side of his first argument in the form of an incomplete hypothetical syllogism: "If I glorify myself, my glory is nothing. It is the Father who glorifies me"; therefore, his glory is real. He continues with another hypothetical syllogism: "If I would say that I do not know him, I would be a liar like you. But I do know him and I keep his word." The point of the argument is very simple: good people will support my case; bad people will not. His final argument provides corroborating natural proof in the form of a witness: "Abraham [a good man] rejoiced that he would see my day; he saw it and was glad." The Jews raise another objection, "You are not yet fifty years old, and have you seen Abraham?" to which Jesus responds, "before Abraham was, I am." The Jews then draw their own conclusions. Jesus' own speech convicts him, and they pick up stones to throw at him.

Both of the key elements of this speech—the assertion or refutation of noble identity and the argument that to agree is just and to disagree is base—appear in many of the speeches within the tragic *agōn*. After Hecuba has poked holes in Polymestor's argument against her by exposing his lack of nobility in killing Polydorus and failing to share the gold with the Argives, she turns to Agamemnon and argues that if he sides with Polymestor, who is impious, disloyal, and a breaker of laws, he will show himself to be base (Euripides, *Hec.* 1187–1237).[137]

---

[135] Lloyd, *The Agon in Euripides*, 32–33.

[136] Ibid., 30–31.

[137] Some other examples: Hippolytus begins his defense by describing his chastity (Euripides, *Hipp.* 983–1006); Menelaus's speech in *Andromache* (645–690)

When the legal debates are situated in the context of the dramatic action of the gospel, the question becomes not who is right or wrong, innocent or guilty, but what motives are exposed and how the *agōn* contributes to the *pathos* of the plot. Neyrey argues that Jesus conducts a *cognito*—a formal component of a Greco-Roman trial in which the judge undertakes a "personal examination of the testimony of witness and plaintiffs" that leads to specific formal charges. At each point in the proceedings when the Jews speak, they provide proof of what Jesus attempts to prove about them: first, they do not remain in his word; second, they are liars.[138] It seems to me that Neyrey's rush to judgment against the Jews in the narrative overlooks the role of the debate in the plot. From the vantage point of an audience that understands Jesus' referents and believes that he has been resurrected, the accusations of the Jews against Jesus prove to be false, but at the level of the drama, his arguments are unsuccessful. At the level of the drama, Jesus' arguments are more provocative than compelling. He repeatedly assents to the accusation that he claims to be God's Son and equal. The proof of that claim obtains not in what has passed, not in his physical birth or the identity of his biological parents, but in a future event, something that has not yet come to pass and therefore would be inadmissible as evidence in any human court of law. In this respect, the legal arguments fit into the pattern of a heroic contest in which the proof of one claim over another rests upon the death by which glory is won rather than a trial that sifts through the facts to determine who should be honored and who should be shamed. In the action of the gospel, Jesus' self-defense serves to push the Jews toward the resolve to execute him. His counteraccusations serve the same purpose, and so we ought to ask whether this purpose governs their form and content and whether we make a categorical error if we treat the charges against the Jews as a reflection of Jesus' condemnation of them in his life or an antagonistic relationship between whomever "the Jews" might represent and the Johannine community.

The resemblance between the tragic *agōn* and Jesus' forensic speeches may be too loose to support an argument for direct literary dependency. Both may be informed by the actual legal proceedings of the courts with which

---

ends his argument that he makes his points out of good will rather than anger and to disagree is to show a hot temper; in her self-defense in *The Trojan Women* (914–965), Helen reviews the nobility of her actions and then argues that to put her to death would be unjust and to pity her would be just; the Theban herald in *The Suppliant Women* (465–510) argues, against Theseus's going to bury the dead Argives in opposition to the Thebans, that all people know that speech about peace is good and speech about war is bad and that wise people do not destroy what they love while brash leaders make errors.

138 Neyrey, *An Ideology of Revolt*, 44–46.

their authors were familiar. In his study of rhetoric in the New Testament, George Kennedy comments that the gospel writers could hardly have avoided hearing or practicing rhetoric, given its pervasive presence in oral and written communication in the Hellenistic world.[139] Michael Lloyd demonstrates that Euripides' dependence upon forensic traditions is more functional than formal.[140] According to Lloyd, the function of the tragic *agōn* is to "concentrate the conflict between two important characters so that it can be isolated and expressed formally in a single scene."[141] Moreover, the debates become the catalyst for *pathos*. When the division between Antigone and Creon cannot be settled with words, Creon resolves to restore his authority by sentencing Antigone to death. Although violation of Creon's command is the charge that brings Antigone before Creon's judgment, the action that constitutes the violation of Creon's authority is her haughty speech. Creon himself states, "This girl knew well how to be insolent then, transgressing the established laws; and after her action, this was a second insolence, to exult in this and to laugh at the thought of having done it" (Sophocles, *Ant.* 480–483 [Lloyd-Jones, LCL]). Whatever the genesis and evolution of their literary form, Jesus' debates serve the same purpose: they dramatize the tension articulated in the prologue between the incarnate Word, the light that comes into the world, and the darkness of the world that obscures the light. Jesus' Sabbath violations set the stage for the action of the gospel: conflict between the authority of the Jews or Jerusalemite leaders to question Jesus and Jesus' authority to speak. Jesus' arguments intensify the conflict instead of bringing understanding or reconciliation; therefore the authorities of the world defend themselves by exercising their power.

A Dialogue in Action:
The Bread-of-Life Discourse

Various verbal gestures, the broad speech patterns that organize and dramatize the conflict, and short, discrete speech-acts fit together to form the dialogues of the gospel. Besides following the development of ideas within the dialogues, one can follow the action constituted by the speech: the thrust of an offensive line and the parry of a defensive reply, displays of vulnerability

---

139 George A. Kennedy, *New Testament Interpretation through Rhetorical Criticism* (Chapel Hill: University of North Carolina Press, 1984), 10.

140 Lloyd, *The Agon in Euripides*, 19–36.

141 Ibid., 131.

and control, and the gestures that signify engagement and those that indicate retreat. In order to illustrate how dialogues function as action, I will guide my reader through the choreography of the bread-of-life discourse (John 6:25–58).

The initial exchange is fraught with language that establishes the context and conditions for the dialogue. The action begins in medias res with a "reflexive pick-up" in which the speaker refers to the present in relation to the past: "When did you come [past action] here [present action]?" (6:25). Francis Moloney calls this line a "trivial question," [142] but in the tight economy of drama, there are no such lines. The word "here" is a verbal gesture that orients the characters to each other within their dramatic space and the audience to the eternal present of theatrical experience. The line works even better in the Greek, where the perfect form γέγονας can signify both moment ("When did you get here?") and duration ("How long have you been here?"). Jesus occupies the represented space into which the crowd enters. The sequence of entrances is one means by which the dramatist can quickly establish an imbalance in the relationship between characters, thereby providing dramatic tension and a catalyst for action.[143] The crowd enters Jesus' domain, placing them in a situation in which they need to establish a relationship with him. An imbalance of attitude is also quickly established. The crowd's enthusiasm is encoded in the use of the polite address "Rabbi" and the gesture of handing the floor to Jesus. Their question invites a speech-act and thus is a "keep on going" cue—the means by which the dramatist keeps the dialogue going and controls turn taking.[144] The question also places the crowd in the vulnerable position of being open to rejection. Jesus' reluctance in initiating a relationship is encoded two ways. First, his use of negatives is a gesture of disdain: "you are looking for me, not because you saw signs, but because you ate your fill of the loaves" (6:26). Second, he redefines the meaning of words to avoid the establishment of common terms. Jesus tells them to work for the food that does not perish; the crowd asks what work it must do; Jesus replies that they must believe. This destabilizing play with words continues throughout the dialogue.

---

[142] Francis J. Moloney, "The Function of Prolepsis in the Interpretation of John 6," in *Critical Readings of John 6* (ed. R. Alan Culpepper; BIS 22; Leiden: Brill, 1997), 134.

[143] With reference to Aeschylus's *Oresteia* trilogy, Richard Beacham explains how the placement of characters in the space of the ὀρχήστρα and the σκηνή and the movement of other characters into that space determine who controls the action. See Richard Beacham and Peter Bowen, *Staging Classical Tragedy* (Princeton, N.J.: Films for the Humanities, 1989), video recording.

[144] Elam, *Semiotics of Theatre and Drama*, 191.

Although Jesus initiates conflict with the use of a negative, he disengages his attack, thereby delaying the rejection and inviting continued interaction, through an apparent offer to them to labor "for the food that endures for eternal life, which the Son of Man will give you" (6:27). This initial speech-act sets the remainder of the action into motion as the offer prompts the crowd's supplication, which is followed by Jesus' denial of their request and their rejection of Jesus.

When the crowd responds to Jesus' offer, they place themselves once again in the vulnerable position of suppliant by asking a question: "What must we do to perform the works of God?" (6:28). The question elicits a reply: "This is the work of God, that you believe in him whom he has sent" (6:29). If the dialogue were to continue in this mode, in which the crowd remains deferential to Jesus, the crowd would logically proceed to accept Jesus; therefore the evangelist has the crowd try to reverse the position of power. Jesus' demand that the crowd do something is met with a reciprocal demand that Jesus do something: "What sign are you going to give us? . . . What work are you performing?" (6:30). By using the second-person pronoun, the crowd also seizes power by exposing Jesus' third-person reference to God's agent as self-referential. The reference to the exodus, "Our ancestors ate the manna in the wilderness," and the quotation of Scripture, "He gave them bread from heaven to eat" (6:31), are verbal challenges that resemble flyting but may be felicitous insofar as they hope that Jesus is the Messiah. Paul Anderson describes the reference to the manna at the end of this demand as both "the throwing of the gauntlet" and a "rhetorical trump."[145] I prefer the first of these analogies in that I take the move to be a "keep on going" cue rather than a move that ends the exchange. Jesus' reply, "Very truly, I tell you, it was not Moses who gave you the bread from heaven, but it is my Father who gives you the true bread from heaven. For the bread of God is that which comes down from heaven and gives life to the world" (6:32–33), seems to cooperate with their request and therefore prompts the completion of the supplication: "Sir, give us this bread always" (6:34). The polite language of address, κύριε, and the acknowledgment that Jesus has something that the crowd needs place them once again in the exceedingly vulnerable position of being wide open for denial.

The supplication in response to Jesus' offer now calls for Jesus to fulfill their request or deny it. The evangelist employs a strategy to maintain the dialogue and avoids bringing it too hastily to its inevitable conclusion. In the dialogue with the Samaritan woman, when Jesus is presented with a similar

---

[145] Paul N. Anderson, "The Sitz im Leben of the Johannine Bread of Life Discourse and Its Evolving Context," in Culpepper, *Critical Readings of John 6*, 16.

request, "Sir, give me this water" (4:15), the evangelist uses the evasive tactic of having Jesus seem to cooperate by requesting the presence of her husband. This keeps the dialogue going instead of sending her away. In the bread-of-life discourse, he changes the direction of interaction by having Jesus turn away from direct challenges and hand the task of response to an absent other: "Whoever comes to me will never be hungry" (6:35). By casting his relationship with the crowd into the past tense, "I said to you that you have seen me and yet do not believe" (6:36), Jesus emphasizes his disengagement from them. He gives them the brush-off. Their request is denied, but in an indirect manner that does not call for a direct response.[146]

The dramatic effect of the shift in person deserves close attention. In verses 25–34, Jesus confines his use of the first-person pronoun to the phrase "I tell you" (6:26, 32), the deictic language of which signifies interaction between the two parties. Otherwise, he refers to himself as the object of the crowd's actions or in the third person as "Son of Man" or "bread of life." Although this use of the third person lends Jesus "an Olympian remoteness" and marks him with the "hubris of the tragic hero, whom the gods mean to destroy," it maintains a social relationship with the crowd.[147] In verses 35–40, Jesus uses self-referential language ("I am the bread of life") and defines experience in terms of "I" ("I will never drive away," "I have come down," "I should lose nothing," "I will raise them up"), thereby relinquishing a social orientation.[148] Jesus' language calls for his demise both dramatically, in that the crowd mirrors his disengagement by referring to Jesus in the third person, and theatrically, insofar as the audience recognizes that Jesus' language signifies his relationship with a transcendent reality to which he will return.[149]

In contrast to the Matthean storyteller, who can allow Jesus to talk for pages and not describe his narrative audience, the Johannine dramatist does not leave characters on stage with nothing to do. The crowd, left without a

---

146 Robert Kysar ("The Dismantling of Decisional Faith," in Culpepper, *Critical Readings of John 6,* 165) perceives that the crowd expresses an "authentic quest and an openness to receive" while Jesus responds with words that "appear harsh and obscure."

147 Madelaine Doran (*Shakespeare's Dramatic Language* [Madison: University of Wisconsin Press, 1976], 136) uses this language to describe Julius Caesar.

148 See Valentin N. Voloshinov, *Marxism and the Philosophy of Language* (trans. L. Matejka and I. R. Titunik; Cambridge: Harvard University Press, 1986), 88. According to Voloshinov, language that describes experience in terms of the self with excessive use of the word "I," rather than in terms of another's point of view, relinquishes both social orientation and the potential for apprehension.

149 Adele Reinhartz (*The Word in the World,* 34–35) situates the "I am" language within the cosmological tale.

dialogue partner, bifurcates into Jews and their silent addressee. Some scholars see the introduction of the term "the Jews" as a sudden change in the dramatis personae, but given that there is no significant interruption of the action, it seems that the identification of the Jews is insignificant or signifies that the crowd is composed of different groups.[150] The internal debate that begins here, "Is not this Jesus, the son of Joseph, whose father and mother we know? How can he now say, 'I have come down from heaven'?" (6:42), and continues elsewhere (7:25–27, 35–36, 40–44, 45–52; 10:19–21) until their resolve to execute him is solidified, is comparable to the agonizing of the chorus in Greek tragedy over how to understand or respond to the protagonist.[151] The task of the audience is not to participate in the debate of the crowd, but to witness it.[152] According to Jean-Pierre Vernant, Greek tragedy leads its audience to recognize the ambiguous nature of language and that the nature of the world is to be in conflict.[153] As we have seen in the discussion of the *agōn*, debate serves a comparable purpose for the audience of the Fourth Gospel. The continuous verbalization of uncertainty dramatizes a characteristic that is attributed to the world in the prologue: the world is without understanding.

Scholarship typically has treated verses 43–51 and 53–58 as revelatory speeches that correct the crowd's misunderstanding.[154] This would make sense if the crowd had misunderstood Jesus, but it has correctly treated Jesus' claim that he is the bread of life as a metaphor for God's heavenly agent. Jesus' so-called clarification, in which he adds the language of "eating" and "flesh" to the metaphoric picture, compounds rather than reduces ambiguity. Instead of explaining with words, Jesus plays with words.

The evangelist begins Jesus' set speech by using a standard technique of building dramatic tension without reestablishing the direct conflict. Jesus is portrayed as listening to the effect of his words upon the crowd when he comments directly upon their speech, "Do not complain" (6:43). Jesus does

---

150 See Kysar, "The Dismantling of Decisional Faith," 165.

151 In chapter 3, I will elaborate on this comparison of the crowd or the Jews with the chorus.

152 As Robert Kysar ("The Dismantling of Decisional Faith," 165) points out in his reader-response criticism of John 6, "The reader cannot entirely share that conflict since he has read 1:1–18 and knows Jesus' true identity."

153 Jean-Pierre Vernant, "Ambiguity and Reversal: On the Enigmatic Structure of Oedipus Rex," in *Myth and Tragedy in Ancient Greece* (ed. Jean-Pierre Vernant and Pierre Vidal-Naquet; trans. P. du Bois; New York: Zone Books, 1988), 114.

154 The theme of misunderstanding is covered extremely well by R. Alan Culpepper, *Anatomy of the Fourth Gospel: A Study in Literary Design* (FF; Philadelphia: Fortress, 1983), 152–65.

not decode what he hears as a message; rather, he categorizes, he ascertains what sort of act it is. In drama, the respondent frequently comments upon the tone or the nature of the speech of another.[155] For example, after Tiresias's opening lines, Oedipus observes, "How despondent you are" (*Oedipus Tyrannus* 319 [Lloyd-Jones, LCL]). The comment upon the speech-act serves an obvious purpose on the performance axis. The playwright controls the actor if the tone of his or her speech is dictated by the response that it evokes. The practice of characterizing the nature of a speech-act also serves a purpose on the dramatic axis in that it often serves as a provocation by which one character maintains control over the direction of the dialogue. Jesus' characterization of the questioning of the veracity of his claim as complaining is the first in a string of thinly veiled or blatant insults in a flyting contest that anticipates a show of arms: "No one can come to me unless drawn by the Father" (6:44), implying that the crowd is not drawn by God, and "Your ancestors ate the manna in the wilderness, and they died" (6:49), a retrospective aspersion against their ancestors. Jesus' description of their failure to accept him precedes and precipitates their rejection of him. He is baiting them. A comparable sequence occurs in Tiresias's dialogue with Oedipus. Tiresias characterizes Oedipus's speech as blame (337–338), invites him to "rage with the most ferocious anger" (343 [Lloyd-Jones, LCL]), and anticipates the assignment of guilt (346–347). At each turn, Tiresias announces the response that he intends his words to provoke from Oedipus. He asks, "Shall I tell you another thing, to make you even angrier?" (365). Jesus' intent may not be so explicit, but the effect of his words should be equally coherent to the audience. Jesus' words about God's rejection of "the Jews" lead to their rejection of him.

As we have noted in the discussion of patterns in dialogues, set speeches in dramas are not systematic treatments of theses that build to a conclusion. They often are reiterations of ideas that progress from thesis to antithesis. A strong rhetorical rhythm rather than an exchange of ideas provides organization to a speech and the illusion of a natural movement of thought. In John 6:44–58, Jesus' speech twists and turns on the two axes of life and death. Johannine scholars typically have used the language of "circle" or "spiral" to describe this movement. Rudolf Schnackenburg observes that "thought 'circles,' repeating and insisting, and at the same time moving forward, explaining and going on to a higher level."[156] John Dominic Crossan describes "formulaic, hypnotic, and almost rhapsodic repetition," while Paul Anderson

---

155 Elam, *Shakespeare's Universe of Discourse*, 48.

156 Rudolf Schnackenburg, *The Gospel according to St. John* (trans. Kevin Smyth; 3 vols; New York: Herder & Herder, 1968), 1:117

characterizes the speech as a "forward moving spiral, combining cyclical-repetitive themes with linear progressive development."[157] But what sort of development occurs? Is it conceptual or is it dramatic?

With the beginning of his antithetically constructed speech, Jesus moves from disengagement to reengagement. When the Jews signal that they have been listening to Jesus by repeating his words in the form of a question, "How can this man give us his flesh to eat" (6:52), Jesus has dropped the third person and addresses his point directly to them: "unless you eat the flesh of the Son of Man and drink his blood, you have no life in you" (6:53). For readers seeking to understand Jesus' meaning, the absolute necessity of eating his flesh is problematic and has generated the Reformation debate over the role of the sacrament—a question that continues to preoccupy many exegetes. Though Jesus' meaning is ambiguous, we can readily recognize what has happened. Jesus has attacked and has escalated the conflict while continuing to play with established themes. The absolute conditional serves as a device for heightening the antipathy between protagonist and people.[158] In *Oedipus Tyrannus*, Sophocles uses a pair of absolute conditionals as a quick thrust and counterthrust in Creon and Oedipus's duel of words:

> CREON: If you believe that obstinacy without sense is worth possessing, you are not thinking wisely.

> OEDIPUS: If you believe that you can harm a kinsman and not pay the penalty, you are unwise. (549–552 [Lloyd-Jones, LCL])

Creon later uses an absolute conditional in arguing that he has no choice but to punish Antigone for her attempt to bury Polynices: "Indeed, now I am no man, but she is a man, if she is to enjoy such power as this with impunity" (Sophocles, *Ant.* 484–485 [Lloyd-Jones, LCL]). The use of the language of absolute condition, which marks the antagonism between characters in the tragedies, plays a large part in producing fatalistic tragic necessity. It serves

---

157 John Dominic Crossan, "It Is Written: A Structuralist Analysis of John 6," *Semeia* 26 (1983): 15; Anderson, "Johannine Bread of Life Discourse," 18.

158 Doran (*Shakespeare's Dramatic Language*, 192) writes that "the antipathy between hero and people" is often "intensified" in tragedy "by the representation of unbridgeable gaps in attitudes through the use of absolute comparisons." Electra speaks this way throughout Sophocles' play by absolutizing the injustice of Clytemnestra's act and the necessity of vindication. To her sister she argues that if the two of them murder Aegisthus, "all should love them, all should reverence them; all should honor them at feasts and among the assembled citizens for their courage" (Sophocles, *El.* 981–984).

the same purpose in the Fourth Gospel by suggesting that characters have no control over the outcome of the action.

As Jesus' speech progresses, the rhetorical rhythm intensifies by becoming hard-hitting. The evangelist exchanges the soft sound of φαγεῖν ("to eat"; 6:50, 51) for the harder sound of its synonym τρώγειν (6:54, 56, 57, 58). Verbal shoves become verbal punches.[159] The force of the word is strengthened through the use of anaphora—the repetition of the same word at the beginning of a series of independent clauses. Through the five verses of 54–58, Jesus uses the same subject, the one who gnaws, ὁ τρώγων, four times.[160] The use of the verb τρώγειν renders the antithesis between eating Jesus' flesh and not eating it a grotesque reference to a cannibalistic meal that is both life-giving and deadly. [161] The absolute contrast between bread that brings life and bread that leads to death may, then, be more a function of the drama than doctrine. Such sarcastic language is designed to end speech by being so offensive that the crowd is prepared to reject him.

Although the purpose of the theatrical exposition of 6:51–58 is to show how its language signifies action, the results have implications for the discussion of the meaning of the text. References to eating Jesus' flesh follow logically from both the feeding of the five thousand and the dialogue it provokes, and they proceed logically to the *pathos* of the gospel. This may be a clever al-

---

[159] Whether τρώγειν is merely a synonym or whether it is intended to be an insulting deployment of a verb used to describe how animals masticate their food is a matter of debate.

[160] In Sophocles' *Electra,* we can hear how a technique similar to anaphora (lost, unfortunately, in translation) works in a speech in which Electra chides her sister Chrysothemis for refusing to abet her in the retaliatory murder of Aegisthus:

ἀπροσδόκητον οὐδὲν εἴρηκας· καλῶς δ' ἤδη σ' ἀπορρίψουσαν
ἀπηγγελλόμην. ἀλλ' αὐτόχειρί μοι μόνη τε δραστέον τοὖργον τόδ· οὐ
γὰρ δὴ κενόν γ' ἀφήσομεν.

You have said nothing that surprises me; I knew well that you would reject what I proposed. Well, I must do this deed single-handed and alone! For I will not leave it unattempted. (1017–1020 [Lloyd-Jones, LCL])

Chrysothemis uses the same figure of speech in response:

ἀλλ' εἰ σεαυτῇ τυγχάνεις δοκοῦσά τι φρονεῖν, φρόνει τοιαῦθ'· ὅταν γὰρ
ἐν κακοῖς ἤδη βεβήκῃς, τἄμ' ἐπαινέσεις ἔπη.

Well, if you think you are showing some sense, think like that! For when you are already in trouble, you will approve my words. (1055–1057)

[161] According to Doran (*Shakespeare's Dramatic Language*, 41), Elizabethan rhetoricians used the word "grotesque" to describe comparable compositions of contraries.

lusion to early Christian consumption of the Lord's Supper, but we ought to distinguish the significance of the statements made in this passage on the dramatic axis and the theatrical axis. The absolute condition in verse 53 is not an invitation to Jesus' narrative audience to partake in a ritual meal; it is an offense. As the speech progresses, Jesus provides the antithetical expression of the verse, but he does not say, "If you eat the flesh and drink the blood, you will have life"; he says, "Those who eat my flesh and drink my blood have eternal life" (6:54). On the dramatic axis, Jesus' signifier has no referent. On the theatrical axis, it is possible and even probable that the first audience contained people who had eaten bread and drunk wine blessed with words such as those found in 1 Cor 11:25 and believed that the terms regarding those who ate Jesus' flesh and drank his blood could or did refer to them. The words, then, affirm their relationship with Jesus and provide assurance of resurrection, but the words do not elevate the ritual of the Eucharist to the means by which salvation is obtained.[162] Perhaps more important, on the theatrical axis, the disparity between how Jesus' words are received prior to his resurrection and how they are taken after that event become clear to the gospel's audience.

When the dialogue reaches its climax, the evangelist delays the conflict with the Jews by interposing a scene between Jesus and his disciples in which we witness their reaction to his words: they reject Jesus. By delaying the dramatization of the reaction of the Jews and the crowd, the evangelist produces two conditions necessary for the plot of the gospel: he begins to isolate Jesus by dramatizing his estrangement from those who might offer him protection, and he provides occasion for new dialogues in which Jesus moves from conditions for rejection to provocation for violence.

This theatrical reading produces an isolated, belligerent, self-absorbed Jesus akin to the tragedian's "dark vision of the hero."[163] When Jesus says that he will not turn away any who come to him and then proceeds to turn as many away as possible, he fits Charles Segal's portrait of Sophoclean heroes who "invite suffering into their lives by a dangerous excess."[164] The dramatic irony of the gospel makes it possible for the audience to avoid this judgment because it knows that Jesus intends to die. His last offensive speech in the

---

[162] Paul N. Anderson (*The Christology of the Fourth Gospel: Its Unity and Disunity in the Light of John 6* [Valley Forge, Pa.: Trinity, 1996], 110–36, esp. 125–26) examines John 6:53–58 in light of Ignatius's understanding of the Eucharist and concludes that Jesus' words affirm participation in the community of faith and are not necessarily the product of a sacramental redactor.

[163] Charles Segal, *Sophocles' Tragic World* (Cambridge: Harvard University Press, 1995), 2 (quoting Bernard Knox).

[164] Ibid.

bread-of-life discourse is predicated upon the paradox that in order for the Jews to have eternal life, they have to kill Jesus. To accept him would foil the plan. So when the crowd would make Jesus king, the police would rather listen than arrest him, and Pilate would release him; Jesus is provided with a motive for his belligerence. As Humphrey Kitto states of the antagonists of Greek tragedy, we should not think of them as "bloodthirsty monsters . . . when the point is that they are quite ordinary people who are persuaded to do a dreadful thing by the supposed demands of the political situation."[165] If we attend to the theatrical conventions of the dialogue's composition, we ought to regard the crowd and the Jews as deserving pity rather than condemnation.

Conclusion

In this discussion I have described many dramatic and theatrical conventions and found them at work in the action and design of the Fourth Gospel. Although the gospel writer consistently makes use of these conventions, he does not make consistent use of them. The conventions seem to serve more as tools to tell the sort of story he wants to tell rather than the constitutive parts of a genre he seeks to realize. Nevertheless, when the conventions are in play, the audience and reader of the gospel ought to acknowledge their purpose and effect if they hope to follow the plot of the gospel rather than construct some form of doctrinal argument.

---

[165] H. D. F. Kitto, *Greek Tragedy: A Literary Study* (3rd ed.; London: Methuen, 1961), 255.

CHAPTER 3

Dramatis Personae and

the Illusion of Identity

EMILY: Do any human beings ever realize life while they live it—
every, every minute?
STAGE MANAGER: No—Saints and poets maybe—they do some.

—Thorton Wilder, *Our Town*

The English word "person," from the Latin *persona* ("mask"), possibly is derived from the words *per* and *sonare*, literally, "that through which the sound comes," probably in reference to the actor's masked performance.[1] At the root of our grammatical usage of first, second, and third persons stands the theatrical tradition of differentiating the principal role (first person) from the secondary and tertiary roles (second and third persons).[2] The etymology of the word reminds us that any notion of person or personality that we apply to a character within a text is based upon the appearance of reality made possible through the artifice of represented speech and action and is constructed with models and presuppositions rooted in our own historically bound consciousness. One enters into a minefield when discussing the nature of literary characters, whether they stand for fictional or historical figures. In order to navigate through this discussion, I will follow the path taken by scholars of the tragedies who focus upon how characters are represented and the relationship of their words to the dramatic situation and who consider questions of the broader social milieu of the literature before hazarding an opinion about the significance of a characterization.

---

[1] Vimala Herman, *Dramatic Discourse: Dialogue as Interaction in Plays* (London: Routledge, 1995), 38.
[2] Observation by John Lyons, *Semantics* (Cambridge: Cambridge University Press, 1977), 638; cited in Keir Elam, *The Semiotics of Theatre and Drama* (London: Routledge, 1980), 134.

Two missteps tend to lead readers to make judgments about characters that lie beyond the bounds of what can be substantiated by their text. The first is illustrated by the question "How many children had Lady Macbeth?" which is used by Lionel Knights to discuss how readers of Shakespeare tend to impute subjectivity to literary and dramatic characters as if they had lives of their own beyond the confines of the text that they inhabit.[3] As Seymour Chatman notes, "Characters do not have 'lives'; we endow them with 'personality' only to the extent that personality is a structure familiar to us in life and art."[4] If readers impose their own experience upon literary figures, treating them as people with complicated psyches, they become vulnerable to a second misstep: treating human nature and human experience as some sort of fixed, unchanging reality. The practitioners of Russian Formalism attempt to evade both of these errors by discussing character simply in terms of function. For example, a formalist would take Orestes' hesitation prior to committing matricide, in Aeschylus's *Choephoroe*, not as a clue to his character but as an instrument of dramatic effect.[5] Limiting the analysis of character to function, however, tends to produce a sort of Proppian universe in which the Gospels, tragedies, and folktales alike are filled with what Wallace Martin describes as "verbal scraps (physical appearance, thoughts, statements, feelings) held loosely together by a proper name."[6] Given that the effect of a play can be to confront its audience with the complexity of human experiences such as death, scholars of the Greek tragedies struggle with this rigid opposition between literature and "real life" and the limitation of character to function.[7] Classicists therefore have come to ask what are the conventions germane or unique to Greek tragedy that represent the dramatic persona as having a subjective existence to which the audience can impute intention or personality

---

[3] L. C. Knights (*How Many Children Had Lady MacBeth? An Essay in the Theory and Practice of Shakespeare Criticism* [Cambridge: Minority Press, 1933]) examines the line of inquiry prompted by Lady Macbeth's line "I have given suck, and know / How tender 'tis to love the babe that milks me" (*Macbeth* 1.7.54).

[4] Seymour Chatman (*Story and Discourse: Narrative Structure in Fiction and Film* [Ithaca, N.Y.: Cornell University Press, 1980], 138) also concedes that denying ourselves this habit "is to deny an absolutely fundamental aesthetic experience."

[5] Example provided by Simon Goldhill, "Character and Action, Representation and Reading: Greek Tragedy and Its Critics," in *Characterization and Individuality in Greek Literature* (ed. Christopher Pelling; Oxford: Clarendon, 1990), 113.

[6] Wallace Martin, *Recent Theories of Narrative* (Ithaca, N.Y.: Cornell University Press, 1986), 18.

[7] P. E. Easterling, "Constructing Character in Greek Tragedy," in Pelling, *Characterization and Individuality,* 90.

and for which it can feel empathy or a desire for identity, and how these conventions work within the action of the play.[8]

In theater, a character is mediated by an actor's performance. The thoughts and wishes that a character expresses through speech are not the actor's thoughts, and the actions do not spring forth from the actor's motivations. As we have noted, method actors try to obscure this fact by reaching into their own memory to call forth their own experiences so that what the audience sees is the real emotions of the actor rather than the emotions of the character that he or she represents. A scandalous example of this, which predates the articulation of the method, occurs in the Charlie Chaplin film *The Kid* (1921), in which the tears of the child are not shed for the Chaplin character but are those of the child actor Jackie Coogan, who was told, moments before the camera began to roll, that if he did not cry, they would shoot his dog. In a more recent film, *Marathon Man* (1976), Dustin Hoffman prepared to depict the suffering of his character by torturing his own body with sleep deprivation, to which his co-star Laurence Olivier commented, "Why don't you try acting, my good man? It's much easier."[9] Greek tragedy, as performed upon the Athenian stage, does not place the same sort of physical demands upon its actors, but it does possess its own conventions for representing the words of an actor as if they proceed out of the subjective consciousness of the character he performs (all Athenian actors were males).

One method of achieving a degree of subjectivity in the construction of a dramatic persona is to give the appearance of an interior life by having the character refer to his or her own thought processes and motivations. Later structuralists, such as A.-J. Greimas and J. Courtès, recognize that the knowledge or ignorance credited to a character is a feature independent of his or her function.[10] Simon Goldhill notes how "the public, masked personae of Athenian tragedy are regularly said to act and claim to act because of their attitudes and states of mind."[11] When a character asks another character what he or she wants and that other character responds, the character appears to have desires and intentions. Goldhill cites an example from *Bacchae:*

---

[8] Christopher Gill ("The Character-Personality Distinction," in Pelling, *Characterization and Individuality,* 2) distinguishes between character, in which a process of decision making is discernable, and personality, that which renders a character empathetic or identifiable.

[9] Olivier recounts this story in an interview, part of which is included in his A&E *Biography.*

[10] Wallace Martin (*Recent Theories of Narrative,* 117) cites A.-J. Greimas and J. Courtès, "The Cognitive Dimension of Narrative Discourse," *New Literary History* 7 (1976): 433–47.

[11] Goldhill, "Character and Action," 114.

DIONYSUS: Do you want to see those women, where they sit together, up on the hills?

PENTHEUS: Why, yes; for that, I'd give a weighty sum of gold.

DIONYSUS: What made you fall into this great desire? (810–812 [Goldhill])

The desire is an epiphenomenon of the statement that desire exists, for the figure can have no such desire nor does the actor possess it.

Such talk of subjective disposition seems natural to the dialogue, and as a result the art is not transparent, but when we attend to the habit of dramatic characters to speak of states of consciousness, we see that the patterns begin to appear repetitive and speech stilted and artificial. The artifice becomes visible when we look at the language of cognition and other interior mental states in the following dialogue, from *Oedipus Tyrannus,* in which Oedipus reveals his suspicions about Creon's treachery:

CREON: *I agree* [ξύμφημί] that what you say is just; but tell me what it is you say I did to you!

OEDIPUS: Did you or did you not *persuade* [ἔπειθες] me that I ought to send someone for the much-revered prophet?

CREON: Yes, *I still stand by the advice* I gave you [καὶ νῦν ἔθ' αὐτός εἰμι τῷ βουλεύματι].

OEDIPUS: How long is it now since Laius . . .

CREON: Did what? *I do not understand* [οὐ γὰρ ἐννοῶ]. . . .

OEDIPUS: How came, it then that this wise man did not tell you this?

CREON: *I do not know* [οὐκ οἶδ']; when *I do not understand* [μὴ φρονῶ], I like to say nothing.

OEDIPUS: But *you know* [οἶσθα] this much, and you would tell me if you were honest.

CREON: What thing? *If I know, I shall not refuse* [εἰ γὰρ οἶδά γ', οὐκ ἀρνήσομαι].

OEDIPUS: That if he had not been in concert with you, he would never have spoken of my killing Laius.

CREON: If he said that, *you must know* [αὐτὸς οἶσθ']; but I claim the right to learn from you as much as you have just claimed to learn from me.

OEDIPUS: You shall learn all you wish: I shall not be proved to be the murderer. . . .

CREON: *Not if you reflect upon the matter as I do* [οὐκ, εἰ διδοίης γ᾽ ὡς ἐγὼ σαυτῷ λόγον]. *Consider first this* [σκέψαι δὲ τοῦτο πρῶτον]. (553–559, 586–576, 583–584 [Lloyd-Jones, LCL]; italics added)

Hardly a line fails to include language suggesting that the characters experience cognitive functions. When we look at a comparable dialogue in the Fourth Gospel between the formerly blind man, his family, and the Pharisees, we begin to appreciate Sophocles' variation of language and technique:

JEWS: Is this your son, who you say was born blind? How then does he now see?

PARENTS: *We know* [οἴδαμεν] that this is our son, and that he was born blind; but *we do not know* [οὐκ οἴδαμεν] how it is that now he sees, *nor do we know* [οὐκ οἴδαμεν] who opened his eyes. Ask him; he is of age. He will speak for himself. . . .

JEWS: Give glory to God! *We know* [οἴδαμεν] that this man is a sinner.

MAN: *I do not know* [οὐκ οἶδα] whether he is a sinner. One thing *I do know* [οἶδα], that though I was blind, now I see.

JEWS: What did he do to you? How did he open your eyes?

MAN: I have told you already, and you would not listen. *Why do you want* [θέλετε] to hear it again? *Do you also want* [θέλετε] to become his disciples?

JEWS: You are his disciple, but we are disciples of Moses. *We know* [οἴδαμεν] that God has spoken to Moses, but as for this man, *we do not know* [οὐκ οἴδαμεν] where he comes from.

MAN: Here is an astonishing thing! *You do not know* [οὐκ οἴδατε] where he comes from, and yet he opened my eyes. *We know* [οἴδαμεν] that God does not listen to sinners, but he does listen to one who worships him and obeys his will. Never since the world began has it been heard that anyone opened the eyes of a person born blind. If this man were not from God, he could do nothing.

JEWS: You are born entirely in sins, and are you trying to teach us? (9:19–21, 24–34; italics added)

The gospel writer is content to use the perfect tense of εἴδω ten times within just a few verses to point to the source of the words within the privacy of the characters' consciousness.[12]

In his analysis of the dialogue with Nicodemus (3:1–21), Robert Kysar notes the prevalent use of the verbs "know" and "believe," verbs referring to the use of the senses, ὁράω and ἀκούω, and reflexive references to speaking.[13] Some of these verbs can be seen within one of Jesus' lines: "*Do not be astonished that I said to you,* 'You must be born from above.' The wind blows where it chooses, and *you hear* the sound of it, but *you do not know* where it comes from" (3:7–8). Kysar's conclusion that "the reader has an auditory experience as a result of the passage"[14] supports my argument that the gospel is intended for audition. It also supports my contention that the audience has an auditory experience of what normally is unheard: the subjective consciousness of another person.

In suggesting that the gospel writer has used the techniques of a dramatist to generate his characters, I anticipate the objection that as the author of a historical narrative, the gospel writer does not create characters. The words representing interior states, such as desire or intent, signify actual referents, the desires or intentions of people who once lived. When Jesus asks the lame man, "Do you want to be made well?" (5:6), the word "want" signifies a desire that the lame man had. Nevertheless, even the reader who believes that the gospel represents historical events ought to acknowledge that the text generates a character that signifies a historical figure. Wallace Martin's explanation of why fictional characters resemble real people can be used to explain the relationship of real people to literary treatments of them:

> I hear verbal reports of the traits and acts of a person who circulates at the edge of my acquaintance. These I piece together with bits of personal observation. From all such fragments, I project a whole: what kind of person is she? A character in fiction of the character of a person in fact is a conjectural configuration. . . . The ultimate reference of fact and fiction is our experience, and it is entirely consistent with experience to say that I understand Huck Finn more or less well than I understand my next door neighbor. Our sense that fictional characters are uncannily similar to people is therefore not something to be dismissed or ridiculed but a crucial feature of narration that requires explanation.[15]

---

[12] Matthew uses the perfect form of εἴδω sixteen times in direct speech, compared with fifty-four such occurrences in the Fourth Gospel.

[13] Robert Kysar, *John's Story of Jesus* (Philadelphia: Fortress, 1984), 33. The list is: οἶδα (3x), θαυμάζω (2x), γινώσκω (1x), πιστεύω (7x), ὁράω (2x), ἀκούω (8x).

[14] Ibid.

[15] Martin, *Recent Theories of Narrative*, 120.

The bits of information provided about a historical figure in a literary piece are fragments that suggest the totality of a person. If we take, for example, Jesus' lines that point to desire, "Give me a drink" (4:7) and "I am thirsty" (19:28), we can see how the gospel writer has provided Jesus with subjectivity to counterbalance the objectification of Jesus in sayings such as "I am the living water." Without language such as this that grounds Jesus in the realm of human experience, he would be Ernst Käsemann's "Son of God walking through the world of man," for whom the trappings of a human life are simply a costume in which his "heavenly glory" is clothed while on earth.[16]

The representation of characters as people with interior lives raises the hermeneutical question "What can we know of them?" Seymour Chatman, whom I cited earlier as one who acknowledges that if characters have personalities, it is we the readers who endow them, presents an "open theory of character," which allows characters totality, mental traits, and uniqueness, and acknowledges that different readers will respond to the potentials evoked by what we find written on the page by constructing personalities. To stop short of drawing inferences about these characters in order to live up to some positivist demand for verification is, for Chatman, a denial of "an absolutely fundamental aesthetic experience." He tries to satisfy the demand of psychological validity by the use of quotation marks: "Iago is 'cold,' not cold."[17] Jacques Lacan, a poststructuralist, finds room for psychoanalysis of characters in the gap that this language of cognition opens up between the demands that the character makes and his or her needs, between "unconscious and conscious," and between "the self of experience and the verbal 'I.'"[18] These gaps allow us to experience and access the workings of desire, but is it the character's psyche or our own that lies on the analyst's couch? Rather than pursue interpretations of the tragedies that hinge upon speculation about personality traits and motives, many classicists recognize the wisdom of John Jones's insight that the discussion of characterization ought not overshadow the discussion of action.[19] Characters' words articulate the drama by representing human activity and experience, particularly that of suffering, rather

---

[16] Ernst Käsemann, *The Testament of Jesus: A Study of the Gospel of John in the Light of Chapter 17* (trans. Gerhard Krodel; Philadelphia: Fortress, 1968), 8–10.

[17] Chatman, *Story and Discourse,* 119–38.

[18] These pairings appear in Martin, *Recent Theories of Narrative,* 121, in his description of Lacan.

[19] John Jones, *On Aristotle and Greek Thought* (London: Chatto & Windus, 1962); cited in P. E. Easterling, "Presentation of Character in Aeschylus," in *Greek Tragedy* (ed. Ian McAuslan and Peter Walcot; Oxford: Oxford University Press, 1993), 13.

than conveying some inner consciousness of hidden desires or repressed emotions. Characters act; they do not behave.

In part because of the centrality of individual and collective voices in the Fourth Gospel and in part because of the surprising activity of its characters (such as Jesus' mother's participation in the miracle at Cana, Pilate's attempts to free Jesus, and Nicodemus's presence at Jesus' burial), scholarly, clerical, and lay readers of every ilk have imputed to its characters motives based upon constructed personalities. Depending upon the reader, Pilate can be weak and vacillating, or honest and well disposed, or strong and calculating.[20] Nicodemus is without faith, or a man of secret faith, or on a trajectory toward open discipleship.[21] Even the Johannine narrator cannot resist explaining the reason for some characters' actions. He tells us why the formerly blind man's parents are afraid to speak, and why Judas reproaches Mary for anointing Jesus, as though he had access to their subjective, private consciousness. Some scholars, such as Raymond Brown, have treated the gospel's cast of characters as representatives of larger groups in the world of the Johannine community. The characters then remain figures without consciousness or personality, but behind them stand real people with a particular mind-set and habits of behavior. According to Brown, the parents of the man born blind represent "Crypto-Christians" who privately believe in Jesus but in public profess to be disciples of Moses.[22] The disaffected disciples of John 6:66 represent members of "the Jewish Christian Churches of inadequate faith" who do not share the same view of the Eucharist held by members of the Johannine community.[23] In the following discussion of Johannine characters, the quest for personality will be set aside in favor of the analysis of the relationship of character to action. Given the centrality of direct speech in the Fourth Gospel, it should come as no surprise that many of the conventions of characterization found in the tragedies also appear in the gospel. Acknowledgment of their presence weighs against conclusions about the personalities of individual characters and focuses attention upon the representation of action.

---

[20] See Helen K. Bond's survey in *Pontius Pilate in History and Interpretation* (SNTSMS 100; Cambridge: Cambridge University Press, 1998), 174.

[21] Winsome Munro surveys negative appraisals of Nicodemus and offers his own, more generous, appraisal in "The Pharisee and the Samaritan in John: Polar or Parallel?" *CBQ* 57 (1995): 710–28.

[22] Raymond E. Brown, *The Community of the Beloved Disciple: The Life, Loves, and Hates of an Individual Church in New Testament Times* (New York: Paulist Press, 1979), 72.

[23] Ibid., 73–74.

Jesus' Identity: What's in a Name?

Scholarly discussion about Jesus in the Fourth Gospel tends to focus on the gospel's Christology and its origins rather than characterization. From where do the titles and the notion of Jesus' preexistence or divine coexistence derive? Is the source some incipient form of Gnosticism or Mandeanism?[24] Is this a development of the Jewish wisdom tradition or some common Jewish eschatological tradition?[25] Do Christian sectarian debates drive the members of the Johannine community to a more radical expression of their Christology?[26] Frequently, when the portrayal of Jesus is discussed, the underlying issue seems to be whether the Christology matches up with the orthodoxy of the verdicts of the Councils of Nicea (325 C.E.) or Chalcedon (451 C.E.), with Ernst Käsemann casting a nay vote in favor of a naively docetic Christology, and Marianne Thompson casting a yea vote by marshaling evidence of Jesus' full humanity (he has flesh and his signs are material) while acknowledging that the gospel affirms Jesus' divinity.[27] In his seminal work on the literary structures of the Fourth Gospel, R. Alan Culpepper discusses Jesus' role as the Logos, his relationship to "the Father," and how Jesus' "I am" statements point to a higher reality. In his analysis of those things typically central to notions of personality—Jesus' limited emotions, lack of reference to his compassion, the absence of children to draw out a tender side—Culpepper suspects that characterization is subordinate to Christology: Jesus is "not of this world" (8:23; 17:14).[28]

In the following analysis, Jesus' identity will be treated not as a reflection of the Christology of the gospel but as a facet of dramatic action.

---

[24] See Rudolf Bultmann, "Die Bedeutung der neuerschlossenen mandäischen und manichäischen Quellen für das Verständnis des Johannesevangeliums," *ZNW* 24 (1925): 100–146; G. W. MacRae, "The Ego-Proclamation in Gnostic Sources," in *The Trial of Jesus* (ed. Ernst Bammel; SBT 2.13; London: SCM, 1970), 129–34.

[25] Regarding wisdom, see Martin Scott, *Sophia and the Johannine Jesus* (JSNTSup 71; Sheffield: JSOT Press, 1992).

[26] See James A. McGrath, *John's Apologetic Christology: Legitimation and Development in Johannine Christology* (SNTSMS 111; Cambridge: Cambridge University Press, 2001).

[27] Käsemann, *The Testament of Jesus*, 26; Marianne Meye Thompson, *The Humanity of Jesus in the Fourth Gospel* (Philadelphia: Fortress, 1988).

[28] R. Alan Culpepper, *Anatomy of the Fourth Gospel: A Study in Literary Design* (FF; Philadelphia: Fortress, 1983), 106–12. See also J. A. du Rand, "The Characterization of Jesus as Depicted in the Narrative of the Fourth Gospel," *Neot* 19 (1985): 30.

Whereas the Jesus of the Synoptic Gospels talks about the kingdom of heaven, the Johannine Jesus talks about himself. Given that Jesus makes explicit claims about his identity, one would expect to have a sense of who Jesus is, but this is precisely the question with which the characters of the gospel contend. Jesus resembles those tragic heroes whose assertions about their own identity and extraordinary claims set them above the realm of ordinary human experience and who incite animosity and efforts to bring them down to human size by those who question their identity.

The Greek tragedians take the theatrical necessity of having characters identify themselves and each other and turn it into a feature of the plot whereby one character seeks to assert his or her own identity and others dispute it or puzzle over who that person really is. Who is a friend and who is an enemy? Who is a stranger and who is kin? Many plays end with realignment or recognition of friendships and relationships in the aftermath of *pathos*. For example, at the beginning of Euripides' *Heracles*, the son of Zeus proves his divine origin by returning from his labors as the savior who, in his own words, takes his family like "tow boats in hand and like a ship drag[s] them" to safety (631 [Kovacs, LCL]). In his absence, they have been threatened with murder by Lycus, who has killed Creon, king of Thebes and father of Heracles' wife, Megara, and who believes that Heracles lies dead in Hades and that Amphitryon has fabricated the story about Zeus lying with his wife. M. S. Silk, in his study of how tragic language makes use of names and titles, notes the paradox within tragedy in which the name—the mark of recognition that society places upon its members—becomes a mark of isolation from that society.[29] Heracles' identity as the son of Zeus alienates him from human society and his own family (how can Amphitryon be his father if Zeus is his father?), and his hubris makes him vulnerable to the vicissitudes of divine jealousy. After he rescues his family, Hera continues her jealous pursuit by inflicting a madness upon him in which he murders his wife and children. Coming to his senses, Heracles contemplates suicide as the consequence of his ignominy, until Theseus demonstrates his friendship by caring for the fallen hero, an act in which Heracles compares himself to "a boat under tow" (1424) and declares, "Whoever desires to get wealth or strength rather than good friends is a fool" (1425). The play ends with Heracles promising to provide the service of burying Amphitryon as any son does for his father, a service in contrast to the heroic deeds that mark his former role as son of Zeus. A similar path can be charted through the Fourth Gospel. Jesus' assertion of

---

[29] M. S. Silk, "Tragic Language: The Greek Tragedians and Shakespeare," in *Tragedy and the Tragic: Greek Theatre and Beyond* (ed. M. S. Silk; Oxford: Clarendon, 1996), 470.

his identity alienates him from his society: he claims the power to name himself, and he rejects the ability of others to name him. His assertions render his identity ambiguous rather than known. Other characters take his self-assertions to be the sort of hubris that renders him God's rival, and like other tragic heroes who are lifted up too high to live among humankind, Jesus must die. Death and suffering are the great levelers of heroes and ordinary people by which *communitas* is reestablished.

Before proceeding with the particular aspects of Jesus' identity, I want to present one other character from the tragic canon to illustrate Silk's point that "the name" becomes a linguistic expression of a character who is "too self-assertive," who goes "too far," and thus necessitates *pathos*.[30] In *Antigone,* Antigone asserts her identity as the sister of the dead Polynices to the exclusion of all other relationships with the living, and in doing so she pronounces her own allegiance to death: "I am his own and I shall lie with him who is my own" (73–74 [Lloyd-Jones, LCL]). The social order, living family members, and political powers have no authority to name her. Antigone's self identification as Polynices' sister comes in conflict with Creon's identification of her as woman and subject. When Antigone is brought before Creon to defend herself for burying Polynices against the king's orders that his body be left unattended, Creon sees her insistence that she acts as a sister as a violation of her role as his subject and a threat to his power. Her bold confession, "I say that I did it and I do not deny it. . . . I knew it [the law]; of course I knew it. . . . It was known to all" (443–448), is received by Creon as an affront: "Indeed, now I am no man, but she is a man, if she is to enjoy such power as this with impunity" (484–485). Her hubris makes her his rival. In Antigone's description of her actions, she consistently refers to Polynices as her brother or kin, while Creon attempts to get her to call him an enemy of the state. She ends his efforts by stating, "I have no enemies by birth, but I have friends by birth" (523), to which Creon replies, "Then go below and love those friends, if you must love them! But while I live, a woman shall not rule!" (524–525). Antigone then treats her death not as the ultimate alienation from human society but as a marriage that unites her with her mother, father, and brother (891–899). Creon's attempts to bolster the legitimacy of his rule create the conditions in which being a sister and being a citizen have become irreconcilable identities. Although Jesus' conflict with various groups of Jews relies upon a transcendent rather than a social or political reality, his allegiance to a kingdom not of this world rather than the world in which he dwells makes his continued residence there as untenable as that of Antigone in Creon's kingdom.

---

[30] Ibid., 465.

The language of identity occupies a conspicuous position in the gospel. The more that Jesus clarifies his identity, the more he makes himself the subject and the object of all action, and the more those around him distance themselves from him. The irony of Jesus' saying "Everything that the Father gives me will come to me, and anyone who comes to me I will never drive away" (6:37) is that most of those who come to him find this talk of "I" and "me" too much to take and are repulsed by it. Insistence that people believe in his name—society's mark of recognition—paradoxically disembodies or dehumanizes Jesus, rendering him alien to that society. Jesus' language for himself—"I am the light of the world," "I am the living water," "I am the bread of life," "I am the way, and the truth, and the life," "I am the resurrection"—distances him from a recognizable name. Moreover, Jesus identifies himself as the "Son of Man" (1:51; 3:13, 14; 5:27; 6:27, 53, 62; 8:28; 12:23, 34; 13:31), a title that the crowd seems not to recognize and a term that seems not to be a confessional title for any of the Jews in the gospel.[31] Efforts to uncover an expected eschatological figure, the Son of Man, in the pre-Christian Jewish literature have turned up nothing conclusive.[32] In effect, Jesus chooses a name that is no name. According to Valentin Voloshinov, words serve as a bridge between oneself and another that give shape to self through another's point of view, but language that describes the I-experience relinquishes social orientation and the potential for apprehension.[33] By describing himself with language that is highly egocentric and asocial, Jesus sets himself apart from familiar and socially intimate relationships and defies identification within the familial and political structures of his society.

Other than John the Baptist, who calls Jesus "the lamb of God," no one in the gospel uses language for Jesus that is so devoid of clear reference to human relationships. One of the principal signs of the individuality of a character is the way that other characters assign him or her a standing within the dramatic world through the use of names and personal or social properties.[34] When the priest addresses Oedipus in the opening of *Oedipus Tyrannus*, he marks his suppliant relationship to the king by adding titles to

---

[31] Frank J. Matera (*New Testament Christology* [Louisville: Westminster John Knox, 1999], 232–33) points to the absence of the term "Son of Man" in any of the confessions and to the fact that the crowd has to ask who this Son of Man is (12:34).

[32] See Delbert R. Burkett, *The Son of the Man in the Gospel of John* (JSNTSup 56; Sheffield: JSOT Press, 1991), 173.

[33] Valentin N. Voloshinov, *Marxism and the Philosophy of Language* (trans. L. Matejka and I. R. Titunik; Cambridge: Harvard University Press, 1986), 88.

[34] Philippe Hamon, "Pour un statut sémiologique du personnage," in *Poétique du récit* (ed. Gérard Genette and Tzvetan Todorov; Paris: Seuil, 1977), 124–25; cited in Elam, *Semiotics of Theatre and Drama*, 132.

Oedipus's name such as "ruler of my land," "mightiest man in the sight of all," and "best of living men" (14–46 [Lloyd-Jones, LCL]). In the exchange between Oedipus and the messenger, the messenger's use of ὦ παῖ ("My son"; 1008) to address the king seems inappropriately familiar until we learn that he is the one who found the infant Oedipus and gave him to Phoebus. In the Fourth Gospel, the secondary characters tend to apply names and titles to Jesus that give him distinction or isolate him within their own social context: prophet, rabbi, Messiah, a teacher who has come from God, a Samaritan with a demon. Naming is used also in attempts to deny this distinctiveness: Jesus is from Nazareth, the son of Joseph, a man. The crowd in the bread-of-life discourse begins by addressing Jesus as "Rabbi," and the Jews end by referring to him in the third person as "this man" (6:25, 52). Jesus rejects the ability of others to name him and asserts his own power of self-identification. He is not the lamb of God but the shepherd who lays down his life. Those who follow him participate unwittingly in this naming game and become the victims of irony. When Jesus proclaims, "I am the resurrection and the life" (11:25)—an allusion to his departure from the world—Martha proclaims him "the one coming into the world" (11:27). Characters persistently try to orient Jesus to their world, whereas Jesus removes himself from the world.

In the Greek tragedies, the name of the protagonist frequently becomes more than a proper name; it is a sign of his tragic identity. Ajax, in a speech in which he describes himself as persona non grata, a noble man without honor, turns his name (Αἴας) into a manifestation of his suffering: "Alas! [Αἰαῖ] Who ever would have thought that my name would come to harmonize with my sorrows? For now I can say 'Alas' a second time" (Euripides, *Aj.* 430–431 [Lloyd-Jones, LCL]). In *Prometheus Bound*, Strength attempts to separate Prometheus's identity from his name by taking its meaning literally: "Falsely the gods call you Prometheus [Προμηθέα], for you yourself need forethought [προμηθέως] to free yourself from this handiwork!" (85 [Vellacott]). Hermes later plays with Prometheus's name by calling him "the mastermind" to indict him for his crimes against Zeus (943). The key to Oedipus's true identity is found in the dissection of his own name. Oedipus is the man with the swollen foot (οἰδέω πούς) that marks him as the child rejected by Laius and Iocaste, and he is Oedipus, who knows (οἶδα) the riddle of the foot (πούς) posed by the Sphinx and in the end proves to be the embodiment of that riddle, the man who confuses generations by being the husband to his mother and the father to his siblings.[35] His name reveals him to be the

---

[35] See Jean-Pierre Vernant, "Ambiguity and Reversal: On the Enigmatic Structure of Oedipus Rex," in *Myth and Tragedy in Ancient Greece* (ed. Jean-Pierre Vernant and Pierre Vidal-Naquet; trans. P. du Bois; New York: Zone Books, 1988), 116.

murderer of Laius and the pollution that curses the city. In all these cases, a person's name becomes more than something bestowed by the community for convenience; it is an extension of the self. In the gospel, this fusion of name and identity is nowhere clearer than in the claim that those who believe in Jesus' name become children of God (1:12). The only way to broach the social isolation generated by Jesus' self-naming is to acknowledge that he is in fact what he calls himself and to concede that he, not the world, identifies himself.

By ignoring the context in which Jesus proclaims his identity, we limit these self-referential statements to the category of christological assertions: Jesus is the bread of life, the light of the world, the way and the truth and the life, the resurrection and the life, and so on.[36] In his study of the "I am" sayings, David Mark Ball argues that the quest for antecedents ignores how these sayings function within their setting in either the dialogues or the entire gospel to portray Jesus as its dominant character.[37] For example, Jesus' insistence upon his coidentity with God, "My Father is still working, and I also am working" (5:17), removes him from ordinary society, which includes those, like the lame man, who break the Sabbath. The Jews seek communion with Jesus until he proclaims, "I am the bread of life" (6:35). Jesus' language calls for his own demise on three levels: metaphorically as an object to be consumed, dramatically as various characters reject him, and theatrically insofar as the audience recognizes that Jesus' language signifies his relationship with a transcendent reality to which he will return.[38]

In the Greek tragedies, characters often hide their identity or the identity of others within the drama while the audience enjoys the irony of the references. In *Alcestis*, Euripides constructs a dialogue with Heracles in which

---

[36] Whether the ἐγώ εἰμι in such statements (6:35, 48, 51; 8:12; 10:7, 9, 11, 14; 11:25; 14:6; 15:1, 5) or those without attributes (4:26; 6:20; 8:24, 28, 58; 13:19; 18:5, 6, 8) ought to be taken as allusions to Exod 3:14, and the use of ἐγώ εἰμι by itself signifies a blasphemous statement, remains a matter of debate. I tend to side, on the whole, with Kenneth L. McKay's emphasis upon the normality of the Greek in all such passages ("'I Am' in John's Gospel," *ExpTim* 107 [1996]: 302–3).

[37] David Mark Ball, *"I Am" in John's Gospel: Literary Function, Background, and Theological Implications* (JSNTSup 124; Sheffield: Sheffield Academic Press, 1996), 256.

[38] Adele Reinhartz (*The Word in the World: The Cosmological Tale in the Fourth Gospel* [SBLMS 45; Atlanta: Scholars Press, 1992], 34–35) situates the "I am" language within the cosmological tale. Her analysis of the generation of the cosmological tale can be adapted to my purposes in that it shows how Jesus' speech generates the dramatic space of the story.

Admetus obscures the fact that his wife, Alcestis, is the object of his mourning. Later in the play, Heracles plays at the same game by withholding the identity of Admetus's future wife, once more Alcestis, whom Heracles has delivered from Hades. In *Bacchae,* in the dialogue in which Pentheus interrogates the disguised Dionysus about the Bacchanalia, the god speaks in much the same manner as Jesus. As Jean-Pierre Vernant puts it, "The gods know and speak the truth but they make it manifest by formulating it in words that appear to men to be saying something quite different."[39] When Pentheus orders his guards to apprehend Dionysus, the god warns,

> You do not know what your life is, or what you are doing, or who you are . . . I am willing to go. For what I should not suffer, I shall not. But be sure that Dionysus will exact punishment for this violence—the god you say does not exit. For in wronging me, you put him in chains. (506–518 [Morwood])

His use of the third person hides his identity as the god.

In the Fourth Gospel, Jesus' proclivity for speaking of himself in indirect terms serves the dramatic purpose of frustrating others' identification of him. When he states, "Destroy this temple, and in three days I will raise it up" (2:19), the audience, even without the narrator's assistance, ought to guess that he means himself, while the Jews ought to have no idea that he means anything other than the temple. Nicodemus begins his first conversation by referring to Jesus' identity as a teacher from God. By the end of the dialogue, after Jesus has questioned his capacity for understanding, the indirect references to Jesus' identity as the Son of Man and God's Son ought to be lost on him. The fact that the audience knows that Jesus is referring to himself leads many commentators to conclude that Jesus no longer addresses Nicodemus but the reader. The gospel writer exploits the subjectivity of intent by producing ambiguity on the dramatic axis and irony on the theatrical axis. Characters find Jesus obscure and oblique, while the audience is privileged and understands Jesus' intent much more clearly. Nevertheless, this Jesus is far from opaque. Though the audience is taken toward some sort of knowledge of Jesus, it continues to experience the inaccessibility of his interior life. Mark Stibbe lays out the abstruseness of the narrator's portrayal of Jesus, beginning with the fact that the Word is not identified as Jesus until verse 17 of the prologue and including how the narrator gives only "occasional, fragmented and laconic glimpses" into "Jesus' thoughts, motives and attitudes."[40] Stibbe finds that Jesus is as abstruse in his speech and action as

---

[39] Vernant, "Ambiguity and Reversal," 117.
[40] Mark W. G. Stibbe, *John's Gospel* (New Testament Readings; London: Routledge, 1994), 9, 11.

the narrator is in his comment, as though Jesus were "a kind of first-century 'Scarlet Pimpernel.'"[41]

Although the Greek tragedies provide us with no character quite like Jesus, who proclaims himself to be the bread of life or the light of the world, we can find similarities in the way that excessive self-identification produces friction. Names tend to signify hubris. When Ajax, realizing that he has killed animals rather than his enemies, calls for his own death as a remedy for his humiliation, he measures the injury to his pride by giving himself titles: "Do you see that I, the bold, the valiant, the one who never trembled in battle among enemies, have done mighty deeds among beasts that frightened no one? Ah, the mockery! What an insult I have suffered!" (Sophocles, *Aj.* 364–367 [Lloyd-Jones, LCL]). When Oedipus declares, "No, it was I that came, Oedipus who knew nothing, and put a stop to her [the Sphinx]" (Sophocles, *Oed. tyr.* 397–398 [Lloyd-Jones, LCL]), the ambiguity and paradox of his name is fully exploited, and the audience recognizes the irony in his boast, for indeed he knows nothing. When the chorus asks Prometheus what he has done to be punished by Zeus, his speech not only describes his deeds, but also makes clear his arrogance through the repeated use of first-person pronouns: "I caused men no longer to foresee their death. . . . I planted firmly in their hearts blind hopefulness. . . . I did more than that: I gave them fire" (Aeschylus, *Prom.* 250–254 [Vellacott]). Hermes provides a contrasting view of Prometheus's nobility by calling him "the thief of fire" (945). When Prometheus resists subordinating himself to Zeus's authority and invites him to assail him with whatever weapons he has by proclaiming, "I am one whom he cannot kill" (1052), Hermes remarks, "Thoughts and words like these are what one may hear from lunatics" (1054–1055). Similarly, Jesus' insistence upon self-declarations of power signifies hubris or even lunacy on the dramatic axis. The Samaritan woman is one of the few characters who respond positively to Jesus' speech, when she says, "He told me everything I have ever done" (4:39), and the temple police correctly note, "Never has anyone spoken like this!" (7:46), but the most frequent response is to discount his assertions as preposterous, the ranting of one demon-possessed (7:20; 8:48, 10:20) or blasphemous (10:33; 19:7). Jesus' repeated claim to seek God's glory rather than his own (7:18; 8:54) answers the unstated but perhaps implicit objection of his opponents that he is glorifying himself.

Jesus' assertions of his own elevated status provoke others to draw a series of comparisons challenging his identity. As the dramatic tension increases, so too does the status of the person with whom Jesus is compared.

---

41 Ibid., 31.

The Baptist and his disciples mark the beginning of the progression: "[He is] the one who is coming after me; I am not worthy to untie the thong of his sandal" (1:27); "Rabbi, the one who was with you across the Jordan, to whom you testified, here he is baptizing, and all are going to him" (3:26). The Samaritan woman asks, "Are you greater than our ancestor Jacob, who gave us the well . . . ?" (4:12). The Jews ask, "Are you greater than our father Abraham, who died?" (8:53). When they take up stones to kill him, they charge, "you, though only a human being, are making yourself God" (10:33). They treat his utterance as unspeakable blasphemy, a capital offense, and call for a physical death to mirror the social death he has already pronounced. Caiaphas's ironic prophecy, "it is better for you to have one man die for the people than to have the whole nation destroyed" (11:50), signifies the final ascent of Jesus to a stature that marks him for death; the world goes after Jesus, so Jesus must die. The high priest may be alluding to the Deuteronomic laws against the enticer (Deut 13:6–11), or he may be describing a political necessity in the world of Roman occupation; in either case, those who proclaim Jesus king or Messiah place him too high above mortals to dwell among them, and send him on the same trajectory toward death as those who call him possessed and a sinner.

Eric Auerbach draws a distinction between the *stasis* of Odysseus, in Homer's *Odyssey,* who "on his return is exactly the same as he was when he left Ithaca two decades earlier," and the dynamic nature of biblical characters whom he describes as "fraught with their development."[42] The development of characters in Greek tragedy is a matter of relationship rather than personality. Michael Hinden describes a movement from estrangement to intimacy:

> In Greek tragedy the protagonist typically is brought, at painful cost, toward a condition of spiritual intimacy with a dramatic community from which earlier he has been estranged. . . . Through assertive action, the protagonist undoes a spiritual bond with the community, which needs to be reestablished before the tensions aroused during the course of the action can be resolved.[43]

In general, I resist such totalizing plot summaries for all of Greek tragedy, but Hinden's pattern fits the Fourth Gospel. Hinden argues, "In tragedy, the hero may be said to absorb that very evil that he seeks to extirpate in others."[44] Although Jesus comes to make God known and to create intimacy with God, he is himself distant and unknowable. If alienation is the communal evil,

---

[42] Eric Auerbach, *Mimesis: The Representation of Reality in Western Literature* (trans. Willard R. Trask; Princeton, N.J.: Princeton University Press, 1953), 16–17.

[43] Michael Hinden, "Drama and Ritual Once Again: Notes toward a Revival of Tragic Theory," *Comparative Drama* 29 (1995): 188.

[44] Ibid., 190.

then Jesus embodies alienation. The action of the gospel until the crucifixion is a movement toward estrangement that is overcome by the death of Jesus, a death that facilitates his resurrection and allows him to abide with his friends. The act of death signifies the act of friendship. After the resurrection, Jesus becomes more human; insofar as he stands in a relationship with other characters, he becomes a social being.

This transformation is reflected in the difference in Jesus' language before and after the passion. The shepherd who knows his sheep by name rarely uses their names prior to his death. The one exception occurs in the "call of the disciples." Jesus says to Simon, "You are Simon son of John. You are to be called Cephas" (1:42). The parallel tradition in Matthew presents a more personable Jesus: "Blessed are you, Simon son of Jonah! For flesh and blood has not revealed this to you, but my Father in heaven. And I tell you, you are Peter, and on this rock I will build my church, and the gates of Hades will not prevail against it" (Matt 16:17–18). In the Fourth Gospel, Jesus greets Nathanael in the third person, "Here is truly an Israelite in whom there is no deceit!" (1:47), and he calls his mother "woman" (2:4).[45] Although Jesus' address to his mother perhaps was not as rude as it may seem to my contemporary readers, it does fit into the pattern of impersonal speech that runs through the first twelve chapters of the gospel. Jesus simply addresses others as "you" or forgoes pronouns altogether by using imperatives, as in, for example, "Give me a drink" (4:7). In the Synoptic Gospels, Jesus' speech is also quite formal, but it is interrupted by terms of intimacy, such as calling the woman who has had a hemorrhage for twelve years "daughter" (Matt 9:22) or addressing Judas as "friend" at his arrest (Matt 26:50).[46]

In the Synoptic Gospels, Jesus is put to death ostensibly for fear that the crowd would make him king. In the Fourth Gospel, the crowd does try to make him king, and he puts them off. The movement is not toward community. The disciples do not go off on a mission to harvest the wheat of the kingdom. Jesus is brought to trial for making himself a god, for setting him-

---

[45] Jesus' use of "woman" rather than "mother" (2:4; 19:26) and the Johannine author's use of epithets rather than the name "Mary" have led to discussions about the possible role of Jesus' mother in the Fourth Gospel as a symbol for the church or Jewish Christianity. Troy W. Martin ("Assessing the Johannine Epithet 'The Mother of Jesus,'" *CBQ* 60 [1998)] 63–73) reviews much of this discussion and rejects it, arguing that the epithet "mother of . . ." was neither uncommon or unusual in its time. Martin agrees with C. K. Barrett that Mary is to be taken as a historical person rather than as an allegorical figure.

[46] See also Matt 9:2; Mark 2:5; 5:34, 41; 10:24; Luke 7:14; 8:48, 54; 12:32; 23:28.

self apart from humanity, and when this charge fails to convict, the priests return to the charge of sedition.

Jesus' transition in the Fourth Gospel from remoteness to the one who abides in the believer begins in the Farewell Discourse when he washes the feet of his disciples and describes his relationship to them as a model of service (13:3–20). As the discourse proceeds, he uses a term of endearment, "little children" (13:33), and commands the disciples to love each other as he has loved them (13:34). Mutual affection rather than belief is the defining characteristic of discipleship. He offers them words of comfort, promising that he will not leave them "orphaned" (14:18) and encouraging them not to be troubled or afraid (14:27). After affirmations of his and God's love and admonishments to them to love each other, he characterizes his death as an act of friendship (15:13). Raymond Brown describes the progression as the arc of a pendulum: the first twelve chapters are its descent, and chapter 13 marks the beginning of the upswing.[47] This change in Jesus' orientation toward other characters continues on the cross, where he seems to enact an adoption in which the Beloved Disciple becomes Jesus' mother's son (19:26–27). In the recognition scene at the tomb, Jesus calls Mary by name (20:16). When he enters the house, he uses benedictions repeatedly, greeting the disciples with, "Peace be with you" (20:19, 21, 26), and ending his encounter with Thomas by saying, "Blessed are those who have not seen and yet have come to believe" (20:29). When he calls to the disciples in the boat, he says, "Children, you have no fish, have you?" (21:5), and invites them, "Come and have breakfast" (21:12) Finally, in his dialogue with Simon Peter, he addresses him by the name "Simon son of John" three times (21:15–17). Jeffrey Staley calls this a movement from the abstract to the personal, as though people are more real to Jesus after he has died than before.[48] Paradoxically, the gospel ends with a much more accessible and human Jesus as a result of his having died.

In his discussion of the resurrection scenes, Andrew Lincoln recalls Rudolf Bultmann's suggestion that this section answers these questions: "Can the disciples still love him, when he is gone? Can the next generation love him, without having had a personal relationship with him?"[49] Lincoln flips these questions around: "Can he still love us when he is gone? Can the next

---

[47] Raymond E. Brown, *The Gospel according to John* (2 vols.; AB 29, 29A; Garden City, N.Y.: Doubleday, 1966–1970), 1:541.

[48] Jeffrey L. Staley, *The Print's First Kiss: A Rhetorical Investigation of the Implied Reader in the Fourth Gospel* (SBLDS 82; Atlanta: Scholars Press, 1988), 69.

[49] Andrew T. Lincoln, *Truth on Trial: The Lawsuit Motif in the Fourth Gospel* (Peabody, Mass.: Hendrickson, 2000), 300; Rudolf Bultmann, *The Gospel of John* (trans. G. R. Beasley-Murray; Philadelphia: Westminster, 1971), 613.

generation still experience his love when he is absent?"[50] If the resurrection scenes answer these questions, they seem to say that Jesus can love the postresurrection community because he has died, that the painful death is in fact Jesus' initiation into the community. Jesus' words "I, when I am lifted up from the earth, will draw all people to myself" (12:32) prove true on the dramatic axis and the theatrical axis.

The Jews as the Corporate Voice of Deliberation

In the Fourth Gospel, the most speaking lines, after those of Jesus, are given to a corporate voice identified by the narrator as "the Jews." From time to time, a smaller group breaks off from the larger collective to speak as leaders or representatives, or the group bifurcates into disputing factions. In the dialogue with John the Baptist, the Jews send a delegation of priests and Levites; in the bread-of-life discourse, the group is identified as "the crowd" out of which the Jews seem to emerge as leaders or a separate entity; at the Festival of Booths, the Pharisees seem to emerge as a faction. The gospel writer is not always careful to identify which aspect of this corporate identity is engaged in the dialogue, and it is impossible to distinguish Pharisees from Levites and priests and Jews in general on the basis of the content of their speech.[51] John's disciples, the Samaritans, Jesus' brothers, and his disciples, including those who are disaffected (6:60–66) and whose identity submerges back into that of the Jews, speak as a group. In Johannine scholarship, the question of the actual identity of groups of characters whom the narrator treats corporately, in particular those identified as "the Jews," has become the focus of historical and post-Holocaust criticism. When the gospel writer speaks about "the Jews," to whom is he referring? Does the indiscriminating representation of them as hostile to Jesus and Jesus' invectives against them amount to a slur against Judaism? If so, James Dunn asks, "Which Judaism? Whose Judaism?"[52] As I have argued in the discussion of the *agōn*, it is possible to account for the passion of these debates as the product of genre con-

---

[50] Lincoln, *Truth on Trial,* 300.

[51] For example, is the referent in 8:31 the same as in 8:59?

[52] James D. G. Dunn, "The Embarrassment of History: Reflections on the Problem of 'Anti-Judaism' in the Fourth Gospel," in *Anti-Judaism and the Fourth Gospel* (ed. R. Bieringer, D. Pollefeyt, and F. Vandecasteele-Vanneuville; Louisville: Westminster John Knox, 2001), 45.

ventions. In the following discussion, I will make a similar case for the
ambiguity of the corporate voice of the Jews by setting aside questions of
identity to look at how the Fourth Evangelist manages their voice in a
manner comparable to the Greek tragedians' use of the chorus.

On the Athenian stage, actors are seldom alone. The play opens with
the *parodos* (πάροδος), the procession of the chorus into the *orchēstra*
(ὀρχήστρα), and closes with the *exodos* (ἔξοδος), its corporate exit. Exceptions to this convention are reserved for important transitions, such as the
movement of action in *Eumenides* from Delphi to Athens, whereby Orestes
returns to the stage followed by the chorus in the role of the Furies in hot
pursuit.[53] While onstage, the chorus employs lyrics and dance that punctuate
the action and translate it into movement or music.[54] In its early manifestation, the chorus seems to have narrated the action, but with the advent of actors, it continues providing information but also participates in the action by
taking on different roles required by the plot; however, its anonymous collective experience stands in contrast to that of the tragic hero, who insists
upon his or her individual identity, name, and lineage.[55] The principal actors
engage in dialogue with the chorus, but the chorus's part usually is limited to
asking questions, imploring, warning, or rejecting suggestions. It never
makes a set of speeches or an argument; consequently, it cannot be a full partner in an *agōn*.[56] For the most part, the chorus is a spectator upon the stage, a
silent witness or observer of the action, whose role as such is to make sense of
what it sees by deliberating about its possible significance. The unity of the
chorus is fractured by its banter about the ambiguity of what it witnesses. By
virtue of its collective character, it can represent confusion and thereby dramatize the ambiguity of the human predicament: the chorus can be physi-
cally seen either not to know its own mind or to be of two minds. The chorus
offers the audience, sitting on high and in possession of hindsight's clarity or
privy to ironic truth, alternative ways of seeing the action from the perspective of one standing before the *skēnē* or in the *orchēstra*.[57]

The chorus in *Oedipus Tyrannus* takes the role of pious citizens of
Thebes who are loyal to Oedipus's reign. After witnessing the debate between

---

[53] Peter D. Arnott, *Public and Performance in the Greek Theatre* (London:
Routledge, 1989), 26.

[54] Ibid., 28.

[55] John Gould, "Tragedy and Collective Experience," in Silk, *Tragedy and the
Tragic*, 222.

[56] See A. M. Dale, "The Chorus in the Action of Greek Tragedy," in *Classical
Drama and Its Influences* (ed. M. J. Anderson; London: Methuen, 1965), 18.

[57] David Wiles, *Tragedy in Athens: Performance Space and Theatrical Meaning*
(Cambridge: Cambridge University Press, 1997), 123.

the blind prophet Tiresias and Oedipus, the chorus engages in an internal debate of its own:

> Who is he that the oracular rock of Delphi sung as having done a deed worse than unspeakable with bloody hands? . . . Grievous, grievous is the trouble caused me by the wise interpreter of omens; I neither believe it nor deny it, but I cannot tell what to say, and fly on the wings of hope, seeing neither the present nor the future. (463–488 [Lloyd-Jones, LCL])

In the end of this speech, the chorus decides not to judge Oedipus, given that he has proven to be wise and the savior of the city in the past. As the action progresses toward the revelation of Oedipus's true identity, the chorus begins to question its understanding of its ruler. In the following dialogue, the chorus tries to temper Creon's indignation at Oedipus's calling him a traitor by inviting him to enter into their own ambiguity:

> CHORUS: Well, this charge was uttered, but perhaps it was forced out by anger rather than by considered thought.
>
> CREON: But was it openly said that the prophet was persuaded by my counsel to speak lies?
>
> CHORUS: This was said, but I know that it was unconsidered.
>
> CREON: But was it with a steady look and from a steady mind that this accusation was pronounced against me?
>
> CHORUS: I do not know; for I cannot judge the doings of my rulers.
> (523–530)

The chorus moves from speaking as though it knows Oedipus's mind to conceding that it does not. In the dialogue between Iocaste and Oedipus, the chorus joins its voice with that of the woman by begging Oedipus to believe Creon. When Oedipus asks the chorus if it knows for what it asks, it replies, "Yes," but when he spells out that believing Creon signifies death or exile for himself, the chorus reveals its inability to decide:

> No, by the foremost of the gods, the Sun! May I perish in the most awful fashion, given by gods and friends, if I harbour this thought! But alas for me, the wasting away of the land tears my heart, if the earlier troubles are to have added to them this trouble sprung from you. (660–667)

The chorus, left alone on stage after the principals have exited, struggles alone to make sense of what it has witnessed, but subsequent deliberations lead it to regret its relationship with Oedipus. The chorus's deliberation dis-

tances it from Oedipus, but it is not a force in the plot; the actual act of deter-
mining Oedipus's fate belongs to Creon, one of the principals.

On occasion, the tragedian splits the chorus so that its internal dialogue
becomes a dialogue between two or more parts. In *Agamemnon,* as the cries of
its king can be heard from inside the palace, the chorus of old men deliberates about what action it should take:

> I say send out heralds, muster the guard, they'll save the house.
> And I say rush in now, catch them red-handed—butchery running on their
> blades.
> . . . .
>
> I'm helpless. Who can raise the dead with words?
> What, drag out our lives? bow down to the tyrants, the ruin of the house?
> Never, better to die on your feet than live on your knees.
> Wait, do we take the cries for signs, prophesy like seers or give him up for
> dead?
> No more suspicions, not another word till we have proof.
> Confusion on all sides—one thing to do. See how it stands with Agamemnon,
> once and for all we'll see. (1373–1390 [Fagles])

True to their role as the chorus, the old men can do nothing other than talk
about their confusion; they debate, stymied from moving forward by the lack
of proof, compelling evidence, or clear knowledge. At the end of *Seven
against Thebes,* the chorus of Theban women splits, one half following Creon
with Eteocles' body and the other half following Antigone with Polynices'
corpse, thereby dramatizing its inability to decide between the two brothers'
competing claims to justice.[58]

Focusing upon the Jews or the disciples as representatives of historical
agents places emphasis upon the product of their deliberation—that is, their
rejection of Jesus. Attending to the action that the Jews or the crowd or the
disciples as a collective represent renders them more like a chorus than any
particular historical association, and emphasis falls upon the thematic relation between their collective voice and a gospel that pits traditional expectations against divine revelation.

In the Johannine dialogues, the majority of the lines of the collective
voice take the form of a question, a speech-act that generally indicates uncertainty or lack of understanding. For example, in the bread-of-life discourse,

---

58 See Martha Nussbaum, *The Fragility of Goodness: Luck and Ethics in Greek
Tragedy and Philosophy* (Cambridge: Cambridge University Press, 1986), 40–41, for
this description of the chorus and the conclusion that the chorus shows that "justice,
even civic justice, is not a simple thing."

the crowd seems first to desire clarity and asks, "Rabbi, when did you come here?" "What must we do to perform the works of God?" and "What sign are you going to give us . . . ?" (6:25, 28, 30). These questions may take on more subtle nuances depending upon their delivery on the performance axis. For example, different intonations could render the last of these three inquiries as a sign of either incredulity or eager anticipation. The crowd eventually moves on to questions that repeat Jesus' statements and indicate their so-called misunderstanding of what he has said: "How can he now say, 'I have come down from heaven'?"; "How can this man give us his flesh to eat?" (6:42, 52). I prefer to characterize this as a failure to come to understanding, because they do not give an actual misinterpretation of his words.

The scenes at the Festival of Booths provide examples of the similarity between how the tragedians and the gospel writer handle the collective voice. When the collective voice speaks to itself, like the Greek chorus, it deliberates about what it has witnessed.

> Is not this the man whom they are trying to kill? And here he is, speaking openly, but they say nothing to him! Can it be that the authorities really know that this is the Messiah? Yet we know where this man is from; but when the Messiah comes, no one will know where he is from. (7:25–27)

The Jews also divide occasionally into two camps to turn the deliberation into an internal debate:

SOME: He is a good man.

OTHERS: No, he is deceiving the crowd. . . .

SOME: This is really the prophet.

OTHERS: This is the Messiah.

OTHERS: Surely the Messiah does not come from Galilee, does he? Has not the scripture said that the Messiah is descended from David and comes from Bethlehem, the village where David lived? (7:12, 40–42)

A comparable debate punctuates Jesus' *paroimia* of the good shepherd. The gospel writer presents the division between many Jews who say, "He has a demon and is out of his mind. Why listen to him?" and others who assert, "These are not the words of one who has a demon. Can a demon open the eyes of the blind?" (10:20–21). The Jews also express their confusion by asking themselves questions—"How does this man have such learning, when he has never been taught?" (7:15), "Where does this man intend to go that we will not find him? Does he intend to go to the Dispersion among the Greeks and teach the Greeks?" (7:35)—for which only Jesus can provide answers.

Like a tragic chorus, the collective Jews never become actors in the Johannine drama. The narrator describes the crowd or Jews wanting to take Jesus by force to make him king but never actually making the move (6:15), wanting to arrest him but no one laying hands on him (7:30, 44; 10:39), and on two occasions taking up rocks that never leave hands (8:59; 10:31). In the tragedies, the chorus describes its own incapacitation. In *Medea*, the chorus hears the cries of the children being murdered within the house and asks itself, "Shall I enter the house? I am determined to stop the death of the children" (1275 [Kovacs, LCL]), but all it can do is hurl names at Medea: "wretched and accursed woman" and "hard-hearted wretch." As the Johannine narrative winds to its conclusion, the collective voice supports Jesus' execution, but that resolution is cast in words suggesting that it continues not to know its own mind. The Pharisees echo Caiaphas's assertion, "You see, you can do nothing. Look, the world has gone after him!" (12:19), and the crowd ends with questions: "How can you say that the Son of Man must be lifted up? Who is this Son of Man?" (12:34). The collective voice of the Jews at the trial petitions for a verdict, but Pilate executes judgment, and it remains a witness to the action. If one is looking for reasons for the gospel writer to omit the trial before the Sanhedrin, the tragic conventions that limit the role of the collective voice may have a hand to play. Pilate may not exercise his authority as freely as he would like to think, but the course of action is determined by the words of a principal character. The group of Jews, like a Greek chorus, may refer to itself as a player, but in the plot it stands at the sidelines, or as John Gould puts it, the members of the chorus are "both the prisoners and the passionately engaged witnesses of the tragic experience."[59]

Although the gospel writer uses the word "Jews" to identify this crowd and the initial conflicts center upon two Jewish institutions, the temple and the Sabbath, Sandra Schneiders's characterization of this conflict as "an idolatrous attachment to the Jewish religious institution and the inbreaking of divine revelation in Jesus" seems excessive.[60] Just as the Pharisees refer to the crowd as "the world," the gospel writer treats the Jews and the world as synonymous. The world as a place without knowledge and incapable of accepting the truth is dramatized in the deliberations of the crowd. The association of the Jews with the response of unbelief stands in juxtaposition with the belief of the audience, to which the narrator alludes in 20:31. The deliberation

---

59 Gould, "Tragedy and Collective Experience," 221.
60 Sandra M. Schneiders, *Written That You May Believe: Encountering Jesus in the Fourth Gospel* (New York: Crossroad, 1999), 82.

of the various groups of Jews is not a device that invites the audience to choose one of two positions; instead, it is an opportunity for the audience to observe the inner workings of the mind of the other, whose perspective it does not share and who makes clear that recognizing Jesus is no easy matter.

The identification of this collective opponent as a deliberating chorus goes only so far in exercising the problem of their designation as Jews. In his discussion of the collective identity of the chorus, John Gould makes observations about the significance of its particular identity that may illuminate the rationale for the gospel writer's choice of the particular term "the Jews":

> [The chorus] brings the presence of a particular collective wider community experience, the sense of a social group with its roots in a wider community, which draws on the inherited stories, all the inherited, gnomic wisdom of social memory and of oral tradition to "contextualize" the tragedy.[61]

The constructed, collective identity of the chorus in Euripides' *Ion* illustrates Gould's point. When the chorus of Athenian women prays to Enodia, daughter of Demeter, to aid in the plot to poison Ion, "May no one else from another house come and rule the city, none save the noble Erechtheids!" (1059–1060 [Kovacs, LCL]), they appeal to the Athenian tradition that its population is indigenous to Attica, having descended from Erichthonius, who, as son of the Earth, sprung from Attic soil. What they know paired with what they do not know becomes the context for the near tragic murder of Ion, who is, in fact, a descendent of noble Erichthonius on his mother's side. The collective Athenian voice presents a homogeneous experience of what it means to be an Athenian by repeatedly insisting without question upon the chorus's earthborn conception. Even though the chorus in *Ion* seems to take an unusually active part in the plot by reminding Creusa of Athenian tradition and law, its deliberations are limited to wondering how to flee the consequences of Creusa's act. It comes to no new understanding but rather continues to spout platitudes and conventional wisdom to its very last breath, and in doing so it reveals the contradictions inherent within an epistemology based upon appearance and tradition. When Ion is revealed to be Creusa's son, the chorus leader proclaims, "[I]n the light of what has just happened, let no one think anything impossible" (1510–1511), but the same voice ends the play saying, "In the end, the noble receive their just reward. But the base, as befits their nature, will never prosper" (1622–1623). Though, in the immediate context of this play's happy ending, this conclusion may seem sound, the Athenian audience, more accustomed to witnes-

---

61 Gould, "Tragedy and Collective Experience," 233.

sing misery than joy at the end of a tragedy, would have recognized the limitations of this "Athenian wisdom."

In the Fourth Gospel, the Jews, by virtue of being Jews, provide the context for the tragic action. Though their deliberation may make some of the Jews or the crowd appear to be sympathetic to Jesus, a basic antipathy is generated by the way that the group represents its own identity. In counterpoint to Jesus' focus upon his divine origin, its claims of having Abraham as father (8:33) places it upon the horizontal plane of the dramatic world. It situates itself within the historical continuum and physical geography constitutive of that plane. The Jews are the descendants of Abraham, and if Jesus opposes them or stands in distinction from them by virtue of his claims or acts, they situate him on that plane by calling him a Samaritan or look to their tradition for precedents: he could be a prophet or a messiah.

Given that Judaism becomes the context in which the Jews try to understand who Jesus is, James Dunn's question "Which Judaism?" becomes particularly relevant.[62] The collective voice deliberates, but it is not divided in the way that factions within Judaism were at odds with each other during the late Second Temple period. There are no Sadducees and Zealots in this gospel, and the picture of the Pharisees, though true to their interest in Sabbath observance, together with the chief priests calling a meeting of the council (11:47) is too felicitous to be true to history. The Synoptic Gospels may place the Pharisees on the Sanhedrin, but the historical record suggests that they were disenfranchised. As Marinus de Jonge demonstrates, asking historical questions such as, "Do the statements in the Fourth Gospel supplement what we know from other sources and do they help to sketch a more coherent picture of Jewish beliefs concerning the Messiah?" ends with a negative answer.[63] De Jonge's conclusion supports my observations:

> Though the persons mentioned in the various stories are meant to be representative, they are more like actors in a play, whose utterances help along the course of events and, even more, the development of thought, than identifiable individuals belonging to clearly defined groups.[64]

De Jonge notes elements that place the messianic beliefs in the Fourth Gospel in tension with Jewish tradition: the expectation that the Messiah will perform many miracles (7:31) finds no supporting Jewish evidence, and the conviction of the crowd that no one knows from where the Messiah will

---

[62] Dunn, "The Embarrassment of History," 45.

[63] Marinus de Jonge, "Jewish Expectations about the 'Messiah' according to the Fourth Gospel," *NTS* 19 (1972–1973): 247, 262.

[64] Ibid., 248.

come from (7:27) suggests that they have no knowledge of the Jewish tradition that he will come from Bethlehem.[65] De Jonge projects this ignorance upon the gospel itself, but it seems to me that the fact that the beliefs of the crowd are a construct is intended to be clear to its audience. Wayne Meeks argues that the title "Messiah" on the lips of the Samaritan woman is "a clear sign of the leveling of different terminologies," so that even the harmonizing of the Samaritan and Jewish traditions is part of the design of the gospel rather than a reflection of history.[66] Judaism and messianic tradition become, in this gospel, orthodoxy without dissenting voices or divergent positions.

This expression of unity that is uncharacteristic of late Second Temple Judaism leads many scholars to look for a period of "normative Judaism," and so the council of Yavneh becomes a reference point, but as Shaye Cohen so forcefully argues, one ought not to treat that council's effects as immediate.[67] Its authority is retrospective rather than historical. Others try to account for the blending of traditions by arguing that the gospel is the product of either a Christian community living in Galilee-Samaria or mutual interaction between Jews and Samaritans in the formation of the traditions; however, the unity of expression and the harmonizing of traditions may be the product of characterization rather than history.[68]

Throughout the Fourth Gospel, the Jews appeal to collective experience and traditions in their attempts to make sense of what they witness, but the results, given what they do not know, fall short of coming to the correct conclusion. The temple in Jerusalem has been under construction for forty-six years; therefore Jesus cannot possibly raise it in three days (2:20). The Jews collectively know Joseph, so how can Jesus come down from heaven (6:42)? They appeal to various messianic traditions as though there were a consensus about them: the Messiah will from an unknown place (7:27), perform signs (7:31), and remain forever (12:34). The disciples, Martha of Bethany, and others who do not reject Jesus are also Jews, and they also frame their understanding of Jesus within a construction of the Jewish tradition: Andrew claims, "We have found the Messiah" (1:41); Nathanael exclaims, "Rabbi, you are the Son of God! You are the King of Israel!" (1:49); Peter calls Jesus "the Holy One of God" (6:69); Martha confesses, "you are the Messiah, the Son of God, the one coming into the world" (11:27). The Jews

---

[65] Ibid., 257, 259.

[66] Wayne A. Meeks, *The Prophet-King: Moses Traditions and the Johannine Christology* (NovTSup 14; Leiden: Brill, 1967), 318 n. 1.

[67] Shaye D. Cohen, "The Significance of Yavneh," *HUCA* 55 (1984): 27–53.

[68] For arguments for Samaritan influence in the development of the tradition, see James D. Purvis, "The Fourth Gospel and the Samaritans," *NovT* 17 (1975): 191.

in the gospel, like the chorus of Athenians in *Ion*, are misled by their tradition. The point is not that tradition is flawed or even that their interpretation of the tradition is false. The problem is with human ways of knowing and how the human act of interpretation will always offer alternatives.

In the context of the action, the choice of the term "the Jews" to identify the crowd is appropriate. The term becomes a problem because that which formerly defined a constructed and theatrical or dramatic normative identity becomes an excluded identity when Christianity emerges as a social and political power. When the dramatic opposition within the gospel is taken as an ontological and soteriological distinction and imposed upon a world in which there are individuals who are Jews rather than Christians, the language leads to the legacy of inquisition, blood libel, pogrom, ghetto, and *Shoah*. Given all this, the choice of the term is lamentable and results in "anti-Judaism" but I hesitate to call the gospel itself anti-Jewish. The tragic genre from which the gospel seems to have emerged as a new literary form but to which it still bears affinity exaggerates conflict and demands characterization of some of its citizens as hostile or ignorant, but it should not necessitate the vilification of one side of the contest. That step is taken when a reader fails to recognize the dramatic conventions at work.

The Second Person: The Uncertain Self

The Fourth Gospel sets itself apart from the Synoptic Gospels by its cast of characters. Some appear only in this story: the disciple Nathanael, Nicodemus, Lazarus, and the Samaritan woman. A striking difference, already discussed here in chapter 1, lies in how the gospel writer handles the movement and dialogues of these characters. A more subtle difference, and again one that relies upon dramatic convention, is found in the way that characters are identified and the role that identification plays in the action. As if to complement our inability to identify these characters beyond the bounds of the gospel, the gospel writer renders them incapable of knowing themselves. Individual secondary characters, like the collective characters, represent a world of bewilderment in which conventions and powers that provide security prove to be an illusion.

Onstage, an actor's identity depends totally upon linguistic or symbolic markers. If the audience does not know that a character has a particular identity, that character does not have that identity. Characters are either greeted by name when they enter or name themselves. *Antigone*, for example, begins with the entrance of Oedipus's two daughters. Antigone speaks first, "My own sister Ismene . . . [h]ave you any knowledge . . . ?" to which Ismene responds, "To me, Antigone, no word about our friends has come" (1–11 [Lloyd-Jones, LCL]). In Greek tragedy, no audience is left wondering, "Who was that masked man?" Without the aid of a narrator to give character sketches, characters also speak about themselves and each other to give important details about their background and desires. In their opening dialogue, Antigone and Ismene take measure of their own and each other's attitudes. Antigone explains the reason for their private encounter: "I summoned you out of the gates of the courtyard because I wished you to hear this alone." Ismene's reply reinforces earlier statements about her own state of ignorance and takes stock of Antigone's disposition: "But what is it? It is clear that you are brooding over something you are going to say" (19–20). Through hearing exchanges such as this, the audience can build a more complete picture of a character and note changes in countenance and mood. In the first part of the play, Antigone is described as a bird screaming its agony over an empty nest; by the end of the play, passion is replaced with reason and calm, and Antigone is portrayed as a bride.[69]

On the whole, the Fourth Evangelist, like the Synoptic authors, uses the narrator to make a clear preliminary identification. For example, he sets up the first dialogue by identifying the speakers as John and the Jews, sent by priests and Levites. Later in the dialogue he emends this qualification by stating that John's interlocutors were sent by the Pharisees. The interlocutors confirm their identity with their own words: "Let us have an answer for those who sent us" (1:22). But like these Jewish agents, the audience of the gospel must still ask of John, "Who are you?" (1:19). The prologue and the narrator identify the speaker only as John. The reader or audience completes the identification of the Baptist only after the second speaker has claimed that he is a "voice of one crying out in the wilderness" (1:23) or when the agents ask him why he is baptizing (1:25).[70] The reader or audience must often infer from the dialogue that the notoriously vague moniker "the Jews" signifies some sort of authority, as it does in the dialogue with the formerly blind man's parents, rather than a crowd, as may be the case in the bread-of-life discourse. Rarely does a character in the gospel fail to make his or her identity or that of another character known to a sufficient degree for the reader to make good sense of the action. The dialogues in which this is not the case tend to be brief encounters with Jesus, who, as we have noted, is not wont to name his con-

---

69 See Arnott, *Public and Performance,* 191.

70 For a reader to make an immediate identification of John with the Baptist, he or she would have to be a rereader or be familiar with the Markan tradition, which begins with the Baptist's witness.

versation partners.[71] Without the narrator's assistance, we would not know that the woman at the wedding of Cana or at the foot of the cross is Jesus' mother, and Nicodemus would be only "a teacher of Israel." But in some cases, such as the dialogue with the Samaritan woman, the narrator provides no more than the speaker.

The episode in which the royal official's request that his son be healed and in which only the narrator provides his identity is the exception in the gospel. This sort of identification is the rule in the Synoptic Gospels, in which entire episodes pass without a single character uttering a line. The healing of Simon's mother-in-law in Mark 1:29–31, for example, passes in silence. In the Matthean version, the pericope ends with a characteristic scriptural proof, "He took our infirmities and bore our diseases" (Matt 8:17), from the disembodied voice of Isaiah. In the Fourth Gospel, characters tend to represent themselves by their speech.

In the economy of the drama, the currency of identification purchases more than the practical ends of the theatrical axis; it becomes part of a naming game in which the winner or loser in the end bears the title in play.[72] The titles of raving savage and wrongdoer, which the chorus and Creon have tried to affix to Antigone, come to land upon Creon's own head. Oedipus and Tiresias accuse each other of being blind, and at the end of the play, Oedipus gouges out his own eyes with Iocaste's golden pins and becomes the one to whom the insult applies. The dialogue in chapter 9 of the Fourth Gospel, which centers on Jesus' identity as a sinner, begins and ends by playing with the identification of sin with blindness. The disciples first ask, "Rabbi, who sinned, this man or his parents, that he was born blind?" (9:2), and the Pharisees conclude by asking, "Surely we are not blind, are we?" to which Jesus responds, "If you were blind, you would not have sin. But now that you say, 'We see,' your sin remains." (9:40–41). In the end, it is the Pharisees rather than the man who prove to be blind, and the Pharisees rather than Jesus to whom the identity of sinner is made to stick. As in the tragedies, once a name comes into play, it applies to someone by the end of the action.

The penchant for self-identification in the gospel tends to be subverted by Jesus' reidentification of himself and others in the course of their dialogues, and in this way, shifting identity becomes part of the action of the gospel. Just as Jesus is not whom people take him to be, others prove not to be who they think they are. The Samaritan woman allies with a Jewish man;

---

71 See, for example, 7:1–9.

72 See Joseph A. Porter, *The Drama of Speech Acts: Shakespeare's Lancastrian Tetralogy* (Berkeley: University of California Press, 1979), 12–27, esp. 12, in which he describes the accusation of traitor in *Richard II*.

Judas, one of the twelve whom Jesus chooses, betrays Jesus; Peter is not the disciple he thinks himself to be; Nicodemus moves from membership with the Pharisees to some ambiguous position that leaves many readers wondering where he belongs. In the conversation with Jesus, the language and markers that a character uses to identify him- or herself, as well as others, lose their power to define identity. Jesus' dialogue with Nathanael sets the course for all subsequent dialogues. Depending upon its delivery, Nathanael's question "Out of Nazareth is it possible for good to come?" (1:46) can be understood as either sarcastic or incredulous.[73] In either case, Nathanael represents himself as one who is discerning. When he acknowledges Jesus, he provides Jesus with three titles: "Rabbi," "Son of God," and "King of Israel" (1:49). Taken all together, Nathanael's lines also mark him as one who interprets his world through the lens of Israelite tradition. Jesus seems to play upon the incredulous aspect of Nathanael's character when he represents Nathanael's belief as based upon slim evidence: "Do you believe because I told you that I saw you under the fig tree?" (1:50). Jesus seems to affirm his association with tradition by greeting him with, "Here is truly an Israelite in whom there is no deceit [δόλος]" (1:47). Raymond Brown and others use this as a datum for treating Nathanael as "a symbol of Israel coming to God," but Jesus' remark may be consistent with his remark about Nathanael's belief, both anticipating and subverting the nature of what Nathanael will say.[74] In an exchange between Socrates and Thrasymachus (Plato, *Rep.* 1.348c), the word εὐήθεια ("guilelessness, simplicity") is applied to those who still trust in communal agreements before discovering that they are made by selfish people to secure power for themselves. Although Jesus uses a different word to describe Nathanael's guilelessness, he seems to be suggesting that Nathanael's power of deduction is naïve rather than astute, and so he says that Nathanael will see greater things and adopts the nontraditional title "Son of Man" (1:51) versus the traditional titles that Nathanael offers. The play with identification continues throughout the gospel. Nicodemus begins his dialogue with Jesus by aligning himself within an association, identified by the narrator as the Pharisees, and characterizing himself as knowledgeable: "Rabbi, we know that you are a teacher who has come from God" (3:2). His self-characterization as one who knows is subverted first by his questioning—"How can anyone be born after having grown old? Can one enter a second time into the mother's womb and be born?" (3:4), "How can these things be?" (3:9)—and then by Jesus' response to this discrepancy in self-characterization when he asks, "Are you a teacher of Israel, and yet you do not understand these things?" (3:10).

---

[73] This is my translation, in which I preserve the Greek word order.
[74] Brown, *The Gospel according to John,* 1:82.

Nicodemus persists in identifying himself with the group when he appeals to the chief priests and Pharisees: "Our law does not judge people without first giving them a hearing to find out what they are doing, does it?" (7:51). The chief priests and Pharisees distance themselves from Nicodemus by asking, "Surely you are not also from Galilee, are you?" and perhaps undermine their own authority by saying to him, "Search and you will see that no prophet is to arise from Galilee" (7:52).[75] This instability of identity within the dramatic world of dialogue and debate characterizes the world as an alienating place for both Jesus and its human denizens.

A significant amount of the dialogue of the Fourth Gospel focuses upon the illusion of identity. When the Samaritan woman draws a sharp distinction between Jesus and her own national identity—"How is it that you, a Jew, ask a drink of me, a woman of Samaria?" (4:9), "Our ancestors worshiped on this mountain, but you say that the place where people must worship is in Jerusalem" (4:20)—Jesus announces that the distinction between Jerusalem and the Samaritans' mountain no longer holds meaning. In the trial with Pilate, the game centers upon the title "King of the Jews" and sovereignty. When Jesus asks Pilate if he questions him at another's bidding, Pilate replies, "I am not a Jew, am I?" (18:35). When Pilate asks Jesus if he is King of the Jews and surmises from Jesus' statement "My kingdom is not from this world" that he lays claim to the title, Jesus avoids accepting it and claims that his role is "to testify to the truth" (18:36–37). Pilate brushes aside this identity with the question "What is truth?" (18:38) and persists in his first line of deduction by referring to Jesus as king when he speaks with the Jews: "Do you want me to release for you the King of the Jews?" (18:39), "Here is your King!" (19:14), "Shall I crucify your King?" (19:15). The guards support him by saying, "Hail, King of the Jews!" (19:3), and despite opposition from the Jews, Pilate places the inscription "Jesus of Nazareth, the King of the Jews" on the cross (19:19). If Pilate uses the title in his own subversive attempts to ridicule Jewish hopes or pretense of power, then he is the victim of irony in that Jesus needs neither Pilate's recognition nor the title of king to hallow his sovereignty. Pilate, like the Pharisees in John 9 and Creon in *Antigone,* has no power to make stable identifications.

The Greek tragedies offer innumerable examples of characters' self-understanding proving false or their ability to identify others proving limited. Sophocles' *Oedipus Tyrannus* provides the classic example of the tragic hero who suffers for ignorance of identity, but other plays provide examples where this is true also of secondary characters. In *Prometheus Bound,* Oceanus

---

75 𝔓66* and 𝔓75*vid* read "the prophet will not arise from Galilee." In fact, at least one prophet, Jonah, did come from a Galilean town (2 Kgs 14:25).

begins, "You shall never say, Prometheus, that you have any firmer friend than Oceanus [a name that speaks against his claims]" (296 [Vellacott]). By the end of the conversation, Prometheus has persuaded Oceanus that in choosing him as a friend he makes an enemy of Zeus, and Oceanus makes a hasty and eager exit. Throughout *Ion*, Euripides plays with the inability of Creusa to put two and two together to discover the identity of her son. Ion greets her, " greeting, O queen! For in your appearance there is nobility. . . . For the most part someone can tell by a person's bearing whether he is well born" (237–240 [Kovacs, LCL]). Creusa, in turn, notes his bearing but does not consider what it signifies, and addresses Ion, "Stranger, your attitude— your wondering at my tears—is well bred" (246). After a long conversation in which she tells a good deal about herself to this stranger, she asks, "But who are you? How blessed in my eyes is your mother!" (308). Ion tells his own story, repeatedly referring to himself as Apollo's own, to which Creusa responds, "Ah me! Another woman suffered as your mother did" (330), and tells her own story. As in the gospel, only divine revelation makes self-understanding possible.

The scene in which the high priest questions Jesus (18:19–24) is perplexing, first because it seems odd that Annas would hold a hearing and second because Annas's identity is withheld until the end of the scene. Moreover, the fact that Annas is not represented by direct speech makes him a rare principal character who inhabits the mimetic space of the action without having a spoken line. Lazarus and Joseph of Arimathea are the only other named characters who do not speak. Add to all this the fact that the guard who does speak identifies Jesus' interlocutor as the high priest, whom the audience knows to be Caiaphas (cf. 18:19 with 18:24). Raymond Brown argues for the plausible historicity of this encounter, and against the possibility that the evangelist is confused about Annas's status, by suggesting that Annas, as former high priest, could still lay claim to the title and was the de facto power controlling Caiaphas.[76] Numerous scholars have suggested that verse 24 ought to follow verse 13, so that Caiaphas becomes the high priest who questions Jesus.[77] Jeffrey Staley describes five instances in the gospel where the implied reader is victimized by a rhetorical strategy in which the evangelist delays the provision of crucial information.[78] Staley later added 18:19–24 to this list.[79]

---

[76] Brown, *The Gospel according to John*, 2:820–21.

[77] Ibid., 821. Brown names Luther, Calmes, Lagrange, Streeter, Durand, Joüon, Vosté, and Sutcliffe.

[78] Staley, *The Print's First Kiss*, 95–118 (4:1–2; 7:1–10; 10:40–11:18; 13:1–30; 20:30–21:25).

[79] Jeffrey L. Staley, "Subversive Narrator/Victimized Reader: A Reader Response Assessment of Text-critical Problems, John 18:12–24," *JSNT* 51 (1993): 79–98.

Modern filmmakers often entrap their audience by withholding clear identification of characters and allowing it to make errors in order to expose the audience's prejudices. The opening scenes of Norman Jewison's film *In the Heat of the Night* (1967) follow the perspective of a white police officer in Sparta, Mississippi, named Gillespie (played by Rod Steiger), who treats a black man named Tibbs (played by Sidney Poitier) as a suspect in a murder investigation. The audience is caught in the stereotypes of the white Southern racist policeman and the victimized black man until the plot takes a sudden turn when Tibbs identifies himself as a homicide detective from Philadelphia and Gillespie invites him to assist in the investigation of the crime. In a more recent film, *The Contender* (2000), directed by Rod Lurie, the president of the United States discusses the nomination of a character named Hanson for vice president. The camera cuts to an office scene in which a man is making love with a woman on top of an expensive desk. The phone rings, and the man picks it up. The viewers are meant to assume (unless they have seen the film's trailer) that the man is Hanson and that he is in his own office. The conversation continues to mislead the audience until the man hands the phone to the woman and says, "The president wants to talk with you." The audience is trapped first by sexist tendencies to assume that vice presidents are male and then by assumptions that office sex is illicit. The man turns out to be Hanson's husband.

In classical drama, confusion about identity is limited to the dramatic axis. In a performance in which actors wear masks, it is necessary to identify them clearly in each scene. The Fourth Evangelist perhaps plays a modern game when he flouts the conventions of the theatrical axis by withholding the identity of Annas. If the audience is intentionally trapped, is the preconception with which the evangelist plays our capacity to name authorities? In a gospel in which anonymity does not undercut credibility—the Samaritan woman, the man born blind, and the disciple upon whose testimony the gospel is based have no names—this makes some sense, although this trick may be too clever, too modern to be credible for a first-century author. The evangelist, or his representative the narrator, demonstrates a consistent disregard for distinctions between Jewish leaders. In the inquisition of John the Baptist, the narrator blurs the difference between the temple authorities and the Pharisees by treating John's interrogators first as representatives of the priests and Levites and then as those of the Pharisees. By drawing attention to different interrogations by Annas and Caiaphas, the narrator makes clear that they are distinct individuals, but by using the title "high priest" to identify both of them, he seems to deny the power of a title to determine a person's identity.

John Gould argues that the language of dramatic persons is part of a metaphor for "the way things are" rather than an enactment of "the way people behave."[80] Language does not just describe the state of affairs; it creates the state of affairs. An effective way of dramatizing the powerlessness of an individual is to show how his or her utterances fail to bring into existence that which they intend. For example, in *Antigone,* when Antigone asks Creon, "Do you wish for anything more than to take me and kill me?"(497 [Lloyd-Jones, LCL]), Creon responds, "Not I! When I have that, I have everything" (498). As it turns out, when he has that, he has nothing, for his son Haemon kills himself as a consequence of Antigone's death and his wife kills herself as a consequence of Haemon's death. In fact, Creon describes himself in the end as "no more than nothing!" (1324). Questions characterize the way things are in the world of the Fourth Gospel. The persistent inquiries and interrogations of Jesus by the other characters in this gospel make the question the most frequently used illocutionary act. Besides their obvious function as a means of initiating and maintaining dialogue, these questions characterize the experience of those who pose them. In general, their questions tend to signify a failure to recognize Jesus. In the interior dialogue of the collective voice, certain knowledge frequently is met with a question that throws it into doubt. When some Jews charge Jesus with having a demon, others rejoin, "Can a demon open the eyes of the blind?" (10:21). When the Jews observe the tears that Jesus weeps before resurrecting Lazarus, they comment, "See how he loved him!" (11:36), but then some among them question the validity of this observation by asking, "Could not he who opened the eyes of the blind man have kept this man from dying?" (11:37). Nicodemus begins with an assertion of certainty, "Rabbi, we know that you are a teacher who has come from God, for no one can do these signs that you do apart from the presence of God" (3:2), but ends with an inarticulate question: "How can these things be?" (3:9). The Samaritan woman, who has become a champion of the faith in our contemporary discourse and to whom Jesus discloses himself to be the Messiah, concludes her invitation to her townspeople to come and see him by asking, "He cannot be the Messiah, can he?" (4:29). Moreover, the failure of questions to provide answers points to the ineffectiveness of the characters' strategies of knowing. After Jesus upsets the commerce of the temple, the Jews ask him, "What sign can you show us for doing this?" (2:18), but Jesus' response, "Destroy this temple, and in three days I will raise it up" (2:19), serves only to provoke another question: "This temple has been under construction for forty-six years, and will you raise it up in three days?" (2:20). Pilate's seemingly cynical question "What is

---

[80] John Gould, "Dramatic Character and 'Human Intelligibility' in Greek Tragedy," *Proceedings of the Cambridge Philological Society* 24 (1978): 43–67; cited in Easterling, "Constructing Character in Greek Tragedy," 91.

truth?" (18:38) illustrates the failure of questions to produce knowledge by expecting no reply.

The resurrection scenes mark a dramatic change in the representation of secondary characters. As the narrator reports, "Now none of the disciples dared to ask him, 'Who are you?' because they knew it was the Lord" (21:12). Once individuals recognize Jesus, they greet him with titles that Jesus does not qualify or reject. Mary cries, "Rabbouni!" (20:16), Thomas, "My Lord and my God!" (20:28), the Beloved Disciple, "It is the Lord!" (21:7), and Peter repeatedly addresses Jesus as "Lord" (21:15, 16, 17, 21). These brief attestations are more like words of praise that acknowledge the relationship of the speaker as suppliant or devotee to the one addressed than confessions of belief. Any certainty that they might express about their relationship to Jesus does not extend to others, for, although Jesus' resurrection may make his identity clearer, it does not make the world a less bewildering place. Peter's last question about the fate of the beloved disciple, "Lord, what about him?" and Jesus' response, "If it is my will that he remain until I come, what is that to you? Follow me!" (21:21–22), bring to mind the last lines of *Oedipus Tyrannus:* "One should wait to see the final day and should call none among mortals fortunate, till he has crossed the bourne of life without suffering grief" (1528–1530 [Lloyd-Jones, LCL]). Jesus' words remind the disciple and the reader of our limited ability to judge a person's circumstances.

Simon Peter and the Beloved Disciple

In proposed reconstructions of the Johannine community, the characterization of Peter in the Fourth Gospel is exploited as a datum to substantiate tensions between Petrine authority and the Beloved Disciple.[81] This argument is based in part upon an intertextual argument. Since Peter is given the role of the foundation of the church in the Gospel of Matthew and not in the Fourth Gospel and since the Beloved Disciple is identified as the authoritative witness upon whose testimony the Fourth Gospel is based, many scholars conclude that the Gospel of Matthew is a document of a Petrine church and the Fourth Gospel is a document of a Johannine community.[82] The

---

[81] For a review of this argument and the opposing view, see A. H. Maynard, "The Role of Peter in the Fourth Gospel," *NTS* 30 (1984): 532.

[82] Although the existence of a Johannine community or "the community of the Beloved Disciple" is treated as a datum by most New Testament scholars, no textual or other empirical evidence, beyond the Fourth Gospel itself, attests to its existence. Moreover, the Fourth Gospel itself makes no clear reference to the establishment of a

footrace to Jesus' tomb, which Simon Peter loses to the other disciple, presumably the Beloved Disciple, and the narrator's attribution of belief to the Beloved Disciple and silence about Simon Peter's mental disposition regarding the empty tomb are also treated as evidence of the Beloved Disciple's superior authority. Against this line of reasoning, I suggest that the contrast in conventions by which these characters are constructed points to each one's role in distinctly different categories. Although both are identified as disciples, in the analysis of characterization discipleship should not be treated as a defining feature by which one can be judged superior and the other inferior. An examination of Simon Peter's speech—the propositional attitudes he posits, how he enters into dialectical relationships, or how he manifests himself as a rhetorical force—points to his role as an actor in the drama, one to whom witness is given.[83] The Beloved Disciple's speech, or lack thereof, points to his role as a bystander, one who can give witness.

Until his final dialogue with Jesus, Simon Peter utters a number of lines that imply a sort of presumption of power. In his first brief dialogue with Jesus, he speaks as the spokesperson for the Twelve:

JESUS: Do you also wish to go away?

SIMON PETER: Lord, to whom can we go? You have the words of eternal life.
   We have come to believe and know that you are the Holy one of God.
   (6:67–69)

Jesus undercuts Simon Peter's ability to speak for the group by noting that one of them is a devil. When, at the supper on the night of Jesus' betrayal, Jesus comes to wash the feet of Simon Peter, the latter singles himself out from the Twelve first by refusing to have his feet washed and then by requesting the distinction of having more than his feet washed. The lack of moderation in his refusal, "You will never wash my feet," is matched by his request to have more washed than what Jesus offered: "Lord, not my feet only but also my hands and my head!" (13:8–9). Later that evening, Simon Peter begins an elaborate speech-act—Raymond Brown sees it as based upon the *paroimia* of the good shepherd—that places Peter in a dialectical relationship with Jesus.[84] Simon Peter begins by asking, "Lord, where are you going?" (13:36). (Oddly, in 16:5, Jesus says, "none of you asks me, 'Where are you going?'")

---

community other than the possibility that Jesus implies its existence when he commands his disciples to "love one another."

   [83] Philippe Hamon's ninth category in a semiotic approach to character; cited in Elam, *Semiotics of Theatre and Drama*, 133.

   [84] Brown, *The Gospel according to John*, 2:49.

Jesus affirms Simon Peter's coidentity with himself by responding, "Where I am going, you cannot follow me now; but you will follow afterward." Simon Peter's next line is different from what we find in the Synoptic Gospels, where he expresses a willingness to die with Jesus. Here he aligns himself with Jesus and his model of the good shepherd by saying, "I will lay down my life for you" (13:37; cf. 10:11). His speech-act seems to prove infelicitous if he intends to fulfill it by defending Jesus at his arrest and when he denies that he is a disciple. Jesus rejects Simon Peter's offer to fulfill that role by predicting that he will deny him, but after the resurrection, he directs him to fulfill it on his behalf. Simon Peter is to tend or feed his flock, and Jesus predicts that Simon Peter eventually will lay down his life and invites him, "Follow me" (21:15–19).

In the denial scene, Simon Peter continues to speak with rhetorical force. His earlier insistence that he is prepared to die is paired with his insistence that he is not a disciple:

WOMAN: You are not also one of this man's disciples, are you?

SIMON PETER: I am not [οὐκ εἰμί]. . . .

UNNAMED CHARACTERS: You are not also one of his disciples, are you?

SIMON PETER: I am not [οὐκ εἰμί].

SLAVE: Did I not see you in the garden with him?

NARRATOR: Again Peter denied it, and at that moment the cock crowed.
     (18:17, 25–27)

I find two significant differences between the Johannine denial scene and those in the Synoptic Gospels. In the Fourth Gospel, Simon Peter does not swear and he focuses upon who he is rather than what he knows. In Mark and Matthew, Peter utters oaths by which he denies knowing Jesus. Although he lies under oath, there is no consequence for his misuse of God's name; his words have no illocutionary force.[85] For the record, we should note that Peter does not make a direct appearance again after the denial scene in any of the Synoptic Gospels. In contrast, Simon Peter's denials in the Fourth Gospel are acts that create a reality in which his statement is true; they have rhetorical force. By saying that he is not a disciple, he is not a disciple. Simon's words οὐκ εἰμί bring to mind Creon's reference to himself as "me who am no more than nothing" (τὸν οὐκ ὄντα μᾶλλον ἢ μηδένα) at the end of *Antigone,* when

---

[85] Exod 20:7 and Lev 19:12 make clear that there is no release from an oath.

niece, son, and wife all lie dead (1324 [Lloyd-Jones, LCL]). Language that denies identity, such as the line "me who am no more than nothing," signifies the action of *pathos* itself insofar as the character semantically kills himself. Simon Peter's denial of Jesus in the Fourth Gospel, in contrast to that in the Synoptic tradition, in which he denies knowledge, is a denial of identity. His "I am not" (18:17, 25), the antithesis to Jesus' insistence "I am," is Simon Peter's catastrophe.

In the final dialogue, Simon Peter's propositional attitude changes when Jesus becomes the subject of his sentences confirming his love: "Yes, Lord; you know that I love you." Jesus seems to note the change in Simon Peter's position from subjective agent to object when he states prophetically, "Very truly, I tell you, when you were younger, you used to fasten your own belt and to go wherever you wished. But when you grow old, you will stretch out your hands, and someone else will fasten a belt around you and take you where you do not wish to go" (21:18). With Jesus' last line, "Follow me," Simon Peter's standing as a disciple has been reinstated, and he will become the good shepherd who lays down his life.

These scenes form a dialectical *peripeteia*. Simon Peter is the tragic character who experiences reversals, the character who in his hubris thinks himself strong only to find that he is weak. The footwashing scene begins with his adamant assertion of his role as helper. The excessive willingness to be washed is a reversal of his position but not of his role. His role reverses when he proves himself unable to live up to his claims for himself. A second reversal comes when he reestablishes his rhetorical relationship with Jesus in which he serves as his agent, but his power to kill has been replaced with a vulnerability to death. The meaning of Jesus' statement "No one has greater love than this, to lay down one's life for one's friends" (15:13) is moved from the arena of conflict, such as the arrest scene, where death may be a consequence of defending one's life, to the field of service, where death is a consequence of not protecting one's own interests. If there is a tragic hero in the Fourth Gospel, it seems to be Simon Peter, and thus it seems wrong to read the gospel as a polemic against him or his leadership.

Simon Peter stands in dialectical relationship with the Beloved Disciple as well as with Jesus. Wherever one is, the other seems to follow. If we take the disciple in 1:35 who is never identified to be the Beloved Disciple, then he became a disciple before Simon Peter did. At the farewell dinner, the Beloved Disciple reclines next to Jesus, and consequently Simon Peter motions to him to find out who Jesus is talking about when he refers to his betrayer (13:23–24). If the other disciple in the trial scene (18:15) is the Beloved Disciple, then he and Peter both pursue Jesus and his captors and enter the high priest's courtyard, where Simon Peter lags behind and betrays Jesus while the

Beloved Disciple follows Jesus to the foot of the cross (19:26). The two dash together to the empty tomb and then leave together (20:3–10). When the disciples return to fishing, the Beloved Disciple recognizes Jesus and lets Simon Peter, who sits or stands next to him, know that it is Jesus on the shore. When Jesus takes Simon Peter aside for a private talk, the Beloved Disciple follows. Richard Bauckham argues that "the beloved disciple is represented as superior to Peter" and that he represents the discipleship of perceptive witness whereas Peter represents service.[86] Martin Hengel and David Beck go further and refer to the Beloved Disciple as the ideal disciple.[87]

Although both may be disciples and appear in the same scenes, something very different is going on in the way that the character of the Beloved Disciple is being constructed. Simon Peter's character emerges through speech and represented action. The Beloved Disciple, except for his words to Jesus, "Lord, who is it?" (13:25), which are prompted by Simon Peter and later rehearsed by the narrator (21:20), and to Peter, "It is the Lord!" (21:7), which prompt Simon Peter to put on his clothes and jump into the sea, is mute. Somewhat like Harpo Marx, he is beloved because he never says anything to give offense. We can pick apart Simon Peter's and Martha's confessions, but the Beloved Disciple says nothing to subject him to scrutiny. Unlike Simon Peter, whose presence in the high priest's courtyard arouses the curiosity of the servants, the Beloved Disciple is not put to the test because he is known to the high priest and goes unquestioned. The narrator, in contrast to his silence about Simon Peter's motives, reports why the Beloved Disciple acts and what he thinks.[88] The Beloved Disciple asks Jesus about his betrayer because Simon Peter has motioned to him to do so (13:24), and he enters the high priest's court because the high priest knows him (18:15). After he sees the linen and cloth in the empty tomb, he believes (20:8), although precisely what he believes remains in question. The narrator resists giving him a name; he draws him in circles by using a retrospective clause, "the disciple whom Jesus loved," which readers (including myself), for their own convenience, have turned into the name "the Beloved Disciple." The terms that point

---

[86] Richard Bauckham, "The Beloved Disciple as Ideal Author," *JSNT* 49 (1993): 35.

[87] Martin Hengel, *The Johannine Question* (Philadelphia: Trinity, 1989); David R. Beck, *The Discipleship Paradigm: Readers and Anonymous Characters in the Fourth Gospel* (BIS 27; Leiden: Brill, 1977), 133–36.

[88] Tom Thatcher ("Jesus, Judas, and Peter: Character by Contrast in the Fourth Gospel," *BSac* 153 [1996]: 440) notes that the narrator also reports Judas's thoughts.

to his existence become an attribute of his identity that result in the questionable conclusion that he is somehow worthy of this love. The narrator attributes authority to his witness and thereby claims authority for his narration. Whereas Jesus predicts Simon Peter's death, he leaves the Beloved Disciple's future as an open story. The narrator hints at the Beloved Disciple's death by explaining what Jesus did not say (21:23). His is a literary rather than a dramatic death; the author of the book is killed by his own narration.

The different methods of representing the characters of Simon Peter and the Beloved Disciple indicate that we should not treat them as alternative models. There is real ingenuity in the design of the Beloved Disciple that does invite the audience to embark upon some sort of journey with him, but we ought to situate this journey in the context of the literary experience. The last references to the Beloved Disciple—the account of the rumor that he would not die (21:23) and the attribution of authorship (21:24)—mark a progression out of a character in a story into that of author in the world. Though the characters in the story are immortal, as they live on beyond the time of the narrative—Simon Peter's death is a certain but future reality and the death of the Beloved Disciple is a potential reality—the author, who lives in the world, is mortal. As he emerges as an author, he must perform a *kenōsis* by giving up his immortality and becoming "obedient unto death."

Another example of an author's use of himself as a character without a real role in his literary work occurs in Plato's dialogues. Hayden Ausland draws attention to the relationship of Plato's anonymity ("Plato" is a nickname meaning "broad forehead") to the form of his writing, which perhaps has some bearing upon how we understand the Beloved Disciple. Curiously, modern readers of Plato's dialogues tend also to ignore their dramatic form and reduce their content to doctrines and equate the ideas of their protagonist with the author, so that we speak about Plato's theory of knowledge or Plato's doctrine of the immortal soul. Those who encourage a mimetic reading of Plato argue that the dialogues do not invite their readers to adopt propositions but rather to stand as critical witnesses to dialogues that end without coming to a conclusion, so that the reader then becomes a participant by continuing the dialogue.[89] There is no authoritative interpretation of the dialogue or answer to the questions, and so the reader must continue asking questions about love, knowledge, justice, and goodness. Because Plato remains anonymous and gives himself only a marginal role in the dialogues, he gains credibility as an objective witness: in *Apology of Socrates,* Socrates names him among his friends present; and in *Phaedo,* he is noted absent due to ill-

---

[89] Hayden W. Ausland, "On Reading Plato Mimetically," *AJP* 118 (1997): 373–74, 386.

ness, but Plato never gives himself a speaking part. First, he does not undermine his own authority by leaving his thoughts exposed to Socrates' scrutiny or the reader's ridicule. Second, he does not detract from Socrates' words or short-circuit the reader's task of interpretation by providing his own commentary on what Socrates says. Plato is the ideal disciple in that he does not try to supplant the master by becoming the philosopher but honors him by being a witness to his dialogues.

Although the English word "testify" is not derived from the Greek word μαρτυρέω, reflection upon its etymology may lead to some insight about the relationship of the Beloved Disciple's witness to Jesus' life and Peter's service. Walter Ong provides this etymology:

> "Contest" comes from the Old French conteste, which in turn derives from the Latin contestari. Testis means a witness and derives from the Proto-Indo-European root trei (three) compounded with stā (stand), to yield the form (unattested in extant literature but pointed to by phonological patternings) *tri-st-i, meaning a third person standing by, as in a dispute between two others. Thus a testis or witness, a "third stander," implies an agonistic situation between two persons which the testis or third person reports from outside.[90]

Ong's lesson in etymology reminds us of what it means to be a witness. In his discussion of verbal dueling in the Iliad, Ward Parks draws attention to the indispensable function that witnesses play in the contest. The fame and glory or honor pursued by the combatants can be achieved only if witnesses attest to it.[91] In many cases, the hero dies in combat, and the witnesses provide the important service of proclaiming his praises in the vaunting at the end of the contest. Thus, Plato as a bystander rather than a dialogue partner is in a position to testify to Socrates' words, and by representing Socrates as the victor in contests of wits, he implicitly praises him. The Beloved Disciple is a bystander in the action of the gospel, and when he emerges out of it as an author, he not only testifies to Jesus' glory but also makes possible the continuation of Jesus' praise by those who receive his testimony.

As far as one believes that Jesus is the Messiah, the Son whom God glorifies, one might identify with the Beloved Disciple's ability to witness to Jesus, but one would hardly identify with what the narrator has not provided: the Beloved Disciple's struggle to understand what he witnesses as it happens and his experience of suffering or love. For that, the narrator provides Simon Peter. Although Jesus announces that Simon will be called "Cephas,"

---

[90] Walter J. Ong, Fighting for Life: Contest, Sexuality, and Consciousness (Ithaca, N.Y.: Cornell University Press, 1981), 45.

[91] Ward Parks, Verbal Dueling in Heroic Narrative: The Homeric and Old English Traditions (Princeton, N.J.: Princeton University Press, 1990), 36–37.

translated "Peter" (1:42), Jesus himself never addresses Peter by either name. In contrast, the narrator, who relies upon the witness of the Beloved Disciple, consistently refers to him as "Simon Peter." The Beloved Disciple, then, is indeed an ideal model of witness, but it is erroneous to think that the witness is to a fixed idea or doctrine or a "strictly forensic concept" rather than to Jesus' glory or Simon Peter's discipleship.[92]

Paul Anderson also pursues the similarity between Johannine and Platonic dialogues but concludes that the dialogic response evoked by the Fourth Gospel is to choose between two ways, one leading to death and the other leading to eternal life?[93] As I have argued with reference to the characterization of the Jews, their deliberation dramatizes the nature of the world instead of presenting a right and a wrong understanding of Jesus. All definitions of who Jesus might be prove to be inadequate, and Jesus pushes beyond the conventions of terms of reference by using titles and names that no institution or tradition can define. The manner in which the Fourth Gospel ends anticipates an ongoing dialogue about who Jesus is, and its references to other stories invites their telling. The gospel's indeterminacy opened a space for the creedal debates of the early church, but the mistake that the church made was to hold councils and promulgate doctrine to end them.

The All-Too-Knowing Narrator

The presence of (and dependence upon) a narrator is perhaps the single efficient datum that undermines an argument that the genre of the Fourth Gospel is more like a play than a history or a biography or a Hellenistic novella. But if we sever the relationship between the Beloved Disciple and the narrator and ask how the narrator is characterized, we find that the voice that represents the ideal is not exactly an omniscient narrator. The narrator in the Fourth Gospel plays a more limited role than, or a qualitatively different role from, that in the Synoptic Gospels. In his capacity as the one who reports action that occurs largely through dialogues rather than narration, the narrator takes the position of a witness who relates the action from a position of hindsight—a role played by the messenger on the Athenian stage. Like the Euripidean messenger, the Johannine narrator violates the limits of his witness by claiming the ability to see into the minds of others. A thorough com-

---

[92] According to Ernst Käsemann (*The Testament of Jesus*, 42), "witness in John is a strictly forensic concept, presupposing the situation of legal proceedings."

[93] Paul N. Anderson, *The Christology of the Fourth Gospel: Its Unity and Disunity in the Light of John 6* (Valley Forge, Pa.: Trinity, 1996), 196, 210–11.

parison of the narration in the Fourth Gospel with the narration in the tragic messenger speeches is beyond the scope of this study, and I do not think that the Johannine narrator should be treated as a later manifestation of a Euripidean messenger, but a comparison of how the two include characters' motivations in their reporting of events, actions, and speech serves as a heuristic device to bring certain propensities of the Johannine narrator into relief.

In her study of Euripidean messenger-speeches, Irene J. F. de Jong notes how the messengers tend to begin and end their stories with explicit references to themselves but only seem to fade into the background when they describe events.[94] Although Euripidean messengers provide factual reports, they are not detached observers, for they express personal opinion, provide epithets, and make comparisons.[95] These messengers habitually draw conclusions about other characters' thoughts and motives, based upon their actions or words, or they violate the bounds of subjectivity and simply tell us what other characters are thinking.[96] De Jong argues that the messenger speeches produce what Gérard Genette calls a "récit motive," "a story in which what characters do is continually motivated."[97] Though the messenger refrains from referring to himself directly, he indirectly expresses his views through the attribution of motive. For example, in a speech describing the death of Neoptolemus (*Andr.* 1085–1165), the messenger describes how suspicion causes the people to gather together, and attributes their attack to anger aroused by Orestes alone. As the fight proceeds, he ascribes emotions or motives to each action.

Like the Euripidean messenger, the Johannine narrator begins and ends the gospel with explicit self-reference and then refrains from referring to himself for the bulk of his narration, allowing the audience to receive the story as though they were witness to its unfolding action; however, by reporting characters' thoughts and motives, the narrator provides more than an objective witness would know. Given our modern propensity to focus upon character, my contemporary readers might object and say that the gospel leaves us in the dark about why characters do what they do. For example, what possesses Nicodemus to cart fifty pounds of myrrh to Jesus' burial? Why does Mary mistake Jesus for the gardener? Why does Peter put his clothes on before jumping into the water? Nevertheless, the Johannine narrator distinguishes

---

[94] Irene J. F. de Jong, *Narrative in Drama: The Art of the Euripidean Messenger-Speech* (MnemosyneSup 116; Leiden: Brill, 1991), 5.

[95] Ibid., 74–96.

[96] Ibid., 25–28.

[97] Ibid., 28.

himself from the other gospel narrators by what he does tell about Jesus and other characters. He explains Jesus' motives for his movements or inner disposition about them:

> When the two days were over, he went from that place to Galilee (for Jesus himself had testified that a prophet has no honor in the prophet's own country. (4:43–44)

> When Jesus realized that they were about to come and take him by force to make him king, he withdrew again to the mountain by himself. (6:15)

> He did not wish to go about in Judea because the Jews were looking for an opportunity to kill him. (7:1)

> Though Jesus loved Martha and her sister and Lazarus, after having heard that Lazarus was ill, he stayed two days longer in the place where he was. (11:5–6)

> Jesus therefore no longer walked about openly among the Jews, but went from there to a town called Ephraim in the region near the wilderness. (11:54)

> He said (in order to fulfill the scripture), "I am thirsty." (19:28)

The narrator also tells about other characters' motivations, some of which seemingly are innocent:

> His disciples had gone to the city to buy food. (4:8)

> A large crowd kept following him, because they saw the signs that he was doing for the sick. (6:2)

> They [the Jews] followed her because they thought that she was going to the tomb to weep there. (11:31)

> Now the slaves and the police had made a charcoal fire because it was cold, and they were standing around it and warming themselves. (18:18)

Others are ignoble or suspect:

> For this reason the Jews were seeking all the more to kill him, because he was not only breaking the sabbath, but was also calling God his own Father, thereby making himself equal to God. (5:18)

> Yet no one would speak openly about him for fear of the Jews. (7:13)

> His [the blind man's] parents said this because they were afraid of the Jews; for the Jews had already agreed that anyone who confessed Jesus to be the Messiah would be put out of the synagogue. (9:22)

He [Judas] said this not because he cared about the poor, but because he was a thief; he kept the common purse and used to steal what was put into it. (12:6)

Nevertheless many, even of the authorities, believed in him. But because of the Pharisees they did not confess it, for fear that they would be put out of the synagogue; for they loved human glory more than the glory that comes from God. (12:42–43)

After he [Judas] received the piece of bread, Satan entered into him. (13:27)

They [the Jews] themselves did not enter the headquarters, so as to avoid ritual defilement and to be able to eat the Passover. (18:28)

Now when Pilate heard this, he was more afraid than ever. (19:8)

Since it was the day of Preparation, the Jews did not want the bodies left on the cross during the sabbath, especially because that sabbath was a day of great solemnity. So they asked Pilate to have the legs of the crucified men broken and the bodies removed. (19:31)

Joseph of Arimathea, who was a disciple of Jesus, though a secret one because of his fear of the Jews, asked Pilate to let him take away the body of Jesus. (19:38)

The doors of the house where the disciples had met were locked for fear of the Jews. (20:19)

The narrator also shows a particular interest in the interior disposition of belief:

Jesus did this, the first of his signs, in Cana of Galilee, and revealed his glory; and his disciples believed in him. (2:11)

After he was raised from the dead, his disciples remembered that he had said this; and they believed the scripture and the word that Jesus had spoken. (2:22)

The man believed the word that Jesus spoke to him and started on his way. (4:50)

So he [the royal official] himself believed, along with his whole household. (4:53)

Nevertheless many, even of the authorities, believed in him. (12:42)

Then the other disciple, who reached the tomb first, also went in, and he saw and believed. (20:8)

The narrator's imputation of belief mirrors the concern for belief expressed in the prologue (1:7, 12) and the epilogue (19:35; 20:31) and Jesus' own interest in the topic.

The longer narratives in the Synoptic tradition describe action rather than interior dispositions. In the following example from the Gospel of Matthew, the gospel writer lets the reader infer the motives of the crowd:

> Jesus went throughout Galilee, teaching in their synagogues and proclaiming the good news of the kingdom and curing every disease and every sickness among the people. So his fame spread throughout all Syria, and they brought to him all the sick, those who were afflicted with various diseases and pains, demoniacs, epileptics, and paralytics, and he cured them. And great crowds followed him from Galilee, the Decapolis, Jerusalem, Judea, and from beyond the Jordan. (Matt 4:23–25)

The crowd seems to follow Jesus in order to be the recipient of a healing or its witness. References to motives are the exception rather than the rule. Matthew tells about Herod's conflicted motives (14:5), and he says that the chief priests and the Pharisees realize that Jesus is referring to them in his parables and that "they wanted to arrest him, but they feared the crowds, because they regarded him as a prophet" (21:45–46). Only at the resurrection does Matthew show any interest in belief: "When they saw him, they worshiped him; but some doubted" (28:17). But this doubt seems inconsequential to Jesus, who commands them to go and make disciples of all nations.

If we consider once again the role of the witness in the heroic contest, a pattern in the Johannine narrator's imputations of motives and thoughts becomes apparent and calls his omniscience into question. In the flyting contest, the hero often imputes to his adversary the eristic motive of desire for honor or the quality of cowardice, or sometimes both. In the speech in which Achilles accuses Aineias of desiring the honors that victory brings, he also reminds him of how on an earlier occasion he ran from Achilles' spear (Homer, *Il.* 20.187). By recounting the tale in a way that magnifies the honor of the victor and the ignominy of the vanquished, the tragic messengers participate in the vaunting at the end of the contest that they narrate. Euripides' *Suppliant Women* provides an excellent example. The play begins following Polynices' failed attempt to take Thebes and Creon's decree that his nephew's body and the Argives' bodies will be left unattended. Adrastus, who as king of the Argives ought to have retrieved the bodies, joins the women in supplication to Demeter and begs Theseus to defend his own honor as well as that of the city by bringing the bodies back to Argos. A Theban herald then arrives, with whom Theseus enters a flyting contest to establish the terms of the conflict: Theseus will try to take the bodies of the sons of Argives who have fought with Polynices and bury them, and the Thebans, ruled by Creon, will oppose him and his army. The actual physical conflict is left to a messenger to recount, and he provides a contrasting picture of Theseus and Creon. According to the messenger, Creon greets Theseus's clear statement of intent with silence and sends his chariots into battle, but he joins the fighting only when his cavalry is winning, as the messenger sees it, so as not to discourage his allies. He clearly paints Creon with the brush of cowardice. In contrast stands the narrator's description of Theseus: "For his part Theseus did not allow his own affairs to be ruined by hesitation" (697 [Kovacs, LCL]). At various points the narrator adds comments, such as "At this point the general did a praiseworthy deed" (707), that draw attention to the merits of Theseus's involvement. When Theseus calls out, "Either stop these Sown Men's hard spears, lad, or it's all over for Pallas Athena!" (710–712) the narrator notes, "That put courage in the hearts of all the Athenian army" (713). At the end of the narration, Adrastus comments on shame that accrues to Theseus when he removes the bodies to wash and attend to them himself. In response, the messenger continues to defend his hero's honor. In the convention of the messenger speech, when the event is a heroic contest, the messenger is neither a disinterested nor an objective witness.

The Johannine narrator contributes to the vaunting of Jesus' victory over death by consistently describing the fear of the Jews and attributing to their love of their own glory their resistance to acknowledging Jesus' superiority. A careful look at the narrator's use of the verb πιστεύω ("believe") shows that in some cases it suggests not some sort of cognitive understanding but a form of reverence (2:11; 4:53; 12:42) and in other cases an attitude of trust (2:22; 4:50). The motivations that the narrator gives to Jesus often undercut any possible shame or cowardice in his actions. He avoids the crowd because he does not desire public honors; his thirst does not signify desire but the fulfillment of Scripture; he evades arrest because it is not his time to die. The attribution of motives is, then, tied to the narrator's role as a witness to a heroic contest.

The narrator possesses a number of other propensities that do not necessarily bear resemblance to any particular model but do give him an identity. He marks himself as a man of a later generation in a number of ways. On two occasions he narrates how the disciples eventually remember what Jesus said and come to understand (2:22; 12:16), and on a third occasion he notes their inability to comprehend Scripture until after Jesus' resurrection (20:9). In the end of his narrative he steps out of narrative time to explain how the report spread that the Beloved Disciple would not die (21:23). He allies himself with Jesus' followers by refraining from using the title "Son of Man" and limiting himself to titles used by characters other than Jesus. Like other followers, he uses fulfillment texts to situate Jesus within the Judaic tradition. His habit of providing ambiguous references to places makes him appear to be from a place other than Judea or Galilee. Nobody has been able to find Bethany beyond the Jordan (1:28), Aenon near Salim (3:23), or Sychar (4:5), and the references to Tiberias (6:1, 23; 21:1) are problematic.[98] Margaret Davies, after reviewing the geographic details, remarks, "The presentation suggests not the report of an eyewitness, nor the reminiscences of a native of Palestine, but the availability of some historical traditions."[99] Davies also refers to other aspects of the gospel's style adopted by the author: "Hebrew, Aramaic and Latin terms provide authentic local colour. Septuagintisms give the narrative a 'religious' aura. The leisurely and repetitive manner serves a didactic purpose and creates a respectful dignity and deliberate solemnity."[100] It is impossible to say what the first audience of the gospel would have thought about the indiscriminate treatment of the Pharisees and priests or the vagueness of geographical references. For a moment, I invite my readers to entertain the possibility that the first audience might have taken the narrator's habits of speech not as a sign of his omniscience but rather as a distinctive feature of his storytelling. The gospel's affinity to drama and the narrator's explicit statement of reliance upon the witness of the Beloved Disciple make him yet another voice in this play of perspective, albeit a guiding one, who seems to maintain a distinct identity as a secondary witness. He is a participant in, rather than the architect of, a tradition of witnessing to Jesus' glory.

Notably Present Characters: Women

Besides the fact that the Fourth Gospel has a more limited cast of characters, we must also consider the composition of the dramatis personae. Feminist exegetes have been attracted to the Fourth Gospel because of the prominent and positive role that it gives women and because, as Sandra Schneiders puts it, "women do not appear in the Fourth Gospel as bloodless representatives of the 'eternal feminine'" but as "strikingly individual and original characters."[101] Martin Scott contends that the gospel gives women a "central position . . . as exemplary disciples" who replace "traditional male

---

[98] See Thomas Brodie, *The Gospel according to John: A Literary and Theological Commentary* (New York: Oxford University Press, 1993), 151, 201, 219.

[99] Margaret Davies, *Rhetoric and Reference in the Fourth Gospel* (JSNTSup 69; Sheffield, JSOT Press, 1992), 285.

[100] Ibid., 27.

[101] Schneiders, *Written That You May Believe*, 99.

figures . . . in their function."[102] For Elisabeth Schüssler Fiorenza, Martha in particular "represents the full apostolic faith of the Johannine community just as Peter does the Matthean community."[103] As tempting as these characterizations of the Johannine women might be for feminist readers, the inclusion of women and their speech may reflect the dramatic concerns of the gospel writer more than his concerns for the socioreligious or political status of women.

Women are strikingly vocal in the Fourth Gospel. In the beginning of the Gospel of Luke, Mary and Elizabeth have long speeches whereas, in the Gospel of Matthew, Mary says nothing and Elizabeth does not appear. Once past the birth narratives, Matthew's and Luke's women are comparatively silent. The Matthean narrator reports the interior thoughts of the hemorrhaging woman as direct speech (Matt 9:21), but in Luke she is mute. Matthew's Canaanite woman has one line (Matt 15:27), and the mother of James and John makes her inappropriate request (Matt 20:21). In Luke, Martha has one line of complaint (Luke 10:40), and a woman's voice can be heard above the crowd saying, "Blessed is the womb that bore you and the breasts that nursed you!" (Luke 11:27). None of the women in either Matthew's or Luke's resurrection account has anything to say. In contrast, the Fourth Gospel's Samaritan woman has nine lines of dialogue with Jesus and two with her community. Martha speaks to Jesus at two separate points, with a total of fives lines, including the confession "I believe that you are the Messiah, the Son of God, the one coming into the world" (John 11:27). Moreover, she has one private line of dialogue with her sister Mary. The mother of Jesus has two lines and Mary of Bethany has one line, but both figure prominently in two episodes each, and Mary Magdalene engages in dialogue with both the angels and Jesus at the empty tomb. Robert Maccini understands this freedom of expression to be a sign of the value that the gospel writer places upon the testimony of individual witnesses, either male or female, rather than a partiality toward women as a class.[104] However, he focuses upon what they say about Jesus and neglects the context of the dialogues and the topics of discussion, both of which may suggest that the

---

[102] Scott, *Sophia and the Johannine Jesus,* 238–45.

[103] Elisabeth Schüssler Fiorenza, "A Feminist Critical Interpretation for Liberation: Martha and Mary—Luke 10:38–42," *Religion and Intellectual Life* 3 (1986): 31. For a rebuttal of her arguments, see Adele Reinhartz, "From Narrative to History: The Resurrection of Mary and Martha," in *"Women Like This": New Perspectives on Jewish Women in the Greco-Roman World* (ed. Amy-Jill Levine; SBLEJL 1; Atlanta: Scholars Press, 1991), 175.

[104] Robert Gordon Maccini, *Her Testimony Is True: Women as Witnesses according to John* (JSNTSup 125; Sheffield: Sheffield Academic Press, 1996), 243–45.

gospel writer is more interested in gender distinctions than our modern concern for equity might allow.

Because Greek tragedy contains more speaking female characters than any other Greek literary genre, classicists also raise questions regarding gender equity. By Mark Griffith's count, a full one-third of speaking roles are given to females in the corpus of thirty-two extant plays, seven of which give more than half the lines to women.[105] What does it signify that women possess rhetorical skill similar to that of the men with whom they speak? Does Euripides give women a public voice by lending women such as Helen the voice of a male actor with which to defend herself, or the women of Troy the opportunity to describe their own suffering? Classicists have found that questions about the social and political position of women in the tragedies have led them in circles. In contrast, questions about the contribution of female characters to dramatic tension and conflict by virtue of their gender reveal a tragedy's capacity to dramatize the anxieties and contradictions of public and private life.[106]

In her analysis of the representation of females by male actors in Greek tragedy, Froma I. Zeitlin emphasizes the phenomenon of women seen and heard onstage in a society in which they are mute.[107] She concludes that the struggles of the female characters for identity and self-esteem are "designed primarily for exploring the male project of selfhood. . . . Functionally women are never an end in themselves, and nothing changes for them once they have lived out their drama onstage."[108] Zeitlin notes, "Tragedy arrives at closures that generally reassert male, often paternal, structures of authority."[109] She makes her case by looking at four indispensable elements of the Greek tragedy: the representation of the body onstage, the arrangement of architectural space onstage, theatrical *mimēsis*, and the plot. When we look for comparable elements in the Fourth Gospel, we find that the female presence contributes to the exploration of Jesus' male selfhood, but unlike the tragedies, the gospel does not reassert male structures.

After examining the representation of the body onstage, Zeitlin observes, "At those points when the male finds himself in a condition of weakness, he too becomes acutely aware that he has a body—and then perceives himself, at the limits of pain, to be most like a woman."[110] Among many ex-

---

[105] Mark Griffith, "Antigone and Her Sister(s): Embodying Women in Greek Tragedy," in *Making Silence Speak: Women's Voices in Greek Literature and Society* (ed. André Lardinois and Laura McClure; Princeton, N.J.: Princeton University Press, 2001), 117.

[106] Ibid., 135.

[107] Zeitlin, "Playing the Other," 68.

[108] Ibid., 69.

[109] Ibid., 86–87.

[110] Ibid., 72.

amples, Zeitlin provides the following from Sophocles' *Women of Trachis*. Heracles has been brought onstage wounded, and he addresses Hyllus:

> Come, my son, bring yourself to do it! Pity me, pitiable in many ways, I who am crying out, weeping like a girl, and no one can say he saw this man do such a thing before, but though racked with torments I never would lament! But now such a thing has shown me as a womanish creature. (1070–1075 [Lloyd-Jones, LCL])

Mourning and lamenting are the province of women in these ancient Mediterranean societies. When Jesus speaks to the disciples about the pain that lies ahead for them, he is explicit: they will become like women.

> Very truly, I tell you, you will weep and mourn, but the world will rejoice; you will have pain, but your pain will turn into joy. When a woman is in labor, she has pain, because her hour has come. But when her child is born, she no longer remembers the anguish because of the joy of having brought a human being into the world. So you have pain now; but I will see you again, and your hearts will rejoice, and no one will take your joy from you. (John 16:20–22)

The association of weeping and mourning with women's activity is substantiated by the progression from the anguish of lament to the pain of childbirth. The men's lament is not like a woman's despair at death but like a woman's cry that anticipates the joy of birth. References to Jesus' own body, particularly those associated most closely with his death, do not explicitly compare him to a woman, but they do seem to play along the borders of emasculation. When Jesus' body becomes the temple (2:19) and the source of living water (4:10–14; 6:35c; 7:37–38), it assumes roles more frequently personified as female. Jesus' claim "Out of the believer's heart [κοιλία = belly, womb] shall flow rivers of living water" (7:38), with its possible reference to himself or to his followers, has no direct source in Scripture. Marcus Joel contends that Jesus is referring to himself and playing with the words of Isa 12:3, "With joy you will draw water from the wells of salvation," and its association with the rites from the Festival of Booths, in which water was taken from the Siloam stream.[111] The Hebrew word for "belly" (מעים) is a pun of sorts on the word for "well" (מעין), or even a homograph in Mishnaic Hebrew (מעיין) that stands for both. Dale Allison associates the quotation with the eschatological images of Zech 13:1 and 14:8 and Ezek 47 in which living water flows out from Jerusalem.[112] In either case, Jesus once more treats his body as the

---

[111] Joel Marcus, "Rivers of Living Water from Jesus' Belly (John 7:38)," *JBL* 117 (1998): 328–30.

[112] Dale C. Allison, "The Living Water (John 4:10–14; 6:35c; 7:37–38)," *SVTQ* 30 (1986): 154.

temple and the source of life. When Jesus' body becomes the source of actual water and blood after it is pierced at the crucifixion, the image suddenly ceases to be a metaphor for Jesus' life-giving spiritual power and becomes dangerously physical, like a woman's life-giving body, from which such emissions come in the form of menses, lactation, and birth fluids.[113] My point is not that Jesus is portrayed as a woman but that the gospel writer represents the body by analogies to the vulnerability of the female body because, in ancient Mediterranean society, female bodies, not those of males, denote suffering. In the following analysis, I will also raise the possibility that the footwashing and Jesus' tears should be placed in this category.

Zeitlin's analysis of theatrical space and the contrast between the outside and public space, represented onstage, and the inside and secret space of women, represented as lying behind a door, do not at first seem to apply to the Fourth Gospel. The gospel does not seem to represent interior space as particularly female or exterior space as particularly male. Jerome Neyrey makes an important observation about private and public space in the gospel: although scenes like the one at the well may be outdoors, they are governed by the conditions of the private world in that they construct a fictive kinship group in which men share food and beverage with women.[114] By engaging in dialogue with the woman at the well, Jesus crosses a boundary from the public world of men, governed by honor, to the private world of women, governed by shame.

In Charles Segal's study of how the tragedians elaborate the dangers that lie at the boundary between male space and female space, he finds that these border crossings open up space to explore the ambiguity of the pain and pleasure of death's commemoration and the interconnectedness of human experience.[115] For example, when men cross over into female space, conversations turn to women's concerns. Although in the tragedies women talk with rhetorical force equal to that of men, they fill their speech with "supplication, prophecies, curses . . . domestic activities such as . . . fetching water . . . descriptions of the miseries of slavery and loss of homeland and family; references to the intimate relations between child and mother or between sexual partners."[116] An examination of the social location of Jesus' encounters with women shows that they tend to be events such as weddings and funerals,

---

[113] Hesiod (*Theog.* 592) states that women are "bellies."

[114] Jerome Neyrey, "What's Wrong with This Picture? John 4, Cultural Stereotypes of Women, and Public and Private Space," *BTB* 24 (1994): 77–91.

[115] Charles Segal, *Euripides and the Poetics of Sorrow: Art, Gender, and Commemoration in Alcestis, Hipploytus, and Hecuba* (Durham, N.C.: Duke University Press, 1993), 8, 12–14, 152–53.

[116] Griffith, "Antigone and Her Sister(s)," 123.

which most readily afford interaction of male and female, and so it is logical that either marriage or death is central to all of Jesus' dialogues with women:

Jesus' Dialogue Partners	Social Location	Topic
MOTHER	A wedding	Wine for a wedding feast
SAMARITAN WOMAN	A well associated with	Fetching water
	the betrothal type-scene	Her marriages
MARY AND MARTHA	Mourning at a tomb	Their brother's death
MARY	A supper at Lazarus's home	Anointing of Jesus' body for burial
MOTHER	A public death	Mother and son union
MARY MAGDALENE	A tomb	Jesus' corpse

Robert Maccini understands this pattern's significance to be naturalistic detail reflective of the cultural milieu;[117] however, at these boundaries between male and female space, gender identification is threatened.

When Jesus enters into the private space of the wedding at Cana, he is confronted by his mother's implicit demand: "They have no wine" (2:3). Despite his disclaimer, "Woman [γύναι], what concern is that to you and me? My hour has not yet come" (2:4), his mother proceeds to instruct the servants to do whatever her son asks. The possible rudeness of addressing his mother as γύναι is a matter of considerable debate, but whatever the case, as Heikki Räisänen remarks, the word γύναι throws the accent upon femaleness here and at the crucifixion (19:26).[118] In Euripides' *Electra*, Electra first gives advice to her farmer husband and then pressures Orestes to murder their mother by arguing, "Don't play the coward and be unmanly but go practice the same guile on her as you used to kill Aegisthus, her husband!" (982–984 [Kovacs, LCL]), and in doing so she takes control of the action by acting through the men. The comic and then negative overtones of Electra's words undermine both men's masculinity and Orestes' heroic stature.[119] The comic

---

[117] Maccini, *Her Testimony Is True*, 246–47.

[118] Cited in Turid Karlsen Seim, "Roles of Women in the Gospel of John," in *Aspects on the Johannine Literature* (ed. Lars Hartman and Birger Olsson; ConBNT 18; Uppsala: Almqvist & Wiksell, 1987), 60.

[119] See Ann Norris Michelini, *Euripides and the Tragic Tradition* (Madison: University of Wisconsin Press, 1987), 228.

elements of the Johannine wedding scene, with the privilege of knowing that Jesus performs a miracle going to only the disciples and the audience, remain obvious to modern readers, but the subtle play upon honor and shame, which perhaps is going on at many levels, may be lost upon them. If the shortage of wine could lead to serious embarrassment for the hosts, as Bruce Malina and Richard Rohrbaugh note, then the mother's interference draws Jesus into the private orbit of shame.[120] In the context of a society in which female assertiveness undermines the male role, when Jesus does what his mother asks, he risks loss of face, but the scene ends with the counterclaim of the narrator, who defends Jesus' honor by concluding that Jesus has revealed his δόξα (2:11).[121] Colleen Conway concludes, "[Jesus' mother] does not move the narrative forward in a disinterested, mechanical way; her actions are in line with the fundamental theological purposes of the Gospel."[122] The scene closes in a way that suits the theological goal of making Jesus' glory manifest, but it does so at the possible expense of Jesus' honor.

As Jerome Neyrey notes in his analysis of John 4, Jesus also risks his male honor by violating social taboos in his conversation with the Samaritan woman.[123] He meets alone with a woman who is not his relative, and he invites impurity by asking for a drink from one who is treated as perpetually unclean.[124] Jesus' disciples are shocked by his conversation with a woman. Turid Karlsen Seim suggests that the narrator discloses their reaction while the disciples do not because it implies a criticism of Jesus; to publicly acknowledge that Jesus' actions are inappropriate would be to shame him.[125]

In the early part of the gospel, Jesus' encounters with women are either set at a marriage or draw marriage into the conversation, but as Jesus moves toward his death, the occasion or themes of conversation also turn toward morbidity and bring Jesus into the female realm of emotional pain and concern for a corpse. The scene of mourning over Lazarus contains elements of

---

[120] Bruce J. Malina and Richard L. Rohrbaugh, *Social-Science Commentary on the Gospel of John* (Minneapolis: Fortress, 1998), 66.

[121] Seim ("Roles of Women in the Gospel of John," 62), who stands in the line of Ernst Haenchen and Heikki Räisänen, argues that Jesus explains that his life is governed by God's will and that Mary accepts this by instructing the servants, "Do whatever he tells you" (2:5).

[122] Colleen Conway, *Men and Women in the Fourth Gospel: Gender and Johannine Characterization* (SBLDS 167; Atlanta: Scholars Press, 1999), 77.

[123] Neyrey, "What's Wrong with This Picture?"

[124] Cf. *m. Nid.* 4:1: "Samaritan women are deemed menstruants from their cradle."

[125] Seim, "Roles of Women in the Gospel of John," 59.

danger for Jesus. Readers sensitive to the categories of honor and shame, such as Malina and Rohrbaugh, notice the challenge to Jesus' honor posed by Mary's public allegation that Jesus could have done something to prevent her brother's death.[126] Jesus' weeping may also signify a border crossing. According to Charles Segal, "for the Greeks after Homer, even more sharply than for us, tears were a gendered category. Although men wept, tears were particularly characteristic of women." Segal therefore concludes that the many examples of men weeping in the tragedies are "a sign of overwhelming catastrophe" and a "temporary lapse of their manliness."[127] The Hebrew tradition offers many examples of male tears, but as in the Greek tradition, these are a sign of extreme emotion and often helplessness. The Jews' reaction to Jesus' weeping, "See how he loved him" (11:36), does not necessarily undo the suggestion that Jesus acts like a woman. In the tragic tradition, a man who suffers from love suffers an affliction or disease.[128] In the anointing scene, Jesus' conduct comes under attack by Judas, and although the narrator imputes ulterior motives for Judas's objection to Mary's display of affection or respect, the objection in its cultural context probably is appropriate. Sirach consistently connects shame with the inability to control one's women and one's money (e.g., Sir 25:21–22), and here Judas draws attention to the inappropriate use of money by a woman.[129] The scene at the cross, in which several women, including Jesus' mother, are present, may also contribute to the tension between shame and honor. Crucifixion is an ignoble death designed to maximize the humiliation of its victim. Several elements of the crucifixion scene underscore Jesus' humiliation and draw attention to his body: the gambling for his garment, his thirst, and the piercing of his side. His treatment recalls the symbolic acts attendant with vaunting at the end of martial combat in the Homeric epics, in which the vanquished is stripped of his armor and his body mutilated.[130] R. Alan Culpepper notes how Jesus' words "I thirst" emphasize "his desperation" or "agony" and "the helplessness of those who love him to respond."[131] The women are witnesses to Jesus' reduction to a state where the one who has proclaimed himself the source of

---

126 Malina and Rohrbaugh, *Social-Science Commentary*, 200.

127 Segal, *Euripides and the Poetics of Sorrow*, 63.

128 Griffith, "Antigone and Her Sister(s)," 123.

129 See Claudia V. Camp, "Understanding a Patriarchy: Women in Second Century Jerusalem through the Eyes of Ben Sira," in Levine, *"Women Like This,"* 28–33.

130 See, for example, Homer, *Il.* 13.618–42. Parks (*Verbal Dueling in Heroic Narrative*) counts over forty such incidents in the *Iliad.*

131 R. Alan Culpepper, "The Death of Jesus: An Exegesis of John 19:28–37," *Faith and Mission* 5 (1988): 64.

living water becomes one who thirsts and is offered vinegar as an expression of either the compassion of his tormentors or their cruel mockery. Paradoxically, what Paul characterizes as humiliation in Phil 2:8–9 is treated as exaltation in this gospel (John 13:1; 17:1).

Several scenes in the last half of the gospel represent private space (a meal and burial) in which one expects to find women but where they are absent in the narrative. In both of these spaces, men take on female roles: Jesus washes feet, and Joseph of Arimathea and Nicodemus prepare his body for burial. On a number of occasions in both Jewish and Greek literature, a man will wash another man's feet, but in all cases, this is an extreme act of humility in which the footwasher takes on the role of servant.[132] In most references to footwashing, the servant is a woman.[133] It may be significant that the other footwashings in the New Testament are performed by women; 1 Tim 5:9–10 lists washing the saints' feet as a prerequisite for placement on the roll of widows.[134] Peter's resistance to having Jesus wash his feet signifies his reception of the act as shameful to himself or Jesus or to both of them, whereas Jesus response, "Unless I wash you, you have no share with me" (John 13:8), suggests a transformation of humiliation into glorification. Segal contends that Euripides, in plays such as *Hippolytus,* in which a character's private endurance of public shame and suffering is set against his public honor as a man of stamina and victory in horseracing, is creating a new notion of honor by revealing a private nobility.[135] Similarly, by having Jesus cross boundaries into the private realm of women's shame, the gospel creates a new notion of glory that anticipates the reversal of the categories of honor and shame at Jesus' crucifixion.

Zeitlin, in her discussion of *mimēsis*—"the art of imitation through which characters are rendered lifelike, and plot and action offer an adequate representation of reality"—argues that in the tragedies women look at the world from a confined and sedentary position and when they reflect upon

---

[132] John Christopher Thomas, *Footwashing in John 13 and the Johannine Community* (JSNTSup 61; Sheffield: JSOT Press, 1991), 40. Thomas cites only three examples besides Jesus: Abraham washes the archangel Michael's feet in *T. Ab.* 3:6–9; Plutarch, *Pomp.* 73.6–7; and young boys wash men's feet in Petronius's *Satyricon*, but in this case, the young men clearly are taking over female roles.

[133] Ibid., 46–56. Thomas cites 1 Sam 25; *Jos. Asen.* 13:15; 20:1–5; Homer, *Od.* 19.308–319, 344–348, 356–358; Athenaeus, *Deipn.* 13.583–584; Herodotus, *Hist.* 6.19; Catullus, *Carm.* 64.158–163; Aristophanes, *Vesp.* 605–611; Plutarch, *Mulier. virt.* 12.249d; 1 Tim 5:9–10.

[134] See also the anointing of Jesus' feet by women: Mark 14:3–9; Luke 7:37–38; John 12:3.

[135] Segal, *Euripides and the Poetics of Sorrow*, 126.

their situation, they see the complexities and paradoxes that men resist.[136] For example, in the tragedies set in the aftermath of the Trojan War, the shame inflicted upon the wives and daughters of the defeated overshadows the glory of male victory. Moreover, the tragedies represent women who, limited by their social status, practice deception and conceal truth in order to achieve their ends and, as a result, recognize that beyond the self that one publicly presents lies a hidden self. Men, on the other hand, accustomed to direct access to power, may treat their public persona as a true and exhaustive representation of the self. Zeitlin proposes that Greek theater used female characters because they presented an opportunity for the masculine self to "play the other," thereby disclosing aspects of the self normally denied to men, such as the emotions of fear and pity, and by "her" example teaching men to recognize an unknown self.[137]

Given that the female characters in the Fourth Gospel are not men representing themselves as female, this discussion might seem irrelevant to the question of why women figure prominently, until we consider how the presence of women draws attention to hidden complexities. Jesus' mother's comment "There is no wine" and its implicit suggestion that Jesus ought to do something about it speak to the ambiguity of his position as a divine agent caught within the ordinary human concerns of social embarrassment. The Samaritan woman, who reveals her own hidden life, opens up a space to explore the realities of Jesus' Jewish maleness, the ultimate privilege of which—access to worship in the temple—Jesus rejects. Her allusion to Jacob as a common ancestor of Jews and Samaritans brings to the surface of the text the contradictions inherent in the systems that divide the two peoples. The encounter with Martha and Mary becomes the occasion for expressions of powerful emotions: Jesus' body shudders and he weeps—something that commentators at least since Augustine have found difficult to reconcile with the idea of a divine agent who possesses the power to resurrect Lazarus and knows the future. Augustine argues that this is not an involuntary action:

> Thou art troubled against thy will; Christ was troubled because He willed. Jesus hungered, it is true, but because He willed; Jesus slept, it is true, but because He willed; He was sorrowful, it is true, but because He willed; He died, it is true, but because He willed: in His own power it lay to be thus and thus affected or not.[138]

---

[136] Zeitlin, "Playing the Other," 84–85.

[137] Ibid., 84–86.

[138] Augustine, *Tract. Ev. Jo.*, 49.18, Christian Classics Ethereal Library, http://www.ccel.org/fathers2/NPNF1-07/npnf1-07-54.htm#P2099_1294739 (accessed January 2002).

Augustine's protest attempts to reduce to simplicity the complexity exposed by the presence of women in the tragedies. Complicity in a divine plan and knowledge about the future do not diminish anguish or anger in the face of human suffering in the present. When Mary anoints Jesus' feet with oil, Jesus turns the respect given to his body into a prophetic act that anticipates its mortality. Women are met with Jesus' disclosure of his identity in a gospel in which Jesus is not always forthcoming. When the Samaritan woman says, "Sir, give me this water, so that I may never be thirsty or have to keep coming here to draw water" (4:15), Jesus seizes the opportunity to break beyond the veil of her feminine secrecy. When a crowd makes a similar request, "Sir, give us this bread always" (6:34), Jesus accuses them of seeing but not believing. Maccini rejects the notion that there is anything symbolic or paradigmatic about these women's witness, and instead he sets them into the context of Jesus' positive reception of the witness of any individual in the Fourth Gospel.[139] Nevertheless, the movement from public to private, the divestment of power and authority of the former and the investment of status to the latter, may be central to the presence of women and their characterization in this gospel.

The representation of women as duplicitous in the Greek tragedies renders women ideal instigators of action that generates the irony or discrepant awareness central to tragic plots. Women who seek to achieve their ends through deception make use of "the riddling doubleness of language."[140] In plots of intrigue in the corpus of extant tragedies, the schemes of women tend to be more successful than those of men, and when men succeed, they do so through the aid of women or by trickery and disguise that threaten to undermine their masculine stature. Ajax wishes that "the whole army may with sword grasped in both hands strike me dead" (Sophocles, *Aj.* 408–409 [Lloyd-Jones, LCL]) because a manly death would reestablish his honor. In his deceptive speech, Ajax claims that, having been softened in his resolve by his wife, he plans to go wash in order to clean the dirt off him, and he describes himself as a suppliant—a role associated with women (646–692). He then commits suicide—a death that, according to Zeitlin, is normally reserved for women.[141] In *Bacchae*, Pentheus, failing to win the power struggle through physical force, is persuaded to exchange his soldier's apparel for the guise of a woman in order to spy upon the women who defy him by worshiping Dionysus, and he is subsequently torn to pieces by them.[142]

Mark Stibbe outlines Jesus' elusive action during the first half of the Fourth Gospel. Jesus withdraws without explanation (5:13; 9:12), makes

---

[139] Maccini, *Her Testimony Is True*, 251.
[140] Zeitlin, "Playing the Other," 73.
[141] Ibid., 82.
[142] Ibid., 83.

mysterious escapes from, or is elusive in, hostile situations or when he questions people's motives (6:15, 22–26; 7:30, 44; 8:59; 10:39), makes mysterious or quiet reappearances (5:14; 6:19; 9:35), and undertakes seemingly impossible or secret journeys (6:1, 20–21; 7:10).[143] Jesus' brothers' suggestion that Jesus is acting secretly and that he ought to show himself to the world (7:4) is a challenge to his honor. Jesus' failure to be forthright with his brothers is hardly an answer to that challenge. Malina and Rohrbaugh argue that because Jesus says that his hour has not yet come, he is not running from the challenge but controlling its timing, and that because his brothers are not loyal to Jesus, he does not owe them the truth.[144] It seems to me that they construct an elaborate theory to protect Jesus' honor when perhaps the thrust of the gospel is to build a strong contrast between the world's inability to honor Jesus and God's glorification of him. Jesus does nothing to protect that honor in private or in public and rejects publicly conferred honorific titles of king and Messiah. In the action of the play, he first avoids the contest in which, by the standards of a society driven by masculine honor, he could assert his power and defend himself, and when the hour comes to display his glory, he surrenders to the religious and political powers. Seen from the perspective of his own society, Jesus undergoes a "feminine" experience.[145]

Zeitlin argues that these feminine forces are the man's undoing: the tragic figure passes from being active to becoming passive, from having control to giving surrender, from sanity to madness, from male experience to a "feminine" experience.[146] At the end of the Fourth Gospel, Peter, who has professed his love for Jesus and has promised to feed his sheep, is pictured with his hands stretched out while being led by a tether to where he does not wish to go—an image that seems to fit the paradigm of the emasculated hero. What differentiates the Greek tragedies, as Zeitlin reads them, and the Fourth Gospel is that the gospel glorifies that emasculated hero. In the play on the otherness of the female in his representation of Jesus, the gospel writer presents a model of male heroism alienated from traditional male heroism. According to Segal, in the plays of Euripides, "the private world, personal ties, and the quality of feelings among men become more important than deeds of physical prowess."[147] We find a similar affirmation of the importance of the private over the public, the personal over the collective, and mutual affection over manifestations of power in the Fourth Gospel.

143 Stibbe, *John's Gospel*, 23.

144 Malina and Rohrbaugh, *Social-Science Commentary*, 143–45.

145 Zeitlin, "Playing the Other," 86.

146 Ibid.

147 Segal, *Euripides and the Poetics of Sorrow*, 126.

At the end of her study of men and women in the Fourth Gospel, Colleen Conway concludes that there is a significant difference between the ways that each gender is portrayed.[148] Women are presented in a positive light, while men stand in varying degrees of illumination. The man who is born blind shines brightly, but Nicodemus seems to remain in the dark. Whereas the women tend to be confident, even bold, and speak forthrightly, the men begin confidently but tend to stumble about as the action progresses and reveal their inconsistencies. Conway wisely resists jumping to the conclusion that this characterization signifies that women are equal disciples with the men, and she presents two possibilities:

> [The characterization] may imply that the positive presentation of Johannine women depends on a presupposition that women stand outside the bounds of recognized structures of authority. On the positive side, the Gospel may be viewed as a polemic against the "world." Not only in the sense of those who reject Jesus, but also precisely those recognized structures.[149]

My findings substantiate her suppositions. Jesus' encounters with women represent dramatically his rejection of the kind of authority that is substantiated with public recognition by men in political office or the conferral of honorific titles. The parallels to the characterization of women in the tragedies, insofar as they are bold and direct, do not signify a threat to Jesus' authority but rather confirm that his authority is not of this world. He does not seek the honor that the world gives; he possesses the glory of God's only Son.

Notably Absent Characters:
Satan and His Minions

The cast of characters in the Fourth Gospel not only is smaller than that in the Synoptic Gospels but also leaves out two categories of characters almost altogether: children and evil figures. The two children who do appear in the plot—the son of the royal official and the boy at the miraculous feeding—never interact with Jesus and are constructed by the speech of other characters. The logic of this is not obvious. Perhaps the presence of a child would humanize Jesus, but given the references to Jesus' emotions in other contexts in the gospel, the absence of children seems more a curiosity than a significant feature. The absence of demonic or satanic figures in dramatized action is more consequential.

---

[148] Conway, *Men and Women in the Fourth Gospel*, 201–5.
[149] Ibid., 205.

Just as the geography of the cosmic tale is represented by speech, so too the characters who fill that space appear for the most part in the minds of characters in the historical tale. As the plot moves toward Jesus' death and resurrection and the collapse of the reality of the historical and the cosmic tales, two exceptions occur: a heavenly voice breaks through the boundaries, and two angels appear at the empty tomb.[150] The diabolical is represented only in the speech of characters and in the opinion of the narrator. The first mention of an underworld character occurs at the end of the bread-of-life discourse when Jesus responds obliquely to Simon Peter's confession that Jesus is the Holy One of God: "Did I not choose you, the twelve? Yet one of you is a devil [διάβολος]" (6:70). The next reference comes when the crowd responds to Jesus' accusation that they are looking for an opportunity to kill him: "You have a demon! Who is trying to kill you?" (7:20). The Jews twice raise the possibility that Jesus is the victim of demon possession (8:48, 10:20). In the light-of-the-world discourse Jesus refers to "the devil" (8:44), in the farewell discourse he refers to "the ruler of this world" (14:30), and in his closing prayer he asks God to protect his disciples from "the evil one" (17:15). The narrator says that before the footwashing, the devil had put it into Judas's heart to betray Jesus (13:2), and Satan enters into Judas after he takes the piece of bread (13:27). These references do not generate a distinct picture of the underworld. The crowd's use of "demon" is clearly diagnostic in that "delusions of grandeur" are attributed to possession. Jesus' use of the term "devil" with reference to Judas seems more metaphoric than indicative of the existence of a real character, and the reference in the bread-of-life discourse seems to allude to the Old Testament notion of Satan as the prosecuting attorney or the lying spirit.[151]

William Domeris suggests that the gospel writer limits the action of the gospel to that which could be portrayed on a stage and therefore restricts supernatural effects by excluding both representatives of evil and the transfiguration.[152] This suggestion finds no support in the tragic tradition that avoids

---

[150] A later gloss, found with many variations in a number of ancient manuscripts and versions, contains a narrated reference to angelic activity at Beth-zatha: "For an angel of the Lord went down at certain seasons into the pool, and stirred up the water; whoever stepped in first after the stirring of the water was made well from whatever disease that person had" (5:4).

[151] William Klassen (*Judas: Betrayer or Friend of Jesus?* [Minneapolis: Fortress, 1996], 141), after reviewing what διάβολος refers to in the Hebrew tradition, deems it likely that Jesus is referring to Judas as an adversary in the legal sense, as in Job 1 and Zech 3:1.

[152] William R. Domeris, "The Johannine Drama," *JTSA* 42 (1983): 29–35. Domeris focuses on the absence of supernatural transfiguration and voices of demons.

neither the representation of the gods nor the denizens of the underworld. Stibbe argues that although the devil is not represented in the gospel, he is at work in the narrative world, albeit fulfilling God's plan by persuading the Jews to kill and Judas to betray Jesus.[153] Graham Twelftree contends that exorcisms are excluded because, as "commonplace and mediated miracles," they are not sufficiently grand in scale to be set alongside the Johannine signs. He supports Stibbe's view by adding that they are excluded so as not "to distract from his [the gospel writer's] view that Jesus' whole ministry was a battle with Satan."[154] However, it is precisely the sort of pericope in which Satan or demons appear that would substantiate these scholars' conclusion about the plot of the gospel. The idea that Jesus engages in combat with Satan rather than the world, represented everywhere in the gospel by historical forces, is an argument from silence. It seems to me that the absence of the demonic brings the gospel more into line with a tragic assessment of the human condition than a view of suffering as the product of supernatural evil. While the gospel writer states that Satan enters into Judas (13:27), he also sets Judas up as one who is antagonistic for purely natural reasons: he loves money (12:6). In the two tales of the Fourth Gospel's plot, two separate forces seem to be at work: on the earthly plane, characters make choices of their own free will; on the heavenly plane, things happen by necessity.

The double determination of a character's actions is a defining feature of Greek tragedy. The Greek tragedians seem to have been preoccupied with the tension between necessity—that is, divine will or fate—and human responsibility for suffering. This tension could be dramatized by having the characters represent the opposing forces in one or another person. In Aeschylus's *Seven against Thebes*, the Argives, chosen by lot, represent fortune (τύχη), while the Thebans, chosen by Etocles, represent choice.[155] More often, the tension is dramatized through debate in which one character explains his or her actions with reference to beliefs and desires while an outside observer attributes actions to some sort of external cause, or vice versa. For example, in *Seven against Thebes*, Etocles sees himself driven by his father's curse, while the chorus accuses him of being motivated by the lust for battle and a craving for blood (670–720).[156]

---

153 Stibbe, *John's Gospel,* 45.

154 Graham H. Twelftree, "Exorcism in the Fourth Gospel and the Synoptics," in *Jesus in Johannine Tradition* (ed. Robert T. Fortna and Tom Thatcher; Louisville: Westminster John Knox, 2001), 138–39.

155 Froma I. Zeitlin, *Under the Sign of the Shield: Semiotics and Aeschylus' Seven against Thebes* (Filologia e critica 44; Rome: Ateneo, 1982), 181

156 See Gill, "The Character-Personality Distinction," 22.

In the Fourth Gospel, this tension between free will and necessity is present in paradoxes found in Jesus' speeches and various dialogues. Jesus characterizes his own motivation as something divorced from his will: "I can do nothing on my own. As I hear, I judge; and my judgment is just, because I seek to do not my own will but the will of him who sent me" (5:30); "I have come down from heaven, not to do my own will, but the will of him who sent me" (6:38). The crowd, represented as deliberating, act as if they have a choice whereas Jesus denies it to them: "Do not complain among yourselves. No one can come to me unless drawn by the Father who sent me" (6:43). Belief and external force are married. Those who do not believe are those who are not granted belief by the Father. On this occasion, Jesus does not attribute to others the true capacity for deliberation, but he is not altogether consistent on this score. Later in the gospel, he does acknowledge the role of the will: "Anyone who resolves to do the will of God will know whether the teaching is from God or whether I am speaking on my own. Those who speak on their own seek their own glory" (7:17); and he attributes freedom to the actions of the Jews: "You are from your father the devil, and you choose to do your father's desires" (8:44). Jesus' own words underscore the ambiguity of human choice and divine determination.

Ironically, while the Jews speak as if their actions are governed by choice, they argue that Jesus is compelled by a demon (7:20; 8:48). The temple authorities treat the belief of Jesus' followers not as the consequence of deliberation but as the result of deception or affliction:

CHIEF PRIESTS AND PHARISEES: Why did you not arrest him?

TEMPLE POLICE: Never has anyone spoken like this!

PHARISEES: Surely you have not been deceived too, have you? Has any one of the authorities or of the Pharisees believed in him? But this crowd, which does not know the law—they are accursed. (7:45–49)

This discussion takes another turn but continues to focus upon whether choice or causality is at work:

NICODEMUS: Our law does not judge people without first giving them a hearing to find out what they are doing, does it?

PHARISEES: Surely you are not also from Galilee, are you? (7:51–52)

Nicodemus presupposes that a decision to act follows an act of careful deliberation. The other Pharisees sarcastically suggest that Jesus' folly is determined by birthplace and that Nicodemus has a choice whether to participate in it. Later, when the chief priests and Pharisees ask the council, "What are we to do?" (11:47)—a question that assumes the power of choice—Caiaphas suggests that the forces of history or the situation indicate that they have no choice.

The choice between Barabbas and Jesus is present in all four gospels, but the Fourth Evangelist layers it with irony. The carefully constructed dialogue between the crowd and Pilate juxtaposes the freedom of choice and the rule of Jewish law, both of which are dramatically rendered impotent under Roman rule, and Jesus' resurrection points to the vanity of Rome's judicial power over life and death. When Pilate offers to allow the Jews to judge Jesus according to their own law, the Jews acknowledge the restriction that Roman law places upon their ability to judge: "We are not permitted to put anyone to death" (18:31). Pilate finds no Roman law with which to condemn Jesus and appeals to a custom that grants the Jews the release of a prisoner at Passover; the crowd chooses Barabbas, a man who has violated Roman law, over Jesus. This choice proves to be an illusion, for Pilate persists in his attempt to release Jesus by repeating that he finds no case against him. The Jews then protest, "We have a law, and according to that law he ought to die" (19:7). Pilate, however, speaks as one not bound by the custom of releasing one prisoner or by Jewish law or Roman law but as one free to release or execute whomever he wishes: "Do you not know that I have power to release you, and power to crucify you?" (19:10). Jesus denies that Pilate has choice: "You would have no power over me unless it had been given you from above; therefore the one who handed me over to you is guilty of a greater sin" (19:11). When Pilate tries to release him, the Jews appeal to Roman law: "Everyone who claims to be a king sets himself against the emperor" (19:12). Pilate succumbs to the apparent necessity of Jesus' death, but by posting on the cross the inscription "Jesus of Nazareth, the King of the Jews," he publicly acknowledges only the compelling power of Roman law. As David Rensberger observes, the gospel writer capitalizes on the irony of Pilate, whose aim is to ridicule the Jews' national hopes, acting as the agent of Roman power by having Jesus' executed, when it is God's will that Jesus die.[157] The gospel provides its audience with a vantage point not shared by characters within the action. The exercise of choice may be an illusion or may lead to ends other than the ones that those characters consider. The compulsions of the moment may be inconsequential or inescapable in the broad sweep of a plot, but from their location in time, the characters do not recognize their limitations. Irony underscores the notion that ignorance of God's will or agency is the cause of suffering.

---

[157] David Rensberger, *Johannine Faith and Liberating Community* (Philadelphia: Westminster, 1988), 92–95.

Character and Ethic in the Fourth Gospel

Perhaps it is simply a reflection of my position as a modern reader conscious of the historical contingency of my own faith that I seek to find some sort of awareness that the disbelief of the crowd or the Jews is not to be treated as a corporate character flaw but as a twist of plot or an accident of history. Choice is an illusion in the theater. As Tom Stoppard so artfully demonstrates in his play *Rosencrantz and Guildenstern Are Dead,* in which two characters from *Hamlet* attempt to act upon their own free will but their actions and fate are determined by the text of Shakespeare's play, a character appears to have free will, but in fact his or her action is determined by the script, by the plot that directs choices. By rendering the characters of the Fourth Gospel like the characters of a tragedy, the writer ought to have made clear that those characters are not to be held accountable, to be pronounced innocent or guilty. Who are the true believers in the gospel? Trond Skard Dokka notes, "Whenever he [Jesus] speaks of those who are not of the world, those who come to him, believe in him, are born anew and the like, his words are without positive reference to given individuals or groups."[158] If we are pressed to name and identify them, we can come up with a Samaritan woman and a disciple whom Jesus loved, maybe John, maybe Lazarus, or his sisters Mary and Martha, or Thomas for all we know. We might name Joseph of Arimathea and Mary Magdalene, who appear without a past to account for their motives. Their actions are determined not by moral courage, not by the integrity of their convictions, but by the plot.[159]

If the Fourth Gospel does not invite us to line up the characters into categories of good and evil, saved and damned, or to view our deliberations as the guarantor of our future, what alternative considerations of our actions might it offer? Martha Nussbaum looks at how Greek tragedy responds to the ethical tradition by which the ancient Greeks tried "to make the goodness of human life safe from luck through the compelling power of reason" through the dramatization of agonizing over conflicting moral claims.[160] She

---

[158] Trond Skard Dokka, "Irony and Sectarianism in the Gospel of John," in *New Readings in John: Literary and Theological Perspectives* (ed. Johannes Nissen and Sigfred Pedersen; JSNTSup 182; Sheffield: Sheffield Academic Press, 1999), 101.

[159] Käsemann (*The Testament of Jesus,* 35–36) describes how the Johannine characters appear to be like puppets—"The light from above, falling upon them, puts them into motion, and only in the circle of his light do they have life"—and how this works against interpreting the gospel as salvation history.

[160] Nussbaum, *The Fragility of Goodness,* 3.

notes that in *Iphigenia at Aulis,* the chorus condemns Agamemnon for sacrificing Iphigenia as he would a heifer and turning his back on goodness so as to avoid a struggle with the gods.[161] Nussbaum argues that the tragedies, *Agamemnon* in particular, allow us to witness the character of human sacrifice:

> We witness . . . the clever way in which the norms of rationality and consistency are pressed to serve where their service will bring safety. We are invited to see how easily, in human lives, with what dexterous sleight-of-hand, human beings substitute human for animal, and animal for human, and stranger for loved one, under pressure endemic to life in a world where choice is constrained by necessity.[162]

The hero is not necessarily the one who avoids falling victim to these pressures but rather is one who deeply regrets what he or she has done, even when forced by fate or circumstance to choose between two evils, and comes to acknowledge a more elusive wisdom than that which formerly made choices seem clear and security attainable.[163] Nussbaum illustrates this point with reference to *Antigone.* The conflict between Creon and Antigone arises because both are equally obstinate and unyielding; each is convinced of the rightness of his or her position. Creon believes that the good of the city can be obtained by acknowledging no other allegiances; therefore, he refuses his duty to bury his nephew Polynices, an enemy of the city, whereas Antigone acknowledges her duty to her dead family. The lesson is not in seeing one as right and the other as wrong but rather in seeing how each handles the consequences of his or her actions. Antigone may evoke our pity in the first half of the play by recognizing that the conflict necessitates her own death, but Creon gains it in the end with his expression of regret, his realization that his demand for allegiance to the civic order carries a price for his household and that he is responsible for their deaths: "Woe for the errors of my mistaken mind, obstinate and fraught with death! You look on kindred that have done and suffered murder! Alas for the disaster caused by my decisions!" (1261–1265 [Lloyd-Jones, LCL]). He concedes that his powers of deliberation to determine justice have led, not by his will, to the death of his son and wife, and he exits with the final line, "I do not know which to look on, which way to lean; for all that is in my hands has gone awry, and fate hard to deal with has leapt upon my head" (1343–1346). Creon gives up his conviction that he can sacrifice duty to one's family without also sacrificing the security of the city, of which the family is a part.

---

161 Ibid., 33 (see Euripides, *Iph. aul.* 1080–1097).
162 Ibid., 38.
163 Ibid., 45.

The Fourth Gospel presents a similar picture of the tension between competing convictions and the illusion of safety. Caiaphas's ironic assertion that it is better for one man to die than for the whole nation to be destroyed, as though security could be bought at so simple a cost, treats death as a political necessity. The Jews at Jesus' trial argue for the legal necessity of Jesus' death, but Roman law backed by Roman political clout overrules the prosecution, and Pilate can find no legal necessity for Jesus' death. In the end, he, like Caiaphas, is compelled by political necessity. Those who cling to civic or political identities end up killing Jesus as easily as though he were a Passover lamb. They are made secure in their position through the death of one man, but in order to avoid the political conflicts of the world, the Jews deny one value or commitment for another. To realize the necessity of Jesus' death, they are made to acknowledge the sovereignty of the Roman emperor: "We have no king but the emperor" (19:15). Pilate brings to mind Agamemnon, who, before he decides to sacrifice Iphigenia, is torn by two evils: "Obey, obey, or a heavy doom will crush me? Oh but doom will crush me once I rend my child, the glory of my house—a father's hands are stained, blood of a young girl streaks the altar" (Aeschylus, *Ag.* 206–211 [Fagles]). But after he makes his choice, the stain disappears: "Pain both ways and what is worse? Desert the fleets, fail the alliance? No, but stop the winds with a virgin's blood, feed their lust, their fury?—feed their fury! Law is law!—Let all go well" (214–217).[164] For the Johannine Pilate, there is no washing of hands, for there is no violation of the law; he places Jesus on the judgment seat or sits upon it himself (the Greek syntax can be interpreted either way) and asks the Jews, who have called for Jesus' death, "Shall I crucify your King?" (19:15). He remains true to Roman law and convicts Jesus only of a crime against the imperial order. He sacrifices truth, in which he holds no store, for a clean conviction. Whether the act of putting the inscription "Jesus of Nazareth, the King of the Jews" in Hebrew, Latin, and Greek over the cross (19:19–20) is sarcasm, an insult to the Jews, or a tacit recognition of Jesus' dignity, Pilate is adamant in his continued allegiance to Roman law and order.

Jesus, like Antigone, is as unyielding in his resolve to meet death as his opponents are resolute in their demand for his death; and like Antigone, the distinction between Jesus' resolve and that of his opponents lies in something other than our weighing out the rightness of his convictions over the wrongness of those of Caiaphas or Pilate. Nussbaum argues, "Antigone, like Creon, has engaged in a ruthless simplification of the world of value which

---

164 Nussbaum's translation (ibid., 35–36) is better: "For it is right and holy . . . that I should desire with exceedingly impassioned passion the sacrifice staying the winds, the maiden's blood. May all turn out well."

effectively eliminates conflicting obligations."[165] Antigone's commitment to her brother, a cold corpse, renders her cold to the living, particularly those who love her: her sister Ismene and her betrothed, Haemon. Antigone's allegiance is to the dead, and so she submits to the powers of the quick and joins her family in death; but as Nussbaum points out, as Antigone approaches death, she realizes that it is upon the living that she depends for her own burial. In the end, she addresses, as her own, the citizens and gods of the city, whom she formerly renounced.[166] What differentiates Antigone from Creon also differentiates Jesus from Caiaphas and Pilate. Nussbaum contends that we can admire Antigone because her "pursuit of virtue is her own":

> It involves nobody else and commits her to abusing no other person. Rulership must be rulership of something; Antigone's pious actions are executed alone, out of a solitary commitment. She may be strangely remote from the world; but she does no violence to it. . . . Finally, and most important, Antigone remains ready to risk and to sacrifice her ends in a way that is not possible for Creon, given the singleness of his conception of value.[167]

Nussbaum's description of Antigone is easily adapted to Jesus. Jesus may be strangely remote from the world, but he does no violence to it. As he says: "If my kingdom were from this world, my followers would be fighting to keep me from being handed over to the Jews. But as it is, my kingdom is not from here" (18:36). His presence in the world shines a light upon its nature as a place of inconsistency, where even one's closest associates or own people are capable of sacrificing one's life for a supposed gain or good. The language of light versus darkness, sight versus blindness, bears more than a passing resemblance to tragic language. Creon's claim to sight that sees "ruin coming upon the citizens instead of safety" and swears by "Zeus who sees all things" (184 [Lloyd-Jones, LCL]) has, in Haemon's words, an ὄμμα δεινὸν, "a strange and terrible eye" (690), and what Creon takes for sight is shown to be blindness by the presence of Antigone, who acts in the open; therefore, in order to hide his folly, he must hide Antigone within a rocky cavern (773–774).[168] Creon is like those whom Jesus describes to Nicodemus who avoid the light lest their deeds be exposed as evil (3:20). He is like the Pharisees who in claiming to see are shown to be blind (9:39–41). The world tries to overcome conflict by the killing of opponents. Jesus conquers the world not by fighting against it but by submitting to its powers. He stands alongside Antigone, Polyxena,

---

165 Ibid., 61.
166 Ibid., 66.
167 Ibid., 66–67.
168 Ibid., 71–72.

Iphigenia, and other men and women sacrificed for a political good, who are ennobled by their death.

The difference between Antigone and Jesus is clear. Antigone goes to her death thinking herself friendless and wronged by the gods. Jesus dies knowing that God has glorified him and will glorify him again (12:28). Antigone descends to her father in Hades, and Jesus ascends to his father in heaven. But I hesitate to draw an end to the dialectic with the Greek tradition here lest the only defense against succumbing to evil be the hope of resurrection. Nussbaum suggests that the good die young in Euripidean tragedy not because of divine malevolence but because those who live a long life inevitably encounter the sort of betrayal of love or principle that turns the good toward revenge and hatred.[169] As a remedy to this "fragility of goodness," Nussbaum offers the Platonic view:

> If we were able to live an entire life inside the Platonic view that the best and most valuable things in life are all invulnerable, we would effectively get revenge, ourselves, upon our worldly situation. We would put the world in good order by sealing off certain risks, closing ourselves to certain happenings. And this world could remain relatively rich in value, since it would still contain the beauty of the Platonic contemplative life. If this is revenge, it may strike us that this is a very attractive and fruitful type of revenge: we effectively get the better of our humanity and keep for ourselves the joys of godlike activity.[170]

In order for my readers to fully appreciate Nussbaum's meaning, they need to read both Nussbaum and Plato. I presuppose that my readers have read the Fourth Gospel and can appreciate that Jesus offers a comparable "revenge." He offers the glory offered by God in lieu of that offered by the world. He offers the abiding love of God in the face of the world's hatred. The Johannine Jesus' consolation resonates with that which Nussbaum finds in Plato's *Symposium* and *Phaedrus:* "There is a beauty in the willingness to love someone in the face of love's instability and worldliness that is absent from a completely trustworthy love."[171] Jesus' love is not dependent upon Simon Peter's fidelity or the world's recognition. The statement "For God so loved the world that he gave his only Son" (3:16) becomes an affirmation of the possibility of enduring life rather than a doctrinal litmus test to determine who will receive this love and who will not. Those who would see the command to love one another as the establishment of an exclusive love, a security against the world, ignore "the truths" of the story that the Fourth Gospel tells. The command

---

169 Ibid., 419.
170 Ibid., 420.
171 Ibid.

calls the disciples to love in the face of uncertain reciprocation, not as a shield against the world. The one who feeds Jesus' sheep extends his hand at his own peril.

If we look at the pattern in the Fourth Gospel in which characters move from the security of conventional or traditional truths toward reception of Jesus and the truth he offers, we see that the movement is also away from former allegiances and roles toward a path of rejection, conflict, alienation, and death. Nicodemus stands out as a member of the Jewish elite who struggles with the competing conflicts of loyalty to the established order and to justice and whose actions seem to acknowledge the injustice of unswerving loyalty to the former by participating in the rites of "marriage to death." In his dialogue with Jesus, he struggles with an understanding of life that is not based upon birth in a mother's womb. He asserts what he knows and becomes subject to Jesus' riddling, and he is left in a position of not knowing or uncertainty. When we encounter him again, he does not retreat to a position of security. His commitment to membership in the Pharisees comes into conflict with his notion of justice. In this, as well as other scenes in which characters are presented with conflicting pictures, those who wish to simplify the picture resort to reducing Jesus, and by extension those who stand by him, to a category easily dismissed. Jesus is a Samaritan, he is demon-possessed, he is mad, he is from Galilee, and so, it seems, is Nicodemus.

Nicodemus's situation brings to mind that of Agamemnon in *Hecuba,* in which he is torn between being of a mind with the Greeks to "crown Achilles' tomb with fresh blood," that of Polyxena, daughter to Priam and Hecuba, and his love for Cassandra, their other daughter (120–129 [Kovacs, LCL]). The ghost of Achilles asks for Polyxena, and the Greek army resolves to honor his request by making her his bride in death. Hecuba pleads to Odysseus on the grounds of justice: he ought to return the kindness of sparing her daughter, for she once spared his life. Odysseus paints a morally unambiguous picture of the sacrifice by arguing for its expediency by asking, "What then will people say if occasion arises to muster the army again and fight the enemy? Will we fight, or will we save our skins since we notice that those who die receive no honor?" (313–316). Polyxena provides the reconciliation of the conflict by finding honor in death rather than disgrace in slavery and servitude. Agamemnon provides reconciliation by allowing her to die a free woman and allowing Hecuba to honor her corpse. Commentators seem compelled to make judgments for or against Nicodemus. Is he in or out, or does he represent some group of secret followers of Jesus contemporary to the gospel writer? Whether he stands by one commitment or the other is perhaps inconsequential to the plot, but his participation in Jesus' burial—an act that allies him with the family of the dead criminal—seems to be an implicit acknowledgment that the alliance to the civic order at the cost of justice is deadly. The civic order does not offer life. In Greek tragedy, the tension between two convictions is often played out over the burial of a corpse. Those who attempt to give the dead an honorable burial seek to restore the honor or status lost in the contest with a victorious enemy. The funeral makes the death glorious, and the hero lives on through commemoration of his or her story. When Hecuba prepares to bury her daughter, she confuses the rituals of a wedding and funeral:

> You, old servant, take an urn, fill it with seawater and bring it here so that I may give my daughter her last bath—bride that is no bride, virgin that is virgin no more—and lay her out for burial. I cannot give her a funeral as she deserves but only as best I may (for what can I do?), gather adornment from the captive women who share this tent with me. (609–615)

By giving Polyxena's body the same treatment it would get if it were being prepared as a bride, Hecuba restores to her dead daughter the wedding of which death has robbed her.[172] Whatever intent we attribute to Nicodemus, be it to give Jesus a proper or even a royal burial or to show his decisive allegiance to him, the gift of myrrh, with its pleasant odor, stands in counterpoint to death and its stench of decay.[173]

Instead of asking, "Who are the children of God?"—that is, inquiring about who is in and who is out—the question that the Fourth Gospel addresses seems to be, "What does it mean to be children of God?" The irony of the gospel, made all the more pronounced by its allegiance to dramatic form, expresses an epistemology of hindsight. Knowledge is a privilege of vantage point. The action of the gospel leaves one with the impression that life lived as children of God, in truth, as opposed to children of a lie, will make clear the competing demands of life. Community may risk betrayal. Friendship may demand self-sacrifice. The righteous may suffer injustice. The certainty that it offers is not a retreat into the kind of false security offered by Caiaphas. Jesus' invitation to Simon Peter to follow him is an invitation to

---

[172] Before going to her death, Polyxena utters this broken lament: "robbed of the bridegroom and wedding I should have had" (416 [Kovacs, LCL]). *Hecuba* offers another, more tantalizing, parallel to Jesus. At Polyxena's sacrifice, Achilles' son holds up a cup of gold filled to the brim with wine or some other beverage and invites his father, "Come and drink the blood of a maiden, dark and undiluted, which is the army's gift and mine!" (536–537).

[173] Nicodemus brings one hundred pounds of myrrh and aloe for the burial of Jesus' body (19:39). The only parallel to the use of this amount of myrrh is found in the description of the phoenix or Bennu bird, which makes a nest of myrrh in which it dies and is resurrected. See Achilles Tatius, *Leuc. Clit.* 3.25.

give up safety. It is not a denial of suffering and death. In order to become children of God, we must freely step into a world of contingency in which we relinquish the security of associations and make ourselves vulnerable to death.

Read as tragedy, the Fourth Gospel takes on an ethical focus that tends to get buried under the doctrinal treatment that seeks definition of membership in a restricted group, be it a catholic or a sectarian orthodoxy. The gospel asserts that some kind of certainty is possible: "you will know the truth, and the truth will make you free" (8:32); "While you have the light, believe in the light, so that you may become children of light." (12:36). However, the ambiguity of the language in which this knowledge is couched does not make it an answer to Pilate's question "What is truth?" This is why Rudolf Bultmann's understanding of belief and knowledge as neither "blind acceptance of dogma" nor "esoteric knowledge in mystagogical teaching" but rather as the "surrender" of a "previous self-understanding" and an openness to God and God's revealer remains so satisfying.[174] The choice presented in the gospel is not between the synagogue and the church but rather between the synagogue and friendship. The Jews, like Creon in *Antigone*, argue that they are compelled by law, whereas Jesus is compelled by friendship. This is why being put out of the synagogue becomes the thing most feared: not necessarily because it refers to a threat in the life of the Johannine community but because it represents an anxiety within Judaism and all human societies. Faced with competing loyalties, we tend to turn to that which makes us feel safe. We face this constantly in the world in which we live. Matthew's Jesus calls us to love our enemies, but the state calls us to kill them. The only way around that tension is to reconcile them by saying that the state acts on behalf of Jesus, but the Fourth Gospel resists this collapse. It maintains the opposition between the agents of the world and the agents of God as distinctly as possible. Nevertheless, nothing in the Fourth Gospel is so simple as the church would have it, with its clean lines of belief and disbelief based upon creedal affirmation. The tidy delineation between belonging and not belonging comes into being when the church becomes like the Fourth Gospel's rendering of the synagogue: something from which one can be expelled.

---

[174] Bultmann, *The Gospel of John*, 435.

CHAPTER 4
Death Becomes Him

All tragedies are finish'd by a death,
All comedies are ended by a marriage;
The future states of both are left to faith,
For authors fear description might disparage
The worlds to come of both, or fall beneath,
And then both worlds would punish their miscarriage;
So leaving each their priest and prayer-book ready,
They say no more of Death or of the Lady.

—Byron, *Don Juan* 3.9

Although Byron's delineation of the difference between tragedy and comedy rings true enough to be cited often, it needs qualification. In Greek tragedy, when marriage is a consequence of military rather than romantic conquest, the heroine sings lamentations rather than odes of joy, and when death arrives too soon in life, the funerary linen becomes a bridal robe and veil. The language of death may mark a wedding, and the language of wedding may mark a death, and the rites performed in these two transitions are confused. A similar confusion occurs in the Fourth Gospel when Jesus appears as the bridegroom whose path leads to a tomb. François-Marie Braun asks, "If Jesus saves men by his Word of truth, if men judge themselves by means of their decisions in His regard, what is the use of the death of a Savior?"[1] Jesus' death in the Fourth Gospel is not about expiation

---

[1] François-Marie Braun, *Jean le théologien. Le mystère de Jésus-Christ* (3 vols.; Paris: Gabalda, 1966), 1.137; cited and translated in Frank J. Matera, "'On Behalf of Others,' 'Cleansing,' and 'Return': Johannine Images for Jesus' Death," *LS* 13 (1988): 161.

or atonement, and Jesus' crucifixion is not treated as humiliation to be reversed by the resurrection.[2] Jesus' death is exaltation. An answer to Braun's question can be found in the Greek heroic tradition, mediated and expanded by the tragedies, in which the beautiful death of the hero is no longer limited to the military combatant but is also granted to the sacrificial victims of Achilles and Agamemnon. In the rhetoric of the gospel, Jesus' crucifixion is represented as the beautiful death of the bridegroom.

The statement "These are written so that you may come to believe that Jesus is the Messiah, the Son of God, and that through believing you may have life in his name" (20:31) suggests to many that the purpose of the Fourth Gospel is to lead the reader to accept or reject Jesus and therefore its rhetoric is deliberative—the form belonging to the public assembly. For some, such as Andrew Lincoln, the legal language of the gospel points to its forensic rhetorical purpose as a sort of tribunal to accuse the Jews and defend Jesus. Aristotle identifies a third kind of rhetoric, found in victory orations and funeral discourses, called epideictic, which praises or disparages.[3] Tragedy, with respect to its rhetorical purpose, belongs to the category of the tribunal only insofar as its audience judges it worthy of a prize. Its primary rhetorical purpose is not to persuade that one competitor is worthier than another but rather to represent an action as laudatory or deplorable. In this respect, tragedy stands in the same category as a victory oration or a funeral discourse. The Homeric epics and Greek tragedies, through their storytelling, served not to entertain so much as to commemorate loss, suffering, and above all death. The action of the gospel, Jesus' verbal contests, and the representation of his death render the rhetoric of the gospel epideictic and place it in the tradition of the tragic commemoration of death.

Jean-Pierre Vernant describes how the Homeric hero overcomes death by embracing it. According to Vernant, "real death lies in amnesia, silence, demeaning obscurity, the absence of fame," whereas "real existence" for the living or the dead "comes from being recognized, valued, and honored" and above all "from being glorified as the central figure in a song of praise, a story

---

[2] Matera, "'On Behalf of Others,'" 161. Ernst Käsemann (*The Testament of Jesus: A Study of the Gospel of John in the Light of Chapter 17* [trans. Gerhard Krodel; Philadelphia: Fortress, 1968], 8–19) makes a forceful case against finding a "christology of humiliation" in the Fourth Gospel.

[3] Aristotle, *Rhet.* 1.3.22. An examination of the task of the various people described as *parakletos* in the Hellenistic literature shows that more often than not their role is to praise their associate through the use of epideictic rhetoric rather than to act as a defense attorney.

that endlessly tells and retells a destiny admired by all."[4] The beautiful death of the hero brings an end to the continuous need for martial contests to prove his excellence. Once he dies in combat, his heroism becomes immortal.[5] In Homer's *Iliad*, Achilles describes this contrast between a life gained by death and a long, deadly life when he decides to return to battle:

> I carry two sorts of destiny toward the day of my death. Either I stay here and fight beside the city of the Trojans, my return home is gone, but my glory shall be everlasting; but if I return home to the beloved land of my fathers, the excellence of my glory is gone, but there will be a long life left for me, and my end in death will not come to me quickly. (9.410–416 [Lattimore])

As he goes into mortal combat with Hector, Achilles underscores that he accepts death as his destiny, and so he dies of his own volition:

> I will accept my own death, at whatever time Zeus wishes to bring it about, and the other immortals. For not even the strength of Herakles fled away from destruction, although he was dearest of all to lord Zeus, son of Kronos, but his fate beat him under, and the wearisome anger of Hera. So I likewise, if such is the fate which has been wrought for me, shall lie still, when I am dead. Now I must win excellent glory. (18.115–121)

Paradoxically, the *Iliad* ends not with Achilles' death, which occurs after the poem concludes, but with that of his enemy, the Trojan hero Hector. Hector, beloved of the gods and shepherd of his people, dies in defeat, and Achilles mutilates his corpse in an act designed to deny him a beautiful death.[6] The gods who love Hector, however, preserve his body from harm even though Achilles drags it about in the dirt behind his chariot for three days.[7] The family of Priam burns its son upon the funeral pyre and performs the rituals designed to honor him, but the *Iliad* itself becomes a commemoration of Hector and grants him the immortality of a glorious death by rendering his death in verse and dwelling upon the humiliation of the corpse and the grief of Hector's family.

In the hands of the tragedians, the trope of the beautiful death becomes the means by which other victims of the Trojan War are elevated to the status of hero or heroine. Euripides makes the beautiful death the action of

---

[4] Jean-Pierre Vernant, "A 'Beautiful Death' and the Disfigured Corpse in Homeric Epic," in *Mortals and Immortals: Collected Essays* (ed. Froma I. Zeitlin; Princeton, N.J.: Princeton University Press, 1991), 57.

[5] Ibid., 51.

[6] Ibid., 67.

[7] Homer pulls back from a complete humiliation of the corpse. Though there is talk of dead heroes being surrendered to the dogs, none is.

Iphigenia at Aulis, and in the clarity with which drama allows us to see, the elements of that death become distinct. Iphigenia's death is beautiful because she dies on behalf of others, through her act of volition she cleanses others of the taint of guilt or the demands of revenge, and in the recognition she gains, she is exalted, she joins the ranks of heroic and divine beings.

Iphigenia comes to Aulis believing that she has been summoned not to die but to become Achilles' beautiful bride, but her union is a "marriage to death."[8] The confusion of nuptial and burial rites points to the complicated dialectic between the experience of men and women, of family and civic politics, and the diverse perspectives that characters may hold regarding the justice, the blessings, or the curses of these events.[9] Euripides exploits this trope of "marriage to death" by fitting the confusion of the rituals of marriage and death into the aesthetic system of his drama (along with conflict, argumentation, and irony) to create a pattern of paradox and ambivalence in which the tragic heroine characterizes herself as a member of a wedding rather than the sacrificial victim of a political system.[10] Iphigenia retains her identity as a bride and renders her death an occasion for familial and national joy.

In Greek tragedy, the paradox of "marriage to death" works because elements of wedding and funeral rituals in Athenian tradition, as well as in many other cultures, are similar. As a result, an element from one may signify metonymy of the other or homology for an element of the other. Weddings and funerals both begin with purification and libations of the bodies, both entail songs and sacrifices, both have processions, and both end with a body laid in a chamber. Some of the actions are symmetrical. In the marriage, the bride is unveiled; in the funeral, the corpse's head is covered in linen. Both rituals facilitate transitions; the rites move the participants through liminal zones. For the bride, the marriage is a death to her former state as a virgin daughter in the household of her father and also a new life in the household of her husband, where the death of her virginity makes possible new fruitfulness. The funeral transports the dead from the household of the living to a new existence in the underworld.

As Iphigenia is being prepared as a sacrifice, an unwitting messenger sees only the preparations for her marriage to Achilles—the ruse that brings

---

[8] Rush Rehm examines "marriage to death" as a trope in *Marriage to Death: The Conflation of Wedding and Funeral Rituals in Greek Tragedy* (Princeton, N.J.: Princeton University Press, 1994).

[9] Ibid. See Rehm's conclusions regarding the Oresteia (57–58).

[10] Ann Norris Michelini (*Euripides and the Tragic Tradition* [Madison: Wisconsin University Press, 1987], 118) makes this claim for Euripides' use of self-contradiction in general.

her to Aulis—and reports the following to Agamemnon and Menelaus, the father and uncle of the bride:

> They are consecrating the young girl to Artemis, the ruler of Aulis, in preparation for her wedding. Who is the bridegroom? Come then, bring the baskets, start the sacrificial rite and garland your heads, and you, King Menelaus, rehearse the wedding song! (433–437 [Morwood])

A few lines later, in a conversation with Menelaus, Agamemnon answers the messenger's question: "As for the wretched virgin—why do I call her virgin? Hades, it seems, will soon marry her" (460). The tears shed by parents at the thought of their loss signify for Iphigenia the separation that marriage brings (650).

Once Iphigenia has reconciled herself to the necessity of her death, she addresses her mother and makes clear the voluntary and selfless nature of her act:

> I have made the decision to die. I want to do this gloriously, to reject all meanness of spirit. Only consider these things with me, mother, and you will see how nobly I am speaking. Greece in all its greatness now looks to me and no one else, on me depends the voyage of the ships across the sea and the overthrow of the Phrygians, and if the barbarians try to seize our women from happy Greece in the future, it lies with me to stop them by ensuring that they pay for the ruin of Helen whom Paris snatched away. Through my death I shall secure all this and my fame as the liberator of Greece will be forever blessed. And indeed it is right that I should not be too much in love with life. You bore me for the common good of the Greeks, not for yourself alone. . . . It is better that one man should see the light of day than any number of women. If Artemis has decided to take my body, am I, a mere mortal, to oppose the goddess? No, it is impossible. No, I give my body to Greece. Sacrifice me and sack Troy. This shall be my lasting monument, this shall be my children, my marriage and my glory. (1375–1398)

Because she treats her death as an act that brings her the immortality of fame and happiness, Iphigenia forbids her mother to mourn:

> CLYTEMNESTRA: In my misery I have good cause for a sorrowing heart.
>
> IPHIGENIA: Stop. Do not make a coward of me. Obey me in what I ask you.
>
> CLYTEMNESTRA: Tell me what it is—you shall have no cause to complain of *me*, at any rate.
>
> IPHIGENIA: Then do not cut off a lock of your hair, or clothe your body in black robes.

> CLYTEMNESTRA: Why do you say this my child—when I have lost you?
>
> IPHIGENIA: But you have not. I have been saved and through me you shall win glory.
>
> CLYTEMNESTRA: What do you mean? Must I not grieve for your death?
>
> IPHIGENIA: No, no. For no tomb will be raised to me.
>
> CLYTEMNESTRA: What? Is not burial customary for the dead?
>
> IPHIGENIA: The altar of the divine daughter of Zeus will be my memorial.
>   (1434–1444)

Iphigenia gives her life freely, and therefore she is not a victim for whom her mother need seek revenge. Moreover, her mother has a share in her glory. In her parting song, Iphigenia refers to her death as a cleansing of Greece's affliction:

> Lead me on—the destroyer of Ilium's city and the Phrygians.
> Give me, bring me garlands to bind my head—here is a lock of my hair to wreathe the altar—and streams of purifying water. Dance your swirling dance for Artemis around the temple, around the altar, for Artemis the queen, the blessed one.
> For with my blood, shed in sacrifice if it must be, I shall wash away the oracle.
> . . . .
> You brought me up to be a light for Greece. It causes me no regret that I die.
>   (1475–1502)

The chorus affirms, "Your glory shall live for ever" (1503), and Iphigenia is led offstage to her execution. The messenger who brings the report of Iphigenia's death to Clytemnestra amplifies its beauty and nobility and characterizes it as an exaltation and departure to reside with the gods:

> She has won glory throughout Greece, glory that will never die. I was there, and I am telling you this as one who saw it. Clearly your daughter has flown away to join the gods. Put an end to your grief and lay aside your anger against your husband. What the gods purpose cannot be foreseen by mortals. They save those they love. For this day has seen you daughter dying and coming back to life. (1605–1612)

Iphigenia's "resurrection" is poetic rather than dramatic. Her eternal life is found in the play itself, which through its performance brings her one of the two forms of immortality known to early classical Greek thought: the immortality of being remembered, as opposed to the immortality of progeny who carry on one's name.[11]

Jesus' resurrection is dramatic and, by virtue of the testimony of other New Testament books, is to be understood as historical. It fits into the Jewish tradition of resurrection to eternal life, but in its representation the gospel writer draws from the language and concepts of classical Greek thought. Jesus' immortality is found in the eternal life of the children of God who believe in his name and in the memory of the community in which he abides. Jesus' death is represented as a "beautiful death"—a voluntary act done on behalf of others, an exaltation, a return to his divine Father—and throughout the action and language that mark the progression of the plot to death runs the thread of the "marriage to death" trope.

Frank Matera provides a detailed account of the texts in the Fourth Gospel that represent Jesus' death as a self-sacrifice on behalf of others. Here I will present a summary of the material that Matera covers and give attention to elements that he neglects that also emphasize the beauty of Jesus' death.[12]

The magnanimous and voluntary quality of Jesus' death is underscored at several points in the gospel, but nowhere so clearly as in the good-shepherd discourse when Jesus describes the actions of that shepherd:

The good shepherd lays down his life for the sheep. (10:11)

And I lay down my life for the sheep. (10:15b)

For this reason the Father loves me, because I lay down my life in order to take it up again. (10:17)

No one takes it from me, but I lay it down of my own accord. I have power to lay it down, and I have power to take it up again. (10:18)

The virtue of laying down one's life on behalf of another is also extolled twice during the farewell discourse, once when Peter claims that he will lay down his life for Jesus (13:37) and a second time when Jesus says, "No one has greater love than this, to lay down one's life for one's friends" (15:13). Matera pays careful attention to the use of the preposition ὑπέρ, and as a result he finds references to death on behalf of others when Jesus equates the bread that he gives "for the life of the world" (ὑπὲρ τῆς τοῦ κόσμου ζωῆς) with his flesh (6:51), and in the allusion to his death in his final prayer: "And for their

---

[11] See Gregory J. Riley, *One Jesus, Many Christs: How Jesus Inspired Not One True Christianity but Many: The Truth about Christian Origins* (San Francisco: HarperSanFrancisco, 1997), 38.

[12] Matera, " 'On Behalf of Others.' "

sakes [ὑπὲρ αὐτῶν] I sanctify myself, so that they also may be sanctified in truth" (17:19).

Jesus refers to his death as exaltation when he speaks of the Son of Man being lifted up (ὑψόω):

> So must the Son of Man be lifted up, that whoever believes in him may have eternal life. (3:14–15)

> When you have lifted up the Son of Man, then you will realize that I am he. (8:28)

> And I, when I am lifted up from the earth, will draw all people to myself. (12:32)

The last of these three juxtaposes the Messiah, who is to stay forever, with the Son of Man, who dies: "The crowd answered him, 'We have heard from the law that the Messiah remains forever. How can you say that the Son of Man must be lifted up?'" (12:34). Both Jesus and a voice from heaven link his death to God's glorification:

> "It is for this reason that I have come to this hour. Father, glorify [δόξασον] your name." Then a voice came from heaven, "I have glorified it [ἐδόξασα], and I will glorify [δοξάσω] it again." (12:27c–28)

> Father, the hour has come; glorify [δόξασον] your Son so that the Son may glorify [δοξάσῃ] you. (17:1)

> I glorified [ἐδόξασα] you on earth by finishing the work that you gave me to do. So now, Father, glorify [δόξασον] me in your own presence with the glory [τῇ δόξῃ] that I had in your presence before the world existed. (17:4–5)

The Greek word δόξα signifies reputation, credit, honor, and glory. New Testament scholars have tended to focus upon the relationship of the language of δόξα to the notion of God's glory (כבוד), God's manifestation in acts of power, found in the Old Testament. It seems possible that the gospel writer has chosen the word δόξα rather than τιμή ("honor"), something given by human beings, or κλέος ("fame"), something preserved by people, in order to emphasize the divine provenance of this glory that accrues to one who manifests God's power. Although the references in these texts are to the soteriology of the Judeo-Christian tradition, when the narrator says, "we have seen his glory" and "From his fullness we have all received, grace upon grace" (1:14, 16), and when Jesus prays on behalf of his disciples, "I have made your name known to those whom you gave me from the world. . . . The glory that you have given me I have given them . . . so that the world may know that you have sent me and have loved them even as you have loved me" (17:6, 22–23), the language is reminiscent of the Greek heroic tradition in which witnesses to a death recognize its victim as a hero by praising his or her name and thereby share in the hero's glory.

The language of descent and ascent typically is used to discuss Jesus' identity, but Matera draws attention to the designation of Jesus' death as a return to the Father. Jesus speaks frequently in enigmatic terms about his departure (7:33; 8:14, 21–22; 13:33, 36; 14:1–3; 16:16), but on one occasion he makes his destination clear: "If you loved me, you would rejoice that I am going to the Father" (14:28). His death is, then, a passage to the abode of immortality.

Matera also identifies cleansing as a Johannine image for the death of Jesus. This designation is dependent upon his reading of the footwashing, which he calls an "action-parable" pointing to the significance of Jesus' death as a "slave-like" death.[13] Matera uses 1 John 1:7–9, "the blood of Jesus his Son cleanses [καθαρίζει] us from all sin. . . . [He] who is faithful and just will forgive us our sins and cleanse [καθαρίσῃ] us from all unrighteousness," in order to cautiously suggest that Jesus' death cleanses sin and unrighteousness.[14] If we situate the act of footwashing within the larger framework of the farewell discourse, we see that the idea that Jesus' death cleanses may also signify something akin to what Iphigenia means when she says that her death washes away the curse of the oracle. In order for Peter to have a part of Jesus (μέρος μετ' ἐμοῦ) (13:8), he must accept that Jesus' death on behalf of his friends is an exaltation and therefore the occasion for celebration. In the speech that follows, Jesus repeatedly asserts that his death is to be received with joy.

> Do not let your hearts be troubled, and do not let them be afraid. (14:27)

> If you loved me, you would rejoice that I am going to the Father. (14:28)

> I tell you, you will weep and mourn, but the world will rejoice; you will have pain, but your pain will turn into joy. (16:20)

> So you have pain now; but I will see you again, and your hearts will rejoice, and no one will take your joy from you. (16:22)

> I am coming to you [God], and I speak these things in the world so that they may have my joy made complete in themselves. (17:13)

For Jesus, there is one way to life, and that is through death, and his path to death is marked by unwavering dedication. He does not ask to be saved from

---

13 Ibid., 171.
14 Ibid., 172.

this hour (12:27), and when Simon Peter attempts to rescue him from arrest, he asks the rhetorical question "Am I not to drink the cup that the Father has given me?" (18:11). Instead of sharing in Jesus' death by performing the sorts of funeral rituals that bring mourners closer to the dead by simulating death through the rending of clothes, the cutting of hair, or the smearing of ashes upon the face, Jesus' disciples have a part of him by performing a ritual associated with hospitality and the joys of friendship. Having a part of Jesus' death is, then, treated as an occasion to rejoice and as the glorification of Jesus' friends as well as himself.

Just as, at the end of the *Iliad*, focalization upon the body of Hector dominates the narrative, the Fourth Gospel dwells upon Jesus' corpse far more than do any of the Synoptic Gospels. Priam provides the Homeric perspective on the centrality of the corpse in the "beautiful death": "For a young man all is decorous [πάντ᾽ ἐπέοικεν] when he is cut down in battle and torn with the sharp bronze, and lies there dead, and though dead still all that shows about him is beautiful [πάντα . . . καλὰ]" (22.71–73 [Lattimore]). Vernant explains,

> At death, when the body is deserted by these [impulses or competing forces], it acquires its formal unity. After being the subject of and medium for various actions, more or less spontaneous, it has become wholly an object for others. Above all, it is an object of contemplation, a visual spectacle, and therefore a focus for care, mourning, and funeral rites.[15]

In the picture of a body at rest in the glory of heroic death, "the blood, the wounds and the grime" testify to his courage and strength and become emblematic of beauty.[16]

The Synoptic Gospels, in comparison with the Fourth Gospel, pay little attention to Jesus' body. Matthew contains accounts of scribes and elders spitting upon Jesus and slapping him (26:67), Jesus' flogging (27:26), and the soldiers dressing him up as the fool's king (27:27–31), but once Jesus is dead, Matthew draws the mind's eye of his reader away from the cross to environmental events: the sky darkens, the curtain of the temple rips, the earth quakes, and tombs open up (27:45–54). The women who witness Jesus' death view him from a distance (27:55), and the gospel provides the reader with a fleeting glimpse of the corpse before it is wrapped in clean linen (27:59) and with brief appearances of the resurrected body (28:9–10, 17–20). Luke dwells upon Jesus' resurrected body with its robust appetite, but in his depiction of a vivacious Jesus upon the cross, there is no hint of

---

[15] Vernant, "A 'Beautiful Death,'" 62.
[16] Ibid., 64.

bodily pain (23:34–46). Pilate twice states his intention to have Jesus flogged (23:16, 22), but no such torture is narrated. The burden of the cross is placed on the shoulders of Simon of Cyrene, leaving Jesus to be attentive to the women bewailing his fate (23:26–31). As he hangs upon the cross, where he ought to be slowly suffocating, Jesus finds the breath to speak words of comfort to a criminal who hangs beside him (23:39–43), and his last words, "Father, into your hands I commend my spirit" (23:46), are uttered in a loud voice. Luke describes no women standing at the base of the cross gazing upon his naked body. The corpse is promptly removed and wrapped, so that when the women lay eyes on Jesus' body in the tomb, they see him covered (23:55).

In the Fourth Gospel, all eyes are upon the body or corpse on the cross, and attention is paid to the signs of suffering that set Jesus apart from others. He bears his own cross like a "real man." The description of the soldiers casting lots for his clothing is followed immediately by the picture of the women standing near the cross where Jesus hangs naked (19:23–25). Jesus describes the experience of his body when he says, "I am thirsty," and the narrator describes how he drinks sour wine from a hyssop branch, utters his final words, bows his head, and gives up his spirit (19:28–30). The eye continues to linger upon the body when the soldiers come to break his legs and look at the body to see that he is dead and when they pierce his cadaver, out of which spews blood and water (19:32–34). After Achilles kills Hector, Homer describes how the Argives "gazed upon the stature and on the imposing beauty of Hektor," and in response to his beauty, they stab at him with their spears (Homer, *Il.* 22.370 [Lattimore]). The Roman soldiers, like the Argives, participate in the mythos of the heroic tradition by denying their enemy a beautiful death. Crucifixion itself and the humiliation of hanging naked and dying a slow death that mutilates the body are institutionalized methods of robbing the enemy of the form of heroic suffering. In dwelling upon Jesus' body and its outrageous treatment, the Fourth Evangelist counters the effect sought by the Romans.

In order to render the Greek hero an enduring object of beauty, his body is burned on a pyre and reduced to white bones, thought to be inedible by animals and incorruptible, and then placed in a burial mound with a σῆμα, a monument, to stand as a permanent reminder of the hero. In the *Iliad*, the gods perform services for the corpse in concert with other human mourners. Aphrodite protects Hector's body from being eaten by dogs and anoints it with oil to prevent skin from tearing while Achilles drags it behind his chariot (23.186–187). Anointing is a service that a woman performs for Jesus. The God of Jesus can do the Greek gods one better: God glorifies Jesus' body through resurrection, and so his body can remain in view to the end of the gospel. Joseph of Arimathea asks for the body, and he comes and removes it. He is joined by Nicodemus, who carries a hundred pounds of myrrh and aloes. Together they take the body, wrap it, and lay it in the tomb. In Matthew, in one synchronous action, Joseph gets the body, lays it down, and wraps it. Then the body disappears behind a great stone that Joseph rolls to the door of the tomb. In the Fourth Gospel, the stone appears in retrospect when Mary discovers it removed. Even once the corpse disappears, it lingers in the focalization upon the linen wrappings and the headcloth that is rolled up in a place by itself in the empty tomb (20:6–7). The audience seems to be invited to imagine what Jesus might have done with the cloths, as though he got up and calmly unwrapped his head, in contrast to Lazarus's exit from his own grave, bound like a mummy fleeing its tomb (11:44). In Luke, Jesus invites the disciples to look at his feet and hands as proof that he is no ghost (24:39). In the Fourth Gospel, the fact that Jesus' hands and side are marred with wounds is made explicit; his sores are the proof of his identity (20:20, 25, 27). He is the one who has endured a painful death, and in standing before them, he becomes the object of rejoicing.

Compared with Euripides' broad treatment of "marriage to death" in a play such as *Iphigenia at Aulis,* in which the heroine expects matrimony and, when she learns that she is to die, continues to speak of her preparations in terms of a wedding, the Fourth Evangelist uses the elements of this trope in light touches. By beginning with a wedding and ending with a funeral, the gospel writer plays out the action on the frame of the traditional ordering of human experience. Alongside Jesus' self-identification as a divine agent and his self-proclamations stands Jesus in the role of the bridegroom. Jesus moves through the ritual landscape that provides the horizons for his society, but against this structure the gospel writer "juxtaposes and transposes elements" to create the radical image of a "marriage to death."[17] The "dominant modes of thinking" expressed by the worldly powers in the gospel lead to the destruction of life writ large—Jesus is not *a* life, but *the* life—and by worldly standards his death ought to be mourned. But human experience is disassembled, and death becomes an occasion for celebration and, like a wedding, an affirmation of life. What could be more ironic than the assertion that eternal life is made possible by death? And what better way to dramatize this paradox than to present it in action that represents the rituals of marriage with Jesus cast in the role of the bridegroom?

An elaborate comparison between Jesus and tragic brides may seem unwarranted because it solves a problem that already has an easy solution. As early as Augustine, Johannine scholars have drawn a straight line from the

---

[17] Rehm (*Marriage to Death*, 139–40) makes a comparable statement about the tragedies.

prophetic tradition of the covenant of marriage, through the romantic themes of the Song of Solomon, and then John the Baptist's identification of Jesus as the bridegroom, to the matrimonial relationship of the church to Christ. More recently, scholars have placed the intertestamental tradition of the messianic wedding on this trajectory as an intermediate point between the Old Testament and the Fourth Gospel. Adeline Fehribach's *The Women in the Life of the Bridegroom* stands as the most recent representation of this exegetical stance. Fehribach argues that the presentation of all the women in the Fourth Gospel anticipates the wedding of the messianic bridegroom, the fruit of which will be the children of God.[18] Several factors lead me to consider the influence of the tragic tradition. The conflation of death and marriage is unanticipated in the Jewish tradition, there is little evidence for the notion of a messianic wedding prior to the New Testament tradition, and though the church as Jesus' bride is suggested in the analogies of the Epistles (e.g., 1 Cor 11:3; Eph 5:23–33) and the allegories of Revelation (Rev 21:2, 9), the association is ambiguous in this gospel.[19] First, overt ecclesiological language is absent. Second, the imagery is not used in a systematic manner. On the whole, the focus of the nuptial language is directed toward the event of Jesus' death rather than the establishment of a covenant relationship.

In the Song of Solomon we find an isolated comparison between love and death: "love is strong as death, passion fierce as the grave" (8:6). The intertestamental novella *Joseph and Aseneth* treats a wedding as a passage from death to life. In Joseph's prayer that Aseneth convert to Judaism in order to become his bride and in the conversion scene, we find language that calls to mind the imagery of the Fourth Gospel. Joseph prays,

---

[18] Adeline Fehribach, *The Women in the Life of the Bridegroom: A Feminist Historical-Literary Analysis of the Female Characters in the Fourth Gospel* (Collegeville, Minn.: Liturgical Press, 1998).

[19] Several pseudepigraphical texts speak of eating with an eschatological figure: *1 En.* 62:14, "They shall eat and rest and rise with that Son of Man forever and ever," describes nothing more than routine life; *3 En.* 48:10 describes a meal at which Jews and Gentiles eat together; *2 Bar.* 29 describes the defeat of the beasts of chaos by the anointed one and a re-creation of the earth's fruitfulness, complete with provision of manna for people to eat. Besides the fact that these are late texts and in some cases Christian, they do not refer to a true banquet, let alone a wedding banquet. No intertestamental text describes the wedding of the Messiah or an eschatological figure. 1QSa refers to the Messiah's participation in the community's rule and meals. In 4QMessAp 2 ii 5–13, the Messiah brings eschatological blessings, including the end of hunger. The rabbinic tradition provides scant material, most of which is quite late. The talmudic texts tend to refer to feasting on the bodies of Leviathan and Behemoth (*b. B. Bat.* 74–75). *Pesiq. Rab Kah.* 6:8 refers to feasting in the garden of Eden.

> Lord God of my father Israel,
> the Most High, the Powerful One of Jacob,
> who gave life to all (things)
> and called (them) from the darkness to the light,•
> and from the error to the truth,
> and from the death to the life;
> you, Lord, bless this virgin,
> and renew her by your spirit,
> and form her anew by your hidden hand,
> and make her alive again by your life,
> and let her eat your bread of life,
> and drink your cup of blessing,
> and number her among your people . . .
> and let her enter your rest
> which you have prepared for your chosen ones,
> and live in your eternal life for ever (and) ever. (8:10–11 [Burchard])

The vocabulary of light, truth, spirit, eternal life, bread of life, and cup of blessing, in its affirmation of continuity and the future, is the language of marriage. Aseneth's conversion in the presence of a heavenly man takes on the trappings of a wedding. She washes herself and dresses in a new linen robe, and comes to the man in her chamber and removes her veil. The man then announces that he gives her to Joseph as a bride and that Joseph will be her bridegroom forever (14:9–15:6). The inversion of this image in which death becomes a marriage appears first in Jewish literature in *Liber antiquitatum biblicarum* (Pseudo-Philo), an imaginative retelling of Old Testament history from Adam to David dating to the first century C.E. Jephthah's daughter unambiguously resembles Iphigenia, who is also sacrificed by her father, when she mourns her untimely death:

> But I have not made good on my marriage chamber,
> and I have not retrieved my wedding garlands.
> For I have not been clothed in splendor while sitting in my woman's chamber,
> And I have not used the sweet-smelling ointment,
> And my soul has not rejoiced in the oil of anointing that has been prepared for
>   me.
> O Mother, in vain have you borne your only daughter,
> because Sheol has become my bridal chamber,
> and on earth there is only my woman's chamber.
> And may all the blend of oil that you have prepared for me be poured out,
> and the white robe that my mother has woven, the moth will eat it.
> And the crown of flowers that my nurse plaited for me for the festival, may it
>   wither up;

and the coverlet that she wove of hyacinth and purple in my woman's
  chamber,
may the worm devour it.
And may my virgin companions tell of me in sorrow and weep for me through
  the days. (40:6 [Harrington])

The language resembles the lament of Euripidean mothers at their child's or
their own death who describe their loss in terms of the rituals in which they
will not partake.[20] The passages from *Joseph and Aseneth* and Pseudo-Philo do
not seem to represent the tip of a Jewish tradition but, rather, cautious
borrowings from the Greek tradition.

The first clear association of death and marriage in the Fourth Gospel
occurs when John the Baptist identifies Jesus first as "the Lamb of God"
(1:29, 36) and then as "the bridegroom" (3:29). The equation is not direct
but rather relies upon a series of progressive associations. Whether "the Lamb
of God" is a sacrificial animal, the paschal lamb, or the suffering servant of
Jeremiah and Isaiah, the lamb is marked for death. The gospel writer points
to the death of the bridegroom in a series of passages linked together by their
vocabulary. The Baptist states, "The friend of the bridegroom, who stands
and hears him, rejoices greatly at the bridegroom's voice. For this reason my
joy has been fulfilled" (3:29). Soon after, Jesus declares, "Very truly, I tell you,
the hour is coming, and is now here, when the dead will hear the voice of the
Son of God, and those who hear will live" (5:25). The wedding party has become a necropolis. The phrase "the hour is coming" recalls the Jesus' reference to his death, "My hour has not yet come," made at the wedding at Cana
(2:4). Adeline Fehribach contends that Jesus' mother's comment there,
"They have no wine" (2:3), places Jesus implicitly in the role of bridegroom
by implying that he has some responsibility to correct the problem.[21] His response does not deny this responsibility but defers it to a future occasion.
Later in the gospel, similar references to an hour yet to come (7:6, 8, 30;
8:20) seem to point to Jesus' passion. Jesus' final words from the cross, "It is
finished" (19:30), support this conclusion. The wine that Jesus provides to
reveal his glory is tied to the blood that he sheds at the hour of his death, in
an elaborate weave of textual patterns: the association of the hour of his glorification with his death, his exaltation with his crucifixion, his mother's
presence at both events, and the emphasis upon water and blood.

A couple of scenes in the gospel seem to cast Jesus in the role of the
bridegroom. Many scholars regard the scene at the Samaritan well as a parody

---

[20] See Euripides, *Alc.* 317–318; *Phoen.* 344–349; *Iph. aul.* 731–741; *Ion*
1474–1076; *Med.* 1026–1027.

[21] Fehribach, *Life of the Bridegroom*, 29.

of the betrothal type-scene.[22] Fehribach treats the entire scene as a symbolic marriage to the Samaritan woman and notes that Jesus uses a cliché for marriage by equating her with a field to be sown (4:35).[23] I tend to see this dialogue as a comic treatment of the type-scene that plays with the elements of marriage. As we have seen in the passage from *Joseph and Aseneth*, eternal life is a gift of marriage. Several biblical passages regarding marriage contain the language of living water or well water. In the Song of Solomon, the bridegroom calls his bride "a garden fountain, a well of living water" (4:15), and Proverbs encourages marital fidelity with the words "Drink water from your own cistern, flowing water from your own well" (5:15–18). After describing God's devotion to Israel as a bride, Jeremiah accuses Israel of infidelity: "they have forsaken me, the fountain of living water" (Jer 2:13).[24] The association of water and life plays on the expectation of the continuity of life through procreation in marriage and the hope of eternal life made possible through Jesus' resurrection, which is contingent upon his death. The scene in which Mary of Bethany anoints Jesus' feet continues the play on courtship but turns comedy to *pathos*. In *Joseph and Aseneth*, Aseneth washes her future husband's feet as a symbol of marital fidelity (20:3–4).[25] Although Mary of Bethany's intent in anointing Jesus may not have been matrimonial, the narrator comments, "The house was filled with the fragrance of the perfume" (John 12:3), using language that finds parallels in texts where the association is with courtship or marriage.[26] In the Song of Solomon, the bride declares, "your anoint-

---

[22] See Robert Alter, *The Art of Biblical Narrative* (New York: Basic Books, 1981), 51–62, for a delineation of the type; see also Lyle Eslinger, The Wooing of the Woman at the Well: Jesus, the Reader, and Reader-Response Criticism, *Journal of Literature and Theology* 1 (1987): 169–70; Jeffrey L. Staley, *The Print's First Kiss: A Rhetorical Investigation of the Implied Reader in the Fourth Gospel* (SBLDS 82; Atlanta: Scholars Press, 1988), 98–103; John Bligh, "Jesus in Samaria," *HeyJ* 3 (1962): 336; Jo-Ann Brant, "Husband Hunting: Characterization and Narrative Art in the Gospel of John," *BibInt* 4 (1996): 211–16, which explores the comic treatment of the type-scene.

[23] Fehribach, *Life of the Bridegroom*, 52–58.

[24] Ibid., 55.

[25] Sjef van Tilborg (*Imaginative Love in John* [BIS 2; Leiden: Brill, 1993], 197–98) cites a number of passages in Greek literature (Athenaeus, *Deipn.* 12.552–553; Apuleius, *Metam.* 10.21; Petronius, *Sat.* 27.57) in which feet are rubbed with ointment as a prelude to sexual intercourse.

[26] Brant ("Husband Hunting") makes the case that Mary's actions are those of a bride and signify the expression of love by a woman for a man rather than a disciple for the Messiah. Adeline Fehribach draws the conclusion that Mary's principal role in the symbolic schema of the messianic wedding is to serve as the bride on behalf of the Jewish people, but Fehribach later subsumes Mary, along with Martha and Lazarus, into the family of Jesus as children of God (*Life of the Bridegroom*, 94, 113).

ing oils are fragrant, your name is perfume poured out; therefore the maidens love you" (1:3); she later adds, "While the king was on his couch, my nard gave forth its fragrance" (1:12). In *Eccl. Rab.* 7:11 we find the following claim: "The fragrance of a good perfume spreads from the bedroom to the dining room." Ruth, Esther, and Judith anoint their bodies with fragrant oils in order to enhance their allure for prospective bridegrooms (Ruth 3:3; Esth 2:12) or, in Judith's case, to entice her victim (Jdt 10:3).[27] When Judas protests that the cost of this extravagant gesture could better have served the poor, Jesus reinterprets the act, which may signify the preparation of his body for union, as preparation for his funeral.

The excessive amount of myrrh and aloes used for Jesus' burial in the Fourth Gospel may also depend upon the image of the deathbed as the bridal bed for its significance. In the Song of Solomon, the woman sings, "My beloved is to me a bag of myrrh that lies between my breasts" (1:13). When she sees Solomon's palanquin in the distance, she asks, "What is that coming up from the wilderness, like a column of smoke, perfumed with myrrh and frankincense?" (3:6). The king in turn sings, "I come to my garden, my sister, my bride; I gather my myrrh with my spice" (5:1).[28] The possibility that Nicodemus offers Jesus a royal burial must also be entertained, but the texts that make this association possible also point to the transformation of a funeral into a joyous occasion. The inclusion of myrrh among the gifts brought by the magi in the Matthean birth narrative (2:11) links the unguent with a royal birth. Josephus's account of Herod's burial, in which Herod appears to be enthroned rather than interred, describes a superabundance of perfumes and spices requiring five hundred servants to carry it (Josephus, *J.W.* 1.673; *Ant.* 17.199).

In some passages, Jesus uses language that suggests that his followers are his bride. When he describes his departure, he uses language evocative of the actions of the bridegroom's preparation for his bride:

> In my Father's house there are many dwelling places [μοναὶ]. If it were not so,
> would I have told you that I go to prepare a place for you [πορεύομαι

---

[27] Tilborg (*Imaginative Love in John*, 196) concludes that Jer 25:10 (LXX) makes the sexual connotations of the anointing clear.

[28] The association of myrrh with death is made explicit in ancient Egyptian poetry: "Death is in my eyes today / Like the scent of myrrh" (from "Dialogue of a Man with His Ba"); but it is also associated with life-giving power: "All the birds of Punt settle upon Egypt, anointed with myrrh / The one that comes first takes my worm [of decay]. Its odor comes from Punt, its claws are full of myrrh" (from "The Bird Catcher"; cited in Josephine Mayer and Tom Prideaux, *Never to Die: The Egyptians in Their Own Words* [New York: Viking, 1938], 70–71, 137).

ἑτοιμάσαι τόπον ὑμῖν]? And if I go and prepare a place for you, I will come again and will take you to myself [παραλήμψομαι ὑμᾶς πρὸς ἐμαυτόν], so that where I am, there you may be also. (14:2–3)

The language of "taking to myself" is nuptial. Hints of "marriage to death" may also be present in the passage: the word μονή appears in a Nabatean inscription in apposition to the word "tomb" and can connote a final resting place as well as dwelling place.[29] Jesus repeatedly uses words homologous with the language of marriage. The play on pain and joy found in the farewell address (16:20–22) depends upon ancient expectations about the experience of marriage for a woman. She was not expected to enjoy the consummation of her marriage, but the birth of the child, itself painful, brings joy. Jesus uses the language of complete joy, also associated with hearing the bridegroom's voice (3:29), to describe the consequence of abiding in his love (15:11), and the figure of the vine branch and the production of fruit to describe the experience of abiding in his love (15:4–7). If we associate this command with the first command to the man and the woman to be fruitful (Gen 1:28), the figure also evokes images of the bonds and progeny of matrimony.

While modern theologians, such as Anders Nygren, who attempted to dissociate the language from that of matrimonial love by creating tidy distinctions between ἀγάπη, φιλία, and ἔρως, seem to have trouble with the relationship between love of Jesus and connubial bliss, early Christian authors did not.[30] *Odes of Solomon* is filled with language and images that blur distinctions between different types of love relationships. The following ode begins with the metaphoric relationship of father and son, but it turns abruptly to the relationship of a man and a woman:

> As the eyes of a son upon his father,
> so are my eyes, O Lord, at all times toward you.
> Because my breasts and my pleasure are with you.
> Do not turn aside your mercies from me, O Lord;
> and do not take your kindness from me.
> Stretch out to me, my Lord, at all times, your right hand,
> and be to me a guide till the end according to your will.
> Let me be pleasing before you, because of your glory,
> and because of your name let me be saved from the Evil One.
> And let serenity, O Lord, abide with me,

---

[29] Mentioned in an essay by J. C. James in *ExpTim* 27 (1915–16): 427–29; cited by Raymond E. Brown, *The Gospel according to John* (2vols.; AB 29, 29A; Garden City, N.Y.: Doubleday, 1966–1970), 2:619.

[30] Anders Nygren, *Agape and Eros* (trans. Philip S. Watson; London: SPCK, 1953).

and the fruits of your love.
Teach me the odes of your truth,
that I may produce fruits in you.
And open to me the harp of your Holy Spirit,
so that with every note I may praise you, O Lord. (14:1–8 [Charlesworth])

In another ode, the gesture of stretching out one's hands as though crucified becomes an invitation to be taken into the bridegroom's arms. The believer begins,

I extended my hands and approached my Lord,
because the stretching out of my hands is his sign.
And my extension is the common cross,
that was lifted up on the way of the Righteous one. (42:1–2)

Christ responds,

Like the arm of the bridegroom over the bride,
so is my yoke over those who know me.
And as the bridal feast is spread out by the bridal pair's home,
so is my love by those who believe in me. (42:8–9)

In this ode, the sign of hands stretched out—a reference to Simon Peter's death in the Fourth Gospel—is associated with the yoke of matrimony. Though it seems unlikely that the gospel writer intended this association, the fact that one of the significant moments in a Greek wedding is when the groom takes the bride by the hand or wrist may have encouraged the author of the ode to make the connection.

The wedding imagery does not lend itself to systematic treatment. The disciples and followers of Jesus are more often the offspring of a union than its partner. Receiving Jesus makes one a child of god (1:12; cf. 11:52), and Jesus invites his followers to become children of light (12:36). While dying on the cross, Jesus institutes some type of familial relationship between his mother and the Beloved Disciple.[31] The precise purpose of this relationship is a matter of speculation, some conclusions informed by ancient custom and others by ecclesiological purposes, but clearly a household is established.[32]

---

[31] Fehribach (*Life of the Bridegroom*, 115–40) presents an elaborate argument that ties this and the entire crucifixion to the Baptist's statements about the Lamb of God and presents the motif of the bridegroom as the establishment of a common patrilineal descent for Jesus' followers through his blood sacrifice. ·

[32] Tilborg (*Imaginative Love in John*, 9) notes that the phrase "It is finished" (τετέλεσται) can mark the completion of a task—in this case, provision for his mother in fulfillment of the commandment to honor one's father and mother (John 19:30; cf. 19:28).

If we use a little imagination, Jesus may also appear in the role of the bride. When Jesus washes the feet of his disciples, he takes on a task suited to either a servant or a bride. When Jesus responds to the Greeks' request to see him, mediated by Philip and Andrew, he describes himself as a grain of wheat:

> The hour has come for the Son of Man to be glorified. Very truly, I tell you, unless a grain of wheat falls into the earth and dies, it remains just a single grain; but if it dies, it bears much fruit. Those who love their life lose it, and those who hate their life in this world will keep it for eternal life. (12:23–25)

The equation of his death with the death of a seed perhaps plays upon the myth of Persephone and its expression in the Eleusinian mysteries, in which the planting of a kernel of grain in the ground and its apparent resurrection were a central ritual. According to Helen Foley, the myth of Persephone played an important role in the marriage ritual for Greek women. The descent of Persephone into the underworld was a figure for a metaphoric death for the woman in marriage.[33] We ought not forget the very real association of death and marriage for women in antiquity (and up until the advent of modern obstetrics), when a significant number died during childbirth. Admittedly, the image may share only an accidental relationship to the mysteries, but Jesus' imagery participates in the paradoxical relationship between life and death upon which he habitually relies when he uses language of glory, hour, life and death, and fruitfulness.

Fehribach does not hesitate to number other items from the Fourth Gospel among the paraphernalia and rituals of a wedding. Her implied reader, who knows the tradition of the messianic wedding, can take the crown of thorns for the wedding wreath and the purple robe as wedding attire.[34] The piercing of Jesus' side, followed by the effusion of blood and water, can be equated with the consummation of the wedding and the conception and birth of children.[35] Like a woman in a Greek romance, Mary Magdelene is a woman searching for the tomb of her husband, and the recognition scene is her reunion with her love.[36] Fehribach provides an elaborate argument that Jesus is the messianic bridegroom whose sacrificial death establishes a patrilineal family; she connects these elements of the gospel with imagery and type-scenes in Genesis, the exodus, the royal psalms, the Greek romances, and the hypothetical tradition of the messianic wedding. Given

---

[33] Helen Foley, "Marriage and Sacrifice in Euripides' *Iphigenia at Aulis*," *Arethusa* 15 (1982): 169.

[34] Fehribach, *Life of the Bridegroom*, 123–24.

[35] Ibid., 125–31.

[36] Ibid., 143–61.

the prominence of the tropes of "marriage to death" and the "beautiful death" in the Homeric and tragic traditions, it seems to me that we need not construct Fehribach's implied reader, who knows a tradition that we can weave together with only a few threads of text, in order to arrive at a gospel writer who couples images of life and future prosperity with Jesus' death.

"Marriage to death" does not exhaust the pattern of paradox in which elements associated with life become agents or omens of death. Bread is a source of life, but when Jesus declares himself to be the "bread of life," he acknowledges that he is an object subject to consumption—that is, to death. He declares, "Whoever eats of this bread will live forever; and the bread that I will give for the life of the world is my flesh" (6:51). Perhaps these words should ring in the ears of the audience when Jesus takes a piece of bread, dips it in a dish, and gives it to the disciple who betrays Jesus to his death (13:26).[37] The meal of bread is a deadly meal.

In the hands of the early church fathers, this material becomes the basis for an elaborate sacramental theory, and ritual confusion is used to move toward doctrinal clarity and orthodoxy. In his treatment of John 3:29, Augustine spins out the metaphor of marriage to support his sacramental theology. Jesus pays the bride price in blood, and his provision of wine at the wedding in Cana is a demonstration of the sacrament of marriage.[38] Just as we know that he who has the bride is the bridegroom, so also we know that she who has the pledges is the bride. The church has the sacraments; therefore the church is the bride.[39]

In contrast to Augustine's systematic movement to doctrinal clarity, the tragedies use the convention of "marriage to death" along with a "beautiful death" to move in the direction of ambiguity and paradox. In the plays based upon the *Iliad,* the quest to reestablish the honor lost by one woman leads to the dishonoring of many men and the shame and death of many women. In *Antigone,* Creon's demand for civic obedience requires the betrayal of filial duty. In *Alcestis,* Admetus's desire for life and demand for the proof of filial devotion call for the death of his spouse. When Alcestis, in turn, demands proof of his devotion through mourning and the promise not to take a new wife, the joy of Admetus's new life turns to mourning and fruitlessness. The paradox points to the disruption of the dichotomies by which we order our lives and our loyalties. By casting Jesus in the role of the bridegroom who

---

[37] Augustine's apologetic on this text (*Tract. Ev. Jo.* 62.1), in which he appeals to 1 Cor 11:27, suggests that those to whom he preached made this connection. Augustine and his audience assume that the bread is dipped in wine. Augustine draws out the image of wine-soaked bread as being blood-stained.

[38] Augustine, *Tract. Ev. Jo.* 13.10, 13; 9.2.

[39] Augustine, *Tract. Ev. Jo.* 13.16.

lies in a tomb rather than in the marriage bed, the Fourth Gospel also points to the paradoxical relationship between life and death, but the gospel also flouts the paradox of "marriage to death." Antigone's death is not a happy ending. When she describes her death as a marriage, it is not an occasion to rejoice. Jesus' death is a different matter: it is a life-giving event, the harbinger of fruitfulness rather than more death or vengeful murder. The Fourth Gospel is not a tragedy; it is a subversion of tragedy. Separation by death is union that brings the gift of eternal life. As David Rensberger suggests, "dogmatic reasoning" cannot bring one to this sort of insight; this concept can be grasped only with the aid of "poetry and paradox, redundancy and self-contradiction."[40]

In his study of the poetics of sorrow in Euripidean tragedy, Charles Segal turns his readers' attention to a Shakespearean play that also gives excessive attention to dead bodies. At the end of *Hamlet,* when the bodies of Hamlet, Laertes, Gertrude, and Claudius are strewn on the stage, Horatio makes this decree:

> Give order that these bodies
> High on a stage be placed to the view;
> And let me speak to the yet unknowing world
> How these things came about. So shall you hear
> Of carnal, bloody, and unnatural acts,
> Of accidental judgements, casual slaughters,
> Of deaths put on by cunning and forc'd cause,
> And, in this upshot, purposes mistook
> Fallen on the inventors' heads: all this can I
> Truly deliver. (5.2.388–396)

The distinction between the witnesses on the dramatic axis and those on the theatrical axis collapses. Horatio calls to the performance of the play that the audience has just seen, the audience becomes the unknowing world, and the play becomes a commemoration of those dead onstage that brings them back to life. Segal suggests that, without being so explicit, the Greek tragedies also end with reference not to ongoing action but to the continuing recollection of the story and characters of the play:

> One source of tragedy's paradoxical pleasure is its always precarious equilibrium between the sadness of loss and the recuperative power of art. The very form and social context of tragic drama surround potentially meaningless suf-

---

[40] David Rensberger, "The Messiah Who Has Come into the World," in *Jesus in Johannine Tradition* (ed. Robert T. Fortna and Tom Thatcher; Louisville: Westminster John Knox, 2001), 23.

fering with the same sense of stability and continuity. In Greek tragedy the closing public acts of mourning and ritual commemoration often imply future survivors and spectators who will hear, remember and learn.[41]

When the narrator turns to his audience at the end of the Fourth Gospel, Jesus' prediction "Very truly, I tell you, anyone who hears my word and believes him who sent me has eternal life, and does not come under judgment, but has passed from death to life" (5:24), his admonition "Those who love me will keep my word" (14:23), his consolation "I have said these things to you so that when their hour comes you may remember that I told you about them" (16:4), and the blessing pronounced upon those who believe without seeing (20:29) become completed speech-acts. The reading of the gospel is the keeping of the word in memory, and members of the audience who believe are the recipients of Jesus' blessing.

---

[41] Charles Segal, *Euripides and the Poetics of Sorrow: Art, Gender, and Commemoration in Alcestis, Hippolytus, and Hecuba* (Durham, N.C.: Duke University Press, 1993), 6–7.

CONCLUSION

The observation that the gospels do not resemble in form or content any previous or contemporary literary work has led New Testament scholars to treat their composition as the product of social forces within the communities for which they were written.[1] This conclusion ignores the complexity of the act of composition. Writing is not a natural, spontaneous gesture but one reliant upon conventions or the artful disregard or inversion of conventions. As Walter Ong explains, writing is a technology that demands that the meaning of words become clear without the gestures or intonation of a speaker and without an existential context: "The need for this exquisite circumspection makes writing the agonizing work it commonly is."[2] An author must decide how and where to begin, how to articulate a plot and limit its action to a coherent series of events in which one calls the next into being. Writers learn this art by emulating the writing of others.

The gospel as a literary form may indeed be sui generis, but the methods of representing time, setting, action, and characters found in the Fourth Gospel are not. As this study has demonstrated, the author of the Fourth Gospel drew upon many of the established and proven methods of dramatic composition found in Greek tragedy in order to construct a story dependent more on the speech of its characters than on that of its narrator. The tragic prologue and epilogue provided the author with a model for how to begin and how to end. The tragedies illustrated how entrances, exits, and a tight economy of represented actions could provide a structure upon which to construct the principal action of a story. They taught that, through speech, characters could represent themselves, the context in which the action took place, and the conflicts comprising the action. They showed how conflict

---

[1] See Larry W. Hurtado, "Gospel Genre," in *DJG*, 276–79.
[2] Walter J. Ong, *Orality and Literacy: The Technologizing of the Word* (London: Routledge, 1982), 104.

could take the form of various speech-acts by following conventions that developed out of oral traditions of verbal dueling such as legal debate and flyting. Greek tragedy presented models of how speech represented in writing could be organized so that the reader who reproduced the sounds of speech and the audience who heard the words could make sense of the thoughts.

This comparison of the Fourth Gospel with Greek tragedies does not facilitate an exhaustive account of every element of the gospel. Some passages, such as the qualifying statement about Jesus' meaning in 21:23, and even episodes, such as the trial of the adulterous woman (7:53–8:11), may be the work of later redactors. The long farewell discourse winds its way along structures germane to classical drama, but nothing like it was performed upon the ancient stage. Episodes that read like dramatic dialogue are laced with a narrative voice uncharacteristic of the tragedies. The sustained attention to Jesus' body and corpse in the final chapter of the gospel is made possible through a subordination of dialogue to narrative. Narrative can do things that dramatic dialogue cannot. It can carry one through action at an accelerated pace by moving the action from one location to the next at a moment's notice, and it can dispense with lengthy speeches to reorient the audience. The narrative voice can allow the reader to focalize a scene independently from any of its characters. Instead of choosing one or another genre with which to tell the story, the Fourth Evangelist seems to have selected techniques for accomplishing whatever task was at hand in writing. The gospel, like the Greek novel or Greco-Roman biography, is an emerging genre that stands at the confluence of many literary traditions and draws from narrative conventions, some of which are found in the Hebrew Bible and some of which appear in the literature of Hellenistic Judaism and in theatrical conventions, to which Johannine scholars have given only passing attention.[3]

Dennis MacDonald gives a lengthy account of why the Gospel of Mark's literary dependence upon the *Odyssey* and the *Iliad* has been neglected. The early association of the gospels with apostles who were eyewitnesses to the events they recounted rendered literary antecedents irrelevant until the rise of higher criticism, and they remain so for those who continue

---

[3] The biographies to which the gospels are often compared are either contemporary or later compositions. Plutarch, the author of fifty biographies, lived from 46 to 120 C.E.; Suetonius, the author of *Lives of the Caesars* and biographies of illustrious authors such as Homer and Virgil, lived from 70 to 160 C.E.; and Diogenes Laertius, the author of *Lives and Opinions of Eminent Philosophers,* lived from 200 to 250 C.E. The ancient Greek or Hellenistic novels generally are thought to date from the mid-first century C.E. to the third century C.E. See Bryan P. Reardon, ed., *Collected Ancient Greek Novels* (Berkeley: University of California Press, 1989), 5.

to think of the gospels as rebroadcasts of events as they happened and speech as it was given.[4] When form critics produced a theory of gospel development, they assigned the gospel writer the task of editing rather than composition, and literary critics have focused upon contemporary genre, such as the biography, rather than its classical antecedents, the works with which boys in the first century C.E. learned to read and write Greek prose.[5]

It seems to me that the neglect of the influence of the tragic tradition in the course of the Christian exegetical tradition is also symptomatic of the urge to find coherence between the gospels and whatever the pressing concerns of the church might be. When the issue was Jesus' relationship to God and the role of the church in salvation, such were the questions put to the texts, and they supplied answers. When the meaning of sacrament came to the fore in Reformation debates, the gospels' sacramental theology became the standing point of debate between Protestant and Catholic scholars. When the women's movement sought scriptural authority for ordination of women, the gospels became a testament to Jesus' validation of female witness. I am not so naive as to claim that I can extract myself from my historical context and its concerns, peer into the mind of the Fourth Evangelist, and then look out through his eyes to see the world and the gospel story as he saw it. In my exploration of what the language of the Fourth Gospel does as opposed to what it means, I find that the gospel puts certainty into question instead of providing answers for our inquiries. Jesus' claims about himself and his counteraccusations against his opponents become movements in a verbal duel that Jesus intends to escalate into a physical confrontation in which he will die a beautiful death. The struggle in which various characters try to place Jesus into an appropriate category and thereby co-opt him into the sociopolitical or religious structures by which relationships in this world are defined does not end with one or more characters getting it right. The names with which characters greet Jesus after his resurrection are spontaneous expressions of joy and praise rather than definitions. By isolating and stylizing these conflicts and struggles, the gospel magnifies the nature of this world as a place of uncertainty instead of debasing its likeness to a caricature in which believers and friends are easily identified by the clarity of their convictions and their unwavering fidelity.

Attention to the theatrical conventions of the tragedies does not simply explain how the story of Jesus' ministry, crucifixion, and resurrection takes the form we find in the Fourth Gospel. Understanding the purpose of these

---

[4] Dennis R. MacDonald, *The Homeric Epics and the Gospel of Mark* (New Haven: Yale University Press, 2000), 170.
[5] Ibid., 170–71.

conventions redirects our reading of antithetical and polemical sayings, as well as lines such as Jesus' "Do not hold on to me," away from the dualistic legacy of Platonism and its Hellenistic and early Christian students, in which words such as "darkness" signify an ontological reality.[6] This ontological treatment of the language of light and darkness and other antithetical pairings compels readers to find their manifestations in this world, or in the world in which Jesus lived, or in the world in which the gospel writer wrote. The Fourth Gospel dramatizes the ambiguity of human experience and the paradox of divine truth. Jesus' presence in the world throws conventional wisdom and traditional certainty into question. The interview with the formerly blind man puts knowledge to the test. Jesus cannot be from God because he does not keep the Sabbath, but then again, how can a sinner bring sight to the blind? Tradition is clear—God spoke to Moses—but the present brings irreconcilable tension. Here is Jesus, who comes from nowhere, and a blind man, born in sin, attests to the gift of sight from one who sins, but God does not listen to sinners. Rather than living with the paradox, the Jews do what most people are inclined to do: drive out those people who stand as living witnesses to confusion, people who demand ongoing, unending deliberation about what is true and right. Pilate would rather kill Jesus than try to answer the question "What is truth?" The debates of the gospel represent tension between institutional and brute facts and the interruption that the incarnation of God's Word brings. Their resolution is not found in the persuasion of one side to the other through the presentation of existing evidence. The cessation of the debate requires a new fact, the resurrection of Jesus, which the contestants can witness only through the escalation of the verbal contest to physical confrontation. Jesus can prove his point only by dying, by letting the power of conventional wisdom and authority exert its full force by nailing him to the cross. Through the employment of dramatic conventions, the Fourth Gospel provides its audience with the experience of unity and clarity unavailable through ordinary human experience but offered by a theatrical performance.

The purpose of the tragic conventions that the Fourth Evangelist employs is not limited to the theatrical experience of following a past action as though you were there or as though it were unfolding before you in the present. The audience takes a role in the performance not as a member of a jury to determine the historical veracity of the events or the guilt or innocence of an individual or a party, nor as a member of an assembly to be persuaded to adopt a sacramental theology or a distinct form of Christology, but as a

---

[6]Note that I distinguish between Platonism and what I read in Plato's dialogues.

congregation to engage in a corporate act of remembering. The audience joins with the gospel writer and his heir the narrator in an act of commemoration by witnessing Jesus' glory through the representation of his life as a heroic contest in which his death becomes exaltation rather than humiliation. The audience is not called to answer christological questions about Jesus' identity but rather to acknowledge that what it has witnessed is not only Jesus' glory but also God's.

I do not mean to suggest that the Fourth Gospel does not affirm the notion that following Jesus leads to salvation but rather to maintain that the awareness of the tragic conventions throws emphasis upon the commandments to love one another; upon the imitation of Christ, in which Simon Peter participates; and above all upon the resurrection that delivers Jesus from death rather than upon some abstract confessional formulation. If one believes that Jesus is the resurrection, that he is what he does rather than the titles people ascribe to him, then one trusts in his name and in future resurrection for those who follow his life and way.

Dennis MacDonald's work has demonstrated that early Christian authors used as their literary inspiration Homer's epics by following their plot elements and literary conventions. Following Gérard Genette's observation that a text that relies on a written antecedent can "transvaluate the values of the hypotext," MacDonald finds that the heroes of the *Acts of Andrew* and the Gospel of Mark replace the imperfections of the Greek gods and heroes with idealized Christian virtues.[7] By placing Jesus within the literary conventions of a Greek tragedy, the author of the Fourth Gospel sets him in relief against the tragic hero and as a result generates a theology that is sharply at odds with that of the tragedies. In the tragedies, the gulf between the human and the divine experience is underscored. The tragedians show that intolerable suffering is the lot of human beings, who are blindly led to their destruction by the gods, and according to Paul Ricoeur, the only deliverance they offer is pity, "weeping with him and purifying the tears with the beauty of song."[8] The Fourth Gospel shows that intolerable suffering is the lot of God in the figure of his Son, Jesus, who is led to his death by the blindness of humanity and who offers deliverance by showing that in willingly subjecting himself to human absurdity, he demonstrates the sublimity of his suffering. The audience of the gospel is

---

[7] MacDonald, *The Homeric Epics,* 2. See also Dennis R. Macdonald, *Christianizing Homer: "The Odyssey," Plato, and "The Acts of Andrew"* (New York: Oxford University Press, 1994).

[8] Paul Ricoeur, *The Symbolism of Evil* (trans. Emerson Buchanan; Boston: Beacon, 1967), 227. Much of the following comparison of tragic and Johannine theology is Ricoeur's work.

therefore enjoined to rejoice in his death rather than pity it. When Hippolytus invites Artemis to look upon his suffering, Artemis responds, "Yes, but the law forbids my shedding tears" (Euripides, *Hipp.* 1396 [Kovacs, LCL]). In contrast, the Son of God weeps at the sight of Mary of Bethany's grief. In tragedy, the gods are shown to be impotent in regard to humankind's mortality, but in the gospel, God becomes mortal, and by his death, humankind gains immortality.[9] In *Alcestis*, Heracles can deliver Alcestis from death, but the joke is that Admetus must then die as he should and Alcestis when she should. In tragedy, death is the enemy that cannot be defeated. The attempts to escape death are like the attempts to escape fate. The hope of tragedy, its cleansing of fear and pity, lies in the beauty of its poetry, in its completeness, and the future that it offers the dead is literary. Tragedy brings life to a close; it exhausts its hero's potential or development, his or her task is accomplished, and so death seems timely.[10] In the Fourth Gospel, death becomes the beginning of resurrected life, animated through the image of the continuity of the vine and its branches, with their potential to bear fruit.[11]

In the tragedies, divine jealousy cannot tolerate the hubris of the hero. The son of a god is his rival, not his partner. Zeus's jealousy binds Prometheus, friend of humankind, to a rock. Aphrodite's jealousy drives Phaedra to fall in love with her stepson Hippolytus, undoing them both. Athena inflicts madness upon Ajax and toys with him in his blindness, and Hera exacts revenge by inflicting Heracles with infanticidal madness, leading him in the end to renounce the gods and accept mortality and to turn to Amphitryon and say, "I regard you, not Zeus, as my father" (Euripides, *Herc. fur.* 1265 [Kovacs, LCL]). Time and again in the tragedies, the gods unleash their undifferentiated power upon human beings, blinding them and driving them mad. It is this theology that leads Socrates, in Plato's *Republic* (2.381d–e [Bloom]), to suggest that the poets ought to be expelled from the city:

[L]et none of the poets tell us that

> The gods, like wandering strangers,
> Take on every sort of shape and visit
>   the cities [Homer, *Od.* 17.485]

and let none tell lies about Proteus and Thetis or bring on an altered Hera, either in tragedies or the other kinds of poetry, as a priestess

---

[9] Ibid., 214.

[10] Susanne K. Langer, "The Great Dramatic Forms: The Tragic Rhythm," in *Feeling and Form: A Theory of Art Developed from Philosophy in a New Key* (New York: Scribner, 1953), 351–68.

[11] See Ricoeur, *The Symbolism of Evil*, 278.

> Making a collection for the life-giving children
> of Inachus, Argo's river. [Aeschylus, *Xanthians* frg. 159]

And let them not lie to us in many other such ways. Nor should the mothers, in their turn, be convinced by these things and frighten the children with tales badly told—that certain gods go around nights looking like all sorts of strangers—lest they slander the gods while at the same time making the children more cowardly.

In this dialogue, Socrates suggests that the young must not "be allowed to hear that Themis and Zeus are responsible for strife and contention among the gods" (2.380a), and he affirms that God, who is good and righteous, is "no lying poet" (2.382d).[12]

In the *Republic,* the tragedians are called liars; in the Fourth Gospel, the storyteller is a true witness. Jesus acts under the guidance of a loving God and dispels the idea that blindness is God's punishment for a man or his parents' sin. Blindness becomes an occasion for God to demonstrate his power to heal. In the Fourth Gospel, Jesus' passion is an expression of God's love. Jesus receives δόξα (divine glory), something abiding and true, rather than κλέος (fame) or τιμή (honor), something dependent upon human recognition and praise. The words "For God so loved the world that he gave his only Son, so that everyone who believes in him may not perish but may have eternal life" (3:16) scrawled upon a placard signify the self-designation of its bearer as the recipient of eternal life. The same words set on the lips of Jesus become an affirmation of the nobility of Jesus' death and the constancy of God's love for his Son and for his creation.[13]

---

[12] The *Republic* is not a treatise but an unfolding dialogue in which Socrates leads his conversation partners to agree to excessive claims. I believe that the state described by the end of the dialogue is not a Socratic or Platonic ideal. If we follow the line of thought in other dialogues, we see that the good state is not dependent upon good laws but rather upon good citizens.

[13] Paul Ricoeur (*The Symbolism of Evil,* 324–26) argues that the polarity of the Adamic myth, in which suffering is punishment for guilt, and the tragic myth, in which suffering is unjust deprivation that is transcended by figure of the suffering servant, provides a view of "senseless and scandalous suffering, anticipates human evil and takes upon itself the sins of the world," giving guilt a "new horizon: not that of Judgment, but that of Mercy." But Ricoeur provides an important reminder of the potency of the tragic myth: "Only a consciousness that had accepted suffering without reservation could also begin to absorb the Wrath of God into the Love of God; but even then the suffering of others, the suffering of children, of the lowly, would renew the mystery of iniquity in his eyes. [Footnote: 'That the theology of love cannot become a systematic theology appears evident.'] Only *timid* hope could anticipate in silence the end of the phantasm of the 'wicked God.' "

BIBLIOGRAPHY

Greek Texts: Translations and Editions

Aeschylus

Agamemnon. Pages 99–172 in *Aeschylus: The Oresteia.* Translated by Robert Fagles. Harmondsworth: Penguin, 1977.

Eumenides. Pages 231–77 in *Aeschylus: The Oresteia.* Translated by Robert Fagles. Harmondsworth: Penguin, 1977.

Prometheus Bound. Pages 20–52 in *Aeschylus: Prometheus Bound, The Suppliants, Seven against Thebes, and The Persians.* Translated by Philip Vellacott. Harmondsworth: Penguin, 1961.

Euripides

Alcestis. Pages 160–281 in *Euripides I.* Edited and translated by David Kovacs. Loeb Classical Library 12. Cambridge: Harvard University Press, 1994.

Bacchae. Pages 44–83 in *Euripides' Bacchae and Other Plays.* Edited and translated by James Morwood. Oxford: Oxford University Press, 1999.

Cyclops. Pages 60–147 in *Euripides I.* Edited and translated by David Kovacs. Loeb Classical Library 12. Cambridge: Harvard University Press, 1994.

Electra. Pages 152–299 in *Euripides III.* Edited and translated by David Kovacs. Loeb Classical Library 9. Cambridge: Harvard University Press, 1998.

Hecuba. Pages 400–519 in *Euripdes II.* Edited and translated by David Kovacs. Loeb Classical Library 484. Cambridge: Harvard University Press, 1995.

Heracles. Pages 310–455 in *Euripides III*. Edited and translated by David Kovacs. Loeb Classical Library 9. Cambridge: Harvard University Press, 1998.

Hippolytus. Pages 124–263 in *Euripdes II*. Edited and translated by David Kovacs. Loeb Classical Library 484. Cambridge: Harvard University Press, 1995.

Ion. Pages 322–511 in *Euripides IV*. Edited and translated by David Kovacs. Loeb Classical Library 10. Cambridge: Harvard University Press, 1999.

Iphigenia among the Taurians. Pages 152–311 in *Euripides IV*. Edited and translated by David Kovacs. Loeb Classical Library 10. Cambridge: Harvard University Press, 1999.

Iphigenia at Aulis. Pages 84–132 in *Euripides' Bacchae and Other Plays*. Edited and translated by James Morwood. Oxford: Oxford University Press, 1999.

Medea. Pages 295–427 in *Euripides I*. Edited and translated by David Kovacs. Loeb Classical Library 12. Cambridge: Harvard University Press, 1994.

Medea. Pages 59–108 in *Euripides I*. Translated by Rex Warner. Edited by David Grene and Richmond Lattimore. The Complete Greek Tragedies 5. Chicago: Chicago University Press, 1955.

Phoenician Women. Pages 212– 397 in *Euripides V*. Edited and translated by David Kovacs. Loeb Classical Library 11. Cambridge: Harvard University Press, 2002.

Suppliant Women. Pages 12–139 in *Euripides III*. Edited and translated by David Kovacs. Loeb Classical Library 9. Cambridge: Harvard University Press, 1998.

The Trojan Women. Pages 14–143 in *Euripides IV*. Edited and translated by David Kovacs. Loeb Classical Library 10. Cambridge: Harvard University Press, 1999.

Sophocles

Ajax. Pages 30–163 in *Sophocles I*. Edited and translated by Hugh Lloyd-Jones. Loeb Classical Library 20. Cambridge: Harvard University Press, 1994.

Antigone. Pages 4–127 in *Sophocles II*. Edited and translated by Hugh Lloyd-Jones. Loeb Classical Library 21. Cambridge: Harvard University Press. 1996.

Electra. Pages 168–321 in *Sophocles I*. Edited and translated by Hugh Lloyd-Jones. Loeb Classical Library 20. Cambridge: Harvard University Press, 1994.

Oedipus at Colonus. Pages 409–608 in *Sophocles II.* Edited and translated by Hugh Lloyd-Jones. Loeb Classical Library 21. Cambridge: Harvard University Press, 1996.

Oedipus Tyrannus. Pages 326–483 in *Sophocles I.* Edited and translated by Hugh Lloyd-Jones. Loeb Classical Library 20. Cambridge: Harvard University Press, 1994.

The Women of Trachis. Pages 132–251 in *Sophocles II.* Edited and translated by Hugh Lloyd-Jones. Loeb Classical Library 21. Cambridge: Harvard University Press, 1996.

Other Ancient Texts and Translations

Aristotle. *The "Art" of Rhetoric.* Translated by John Henry Freese. Loeb Classical Library 193; Cambridge: Harvard University Press, 1982.

———. *Poetics.* Edited and translated by Stephen Halliwell, W. Hamilton Fyfe, and Doreen C. Innes. Loeb Classical Library 199. Cambridge: Harvard University Press, 1995.

Augustine. *Tractates on the Gospel of John* in *St. Augustin: Homilies on the Gospel of John; Homilies on the First Epistle of John Soliloquies.* Vol II. Translated by James Innes. Edinburgh: T&T Clark, Edinburgh, 1873. Repr., Christian Classics Ethereal Library. http://www.ccel.org.

Homer. *The Iliad.* Translated, with an introduction, by Richmond Lattimore. Chicago: University of Chicago Press, 1951.

Joseph and Aseneth. Translated by C. Burchard. Pages 177–247 in vol. 2 of *The Old Testament Pseudepigrapha.* Edited by James H. Charlesworth. 2 vols. Garden City, N.Y.: Doubleday, 1983–1985.

Novum Testamentum Graece. Edited by Barbara Aland et al. 27th ed. Stuttgart: Deutsche Bibelgesellschaft, 1993.

Odes of Solomon. Translated by J. H. Charlesworth. Pages 725–79 in vol. 2 of *The Old Testament Pseudepigrapha.* Edited by James H. Charlesworth. 2 vols. Garden City, N.Y.: Doubleday, 1983–1985.

Plato. *The Republic.* Translated, with notes and an interpretive essay, by Allan Bloom. New York: Basic Books, 1968.

Pseudo-Philo. Translated by D. J. Harrington. Pages 298–377 in vol. 2 of *The Old Testament Pseudepigrapha.* Edited by James H. Charlesworth. 2 vols. Garden City, N.Y.: Doubleday, 1983–1985.

Quintilian. *The Instituto Oratoria of Quintilian.* Translated by H. E. Butler. Loeb Classical Library 127. Cambridge: Harvard University Press, 1943.

Critical Scholarship

Works on the Fourth Gospel

Abbott, Edwin A. *Johannine Grammar.* London: Black, 1906.

Allison, Dale C. "The Living Water (John 4:10–14; 6:35c; 7:37–38)." *St. Vladimir's Theological Quarterly* 30 (1986): 142–57.

Anderson, Paul N. *The Christology of the Fourth Gospel: Its Unity and Disunity in the Light of John 6.* Valley Forge, Pa.: Trinity, 1996.

———. "The Sitz im Leben of the Johannine Bread of Life Discourse and Its Evolving Context." Pages 1–59 in *Critical Readings of John 6.* Edited by R. Alan Culpepper. Biblical Interpretation Series 22. Leiden: Brill, 1997.

Ball, David Mark. *"I Am" in John's Gospel: Literary Function, Background, and Theological Implications.* Journal for the Study of the New Testament: Supplement Series 124. Sheffield: Sheffield Academic Press, 1996.

Barrett, C. K. *The Gospel according to St. John.* London: SPCK, 1978.

Bauckham, Richard. "The Beloved Disciple as Ideal Author." *Journal for the Study of the New Testament* 49 (1993): 21–44.

———, ed. *The Gospels for All Christians: Rethinking the Gospel Audiences.* Grand Rapids: Eerdmans, 1998.

Beck, David R. *The Discipleship Paradigm: Readers and Anonymous Characters in the Fourth Gospel.* Biblical Interpretation Series 27. Leiden: Brill, 1977.

Bieringer, R., D. Pollefeyt, and F. Vandecasteele-Vanneuville, eds. *Anti-Judaism and the Fourth Gospel.* Louisville: Westminster John Knox, 2001.

Bligh, John. "Jesus in Samaria." *Heythrop Journal* 3 (1962): 329–46.

Bond, Helen K. *Pontius Pilate in History and Interpretation.* Society for New Testament Studies Monograph Series 100. Cambridge: Cambridge University Press, 1998.

Bowen, Clayton R. "The Fourth Gospel as Dramatic Material." *Journal of Biblical Literature* 49 (1930): 292–305.

Brant, Jo-Ann. "Husband Hunting: Characterization and Narrative Art in the Gospel of John." *Biblical Interpretation* 4 (1996): 205–23.

Brodie, Thomas. *The Gospel according to John: A Literary and Theological Commentary.* New York: Oxford University Press, 1993.

Brown, Raymond E. *The Gospel according to John.* 2 vols. Anchor Bible 29, 29A. Garden City, N.Y.: Doubleday, 1966–1970.

———. *The Community of the Beloved Disciple: The Life, Loves, and Hates of an Individual Church in New Testament Times.* New York: Paulist Press, 1979.

Bultmann, Rudolf. "Die Bedeutung der neuerschlossenen mandäischen und manichäischen Quellen für das Verständnis des Johannesevangeliums." *Zeitschrift für die neutestamentliche Wissenschaft und die Kunde der älteren Kirche* 24 (1925): 100–146.

———. *The Gospel of John*. Translated by G. R. Beasley-Murray. Philadelphia: Westminster, 1971.

Burkett, Delbert R. *The Son of the Man in the Gospel of John*. Journal for the Study of the New Testament: Supplement Series 56. Sheffield: JSOT Press, 1991.

Campenhausen, Hans von. "The Events of Easter and the Empty Tomb." Pages 42–89 in *Tradition and Life in the Church*. Translated by A. V. Littledale. Philadelphia: Fortress, 1968.

Carson, D. A. *The Gospel according to John*. Grand Rapids: Eerdmans, 1991.

Cohen, Shaye D. "The Significance of Yavneh." *Hebrew Union College Annual* 55 (1984): 27–53.

Connick, C. M. "The Dramatic Character of the Fourth Gospel." *Journal of Biblical Literature* 67 (1948): 159–69.

Conway, Colleen M. *Men and Women in the Fourth Gospel: Gender and Johannine Characterization*. Society of Biblical Literature Dissertation Series 167. Atlanta: Scholars Press, 1999.

———. "The Politics of the Johannine Drama." Paper presented at the annual meeting of the Society of Biblical Literature. Nashville, Tenn., November 2000.

Crossan, John Dominic. "It Is Written: A Structuralist Analysis of John 6." *Semeia* 26 (1983): 3–21.

Culpepper, R. Alan. *Anatomy of the Fourth Gospel: A Study in Literary Design*. Foundations and Facets. Philadelphia: Fortress, 1983.

———. "The Death of Jesus: An Exegesis of John 19:28–37." *Faith and Mission* 5 (1988): 64–70.

———. *The Gospel and Letters of John*. Nashville: Abingdon, 1998.

D'Angelo, Mary Rose. "A Critical Note: John 20:17 and Apocalypse of Moses 31." *Journal of Theological Studies* 41 (1990): 481–503.

Davies, Margaret. *Rhetoric and Reference in the Fourth Gospel*. Journal for the Study of the New Testament: Supplement Series 69. Sheffield: JSOT Press, 1992.

Dodd, C. H. *The Interpretation of the Fourth Gospel*. Cambridge: Cambridge University Press, 1953.

———. *Historical Tradition in the Fourth Gospel*. Cambridge: Cambridge University Press, 1963.

Dokka, Trond Skard. "Irony and Sectarianism in the Gospel of John." Pages 83–107 in *New Readings in John: Literary and Theological Perspectives*.

Edited by Johannes Nissen and Sigfred Pedersen. Journal for the Study of the New Testament: Supplement Series 182. Sheffield: Sheffield Academic Press, 1999.

Domeris, William R. "The Johannine Drama." *Journal of Theology for Southern Africa* 42 (1983): 29–35.

Duke, Paul D. *Irony in the Fourth Gospel.* Atlanta: John Knox, 1985.

Dunn, James D. G. "The Embarrassment of History: Reflections on the Problem of 'Anti-Judaism' in the Fourth Gospel." Pages 41–60 in *Anti-Judaism and the Fourth Gospel.* Edited by R. Bieringer, D. Pollefeyt, and F. Vandecasteele-Vanneuville. Louisville: Westminster John Knox, 2001.

Eslinger, Lyle. "The Wooing of the Woman at the Well: Jesus, the Reader, and Reader-Response Criticism." *Journal of Literature and Theology* 1 (1987): 167–83.

Fehribach, Adeline. *The Women in the Life of the Bridegroom: A Feminist Historical-Literary Analysis of the Female Characters in the Fourth Gospel.* Collegeville, Minn.: Liturgical Press, 1998.

Felton, Tom, and Tom Thatcher. "Stylometry and the Signs Gospel." Pages 209–18 in *Jesus in Johannine Tradition.* Edited by Robert T. Fortna and Tom Thatcher. Louisville: Westminster John Knox, 2001.

Flanagan, Neal. "The Gospel of John as Drama." *The Bible Today* 19 (1981): 264–70.

Fortna, Robert T. "Theological Use of Locale in the Fourth Gospel." *Anglican Theological Review* 3 (1974): 58–95.

———. *The Fourth Gospel and Its Predecessors: From Narrative Source to Present Gospel.* Philadelphia: Fortress, 1988.

———. "Jesus Tradition in the Signs Gospel." Pages 199–208 in *Jesus in Johannine Tradition.* Edited by Robert T. Fortna and Tom Thatcher. Louisville: Westminster John Knox, 2001.

Fowler, D. C. "The Meaning of 'Touch Me Not' in John 20:17." *Evangelical Quarterly* 47 (1975): 16–25.

Giblin, Charles H. "Two Complementary Literary Structures in John 1:1–18." *Journal of Biblical Literature* 104 (1985): 87–103.

Harris, Elizabeth. *Prologue and Gospel: The Theology of the Fourth Gospel.* Journal for the Study of the New Testament: Supplement Series 107. Sheffield: Sheffield Academic Press, 1994.

Hedrick, Charles B. "Pageantry in the Fourth Gospel." *Anglican Theological Review* 15 (1933): 115–24.

Hengel, Martin. *The Johannine Question.* Philadelphia: Trinity, 1989.

Hitchcock, F. R. Montgomery. "The Dramatic Development of the Fourth Gospel." *Expositor* 4 (1907): 266–79.

———. *A Fresh Study of the Fourth Gospel.* New York: Gorham, 1911.

————. "Is the Fourth Gospel a Drama?" *Theology* 7 (1923): 307–17.

Hooker, Morna. "John's Prologue and the Messianic Secret." *New Testament Studies* 21 (1974): 40–58.

Jasper, Alison. "Interpretative Approaches to John 20:1–18: Mary at the Tomb of Jesus." *Studia Theologica* 47 (1993): 107–18.

Jonge, Marinus de. "Jewish Expectations about the 'Messiah' according to the Fourth Gospel." *New Testament Studies* 19 (1972–1973): 246–70.

Käsemann, Ernst. *The Testament of Jesus: A Study of the Gospel of John in the Light of Chapter 17*. Translated by Gerhard Krodel. Philadelphia: Fortress, 1968.

Kimelman, Reuven. "Birkat Ha-Minim and the Lack of Evidence for an Anti-Christian Jewish Prayer in Late Antiquity." Pages 226–44, 391–403 in vol. 1 of *Jewish and Christian Self-Definition*. Edited by E. P. Sanders. 3 vols. Philadelphia: Fortress, 1980–1982.

Klassen, William. *Judas: Betrayer or Friend of Jesus?* Minneapolis: Fortress, 1996.

Koester, Craig. "Spectrum of Johannine Readers." Pages 5–19 in vol. 1 of *What Is John? Readers and Readings of the Fourth Gospel*. Edited by Fernando Segovia. 2 vols. Society of Biblical Literature Symposium Series 3, 7. Atlanta: Scholars Press, 1996–1998.

Kraft, H. "John 20:17." *Theologische Literaturzeitung* 76 (1951): n.p.

Kysar, Robert. *John's Story of Jesus*. Philadelphia: Fortress, 1984.

————. "Johannine Metaphor—Meaning and Function: A Literary Study of John 10:1–18." *Semeia* 53 (1991): 81–111.

————. "The Dismantling of Decisional Faith." Pages 161–81 in *Critical Readings of John 6*. Edited by R. Alan Culpepper. Biblical Interpretation Series 22. Leiden: Brill, 1997.

Lee, E. Kenneth. "The Drama of the Fourth Gospel." *Expository Times* 65 (1954): 173–76.

Lincoln, Andrew T. *Truth on Trial: The Lawsuit Motif in the Fourth Gospel*. Peabody, Mass.: Hendrickson, 2000.

Maccini, Robert Gordon. *Her Testimony Is True: Women as Witnesses according to John*. Journal for the Study of the New Testament: Supplement Series 125. Sheffield: Sheffield Academic Press, 1996.

MacRae, G. W. "The Ego-Proclamation in Gnostic Sources." Pages 129–34 in *The Trial of Jesus*. Edited by Ernst Bammel. Studies in Biblical Theology 2.13. London: SCM, 1970.

Malina, Bruce. *The Gospel of John in Sociolinguistic Perspective*. Edited by Herman C. Waetjen. Berkeley: Center for Hermeneutical Studies in Hellenistic and Modern Culture, 1985.

Malina, Bruce J., and Richard L. Rohrbaugh. *Social-Science Commentary on the Gospel of John*. Minneapolis: Fortress, 1998.

Marcus, Joel. "Rivers of Living Water from Jesus' Belly (John 7:38)." *Journal of Biblical Literature* 117 (1998): 328–30.

Martin, Troy W. "Assessing the Johannine Epithet 'The Mother of Jesus.'" *Catholic Biblical Quarterly* 60 (1998): 63–73.

Martyn, J. Louis. *History and Theology of the Fourth Gospel.* Rev. ed. Nashville: Abingdon, 1979.

Matera, Frank J. "'On Behalf of Others,' 'Cleansing,' and 'Return': Johannine Images for Jesus' Death." *Louvain Studies* 13 (1988): 161–78.

———. *New Testament Christology.* Louisville: Westminster John Knox, 1999.

Matson, Mark A. "The Temple Incident: An Integral Element in the Fourth Gospel's Narrative." Pages 145–54 in *Jesus in Johannine Tradition.* Edited by Robert T. Fortna and Tom Thatcher. Louisville: Westminster John Knox, 2001.

Maynard, A. H. "The Role of Peter in the Fourth Gospel." *New Testament Studies* 30 (1984): 531–48.

McGrath, James A. *John's Apologetic Christology: Legitimation and Development in Johannine Christology.* Society for New Testament Studies Monograph Series 111. Cambridge: Cambridge University Press, 2001.

McKay, Kenneth L. "'I Am' in John's Gospel." *Expository Times* 107 (1996): 302–3.

Meeks, Wayne A. "Galilee and Judea in the Fourth Gospel." *Journal of Biblical Literature* 85 (1966): 159–69.

———. *The Prophet-King: Moses Traditions and the Johannine Christology.* Novum Testamentum Supplements. Leiden: Brill, 1967.

———. "The Man from Heaven in Johannine Sectarianism." *Journal of Biblical Literature* 91 (1972): 44–72.

Miller, Ed L. "The Logic of the Logos Hymn: A New View." *New Testament Studies* 29 (1983): 552–56.

Moloney, Francis J. "The Function of Prolepsis in the Interpretation of John 6." Pages 129–48 in *Critical Readings of John 6.* Edited by R. Alan Culpepper. Biblical Interpretation Series 22. Leiden: Brill, 1997.

Muilenburg, James. "Literary Form in the Fourth Gospel." *Journal of Biblical Literature* 51 (1932): 40–53.

Munro, Winsome. "The Pharisee and the Samaritan in John: Polar or Parallel?" *Catholic Biblical Quarterly* 57 (1995): 710–28.

Neyrey, Jerome. *An Ideology of Revolt: John's Christology in Social-Science Perspective.* Philadelphia: Fortress, 1988.

———. "'I Said: You Are Gods': Psalm 82:6 and John 10." *Journal of Biblical Literature* 108 (1989): 647–63.

————. "What's Wrong with This Picture? John 4, Cultural Stereotypes of Women, and Public and Private Space." *Biblical Theology Bulletin* 24 (1994): 77–91.

————. "The Trials (Forensic) and Tribulations (Honor Challenges) of Jesus: John 7 in Social-Science Perspective." *Biblical Theology Bulletin* 26 (1996): 107–24.

Nicholson, Godfrey C. *Death as Departure: The Johannine Descent-Ascent Schema.* Society of Biblical Literature Dissertation Series 63. Atlanta: Scholars Press, 1983.

O'Rourke, J. J. "The Historic Present in the Gospel of John." *Journal of Biblical Literature* 93 (1974): 585–90.

Painter, John. *The Quest for the Messiah: The History, Literature, and Theology of the Johannine Community.* Nashville: Abingdon, 1993.

Peterson, Norman R. *The Gospel of John and the Sociology of Light: Language and Characterization in the Fourth Gospel.* Valley Forge, Pa.: Trinity, 1993.

Phillips, Gary A. "'This Is a Hard Saying. Who Can Be Listener to It?' Creating a Reader in John 6." *Semeia* 26 (1983): 23–56.

Pierce, Edith Lovejoy. "The Fourth Gospel as Drama." *Religion in Life* 29 (1960): 453–54.

Purvis, James D. "The Fourth Gospel and the Samaritans." *Novum Testamentum* 17 (1975): 161–98.

Quasten, Johannes. "The Parable of the Good Shepherd: Jn. 10:1–21." *Catholic Biblical Quarterly* 10 (1948): 1–12, 151–69.

Rand, J. A. du. "The Characterization of Jesus as Depicted in the Narrative of the Fourth Gospel." *Neotestamentica* 19 (1985): 18–36.

Reimer, Martha. "The Functions of οὖν in the Gospel of John." *START* 13 (1985): 28–36.

Reinhartz, Adele. *Befriending the Beloved Disciple: A Jewish Reading of the Gospel of John.* New York: Continuum, 2001.

————. "From Narrative to History: The Resurrection of Mary and Martha." Pages 161–84 in *"Women Like This": New Perspectives on Jewish Women in the Greco-Roman World.* Edited by Amy-Jill Levine. Society of Biblical Literature Early Judaism and Its Literature 1. Atlanta: Scholars Press, 1991.

————. "Jesus as Prophet: Predictive Prolepses in the Fourth Gospel." *Journal for the Study of the New Testament* 36 (1989): 3–16.

————. "The Johannine Community and Its Jewish Neighbors: A Reappraisal." Pages 111–38 in vol. 2 of *What Is John? Literary and Social Readings of the Fourth Gospel.* Edited by Fernando Segovia. 2 vols. Society of Biblical Literature Symposium Series 3, 7. Atlanta: Scholars Press, 1996–1998.

————. *The Word in the World: The Cosmological Tale in the Fourth Gospel.* Society of Biblical Literature Monograph Series 45. Atlanta: Scholars Press, 1992.

Rensberger, David. *Johannine Faith and Liberating Community.* Philadelphia: Westminster, 1988.

————. "The Messiah Who Has Come into the World." Pages 15–24 in *Jesus in Johannine Tradition.* Edited by Robert T. Fortna and Tom Thatcher. Louisville: Westminster John Knox, 2001.

Ridderbos, Herman. "The Structure and Scope of the Prologue of the Gospel of John." *Novum Testamentum* 8 (1966): 180–201.

Robinson, John A. T. "The Parable of John 10:1–5." *Zeitschrift für die neutestamentliche Wissenschaft und die Kunde der älteren Kirche* 46 (1955): 233–40.

————. "The Relation of the Prologue to the Gospel of St. John." Pages 65–76 in *Twelve More New Testament Studies.* London: SCM, 1984.

Rohrbaugh, Richard L. "The Gospel of John in the Twenty-First Century." Pages 257–63 in vol. 2 of *What Is John? Readers and Readings of the Fourth Gospel.* Edited by Fernando Segovia. 2 vols. Society of Biblical Literature Symposium Series 3, 7. Atlanta: Scholars Press, 1996–1998.

Schnackenburg, Rudolf. *The Gospel according to St. John.* Translated by Kevin Smyth. 3 vols. New York: Herder & Herder, 1968.

Schneiders, Sandra M. *Written That You May Believe: Encountering Jesus in the Fourth Gospel.* New York: Crossroad, 1999.

Schüssler Fiorenza, Elisabeth. "A Feminist Critical Interpretation for Liberation: Martha and Mary—Luke 10:38–42." *Religion and Intellectual Life* 3 (1986): 21–36.

Scott, Martin. *Sophia and the Johannine Jesus.* Journal for the Study of the New Testament: Supplement Series 71. Sheffield: JSOT Press, 1992.

Segovia, Fernando F. "The Journey(s) of the Word of God: A Reading of the Plot of the Fourth Gospel." *Semeia* 53 (1991): 23–54.

Seim, Turid Karlsen. "Roles of Women in the Gospel of John." Pages 56–73 in *Aspects on the Johannine Literature.* Edited by Lars Hartman and Birger Olsson. Coniectanea biblica: New Testament Series 18. Uppsala: Almqvist & Wiksell, 1987.

Smith, D. Moody. *John among the Gospels: The Relationship in Twentieth-Century Research.* Minneapolis: Fortress, 1992.

Staley, Jeffrey L. *The Print's First Kiss: A Rhetorical Investigation of the Implied Reader in the Fourth Gospel.* Society of Biblical Literature Dissertation Series 82. Atlanta: Scholars Press, 1988.

————. "Subversive Narrator/Victimized Reader: A Reader Response Assessment of Text-critical Problems, John 18:12–24." *Journal for the Study of the New Testament* 51 (1993): 79–98.

Stibbe, Mark W. G. *John as Storyteller: Narrative Criticism and the Fourth Gospel.* Society for New Testament Studies Monograph Series 73. Cambridge: Cambridge University Press, 1992.

———. *John's Gospel.* New Testament Readings. London: Routledge, 1994.

Strachan, Robert H. *The Fourth Evangelist: Dramatist or Historian?* New York: Doran, 1925.

Talbert, Charles H. "Artistry and Theology: An Analysis of the Architecture of Jn 1,19–5,47." *Catholic Biblical Quarterly* 32 (1970): 341–66.

Thatcher, Tom. "Jesus, Judas, and Peter: Character by Contrast in the Fourth Gospel." *Bibliotheca sacra* 153 (1996): 435–48.

———. *The Riddles of Jesus in John: A Study in Tradition and Folklore.* Society of Biblical Literature Monograph Series 53. Atlanta: Scholars Press, 2000.

———. "The Riddles of Jesus in the Johannine Dialogues." Pages 263–81 in *Jesus in Johannine Tradition.* Edited by Robert T. Fortna and Tom Thatcher. Louisville: Westminster John Knox, 2001.

Thomas, John Christopher. *Footwashing in John 13 and the Johannine Community.* Journal for the Study of the New Testament: Supplement Series 61. Sheffield: JSOT Press, 1991.

Thompson, Marianne Meye. *The Humanity of Jesus in the Fourth Gospel.* Philadelphia: Fortress, 1988.

Tilborg, Sjef van. *Imaginative Love in John.* Biblical Interpretation Series 2. Leiden: Brill, 1993.

Tovey, Derek. *Narrative Art and Act in the Fourth Gospel.* Journal for the Study of the New Testament: Supplement Series 151. Sheffield: Sheffield Academic Press, 1997.

Twelftree, Graham H. "Exorcism in the Fourth Gospel and the Synoptics." Pages 135–44 in *Jesus in Johannine Tradition.* Edited by Robert T. Fortna and Tom Thatcher. Louisville: Westminster John Knox, 2001.

Whitacre, Rodney A. *Johannine Polemic: The Role of Tradition and Theology.* Society of Biblical Literature Dissertation Series 67. Chico, Calif.: Scholars Press, 1982.

Wikenhauser, Alfred. *Das Evangelium nach Johannes.* 3d ed. Regensburger Neues Testament 4. Regensburg: Pustet, 1961.

Windisch, Hans. "Der johanneische Erzählungsstil." Pages 174–213 in vol. 2 of *Eucharisterion: Studien zur Religion und Literatur des Alten und Neuen Testaments.* Edited by Hans Schmidt. 2 vols. in 1. Forschungen zur Religion und Literatur des Alten und Neuen Testaments 36. Göttingen: Vandenhoeck & Ruprecht, 1923. English translation, "John's Narrative Style." Pages 25–64 in *The Gospel of John as Literature: An Anthology of Twentieth-Century Perspectives.* Edited by Mark W. G.

Stibbe. Translated by David E. Orton. New Testament Tools and Studies 17. Leiden: Brill, 1993.

Wyatt, Nicolas. "Supposing Him to Be the Gardener (John 20,25): A Study of the Paradise Motif in John." *Zeitschrift für die neutestamentliche Wissenschaft und die Kunde der älteren Kirche* 81 (90): 21–38.

Works on Classical Tragedy

Arnott, Peter D. *An Introduction to Greek Theatre*. New York: St. Martin's, 1967.

———. *Public and Performance in the Greek Theatre*. London: Routledge, 1989.

Calame, Claude. "Vision, Blindness, and Mask: The Radicalization of the Emotions in Sophocles." Pages 17–37 in *Tragedy and the Tragic: Greek Theatre and Beyond*. Edited by M. S. Silk. Oxford: Clarendon, 1996.

Dale, A. M. "The Chorus in the Action of Greek Tragedy." Pages 17–27 in *Classical Drama and Its Influences*. Edited by M. J. Anderson. London: Methuen, 1965.

Dunn, Francis M. *Tragedy's End: Closure and Innovation in Euripidean Drama*. Oxford: Oxford University Press, 1996.

Easterling, P. E. "Constructing Character in Greek Tragedy." Pages 82–99 in *Characterization and Individuality in Greek Literature*. Edited by Christopher Pelling. Oxford: Clarendon, 1990.

Foley, Helen. "Marriage and Sacrifice in Euripides' *Iphigenia at Aulis.*" *Arethusa* 15 (1982): 159–80.

Gill, Christopher. "The Character-Personality Distinction." Pages 1–31 in *Characterization and Individuality in Greek Literature*. Edited by Christopher Pelling. Oxford: Clarendon, 1990.

Goldhill, Simon. "Character and Action, Representation and Reading: Greek Tragedy and Its Critics." Pages 100–127 in *Characterization and Individuality in Greek Literature*. Edited by Christopher Pelling. Oxford: Clarendon, 1990.

Gould, John. "Tragedy and Collective Experience." Pages 217–43 in *Tragedy and the Tragic: Greek Theatre and Beyond*. Edited by M. S. Silk. Oxford: Clarendon, 1996.

Griffith, Mark. "Antigone and Her Sister(s): Embodying Women in Greek Tragedy." Pages 117–36 in *Making Silence Speak: Women's Voices in Greek Literature and Society*. Edited by André Lardinois and Laura McClure. Princeton, N.J.: Princeton University Press, 2001.

Hadas, Moses. *Hellenistic Culture*. New York: Columbia University Press, 1959.

Jong, Irene J. F. de. *Narrative in Drama: The Art of the Euripidean Messenger-Speech.* Mnemosyne, bibliotheca classica batava: Supplementum 116. Leiden: Brill, 1991.

Käppel, Lutz. *Die Konstruktion der Handlung der Orestie des Aischylos: Die Makrostruktur des "Plot" als Sinnträger in der Darstellung des Geschlechterfluchs.* Zetemata 99. Munich: Beck, 1998.

Kitto, H. D. F. *Greek Tragedy: A Literary Study.* 2d ed. New York: Doubleday, 1950. 3d ed. London: Metheun, 1961.

Lloyd, Michael. *The Agon in Euripides.* Oxford: Clarendon, 1992.

MacIntosh, Fiona. "Tragic Last Words: The Big Speech and Lament in Ancient Greek and Modern Irish Tragic Drama." Pages 414–25 in *Tragedy and the Tragic: Greek Theatre and Beyond.* Edited by M. S. Silk. Oxford: Clarendon, 1996.

Meier, Mischa. Review of Lutz Käppel, *Die Konstruktion der Handlung der Orestie des Aischylos: Die Makrostruktur des "Plot" als Sinnträger in der Darstellung des Geschlechterfluchs. Bryn Mawr Classical Review,* September 5, 1999, n.p.

Michelini, Ann Norris. *Euripides and the Tragic Tradition.* Madison: University of Wisconsin Press, 1987.

Murray, Gilbert. *Euripides and His Age.* Home University Library of Modern Knowledge 73. New York: Holt, 1913.

Nussbaum, Martha. *The Fragility of Goodness: Luck and Ethics in Greek Tragedy and Philosophy.* Cambridge: Cambridge University Press, 1986.

Padel, Ruth. "Making Space Speak." Pages 336–65 in *Nothing to Do with Dionysos? Athenian Drama in Its Social Context.* Edited by John J. Winkler and Froma I. Zeitlin. Princeton, N.J.: Princeton University Press, 1990.

Rehm, Rush. *Marriage to Death: The Conflation of Wedding and Funeral Rituals in Greek Tragedy.* Princeton, N.J.: Princeton University Press, 1994.

Reinhardt, Karl. "Illusion and Truth in Oedipus Tyrannus." Pages 65–102 in *Modern Critical Interpretations: Sophocles' Oedipus Rex.* Edited by Harold Bloom. New York: Chelsea House, 1988.

Segal, Charles. *Euripides and the Poetics of Sorrow: Art, Gender, and Commemoration in Alcestis, Hipploytus, and Hecuba.* Durham, N.C.: Duke University Press, 1993.

———. *Sophocles' Tragic World.* Cambridge: Harvard University Press, 1995.

Silk, M. S. "Tragic Language: The Greek Tragedians and Shakespeare." Pages 458–96 in *Tragedy and the Tragic: Greek Theatre and Beyond.* Edited by M. S. Silk. Oxford: Clarendon, 1996.

Taplin, Oliver. *Greek Tragedy in Action.* Berkeley: University of California Press, 1978.

Vernant, Jean-Pierre. "Ambiguity and Reversal: On the Enigmatic Structure of Oedipus Rex." Pages 82–112 in *Myth and Tragedy in Ancient Greece*. Edited by Jean-Pierre Vernant and Pierre Vidal-Naquet. Translated by P. du Bois. New York: Zone Books, 1988.

———. "A 'Beautiful Death' and the Disfigured Corpse in Homeric Epic." Pages 50–74 in *Mortals and Immortals: Collected Essays*. Edited by Froma I. Zeitlin. Princeton, N.J.: Princeton University Press, 1991.

Whitman, Cedric H. *Euripides and the Full Circle of Myth*. Cambridge: Harvard University Press, 1974.

Wiles, David. *Tragedy in Athens: Performance Space and Theatrical Meaning*. Cambridge: Cambridge University Press, 1997.

Zeitlin, Froma I. *Under the Sign of the Shield: Semiotics and Aeschylus' Seven against Thebes*. Filologia e critica 44. Rome: Ateneo, 1982.

———. "Playing the Other: Theater, Theatricality, and the Feminine in Greek Drama." Pages 63–97 in *Nothing to Do with Dionysos? Athenian Drama in Its Social Context*. Edited by John J. Winkler and Froma I. Zeitlin. Princeton, N.J.: Princeton University Press, 1990.

Zwierlein, Otto. *Die Rezitationsdramen Senecas*. Beiträge zur klassischen Philologie 20. Meisenheim am Glan: Anton Hain, 1966.

Works on Theater Criticism and Theory

Austin, J. L. *How to Do Things with Words*. New York: Oxford University Press, 1962.

Bakhtin, Mikhail. "Forms of Time and of the Chronotope in the Novel." Pages 84–258 in *The Dialogic Imagination: Four Essays*. Edited by Michael Holquist. Translated by Caryl Emerson and Michael Holquist. Austin: University of Texas Press, 1981.

Berger, Harry Jr. *Imaginary Audition: Shakespeare on Stage and Page*. Berkeley: University of California Press, 1989.

Brook, Peter. *The Empty Space*. New York: Atheneum, 1968.

Bühler, Karl. "The Deictic Field of Language and Deictic Words." Pages 9–30 in *Speech, Place, and Action: Studies in Deixis and Related Topics*. Edited by Robert J. Jarvella and Wolfgang Klein. Chichester, N.Y.: Wiley, 1982.

Chatman, Seymour. *Story and Discourse: Narrative Structure in Fiction and Film*. Ithaca, N.Y.: Cornell University Press, 1980.

Doran, Madelaine. *Shakespeare's Dramatic Language*. Madison: University of Wisconsin Press, 1976.

Elam, Keir. *The Semiotics of Theatre and Drama*. London: Routledge, 1980.

———. *Shakespeare's Universe of Discourse: Language Games in the Comedies*. Cambridge: Cambridge University Press, 1984.

Fillmore, Charles J. "Towards a Descriptive Framework for Spatial Deixis." Pages 31–59 in *Speech, Place, and Action: Studies in Deixis and Related Topics.* Edited by Robert J. Jarvella and Wolfgang Klein. Chichester, N.Y.: Wiley, 1982.

Genette, Gérard. *Narrative Discourse: An Essay in Method.* Translated by Jane E. Lewin. Ithaca, N.Y.: Cornell University Press, 1980.

Halliday, M. A. K. *Language as a Social Semiotic: The Social Interpretation of Language and Meaning.* London: Edward Arnold, 1978.

Herman, Vimala. *Dramatic Discourse: Dialogue as Interaction in Plays.* London: Routlege, 1995.

Hinden, Michael. "Drama and Ritual Once Again: Notes toward a Revival of Tragic Theory." *Comparative Drama* 29 (1995): 183–202.

Honzl, Jindrich. "The Hierarchy of Dramatic Devices." Pages 118–27 in *The Semiotics of Art: Prague School Contributions.* Edited by Ladislav Matejka and Irwin Titunik. Cambridge: MIT Press, 1976.

Ingarden, Roman. "The Functions of Language in the Theater." Pages 377–96 in *The Literary Work of Art: An Investigation on the Borderlines of Ontology, Logic, and Theory of Literature.* Translated by George G. Grabowicz. Evanston, Ill.: Northwestern University Press, 1973.

Issacharoff, Michael. "Space and Reference in Drama." *Poetics Today* 23 (1981): 211–24.

Knights, L. C. *How Many Children Had Lady MacBeth? An Essay in the Theory and Practice of Shakespeare Criticism.* Cambridge: Minority Press, 1933.

Langer, Susanne K. *Feeling and Form: A Theory of Art Developed from Philosophy in a New Key.* New York: Scribner, 1953.

Ong, Walter J. *Orality and Literacy: The Technologizing of the Word.* London: Routledge, 1982.

Peirce, Charles Sanders. *Elements of Logic.* Vol. 2 of *The Collected Papers of Charles Sanders Peirce.* Edited by Charles Hartshorne and Paul Weiss. 6 vols. Cambridge: Harvard University Press, 1931–1935. Repr., Bristol: Thoemmes, 1997.

Pfister, Manfred. *The Theory and Analysis of Drama.* Translated by J. Halliday. Cambridge: Cambridge University Press, 1988.

Porter, Joseph A. *The Drama of Speech Acts: Shakespeare's Lancastrian Tetralogy.* Berkeley: University of California Press, 1979.

Rozik, Eli. "The Functions of Language in the Theatre." *Theatre Research International* 18 (1993): 104–14.

Schechner, Richard. *Performance Theory.* London: Routledge, 1988.

Ubersfeld, Anne. *Reading Theatre.* Translated by Frank Collins. Toronto: University of Toronto Press, 1999.

Vellacott, Philip. *Ironic Drama: A Study of Euripides' Method and Meaning.* Cambridge: Cambridge University Press, 1975.

Veltrusky, Jirí. "Basic Features of Dramatic Dialogue." Pages 128–33 in *The Semiotics of Art: Prague School Contributions.* Edited by Ladislav Matejka and Irwin Titunik. Cambridge: MIT Press, 1976.

Voloshinov, Valentin N. *Marxism and the Philosophy of Language.* Translated by L. Matejka and I. R. Titunik. Cambridge: Harvard University Press, 1986.

Other Works Consulted

Alter, Robert. *The Art of Biblical Narrative.* New York: Basic Books, 1981.

Auden, William H. "The Christian Hero." N.p. in *Tragedy: Vision and Form.* Edited by Robert W. Corrigan. San Francisco: Chandler, 1965.

Auerbach, Eric. *Mimesis: The Representation of Reality in Western Literature.* Translated by Willard R. Trask. Princeton, N.J.: Princeton University Press, 1953.

Ausland, Hayden W. "On Reading Plato Mimetically." *American Journal of Philology* 118 (1997): 371–416.

Burridge, Richard A. *What Are the Gospels? A Comparison with Graeco-Roman Biography.* Society for New Testament Studies Monograph Series 70. Cambridge: Cambridge University Press, 1992.

Calame, Claude. *Poétique des mythes dans la Grèce antique.* Hachette Université: Langues et civilisations anciennes. Paris: Hachette, 2000.

Clover, Carol J. "The Germanic Context of the Unferth Episode." *Speculum* 55 (1980): 444–68.

Cowley, Malcolm, ed. *Writers at Work: The Paris Review Interviews.* New York: Viking, 1958.

Culbertson, Diana. *The Poetics of Revelation: Recognition and the Narrative Tradition.* Macon, Ga.: Mercer University Press, 1989.

Easterling, P. E. "Presentation of Character in Aeschylus." Pages 12–28 in *Greek Tragedy.* Edited by Ian McAuslan and Peter Walcot. Oxford: Oxford University Press, 1993.

Greimas, A.-J., and J. Courtès. "The Cognitive Dimension of Narrative Discourse." *New Literary History* 7 (1976): 433–47.

Hadas, Moses. *The Third and Fourth Books of the Maccabees.* New York: Harper, 1953.

Hock, Ronald F. "Homer in Greco-Roman Education." Pages 56–77 in *Mimesis and Intertextuality in Antiquity and Christianity.* Edited by Dennis R. MacDonald. Harrisburg, Pa.: Trinity, 2001.

Hurtado, Larry W. "Gospel Genre." Pages 276–79 in *Dictionary of Jesus and the Gospels.* Edited by Joel B. Green, Scot McKnight, and I. Howard Marshall. Downers Grove, Ill.: InterVarsity, 1992.

Kennedy, George A. *New Testament Interpretation through Rhetorical Criticism*. Chapel Hill: University of North Carolina Press, 1984.

Laistner, M. L. *Christianity and Pagan Culture in the Later Roman Empire*. Ithaca, N.Y.: Cornell University Press, 1951.

MacDonald, Dennis R. *Christianizing Homer: "The Odyssey," Plato, and "The Acts of Andrew."* New York: Oxford University Press, 1994.

———. *The Homeric Epics and the Gospel of Mark*. New Haven: Yale University Press, 2000.

Marrou, Henri I. *A History of Education in Antiquity*. Translated by George Lamb. New York: Sheed & Ward, 1956.

Martin, Wallace. *Recent Theories of Narrative*. Ithaca, N.Y.: Cornell University Press, 1986.

Mayer, Josephine, and Tom Prideaux. *Never to Die: The Egyptians in Their Own Words*. New York: Viking, 1938.

Nygren, Anders. *Agape and Eros*. Translated by Philip S. Watson. London: SPCK, 1953.

Ong, Walter J. *Fighting for Life: Contest, Sexuality, and Consciousness*. Ithaca, N.Y.: Cornell University Press, 1981.

Parks, Ward. *Verbal Dueling in Heroic Narrative: The Homeric and Old English Traditions*. Princeton, N.J.: Princeton University Press, 1990.

Ricoeur, Paul. *The Symbolism of Evil*. Translated by Emerson Buchanan. Boston: Beacon, 1967.

Riley, Gregory J. *One Jesus, Many Christs: How Jesus Inspired Not One True Christianity but Many: The Truth about Christian Origins*. San Francisco: HarperSanFrancisco, 1997.

Searle, John R. *The Construction of Social Reality*. New York: Free Press, 1995.

Sutton, Dana F. *Seneca on the Stage*. Mnemosyne, bibliotheca classica batava: Supplementum 96. Leiden: Brill, 1986.

INDEX
Modern Authors

INDEX

Subjects

INDEX

Ancient Sources